Poet, priest and prophet
The life and thought of Bishop John V. Taylor

'Bishop John Taylor was one of the most significant church leaders of the twentieth century ... his example stays with us.'
The Most Revd and Rt Hon. Dr George Carey, Archbishop of Canterbury

'A book to remind those who have forgotten Taylor's missionary significance, and to refresh those who need it.'
Canon Tim Dakin, CMS General Secretary

'A major contribution to Christian thinking in the modern era.'
Fr Larry Nemer, Director, Mill Hill Institute

Does Christian evangelism promote sectarianism and violence, or can it contribute to harmony and peace in the global village? Can Christians extol the true significance of Jesus Christ without demeaning others? Who is God and how does God's nature shape ours? This book tackles these and other vital issues by giving the first major account of the life and thought of one of the twentieth century's greatest religious thinkers. John V. Taylor was a missionary statesman, ecumenist, Africanist, sometime General Secretary of the Church Missionary Society, and later Anglican Bishop of Winchester. His work offers a theology and practice of Christian mission which is faithful to scripture while fully facing the facts of the contemporary world at the beginning of the third millennium. Taylor is author of major works such as *The Go-Between God*, his book on the Holy Spirit, and *The Christlike God*, where he outlines the distinctive Christian insight into God as the patient, generous, self-sacrificing Love we see in Jesus. Here is an example and tutor to any thoughtful Christian. Consistently incarnational and sacramental in his approach, Taylor seeks to live out the truths he discovers in his daily ministry as poet, priest and prophet – inviting those around him to share the way of Christ.

David Graeme Wood has served as a priest in six parishes in two metropolitan dioceses of the Anglican Church of Australia. Educated at the University of Melbourne, the United Faculty of Theology and Monash University, he has degrees in art history, women's studies and theology. Ordained by the Archbishop of Melbourne in 1979, he has been an Examining Chaplain and Director of Vocations, Secretary to the Commission on Multicultural Affairs of the Victorian Council of Churches, Moderator of the Summer School in Ecumenism, an Executive Member of the Council of Christians and Jews, and Canon of St George's Cathedral Perth. His first book, *Is God a Boy's Name?: Inclusive Language for the Liturgy*, was published in 1991. He has taught at Trinity College in Melbourne and Wollaston College in Perth, and is currently engaged in designing and teaching courses in missionary theology for Trinity OnLine, and sacramental theology for the Anglican Institute of Theology. His doctoral thesis was on the theology of Bishop John V. Taylor.

for my parents
Betty and Bill
and for my God-children
Benjamin, Graeme, David and Abigael

Poet, priest and prophet

The life and thought of Bishop John V. Taylor

DAVID WOOD

CHURCHES TOGETHER
IN BRITAIN AND IRELAND

Churches Together in Britain and Ireland
Inter-Church House
35-41 Lower Marsh
London SE1 7SA
Tel: +44 (0)20 7523 2121; Fax: +44 (0)20 7928 0010
info@ctbi.org.uk or (team)@ctbi.org.uk
www.ctbi.org.uk

ISBN 0 85169 272 9

Published 2002 by Churches Together in Britain and Ireland

Produced by Church House Publishing

Further copies available from CTBI Publications, 31 Great Smith Street, London SW1P 3BN Tel: +44 (0)20 7898 1300; Fax: +44 (0)20 7898 1305; orders@ctbi.org.uk; wwww.chbookshop.co.uk

Cover photograph: Painting by M. Bohusz Szysko. Presented to the Church Mission Society (CMS) by friends in 1977. Copyright © CMS and reproduced by permission.

Designed by Church House Publishing

Typeset in 10.5 on 12pt Palatino by Vitaset, Paddock Wood, Kent

Printed by Bookcraft Limited, Midsomer Norton, Somerset

Contents

List of Plates   vi

Foreword   vii

Acknowledgements   ix

Copyright Acknowledgements   xii

Chapter 1   Christ and religion: theological exploration with John V. Taylor   1

Chapter 2   Setting out   17

Chapter 3   Mukono   25

Chapter 4   Way of the Cross   47

Chapter 5   Primal vision   69

Chapter 6   All the world   80

Chapter 7   Theology come of age   103

Chapter 8   Winchester   131

Chapter 9   Christlike God   183

Notes   223

Bibliography   254

Index   269

Plates

Between pp. 148 and 149

1. John with parents, Irene and Ralph.

2. John aged 4 with mother and sister Aileen.

3. Marriage, October 1940.

4. Family at Mukono, 1953 or 1954.

5. The warden of Mukono with an ordinand and his family in the Training Village.

6. Farewell from CMS, late 1974 or early January 1975 (photograph courtesy of John Harwood).

7. Before the Enthronement. Winchester, 8 February 1975 (photograph courtesy of *Hampshire Chronicle*).

8. John at his Enthronement (photograph courtesy of E. A. (Bob) Sollars, Winchester).

9. The 93rd Bishop of Winchester with one of the flock.

10. Visiting Pope Paul VI. Typically, the Bishop presented the Pope with a recording by Winchester Cathedral Choir (photograph courtesy of Fotografia Felici, Rome).

11. Parish visit. The Bishop of Winchester with his chaplain, Ron Diss.

12. Pilgrims. John Taylor and chaplain Ron Diss walking from Dorchester to Winchester 1979, 1300 years after Bishop Hedda relocated the See city (photograph courtesy of *Hampshire Chronicle*).

13. Peggy and John with Ugandan priest in Britain.

14. Diamond wedding anniversary, October 2000. From left to right: Peggy, Peter, John, Veronica and Joanna.

Foreword

Bishop John V. Taylor has had an impact on Anglicans and those of other Christian traditions in recent decades comparable only to that of Archbishop Michael Ramsey. Both men represented an exhilarating largeness of spirit and imagination; they made you believe that this largeness was the native air of Christians, and that to live in such an atmosphere was the most desirable thing in the world. In other words, they made the reality of the Church a missionary reality because they made it compellingly attractive, an environment in which could be found the secret of true and joyful vision.

Vision and mission are both words that will always be associated with John. I remember first hearing of him when people spoke to me in the late sixties about his work – about the CMS newsletters, and how they had changed the frame of reference for so many trying to think about mission in contemporary and intelligent ways; then later about the various books, which I learned to know and love for myself. And I even remember thinking, when he became Bishop of Winchester, that there must be something to be said for the Church of England after all ... Some people have this effect, of making the muddled and tired institutions they serve seem worthwhile after all, dignified and brightened by the service offered to them.

I only came to know John personally after his retirement. In Oxford, he was a wonderful background presence for many of us, a reminder of ways of doing theology that could only come from somewhere other than the academic 'mainstream', and were all the more richly three-dimensional for that. To be with him was always to be recalled to what mattered. His poems above all went straight through any ecclesiastical baggage to the things that struck the heart.

It is a joy to commend this marvellously comprehensive study. A lot of people will have longed to see justice done in this way to both man and work. I hope this book will not only keep the memory alive of a great saint and thinker, but also rekindle the vision he brought to such fullness in Africa and then matured in the years of pastoral and teaching ministry that followed. I hope too that the book will move us to pray that the Church will go on being capacious enough to nourish and utilize people of his exceptional and unchurchy gifts, his depth and his warmth.

The Most Revd Dr Rowan Williams
Archbishop of Wales

Acknowledgements

THIS WORK began as a Ph.D. dissertation in 1992, finally presented to Monash University in Melbourne in 2000. For all but the last few months it was a spare-time occupation, and I would like to thank two Christian communities – St John the Divine Croydon and Christ Church Claremont – who appreciated and loved a parish priest devoted to reading and writing. They were good enough to recognize that whatever disturbed, inspired and enlightened me, also informed my preaching, teaching and pastoring, and was a valuable gift to them as well. In seeing serious theological study as one way in which I cared for the church and fulfilled my ordination vows, they set me free to devote time and energy to intellectual exploration and spiritual discovery – time and energy which might otherwise have been spent on more obviously practical matters. Their generosity and understanding encouraged me to persevere, and the results shared in conversation and communion enriched our shared life as disciples of Christ.

When I began this work through the School of Social and Political Inquiry at Monash, the Revd Dr Larry Nemer SVD of the Yarra Theological Union agreed to supervise the work. After the university required one of its own faculty to undertake this primary supervisory role, the Revd Dr Gary Bouma, Professor of Sociology, kindly agreed to do so. I am extremely grateful for the warm interest and support of Fr Bouma, for helpful criticism and careful direction. Knowing when to push me hard and when to make allowances ensured that this project was completed rather than aborted, with our long-standing friendship surviving intact. Fr Nemer, meanwhile, very graciously consented to continue as auxiliary (and unpaid) supervisor, and I am more grateful than I can say for his meticulous attention to detail and vision for the whole even after he was appointed Director of the London Missionary Institute. Thankfully, this friendship is another to safely survive the rigours of academic supervision.

Early on, when I was feeling diffident, it was Fr Nemer who encouraged me to contact John Taylor. Having himself enjoyed wonderful hospitality and friendship from the retired Max Warren when writing his own doctoral thesis, Fr Nemer convinced me not to be shy in approaching Bishop John. His response was immediate and warm, and he and Peggy generously welcomed my visits to their Oxford home over the last six years of his life. Our meetings, conversations and correspondence proved to be enjoyable and deeply formative. It is a matter of particular satisfaction to me that Bishop John read the completed work and graciously approved my efforts in his final months.

The encouragement, help and hospitality I received from Bishop John's family and friends has made the work both possible and delightful. Others have also been generous in sharing their research and stimulating my thought along the way. In particular I record my thanks to Bishop John Austin Baker, Bishop Simon Barrington-Ward, Paul Bates, Daphne Bowers and the Revd Ray Bowers, the Revd Michael Brierly, the Rt Revd Lord Coggan of Canterbury and Sissinghurst, Bishop David Conner, the Revd Sarah Cowdell, Canon Ron Diss, Glynne Evans, the Revd Jack Hodgins, Pat Hooker and Canon Dr Roger Hooker, Bishop Bill Ind, Sally James and Bishop Colin James, Canon Dr Graham Kings, Professor Ross Langmead, Bishop Michael Manktelow, Archdeacon Trevor Nash, Dean Michael Perham, Barbara and Graham Phillips, Canon J. W. D. Simonson, Juliet Teare and Canon Robert Teare, and Mary Tomsen (Buckley). Since Bishop John's death I have been greatly helped in preparing the manuscript for publication and gathering photographs by his daughters, Joanna Woodd and Veronica Armstrong. I would also like to thank Edward Armstrong for sharing remembrances of his grandfather.

I am grateful for the assistance of expert staff at the Church Mission Society Library at Partnership House, the Lambeth Palace Library, the Hampshire Record Office, the United Faculty of Theology Library in Melbourne, St Mark's Library at the General Theological Seminary, and the Burke Library at the Union Seminary Library in New York City. For providing the perfect environment for completing the work I am indebted to the Community of the Holy Spirit. Living with them in their New York convent for some weeks in 1997 and again for four months in 1999 has been for me a new experience of the Christlike God. Sister Catherine Grace, Sister Domenica, Sister Élise, Sister Faith Margaret, Sister Heléna Marie, Sister Jerolyn Mary, Sister Lesley, Sister Madeleine Mary, Sister Maria Felicitas, Sister Mary Christabel, Sister Mary Elizabeth, Sister Mary Martha, and Sister Penelope Mary – only you really know how much I owe you.

Particular friends have reviewed various drafts of the book and I have profited gladly from their insights and thoughtful comments. In particular I gratefully acknowledge the enthusiasm and encouragement of Dr Jan Chaney, Freda Coish and the Revd Colin Coish, the Revd Professor Mitties DeChamplain, the Revd Ron Dowling, Bishop Brian Farran, Sister Catherine Grace CHS, Canon Theresa Harvey, Liz and Chris Haynes, Elizabeth Millett, the Revd Sean Mullen, the Revd Dr Brian Porter, Wayne Simes, Dorothy and Jay Roth, Tony White, Mary and Tom Williams. My indebtedness to the Revd David Moore and the Revd Christine Simes for endless love and support, criticism and insight, can hardly be exaggerated. Juggling parish and diocesan responsibilities with the business of research and writing would have been impossible without the professionalism, loyalty and good humour of my secretary Maria Barry. Since I moved to Perth in 1994, Archbishop Peter Carnley has enthusiastically supported this work and funded primary research by annual scholarship grants. I am indebted to him and to his wife Ann for their loving care through thick and thin.

My association with Simon Barrow at Churches Together in Britain and Ireland has been one of growing admiration and real enjoyment since he first expressed interest in publishing this book. Quickly I came to respect his opinions and trust his judgement. Working closely with him has been easy, as well as great fun. I am also very grateful for the expertise and cheerful efficiency of Sarah Roberts and her staff at Church House Publishing.

David Wood

Copyright Acknowledgements

Church Mission Society (CMS): Extracts from the following writings by John V. Taylor: annual letter to CMS, September 1951; *Were you There? An African Presentation of the Passion Story*, Highway Press, 1951; 'Vespers', written for 'Southward Bound', 1966; and *Newsletter 297*, October 1966, are reproduced by permission of CMS.

Estate of John V. Taylor: All extracts from the poetry and prose writings of John V. Taylor except those listed on this page are used by permission of the estate of the late John V. Taylor.

Faber & Faber Ltd: Extract from T. S. Eliot, 'Little Gidding' from *The Four Quartets* in *Collected Poems*, Faber & Faber, 1974, p. 215 is reproduced by permission of the publishers.

Harcourt Inc: Excerpt from 'Little Gidding' in *Four Quartets*, copyright 1942 by T. S. Eliot and renewed 1970 by Esme Valerie Eliot, reprinted by permission of Harcourt, Inc.

Routledge: Extract from 'The Gospel of Thomas 77' from Richard Valantasis (ed.), *The Gospel of Thomas, Routledge*, 1997.

SCM Press: Extracts from John V. Taylor, *The Primal Vision*, SCM Press, 1963; *The Go-Between God*, SCM Press, 1972; *The Christlike God*, SCM Press, 1992; and the poem 'Christians and pagans' from Dietrich Bonhoeffer, *Letters and Papers from Prison*, revised, enlarged edition, SCM Press, 1971, p. 348 are reproduced by permission of the publisher.

Scribner, an imprint of Simon & Schuster Adult Publishing Group: 'Christians and pagans' from Dietrich Bonhoeffer, *Letters and Papers from Prison*, revised, enlarged edition, copyright © 1953, 1967, 1971 by SCM Press Ltd.

World Council of Churches, Geneva: Extract from John V. Taylor: *Weep Not for Me: Meditations on the Cross and Resurrection*, Geneva, WCC Risk Books No. 27, 1986.

CHAPTER ONE

Christ and religion: theological exploration with John V. Taylor

Church at the crossroads

IN 1962 Hendrik Kraemer, that doyen of contemporary thinkers about the Christian mission as Max Warren called him,[1] published a small book called *Why Christianity of all Religions?* It was the question of the moment, and nearly forty years later it remains *the* question – and not for Christians alone, but for all human beings who search for meaning. Why Christianity, or, better, why Christ? Why Muhammed, or Islam? Why the Buddha, or Buddhism? Why Judaism? Why this religion, rather than that? Indeed, why believe at all? Is it possible to have faith, or has humanity 'come of age' in a way that renders any and all religion redundant? And if we are to believe, or if some are to believe, how can believers and non-believers live together harmoniously and peacefully?

My interest in all this is both personal and immediate. The question 'why Christ?' is certainly the urgent question for me as a Christian and as a Christian priest at the start of the third millennium of the Common Era.

> Jews from around the world can now fax their prayers to the Wailing Wall in Jerusalem. Fortunetellers in China provide computer-generated astrological charts. Telecommunications satellites link isolated religious communities at separate ends of the earth; American television offers its viewers Christian preachers and Buddhist teachers.[2]

Daily we are confronted by these issues, and in all my work of preaching, teaching, pastoral care and leadership in a local Christian community in a post-Christian society I must address myself to the questions and help others to address them – and do so in faith rather than in fear. At every turn these disparate questions focus in the supreme question: who is God? This forces Christians to concentrate their attention on the very heart of their faith and of all Christian theology, christology – not by worrying about the uniqueness of Jesus of Nazareth, but by exploring the Christlikeness of God.[3]

Concerns over the uniqueness of Christ among the religions of the world frequently seem to be driven by Christian anxiety which is betrayed by the language even of those who wish to welcome the contemporary plural religious scene. Their choice of words gives the game away to the reader – we are faced with an 'intellectual and spiritual threat', a 'problem' or a 'challenge'.[4] 'Challenge' in Christian rhetoric often masks naked fright! Church circles seem unaware that the real question for us is 'What is God up to in a religiously plural world?'[5] There is not much sense among Christians that in the plural religious scene God is offering humanity a new opportunity, nudging each religion out of its tendency to introspective self-reference,[6] forcing us all out of our self-enclosure to become public, so that we insistently interrogate one another and enter into a lively, healthy and life-giving cross-fertilization, a healthy 'theology of cross-reference'.[7]

Bishop John Vernon Taylor offers the Christian Church a way to live which both honours the freedom of the divine Spirit to blow where it will through all religions and none and also holds firmly to the essence of the distinctively Christian revelation of God's nature and being. The God who is everywhere active and who is nowhere without witnesses, however strange and hard to recognize, is none other than the God ultimately disclosed in Jesus, the God who is Christlike, and in whom there is no unChristlikeness at all.[8]

We are aware as never before that we live in a sea of faith, indeed, in a sea of faiths, a time of great scepticism and great credulity, when all truth is relative and privatized – my truth competing with your truth. Popular wisdom decrees that my opinion is as good or as bad as your opinion, no more and no less; everything gains a hearing, and nothing is heard. All religions being simply different paths up the same mountain is a recipe for dangerous indifference, not happy tolerance. If all religions are true, no religion need be taken seriously or seriously considered. Believe or not, as you please. One way or another, who cares?

As Hendrik Kraemer says –

> For the first time since the Constantine victory in A.D. 312 and its consequences, the Christian Church is heading towards a real and spiritual encounter with the great non-Christian religions. Not only because the so-called younger Churches, the fruit of modern missions, live in the midst of them, but also because the fast growing interdependence of the whole world forces the existence and vitality of these religions upon us, and makes them a challenge to the Church to manifest in new terms its spiritual and intellectual integrity and value.[9]

Even more acutely than in Kraemer's day, we live now in a melting pot of peoples and cultures, a plural society in terms of religion and everything else which, more approvingly, we might call a garden of many colours.[10] On the other hand, we may be afraid that choking weeds are thriving among the flowers. In the Churches this is a time of hope for some, and fear for others, a time for opening up in wonder to the incredible diversity of faithful people or a time for strengthening the walls of the city of God against pagan intruders and potential plunderers.

Individuals living in a plural society are not usually plural in their own religious commitments, although it is probable that we are all influenced rather more than we think by prevailing popular culture, drawing good ideas and attitudes from different sources and blending them. All are relativists whether we like it or not. Even those who claim to see things in black and white, consciously struggling to keep ideas and ideologies in water-tight compartments without compromise, contamination or capitulation, are rarely as pure as they pretend. The waters are muddy, the environment is sophisticated and polluted. None of us has access to a single pristine mountain stream.

Until very recently, the apparently exclusive texts of the New Testament did not overly trouble most Christians.[11] In theory, of course, the existence of other religions always posed a challenge to Christianity, and early fathers and doctors of the Church as well as later theologians and apologists addressed themselves to these questions with varying degrees of ingenuity. In a sense, however, even for the experts the difficulties hardly seem to have been overwhelming. As late as the first decades of the twentieth century many or most continued to believe in 'the evangelization of the world in this generation'.[12] If the Christian mission had failed, it had only failed *thus far* – it was now only a matter of resources and time. But by the end of the second millennium a slogan such as 'the evangelization of the world in this generation' seemed little short of absurd. This demonstrates just how far we have moved from the mind-set of our great-grandparents. The old confidence – perhaps the old arrogance – is gone; was it ever justified? All the gospel images of the kingdom, after all, are minority images – salt, light, yeast. Were they ever meant to dominate? Was Christendom the aberration, rather than the norm? In establishing decades of evangelism or evangelization to greet the third millennium, even popes and bishops have the good sense not to predict exact results or set precise goals, deliberately making it difficult or impossible to measure success or failure.

Uncancelled mandate

That Christianity, like its cousin Islam, but unlike its parent faith Judaism, is a missionary religion is a given.[13] That Christianity is essentially missionary in nature is simply an intrinsic fact of history.

Jesus of Nazareth proclaimed the good news of the coming kingdom, the coming reign or dominion of God, and called disciples. 'Follow me' was his invitation to all seekers after truth, and this invitation was issued from start to finish of his ministry. Those seeking God needed to be with Jesus, journeying with him, hearing his public preaching, tutored in the more intimate circle of followers and friends, praying with him, eating and drinking with him, sharing every aspect of his daily walk with God.

Even so, the so-called 'great commission' is not the sole missionary commission in the Christian Scriptures. It is, however, the best known, even to the eclipse in the Christian mind of the other principal contender, seeming to make clear that Christians must make more Christians. 'Go, therefore, and make disciples of all nations, baptizing them in the name of the Father, and of the Son, and of the Holy Spirit.'[14]

In the Gospel of John, however, we find the whole notion of mission expressed quite differently and distinctively. Christians, according to the fourth evangelist and his community, are sent out just as Jesus is sent out. 'As the Father sent me, so I send you.'[15] In other words, God is *the* missionary. God is overflowing, creative, sacrificial Love, self-giving and self-sacrificing, and Christian mission is participation in this one mission of God in the world.[16] The only true mission is primarily God's own going forth to the world in the Son and Holy Spirit. God's mission is the only true mission.

> It is for us to choose whether we shall be caught up into God's mission and participate in it, and so be the Church, or not. The triune God remains till the last day the One who carries on this mission to the uttermost part of the globe, to the uttermost area of human need, and to the uttermost extreme of self-giving.[17]

The implications of the Johannine tradition are worth spelling out and holding in tension with the Matthean tradition. For the mission to be genuine participation in the one mission of God-in-Christ, our mission must be Christlike, mission as we experience it in Jesus of Nazareth, in Christ's own way, in God's good time,[18] proclamation not propaganda, for propaganda smacks too much of human stratagem. It is never proselytizing, for God does not proselytize. God calls and waits and judges, seeks and serves and suffers.[19] We are not authorized to engage in mission that is not founded and modelled on Christ's mission. The way we think about mission and the way we carry it out is patterned for us in advance by the pioneer of our faith. Crucially, God alone sees the End when the mission will be completed, for Christ is perfector of faith as well as pioneer, and so Christian missionaries can be properly agnostic about the outcomes of mission. Will we make more Christians? Will we, in the end, perhaps, make everyone Christian? Is this the goal of Christian mission? Is this God's will and plan? The answer, if we are honest, is that we don't and can't know. The future is in the hands of God. Just as the Beginning belongs to God, so the End belongs to God. What is required of us is humility and, within the context of such humble honesty in the face of mystery, faithfulness in word and deed, at whatever cost. We are called to faithfulness in action for truth, for justice, mercy, compassion; faithfulness in speaking the name of Jesus when the time is right, bearing witness by explicit word as occasion arises, to God whose we are and whom we serve.[20] Success, in terms of growth in numbers or even quality of committed Christians, is not our business. Conversion of heart belongs always to God alone, for the activity of the Spirit in human beings is beyond any possibility of our manipulation, even beyond our comprehension.

Regardless of our model of mission, however, it is impossible for Christianity to renounce the missionary commission of the missionary Lord, so integral is it to the faith. 'The Church exists by mission as a fire exists by burning.'[21] The missionary mandate has not been cancelled,[22] but how do we express it with integrity today and tomorrow and exercise it sensitively rather than aggressively? Is it possible to exercise Christian ministry and mission with genuine respect for others made in the image of God?[23] Can we honour and reverence the holy no matter where and in whom it is found, and however strange or disturbing it may be?

Those touched by the Spirit of Christ inevitably ask themselves such questions. If we cannot excise evangelism from the Christian agenda, it is encouraging to see widespread confusion about content and style, concern about the ethical issues involved in any contemporary proclamation of the gospel, and newfound humility in place of unthinking triumphal violence. If we have somehow lost our nerve, this loss of nerve is welcome. For one thing, it is honest. It faces the fact that there has been what Hendrik Kraemer calls an 'earthquake' in our world, and one result must be the emergence of a humbler Church.

The Second World War deprived Europe for good and all of its former place at the centre of the world. Since then the daily spectacle has been of nations achieving their independence and sovereignty. The Asian countries broke free; and no one can calculate or predict what the outcome of that is likely to be. They are in the throes of spectacular, painful and often alarming struggles to become real nations and reach stability as states. Africa was already well and truly awakened and took a leap out of 'the primitive state' straight into the full and complex life of modernity manufactured by the West. 'It has become the arena of a great spiritual struggle in which the issue is whether African "paganism" is to be replaced for the most part by incorporation into Islam or incorporation into the Christian Church.'[24]

All this was the stuff of day to day life, ministry and mission for the principal Anglican missionary society, the Church Missionary Society, through the general secretaryships of Max Warren and John Taylor. Their knowledge of the developing world was unrivalled, and their creative and sensitive leadership crucial as the map of the world changed colour, as the British Empire died and the Anglican Communion of independent churches was born. As more and more peoples stood on their own feet and took responsibility for their own destiny in the modern world, mission in this second half of the twentieth century gradually became a matter of partnership between sister churches rather than dependence on mother.

The transformation of the vast world into the global village turned out to be a very mixed blessing.[25] It enriches us by heightening our awareness and understanding of each other, while simultaneously impressing on us a new sense of uncertainty and impermanence. 'Economic, financial, and technical forces have created a global system that is far more powerful than most existing states. The secular powers shaping human life are increasingly transnational.'[26]

Why Christ?

In this environment sensitive mutual awareness is crucial, not least to replace lazy or wishful thinking, xenophobia and bigotry. The conventional wisdom seems to be that all religions boil down to the same essence, teaching basically the same truths, all simply different paths to the same god. This approach is undoubtedly fuelled by good intentions and born of a genuine desire for reconciliation between believers and a genuine longing for human harmony.

Regardless of motivation, however, this argument fails to convince because it is simply incompatible with reality. It fails to pay adequate attention to the facts of life. All religions make truth claims. Some of these truths coincide, others are complementary, while others again are contradictory. Not all the spiritual food in the smorgasbord is equally digestible or nourishing. Hans Küng found a striking way of encapsulating this reality by comparing the deaths of great religious leaders.

> Anyone who thinks that all religions and their 'founders' are alike will see the differences which appear if they compare the deaths of such men. Moses, Buddha, Confucius, all died at a ripe old age, successful despite many disappointments, in the midst of their disciples and supporters, their 'span of life completed' like the patriarchs of Israel. According to the tradition, Moses died in sight of the promised land, in the midst of his people, at the age of 120 years, his eyes undimmed, his vigour unfaded. Buddha died at the age of eighty, peacefully, his disciples around him, after he had collected in the course of his itinerant preaching a great community of monks, nuns and lay supporters. Confucius returned in old age to Lau ... after he had spent his last years in training a group of mainly noble disciples, to preserve and continue his work, and in editing the ancient writings of his people, to be transmitted to posterity only in his version. Muhammad, after he had thoroughly enjoyed the last years of his life as political ruler of Arabia, died in the midst of his hareem in the arms of his favourite wife. On the other hand we have a young man of thirty, after three years at most of activity, perhaps only a few months. Expelled from society, betrayed and denied by his disciples and supporters, mocked and ridiculed by his opponents, forsaken by humankind and even by God, he goes through a ritual of death that is one of the most atrocious and enigmatic ever invented by our ingenious cruelty. Jesus' violent end was the logical conclusion of his proclamation and his behaviour.[27]

Factual and undisputed historical knowledge, however, may help to clarify our thinking and be indispensable to any genuine inter-faith encounter, but it also increases our anxiety. It is precisely our *knowing more* which undermines confidence in us and in our structures of meaning, so that we still find ourselves 'tossed about on a sea of doubt and uncertainty'.[28]

Another real breeding ground of doubt, questioning and uncertainty in the Western world is the relativism resulting from a whole series of scientific discoveries. Since everything is comparative, we live in a perpetual state of uncertainty, inquiry and experiment. There is absolutely no absolute; the only certainty is change. The multiplicity of religions is simply something more to be experienced, spirituality is yet another leisure industry. Where there are no absolutes, it is impossible to argue that Christianity, considered as a concrete, historical phenomenon and just one more religion, is absolute in any sense, true where others are not, or somehow only true. 'If we take the word in the absolute sense invariably ascribed to it in ordinary usage, then *there is no true religion.*'[29]

> If one looks at the thing honestly, there are only religions which present interwoven threads of truth and error which it is impossible to disentangle. Christianity as a religion, which has unfolded in an historical setting, is just like other religions in being a body of human ideas and institutions which is 'passing away', as all things human do, and so cannot possibly be absolute. Christianity is therefore not absolute. It is not even in all respects the 'best' religion, if by that we mean the religion which has found the best and noblest way of expressing religious truth and experience.[30]

If Christians are to speak in terms of absolutes at all, it is not Christianity we must speak of, but the Christ at its heart. 'Why Christ?' is always the more precise formulation of the real question. 'What is absolute is not Christianity but the revelation of God in Jesus Christ. He has no need of our proofs. He simply reigns from the cross, even were no one to recognise the fact.'[31]

Hendrik Kraemer, Max Warren and the subject of this study, John Taylor, all belong to one family of thinkers. This distinguished tradition becomes the distinctive Anglican stance, offering an attractive basis for thinking through complex and contentious issues of mission and evangelism at the turn of the millennium. Already at the Anglican Congress in Toronto in 1963, we find Max Warren, on the eve of retiring from CMS, and in the presence of his chosen successor, saying precisely the same thing as Kraemer, albeit with a considerably larger dose of poetry.

> In the beginning, God. In the end, God. And surely we have to learn to say, 'in the middle, God. In the centre, at the heart of things, God.' God has

revealed himself in divers manners. We should be bold to insist that God was speaking in that cave outside Mecca; that God brought illumination to the man who once sat under the Bo tree; that the insight into the reality of the moral struggle and of our freedom to choose the right, which was given to Zoroaster, came from God; that it was God who spoke to a simple Japanese peasant woman a hundred years ago, and that God is at work among the four million Japanese who follow her teaching; that indeed the God of a hundred names is still God. Thus boldly to insist is in no way whatever to hesitate in affirming what we believe, that in a quite unique way he revealed himself in Jesus Christ our Lord. I wish I knew how best to insist on that uniqueness. Perhaps I must content myself with the Incarnatus of our Creed and say simply that once upon a time the Word was made flesh at Bethlehem.[32]

Hendrik Kraemer, himself a Christian theologian with some first-hand experience of other religions, alerts us to the failure of theologians to engage satisfactorily with religious plurality. He points us to the missionaries and their experience of Christian mission in particular cultures, with people who have histories, faces, names, hopes and fears. We must pay attention to the experiences and learnings of the missiologists. Max Warren's knowledge of the missionary scene was unrivalled, but his first-hand experience was almost as limited as Kraemer's.[33] It could be argued that John Taylor is both Kraemer and Warren with significant first-hand missionary experience added to the recipe.

This is why John Taylor really comes into focus. With ten years living the gospel as a missionary in Uganda, and another five years working for the International Missionary Council – he is accustomed to living with, listening to, reflecting on, and writing about Christian mission in the real world and in the actual situation of the local church. The essential foundation for his years as Africa Secretary and later General Secretary of the Church Missionary Society was laid in the field, and this African experience is also essential to understanding his ministry as Bishop of Winchester. John Taylor came early to the conviction that the churches must 'pay attention to the facts'[34] and would know the disappointment of finding theologians so enmeshed in book learning as to be uninterested in the facts of lived experience.[35]

Christian presence in the world, paying attention to the facts, taking historical events seriously, genuine engagement with the textured world of experience, facing up to the challenge presented to a Church on trial by religious plurality – these are the constants of John Taylor's ministry. Evangelism means calling people to believe something radically different from what currently is accepted as public truth, for a conversion of both heart and mind. 'A serious commitment to evangelism, to the telling of the story that the Church is sent to tell, means a radical questioning of the reigning assumptions of public life.'[36]

Thesis

The question addressed by this book is the extent to which John Taylor has made an original contribution to theology and missiology, and how his seminal ten years in Uganda informed and directed his subsequent thinking, writing and ministry.

The old conviction that all non-Christian religion is idolatry whose devotees are going to hell provides powerful and urgent motivation for evangelism. Salvation equals saving the lost in this narrow sense, and their peril demands immediate and sustained action. John Taylor is emphatically not in the business of reinstating these traditional missionary motives, which he thinks are mistaken, a misreading of the gospel committed to us. But if there is no authentic power left in such threadbare imperial theology, what will replace it? Are we sufficiently concerned to proclaim the gospel as public truth, and what will motivate us to act?

The Church's loss of conviction stems, John Taylor suggests, from the fact that what Christians say they believe so inadequately describes what we commonly experience. Making connections between doctrine and normal experience becomes for John Taylor one of the most urgent tasks of mission. 'Perhaps the only connection that can now be unmistakably brought home to our Western civilization in its affluent meaninglessness is that between its own experience of decline and the theology of judgement.'[37] But there are no grounds for gloom in this prognostication, for the mission is not ours but God's, and if the flesh-taking of the Incarnation is the pattern rather than the exception which shows us what God is really like, then the hope is that this Word will now grasp and mould our own flesh. If Christ lives in and through the Christian people, then our contemporary mission will presumably be as diverse in its range and style as his. It will also be equally gracious and life giving, for it will be none other than Christ acting now for the life of the world.

These contemporary incarnations of Christ will initially involve Christian and non-Christian alike in a process of un-learning fixed ideas and images of God. Christ, living now in his followers and friends, joins all honest seekers after truth, searching the great perennial human questions about pain and loss, suffering and evil, but the distinctively Christian question is always 'Does God bleed?' The religiously plural context of contemporary mission sharpens our articulation of the Christian contribution. John Taylor teaches that accepting pluralism as God-given is not so much a threat to faith as an invitation to radical trust, because it is God's invitation for the Church to embrace God's own way in the world, the way of the cross. Our distinctive Christian contribution to the universal human conversation present and future means sharing the stupendous revelation that God is not some vague mystery or even that God is love, but that God is Christlike. This unique penetration of the divine mystery – alongside real insights from other religious experience – allows everyone to glimpse precisely the kind of love burning in the heart of the only true God. If Christ shows us that only a *wounded* God will do, our peculiarly Christian witness necessitates pointing directly – by the way we live as much as by what we say – to God's everlasting self-sacrifice.

Methodology

Making connections between Christian doctrine and ordinary experience is personal and it begins in oneself, so this work looks at John Taylor's theology, and particularly his theology of mission, as it is expressed in his own life as Christ's disciple. The biographical element is intentional and deliberate, central and inescapable in this study. One whose theology is so intensely and insistently incarnational must himself be incarnate for us and with us. The Christian doctrine of the Incarnation can be said to represent the Church's paramount discovery that in Jesus of Nazareth truth spoken via a prophet deepens into truth in personhood, as if prophecy necessitates and enlists, indeed *becomes* biography. 'In the New Testament, "truth through personality" is not, as in Islamic tradition, a secondary, ancillary, vehicle of revelation – it is crucial and definitive.'[38] 'Biography', claims Kenneth Cragg, 'has always been the first clue to theology, and in Christian tradition the reality of God is believed to have been biographized in Jesus as the Christ – the divine Word expressed in human terms and engaged with just those issues of wrong and mysteries of meaning which most bewilder and oppress the human self.'[39] This insight of Bishop Cragg is integral to John Taylor's own teaching. God creates and loves and redeems the whole person, not just the religious bits, and because salvation is *for* the whole person, the gospel must be conveyed *by* the whole person – including what we tell (proclamation), what we are (life and witness) and what we do (service, ministry and mission).[40]

Witness is a way of living, or, better, a way of the crucified and raised Christ living in particular individual disciples and in whole Christian communities. 'Because the ultimate power and eternal meaning which we call God has been perfectly disclosed in one human life we have learned to see the same meaning shining just below the surface of our most casual and humdrum experiences.'[41] To witness is to remember this so that others can catch sight of Christ and touch the hem of his garment.[42] This encounter is always orchestrated by the Holy Spirit, the go-between God who enables us consciously to enjoy God's gift of communion. We are to testify *from* our experience and also to offer testimony *in* our experience, as both eyewitnesses and evidence,[43] concerned with showing even more than with speaking.[44] In a time when fatal distinctions between objective and subjective knowledge poison all seeking after truth, this study champions the centrality of the person and the personal. In order to believe that truth is still knowable, all our knowing has to be personal commitment, without any external guarantee that we may not be mistaken. All knowing involves struggle, tentative exploration, feeling one's way.

> The alternative to subjectivity is not an illusory claim to objectivity, but the willingness to publish and to test. The proper answer to the charge of subjectivity is world mission, but it is world mission not as proselytism but as exegesis.[45]

So we must examine the telling of the great story through the telling of particular stories, of one little story at a time. Repeatedly, there is something magnetic and exciting noted about the person of John Taylor.[46] You cannot fully appreciate his significance unless you see and hear him. The personal magnetism is compelling. One astute observer sees this clearly:

> Holy Week 1984. The chapel of the Ecumenical Centre in Geneva. A crowd of people, gathered in circular formation, intently listening to a man dressed in a faded purple cassock as he quietly leads them deeper into the mystery of God, of the cross. A community of seekers, glad and heartened at not being fobbed off with easy answers, seeing in this man, John Taylor, with his scarred eyes and humorous mouth someone who had also suffered and doubted and been tempted, a fellow pilgrim.[47]

This reflects my own experience in a retreat house on the outskirts of Rome in 1990. Morning after morning, in the intense July heat, the bishop appeared dressed in purple shirt and pectoral cross to lecture to clergy from three continents dressed in shorts and sandals. Always, there was a sense of occasion, yet without any personal grandstanding. This was plainly not episcopal power dressing, for at other times John Taylor was indistinguishable from the rest of us and mixed freely with everyone. At breakfast he wore an open-necked shirt, but he changed before his lectures and then again afterwards. The signal was clear: the lectures dealt with a tremendously important subject, demanded serious intellectual endeavour and required a certain formality. We were honoured to find that we ourselves merited such marks of respect.

I had already fallen under the spell of John Taylor through reading *The Go-Between God*, but it was those weeks in Rome, sitting at his feet each day, soaking up the words, captivated by the word-smith, that made this awakening of imagination to the theological quest permanent. This is one reason why it is necessary to quote John Taylor's own words at greater length than is customary, for we miss the authentic tone of voice if we avoid the performance and artistry of the preacher. This priest and prophet is also poet.

If, as the great Australian poet Les Murray contends, every religion is a long poem, then perhaps only poets can really be theologians,[48] a statement that will infuriate most theologians. Does it mean the best theologians are intuitive, rather than rational and precise? Perhaps. More significantly, however, it means that real theologians must be people of imagination, capable of thinking and writing evocatively, advancing by hints and glimpses, identifying and sharing insights.[49] Imaginative, evocative theology, however, may well be unsystematic, and therefore academically unpopular. At least one professor who assigned *The Go-Between God* as a textbook admitted to his students that, given the subject, this is possibly inevitable. 'The Holy Spirit may never sit still long enough to allow a detailed, full-length portrait.'[50] In other words, the unsystematic theology of John Taylor may itself reveal the truth about the nature of God. Can the untidy God of surprises ever be truthfully delineated in human systems?[51]

The emphasis in this study, then, is on what Kenneth Cragg calls 'biographies of mind', or intellectual biography.[52] Like Bishop Cragg himself, we employ this method in the hope that it 'may serve to focus what is at stake in contemporary pluralism and do so effectively for being intimate and personal'.[53] If the two biblical words for time, *chronos* (time measured horizontally, time which passes) and *kairos* (time measured vertically, the appropriate time or the critical hour) can be applied to individual lives, then biography as theology seems to be demanded. Most of us live relatively insignificant lives, time passes; but there are a few whose existence encapsulates something of greater significance.[54]

Theology, then, cannot only be 'faith seeking understanding' as an intellectual exercise, any more than it is a talking head or a writing hand.[55] Theology is *thought* and *taught* and *lived*, always ministered, never simply proclaimed. All truth, and all theology, is relational,[56] and any response of faith to life, any relating of life to faith, must be autobiographical. 'Negotiation and situation' are always part of an internal conversation,[57] 'for that is where life is consciously happening and faith is inwardly reached and trusted'.[58] Inevitably, such a quest articulates the explorer's own theology seen through the lens of John Taylor's life and work and thought. Following in his footsteps and those of his principal influences, especially Dietrich Bonhoeffer, such theology is in the end my own, authentic rather than derivative because it is the product of my own tears and the humus of my own life. Only so does it become an invitation to further revelation, as opposed to providing a defence shield or safe hiding-place. Biography and autobiography involve emerging from the shadows and declaring one's hand. True theologizing demands coming out, and truth is not merely proposition or statement, but always a transaction with the hearer, a dialogue between what we have to say and the one to whom it is said. I do not know what I think until I hear what I say, until I see how my words are received. I do not know what I believe until I am living through crisis. Linguistically, conversation and conversion are linked because theology is forged in dialogical encounters. Inter-faith dialogue is simply an extension of that intra-faith dialogue in which the household of faith is enlarged, despite fears that renovation will destroy the house we know and love, permanently changing its aspect and its face. According to John Taylor, God's surprise for those with the courage to face their fears and overcome them with trusting faith – is that Christ, the Man in the midst,[59] Christ who is Everyman,[60] turns out to be at home in this many-roomed mansion, albeit as a disruptive and disturbing guest![61]

If we are made in the divine image, human relationships, biographical stories, must be central to the theological quest, for the last thing God can be is an individual.[62] Not surprisingly, for sixteen of the twenty Christian centuries 'mission' was used exclusively of the Trinity; applied to human activity, it really describes a reflection here and now of the divine life as it is from before the foundation of the world.[63]

This methodology has its dangers, not least that I may objectify one who long ago became a subject for me, and so find that the real John Taylor slips through my fingers. The meeting of *thou* with *Thou*, or indeed simply of *thou* with *thou*, generated by God the Spirit, lasts only so long as truth faces truth.[64] The truth about something or someone is like a string of adjectives, but the truth *of* something or someone must always be experienced as a noun or pronoun.

> It demands that I meet it in my own integrity. If I respond with pretension or begin to play a part, the other withdraws, because my attention is now turned upon myself. As soon as I dramatise myself as an aspiring Mallory I lose the truth of the real Kilimanjaro and am left with a fantasy mountain of my own creation. As soon as I pretend to see in the Titian the things other people have said I ought to see, it ceases to speak with its own authority, for the scribes have taken over.[65]

Troubled creatures that we are, this living out of belief, trust and faith will inevitably be patchy. Large stretches of any one of us remain unredeemed. Even saints have their dark sides and John Taylor was no exception. Biography, not hagiography, is the stuff of theology.[66] Like Scripture and the Church's living tradition and history, biography intends to be historically true, if not always free of legend and embellishment. Biography as a true *human* story is the form of story most nearly suited to Christian faith.[67] 'In the words and wounds of Jesus as the Christ there has been a divine disclosure of God, a biography, as it were, "a writing-in-life" where the divine has been defined, denoted, described and dramatized.'[68]

Biography as theology cannot, of course, replace propositional theology. It is not intended to do so. It complements, disturbs and enhances it, however, not least by continually asking propositional theology if this religion makes us more human or less.[69] Another person's life story affirms, undermines or revolutionizes our understanding of the tradition we inherit, and helps us recover lost aspects of the tradition and question aspects we hold sacred.[70]

> Theology needs life stories not just for illustrative purposes and not just to give personal examples of doctrine and morals. Rather, our theology must

be adequate to lives such as these lives; we seek to shape in our times a faith adequate to the intensity and spiritual seriousness of these life stories.[71]

To attempt a biography of mind, expecting to discover theology in biography and biography in theology, inevitably means that the results are illuminating and suggestive, fragmentary and partial. Hans Keller wisely observes that in our biography-obsessed age we like to think that the life explains the work, whereas more often the work explains the life.[72] The interest lies in how closely the two are interrelated. Who is this person who writes so beautifully? Does he manage to practise what he preaches?

In asking such questions, we must beware of falling between two stools. On the one hand, it is impossible to tell the whole story of John Taylor's life, to write a full biography that looks at every single moment giving rise to theological reflection, watching him act out his convictions hour by hour. As John Updike says, 'description solidifies the past and creates a gravitational body that wasn't there before', but there is also 'a background of dark matter – all that is not said', which 'remains, buzzing'.[73] Description, therefore, already involves some distorting of the plain facts, offering a solidity that was not actually present in the fluid reality of the life as actually lived. This book is plainly not an attempt at biography in that sense.

Some activities of the mind, on the other hand, are also not here, for the life of the mind can be glimpsed only as a series of cameos rather than as a coherent whole. But how can theology touch us if it comes sanitized, divorced from the ordinary and the everyday, gloriously independent of personal experience, emotions and vicissitudes, the theologian without her or his humanity? How can a person be real without shadows, mistakes, deliberate as well as accidental wrong turns?[74] This particular intellectual biography aims to record some of the more seminal moments in a very rich life, and is, necessarily, fragmentary. Anything more ambitious would introduce a false note of triumphalism.

Characteristics of a theologian

John Taylor says of himself that he has no theological system, that he is not really a theologian, but simply a man in his humanity learning by looking at what is going on inside himself as he lives in the world, open to its influences.[75] At the start of his three major books he goes out of his way to disclaim any authority for his own theology. He is merely 'a bagman'[76] or 'a borrower and retailer of other men's ideas',[77] or, to use St Paul's phrase, a *spermologos*, a 'snapper up of others' words', who has enjoyed a 'free-range pecking', and produced 'a collection of other people's flowers'.[78] Some critics would agree that he is not a theologian in the formal sense, and that he offers no coherent or systematic theology; he is simply an anthologist.[79] Indeed, the charge might be made that the result of John

Taylor's explorations and efforts is unsystematic theology, at best abhorrent and unforgivable to professional theologians, at worst subjective and
whimsical.[80]

Acknowledging these realities and dangers, my contention is that it is
precisely in John Taylor's fragmentary, tentative exploration, and
particularly in the brilliantly creative way in which insights and ideas are
gathered, juxtaposed, or simply held together in tension, that he makes
his unique contribution.[81] Indeed, it is in his willingness to admit others to
his own unfinished internal dialogue, allowing us to share his struggles
and strategies for continuing belief and trust, that John Taylor's theology
bursts into flame, exciting, stimulating, rescuing, evoking new dimensions
in ways not open to more constrained practitioners.[82] We might, however,
want to ask, must 'subjectivity' and 'whimsicality' always be pejorative?
Genuinely creative people do not necessarily come up with anything not
seen before, so much as combine components that are strange to one
another. Creativity lies in these new associations, surprising connections
between things we already know, combinations which make the familiar
strange again, arresting attention, disturbing complacency, inviting further
exploration.

In what has been called his eclectic 'weaver bird' theology, John Taylor
offers something rare – a genuinely honest theology, without the
pretension of artificial or arbitrary order imposed on an untidy world.[83] He
has the intellectual or theological expertise to produce a splendid
theological edifice, but he lacks the passion to do so. Such a theology, for
him, would lack integrity. However impressive, it would ultimately be
unreal in failing to pay attention to all the facts, messy, contradictory and
distressing facts as well as the delightful and exciting. These facts are ragged
around the edges, like the back view of the weaver's loom,[84] and cannot
be systematized; any systematic theology is too grand a project and
something of an illusion, perhaps a mirage. It was Ralph Waldo Emerson
who castigated 'foolish consistency' as 'the hobgoblin of little minds,
adored by little statesmen and philosophers and divines'.[85] John Taylor's
humble theology may be the only theologizing open to any of us today.
Anything grander is simply too arrogant to gain a respectful hearing in so
diverse and plural a world. Anything more comprehensive is a proud
delusion inconsistent with the authority of Jesus Christ. It may be, of
course, that we are so intent on conquering that we cannot help shouting,
but while this technique seems to do well in terms of numbers, loudhailer
evangelism is ultimately doomed to failure, because it is basically
inconsistent with the way of Christ, for in all the records we have his own
temper and practice are consistently gentle.

Paying attention to the facts means that now we know only in part.
There is no viable Christian alternative. This realization makes for modest
theology, arising out of faith *humbly* and *humanly* seeking understanding.
A question asked by the biographer of Dietrich Bonhoeffer may also be

asked of John Taylor, Bonhoeffer's disciple: 'Does not the conviction that he carries derive from the incompleteness of the man and his answers, because he presents us, not with a finished doctrine, but with an active process of learning?'[86] It is worth remembering that the root of the words humiliation and humility is *humus*.

> To be down in the straw and the dung and the refuse – Paul's words – is to become the soil in which the seed of Christ's manhood falls and dies and brings forth the harvest. Here is the meeting of the four elements: we the earth, and the Spirit the wind, the water and the fire.[87]

CHAPTER TWO

Setting out

JOHN TAYLOR was born in 1914. He was brought up in the Church of England, the son of a priest in the English evangelical tradition who ended his ministry as Bishop of Sodor and Man. When John Taylor was four years old his father, John Ralph Strickland Taylor, became headmaster of a small independent school on the coast north of Dover, St Lawrence's at Ramsgate. Here visitors from all parts of the world were invited to lecture or preach in the school and were also house-guests of the headmaster and his family. This meant that from an early age, John Taylor was in close contact with Indian, Chinese and African church leaders. The influence of this rather exotic and cosmopolitan environment, combined with the daily sight of the sea and the horizon, shaped his imagination. In his own words, it 'created for me a beckoning world beyond my immediate rather flat and colourless surroundings'.[1]

This romantic fascination with geography is not to be despised as a spark to ignite a sense of vocation. If mission is apostolic, from the Greek απoστoλoς (*apostolos*), one who is *sent*, you can only be sent from where you are to somewhere else. Nothing could be more logical or obvious. 'If you stay where you were before, you have not been sent, or at least you have not gone.'[2]

Mission, by definition, involves going elsewhere. At first, this elsewhere was understood quite literally. It meant physical relocation.[3] Only gradually and painfully would the mature John Taylor discover that the mission field may not be a *geographical* elsewhere, but a *cultural* elsewhere. It may involve an emotional or spiritual relocation, a going to people who speak with a different accent or have a different background. Nevertheless, it follows that the image of journey is always a valid metaphor of mission, and the first crucial step is out of your own shoes into the shoes of another person, or, even more significantly, out of your own ears into the ears of the person you are talking with, in order to hear your own words as the other hears them. Standing in another's shoes, or sitting where others sit, are classic metaphors of missionary technique, but stepping out of your own ears into the ears of a conversation partner seems to be a characteristically John Taylor formulation, learnt through painful experience.[4]

> My germinal *yonderlust* might just as well have led me towards the colonial service or into social anthropology or even psychiatry were it not for the

religious motivation which my parents gently and consistently imparted to me throughout my childhood.[5]

In fact John Taylor's service in the Church's mission, in Africa, London and Winchester, led him in various ways to be social anthropologist and even colonial civil servant at a time when the Empire was breaking up as British colonies achieved independence – and pastoral ministry always gives scope for amateur psychiatric analysis!

As a child growing up in such an environment, John Taylor was also acquiring heroes, populating his imagination by reading romantic missionary biographies, so that from the age of ten or eleven he was imbued with the desire to share and help, and with the certainty that Jesus Christ was somehow central to this process. 'Of those to whom much is given much will be required' is gospel seed, but it finds particularly fertile soil in the imperial mind, in the England of empire, of colony and even of commonwealth. Not surprisingly then, by the time he was sixteen John Taylor was sure he should prepare himself for service abroad. In what capacity he was not clear. Slowly and steadily – almost inevitably, given the culture of home and school and Church – he was absorbing the view that the missionary is the first-class Christian, the heroic Christian.[6] His subsequent decision to seek ordination was taken with this general missionary aim in view. He never seems to have imagined that his ministry would be in England, apart from his initial training which routinely included some years as a curate in a parish.

Tertiary education followed the usual privileged pattern. He went to Trinity College, Cambridge, to take a degree in English literature and history, followed by theology at St Catherine's College, Oxford.[7] From 1936 he was at Wycliffe Hall, a theological college in the evangelical tradition situated in Oxford, where his father was now principal. Apart from his time at Cambridge, it could be argued that he never left home and that his headmaster and then his principal was always his own father! This would certainly be traditional education with a twist,[8] but is, however, stretching things just a bit far. In fact, by the time John Taylor went to secondary school his father was no longer headmaster, and returning to live close to his family at Wycliffe after three years away in Cambridge can hardly be construed as a return to the nest.

The choice of Wycliffe was deliberately made. Ridley Hall at Cambridge was considered, but it seemed to John Taylor, his father and other advisers that little lively and warm inspirational theology was offered at that time by the members of the Cambridge divinity faculty.[9] This was just before great scholars like C. H. Dodd began to make their mark. To avoid a rather dull situation, the shift to Oxford was deemed best. Joe Fison, Douglas Harrison, Alan Thornhill, Stephen Neill and F. W. Dillistone were all then teaching at Oxford. At the same time John Taylor naturally gravitated to a group of students who were all thinking in terms of service abroad. The culture of this group involved schoolboy camps and beach missions, and he joined that circuit as a leader and speaker.

Made deacon in Advent 1938, he was ordained to the priesthood at Michaelmas 1939 and, because the war was just beginning, the priesting took place in the crypt of St Paul's Cathedral rather than in the great metropolitan church itself. The ordaining bishop for his diaconate was the famous Arthur Foley Winnington-Ingram, who had been Bishop of London for longer than anyone could remember.[10] John Taylor was priested, however, by one of the suffragans during the vacancy before Geoffrey Fisher became diocesan. His first curacy was at the famous central London Church of All Souls, Langham Place, a centre of evangelical life and influence in the capital and beyond. He remained there for two years. The vicar, Harold Earnshaw-Smith, while not as famous as his successor John Stott, was undoubtedly one of the really big names on the evangelical scene at that time.

There was a particular taste to conservative evangelicalism in those days, a narrowness and a lack of intellectual force, for evangelicals tended to be a rather dispirited rump. The Oxford Movement and the Catholic Revival in the Church of England had transformed the whole Church. These were salad days for everyone but evangelicals, when Anglo-Catholicism was at its most triumphant, and not least in the Diocese of London. John Taylor, possibly due to his father's influence, had never imbibed this particular ghetto mentality, characterized by evangelical narrowness, or its characteristic earnestness; besides, he had a sense of humour.[11] The best of the evangelicals at Cambridge, and later at Oxford, were able to laugh at the whole thing.[12]

John Taylor came now under the influence of Max Warren, the young and attractive Vicar of Holy Trinity, Cambridge, a landmark in town and university life because of its association with Charles Simeon and the Evangelical Revival. He also joined the Cambridge Inter-Collegiate Christian Union, even though it considered Max Warren dangerously unsound! John Taylor would become CICCU prayer secretary and, later, vice-president. He was an exact contemporary of Robin Woods,[13] who became president of the Student Christian Movement at about the same time. Where the CICCU tended to be exclusive and biblically conservative, the SCM was ecumenical and more liberal in its attitudes. From the day of their appointment John Taylor and Robin Woods broke all the rules, risking contamination by forming a lasting friendship and breakfasting together every Sunday.

Conservative evangelicals at this time were not all biblical fundamentalists, but they were certainly cautious in their biblical criticism. Some at least were ready to be flexible, and they were open to new insights. While they were not totally hostile to biblical criticism, they were slow to change. At Wycliffe there was no great conflict between in-house theology and what was learnt in the schools of the university.[14] In this, John Taylor was more fortunate than some of his contemporaries. At Trinity College, Bristol, Kenneth Cragg's faith and life negotiation was delayed by highly protective tuition.[15] Biblical criticism should be noted for examination purposes, but otherwise dismissed as untrue.[16] For all its intellectual openness, there was, nevertheless, at Wycliffe a typically strong and abiding belief in the power of the gospel to bring about change in people's lives. The shared conviction was that, by its plain meaning and the grace of the Holy Spirit, the evangel could work the miracle of conversion of heart.

There was also a characteristic evangelical conviction about the absolute priority of conversion. For his part, however, John Taylor was wary. Even then there was an independent streak and an instinctive rejection of overly simple answers to complex questions. He was honest enough to see that conversion is a pastoral activity and process, not just a matter of saying 'down on your knees, change direction, give yourself to Christ'. People are different, people are complex and subtle, sometimes inconsistent, even contradictory. Surrendering one's life to Christ may take a longer or shorter time, involving false starts, wrong turns and reversals as much as good intentions and generous commitments. In any event, it will be anything but a straightforward transaction. And he knew too that he could point to no spectacular moment of conversion in his own life.[17] This was undoubtedly something of a liability for any young evangelical. In this particular atmosphere, immersed in this culture of conviction, he sometimes felt like a man with no trumps in his hand.[18] While this made him cautious, the fact that he could not point to any spectacular conversion experience himself was not too serious. It was not exactly mandatory. It was acceptable to have grown up in the tradition. No wonder John Taylor never much cared for first-born/second-born distinctions.[19]

All Souls, Langham Place was not something he sought out or negotiated for himself. You didn't put yourself forward. You waited to be asked. In the natural (or providential) course of events, Earnshaw Smith came to one of the seaside children's missions as a speaker. He met John Taylor and quite soon after invited him to be his next curate or, in the language of the time, 'offered him a title' without which he could not be ordained. John Taylor was more than lucky in this encounter. Earnshaw Smith was a superbly beautiful preacher. In his curate's words, he was 'glowing' in the pulpit.[20] This was not great elocution, not great rhetoric, but there was warmth and life. He taught John Taylor to love the beauty of the Church's traditional liturgy. It was simple evangelical worship, faithful to the Prayer Book and deeply reverent. At the Lord's Table they took up their positions at either end – the book-ends position as it was known derisively in some circles.[21] Apart from such party symbols, Earnshaw Smith knew how to order worship. He also made sure that John Taylor could use his voice and that he had experience of other places and styles of worship – sending him to an elocutionist and giving him occasional Sundays off so that he could experience for himself what other churches were doing.

It was here at All Souls that John Taylor met Peggy, then a violin student at the prestigious Royal College of Music. The church organist invited John Taylor to give some Bible readings at the RCM, and he remembers that by about his third visit he began to be more aware of one of the students. They got secretly engaged in his first year at All Souls, but in those days the Bishop of London would not allow curates to marry in their first few years of ministry. They waited, and John Taylor settled with his vicar that they should marry between leaving London and moving to his second curacy. They were married in St Giles's in Oxford and, with the thought of missionary service overseas always in his mind, John Taylor warned Peggy that there was a health risk attached. The realization of this long-cherished hope of missionary service was not optional. She was happy to take the risk.

From the centre of London John Taylor moved north to the Diocese of Liverpool, to St Helen's in Lancashire, for a further three years. This was a common trend among catholic Anglicans as much as among evangelicals. In the great northern parishes a completely different experience of ministry awaited establishment men, all of them largely the products of the great public schools and the two ancient universities. Socially, there was little comparison between the more affluent south and the poor industrialized north. Nevertheless, his experience of pastoral and priestly ministry in both London and Liverpool confirmed John Taylor's evangelical heritage by personal experience of the joy of seeing others find a living relationship with Jesus. At the same time, however, this experience also broadened his heritage in a more catholic direction, for he experienced at first hand the necessity of the living Church for the nurture of this living relationship.

As he tasted the difference of cultural elsewhere in the back streets of London's West End and the poorer industrial north, so his sense of a great divide between ministry at home and ministry abroad dimmed and began to seem far less significant. Clearly this home turf was part of the mission field, and in ways he had never previously realized or considered. This broadening sense of mission meant that nice sharp edges in understanding and motivation blurred, becoming more subtle, more nuanced, more sensitive to the complexities of real life. Faith and life were negotiating. 'How right they should, if life is to be faithful, and faith is to be alive.'[22] To put it another way, a way that would become central to John Taylor's vision and theology, he was beginning to pay close attention to the facts, to ordinary everyday experience, doing his theology for and with real people in particular circumstances and in the light of actual events. So while he was still in a sense ready to go, receiving no further call and being unable even to imagine what further signal he was waiting for, he felt himself to be at some kind of turning point, at an unposted crossroads. He needed a sign.

At this juncture John Taylor again encountered Max Warren, by now newly appointed General Secretary of the Church Missionary Society. He talked with him about his vocation in the light of his changing perceptions of mission. Without seriously considering devoting himself to parochial life, he wondered about teaching theology. He knew he would not be acceptable teaching theology in Oxford or Cambridge – he didn't have the required First Class honours degree. Perhaps his Second Class degree fitted him for a 'second rung of the ladder' teaching post in a theological college in England? Certainly it would be good enough for overseas! Should he still go on thinking about working in the younger Churches of Africa or Asia?

> For some years I had been willing, and indeed anxious, to serve overseas but nothing had happened to clinch the matter. Those were days when people expected an unmistakable call to 'the mission field', and I only half believed it because I could see no fundamental difference between the ministry of the gospel in Britain or anywhere else. In considerable anxiety I explained to Max that I felt I should be able to look at a particular appointment overseas and weigh it up with the same amount of prayer and practicality as I would another opening in this country, and that I could no more present myself to a missionary society, saying, 'I am called to work with you', than I could throw myself at an English diocesan bishop with the same cry. Max understood. In fact he was more severely down-to-earth than I. He asked a lot of questions about my family situation, capabilities and interests, promised to let me know when an opening occurred which he thought I might fit, and asked me to get in touch before accepting any new offer that might be made in this country. Six months later we each kept our side of the bargain on the same day.[23]

This is astonishing. It is astonishing not just in terms of the six-months-to-the-day rendezvous. What is truly remarkable is two young evangelical priests, who have met before but do not know one another well, managing such an unusual degree of mutual personal honesty. John Taylor takes the risk of confessing uncertainty about what in the evangelical and missionary subculture he was taught to believe as certain: mission means being sent from here to there, and everything along the way is preparation for this apostolate. But now he finds he only half believes that mission means being sent from here to there, and he is anxious. Is this betrayal? Is it unfaithfulness? Clarity gives way to doubt. Security is dissolving. The way to sort things out is prayer. He prays, but nothing is clarified for him, nothing happens to clinch the matter – as it should if God is God and John Taylor is praying aright. He expects an unmistakable call to what he knows as 'the mission field', but finds himself already in a mission field with no dramatic call to leave it for another more distant and exotic. In London and Liverpool, long before his decade in Uganda and the following years as a research worker for the International Missionary Council, John Taylor is discovering that 'the whole world is the mission field'.[24] The geographical concept of the missionary task is already out of date. The mission is not from the West to elsewhere, but from the Church to the world.

In the West as well as in the East the Church stands in a non-Christian world. However deep may be the difference between a pre-Christian and a post-Christian society, the Gospel stands over and against all cultures, including that of the West, and all religion, including 'Christianity'. If what is said about the Mission and the missionary does not apply to all parts of this world-wide Church, it is probably not true or needs re-phrasing.[25]

His time serving as a foreign missionary and researcher simply confirms what he has learnt in his own pastoral experience in hard-pressed English parishes, and from his reading in Barth and Bonhoeffer and their followers. His theological reflection on experience enables him to see well into the future.

The Church is everywhere foreign to the world. As a human association, and even more, as the Body of its Incarnate Lord, it is rooted in the cultures within which it stands and partakes of them to an extent no one has yet measured. Nevertheless it remains everywhere a community *sui generis*, belonging to a Head whose authority transcends all other allegiance, and whose task sets it apart from the world. The true growth of any branch of the Church, therefore, is not to be measured by the extent to which it has become indigenous, nor the amount of autonomy which it enjoys, but by the degree to which it is a responsible Church, aware of the demands of God in its own conscience, responding to the Word of God in the terms of its own environment, and offering its own obedience in its own ways.[26]

To be straightforward about all this may harm his reputation within evangelical culture. His honesty is a step too far. In the Church honesty may not be welcomed, let alone met with honesty. In Max Warren, fortunately, it is. Max Warren is not scandalized or panicked. 'Max understood.'[27] Max Warren doesn't commiserate or condemn, panic or preach or push. Max Warren doesn't try to force the required religious experience where there is none, or write off the individual for lack of it. Indeed, he is even more severely practical than John Taylor himself. He looks at the situation honestly, simply attending to things as they are rather than as either party wishes them to be. He asks a lot of questions, drawing John Taylor out. He offers an attentive ear. He really listens. He doesn't come up with any premature or artificial solutions, trying to solve the problem or save the situation. He takes the wise precaution of asking John Taylor to discuss with him any offer that might come his way before accepting, but beyond that he simply reassures by quietly sharing the bewilderment and refusing to force matters. Here is someone strong enough, steady and sufficiently secure in himself to meet honesty with honesty. Here is someone faithful enough to trust that the future will unfold, that the future is God's, that directions will become clear. There is no crippling idealism in this exchange. Family circumstances are taken into account, gifts and abilities are part of the equation. Schooled in the same language of mission, call and prayer, Max Warren is nevertheless free to dispense with them or move beyond them without undue fear. 'It was the most common sense thing in the whole business of mission that had ever been said to me.'[28]

So everything continued as usual. The crisis came only when John Taylor was offered a suitable parish in North London. Now he was forced to decide whether to take up the new appointment and commit himself to the life and work of a parish priest for the next four or five years, possibly longer. Although he would have welcomed the freedom of a parish priest and the authority that comes with it, he found the offered parish easy enough to decline because his current work was already more demanding. There was no need to discuss it with Max Warren and he didn't get as far as informing him of his decision. A letter from Max Warren offering him a post overseas with CMS was waiting when John Taylor returned from London having just refused the offered parish! John Taylor could, the letter suggested, go to Bishop Tucker College at Mukono, the theological seminary of the Church of Uganda, working with candidates for the priesthood and training primary school teachers. He would begin as assistant Warden, apprenticed to an experienced theological teacher familiar with the culture and language.

Here was a sign. This seemed to be the sign and the call John Taylor had been awaiting. There was nothing pious about it. It was all presented in matter-of-fact fashion. He felt it to be the beginning of what he had been preparing for all his life, and he confidently expected to be embarking now on the real phase of his life's work.

One frustration for John Taylor was not to be allowed to set sail for Africa immediately. CMS insisted he prepare himself by acquiring a diploma in education from the University of London. For a year he became a student again. Itching to begin his real work, this delay was hard to take. In the event, however, he enjoyed the study and found CMS had been wise in its requirement. Again and again throughout his ministry, not only at Mukono, John Taylor would draw on this year's learning.[29]

Because of the war, John Taylor set out for Africa alone. It would be eighteen months before Peggy could join him, finally taking matters into her own hands after waiting patiently for CMS to arrange passage for her. Pregnant, Peggy waited on her own in England with one small child, Joanna, to care for and then a new-born baby as well. Their second child, Peter, was twelve months old before he met his father.

CHAPTER THREE

Mukono

Bishop Tucker College

THE HILL of Mukono, the 'right hand of the kings of Buganda', stands about twelve miles to the east of Kampala, the capital of Uganda. In 1905 an outbreak of sleeping sickness had driven the county-chief from his old seat of government and he set up his new headquarters at Mukono. The missionaries who had been his neighbours moved with him and were given permission to build around the side of the hill. The two oldest of the existing mission houses were started that year and the first school was opened just below them. In 1913 the bishop's divinity class, previously trained in Kampala, was moved out to Mukono and the first theological college, a large building of mud walls and thatch, was put up to accommodate the students. At the end of the 1914–18 war a main building was erected to commemorate Uganda's great bishop and missionary-statesman, Alfred Tucker, comprising a chapel, assembly hall, library, classrooms and offices. 'It is one of the most attractive buildings in the country; the satisfying lines of its brick and tiles have mellowed to a golden-brown which blends happily with the green forest and blue hills that lie beyond.'[1]

So writes a happy Warden of Mukono, John Taylor, some time into his ministry. The combination of theological college and teacher-training college was natural enough given the history of the Uganda church. In the early days every Church worker was also a teacher in the local bush school. In fact, church and schoolroom were often the same building. By the time John Taylor was principal, however, the advantages and disadvantages of this marriage were plain.

> The ethos of a theological college is necessarily different from that of a teacher-training centre. The discipline of boys of seventeen is not the same as that of adults. Teacher-training was financed and inspected and guided by government, but the Theological College was the responsibility solely of the Church.[2]

So much for the difficulties; what of the advantages? Having theological college and teacher-training on the same hill in a single compound,

> helps young teachers to believe in their work as a vocation within the Church, and it trains schoolmasters and clergy in mutual co-operation, so

avoiding that separation of the professions which is a symptom of the modern break-down of community.[3]

This marriage became a ménage à trois in 1940 when for the first time some of the ordinands were invited to bring their wives into a special class. A row of six mud-and-thatch cottages was built by private subscription to house them, and there six men lived, each with their wife and two of their children. In order that the women might attend classes, a crèche was started for their children under the care of an African girl, and this grew into a nursery school. After a few years the government became interested in the Women's Training Centre and through their Department of Social Welfare agreed to finance this part of the work and pay for the building of a better village in which the training could be carried on. The result was twelve cottages in colour-washed brick and tile, with separate kitchens, standing in a horse-shoe pattern around the new teaching block and the new nursery school, as well as houses for the missionary-in-charge and her African assistant. 'So it is a large and diverse family that is roused each day by the throb of the four college drums, dedicated in the chapel, bearing the names of the four archangels of God.'[4]

So casual a mention of these drums in John Taylor's pamphlet about Mukono disguises the fact that his work there began in crisis, of which the drums are symbolic.

Revival: crisis and opportunity

Expecting to be only Assistant Warden, very soon after his arrival John Taylor found himself Warden, in sole charge and with full responsibility, when his predecessor, John Jones, suddenly resigned and returned to the Church in Wales.[5] There was a hand-over period of only three weeks, although John Taylor was helped by inheriting John Jones's teaching notes.

John Jones was broken by the East African Balokole Revival.

> Where Christianity grows strong, where it escapes the dullness we have detected in none too intelligible services, a puritanical morality, and a preoccupation with schooling, which is useful but hardly for most people the business of a lifetime, it does so by sprouting a variety of associations.[6]

One such association was the East African Balokole Revival. Essentially lay and egalitarian, with good male–female relations, for all its narrowness and intensity and divisiveness it avoided schism. It resolutely refused to become a Church in its own right, and it managed to avoid hierarchism. For these achievements at least, the Revival movement should be honoured. Most of the clergy were opposed to it, yet, ironically, most of the first group of African bishops came from its ranks – great names like Sabbiti, Shalita, Luwum and Kivengere among them. Growing out of the

Rwanda Mission, an intensely conservative evangelical wing of CMS, it was largely staffed by Cambridge men recruited from the Cambridge Inter-Collegiate Christian Union (CICCU), that same fundamentalist alternative to the liberal and ecumenical Student Christian Movement (SCM) which John Taylor had served as Vice-President.

Of these recruits the most influential was Joe Church, who arrived in Rwanda in 1927, imbued with a volatile mixture of Keswick evangelical-ism and the Oxford Group (Moral Rearmament) practice of public confession.[7] Church became friendly with Simeoni Nsibambi, a wealthy landowner, and his brother Blasio Kigosi. As a result, Dr Church was helped at his hospital by a flow of young Ganda Christians coming to work in Rwanda. This relationship produced the Revival. The conventions which resulted in various places always followed the same pattern, centring on an impassioned appeal to 'awake'. Sin, repentance, 'coming out of Egypt', separation from sinners and occasions of sin, and the Holy Spirit – these were favourite topics, always leading up to public confession of guilt.

The Revival seems to have been distinctly apolitical, with a spirituality of separation not transformation, very 'vertical' and individualistic in its concentration on personal sin, rather than 'horizontal' and communal in concern for righteousness and social and political justice. Holiness was acquired by retreat into a holy huddle, by removing oneself from the temptations of this 'naughty' world. Holiness demanded associating only with the 'saved' and the good – a spirituality with support in the New Testament and a long pedigree in Christian history, although it is arguably a denial of the gospel. New Testament voices calling for exclusive communities do not, after all, include the voice of Jesus. Unlike some of his followers, he deliberately chose to eat with sinners, regularly defiling himself and polluting his own ritual purity – touching the sick, socializing with outcasts, cleansing lepers, even coming into physical contact with the dead. By contrast with this, the Revival was characterized by

> an almost hysterical confession of 'sin', a fixation on the 'saving blood' of Christ, an unqualified condemnation of everything the Balokole or 'saved ones' did not regard as acceptable. To their neighbours the impression the Balakole gave could be much the same as that which members of a Spirit-filled Church produced elsewhere: an at times almost uncontrollable and infectious frenzy of enthusiasm.[8]

Dr Church, Nsibambi and their allies had two targets. One was the so-called 'dead' state of the Ganda Church fifty years after its mass conversion – a mix of establishment Anglican and Ganda traditionalist attitudes. This 'dead' church tolerated chiefly polygamy, and was characterized by rather staid and stuffy worship in strict conformity with the rubrics and liturgy of *The Book of Common Prayer* of 1662, coupled with *Hymns Ancient and Modern*. No concession was made to Africa by acknowledging or using traditional African dance or drama or music. The other target was 'modernism', which Dr Church and other Rwanda missionaries with their CICCU background discovered in everyone a little less fundamentalist than themselves, and especially in J. C. Jones, warden of the theological college of Mukono.[9]

In October 1941 thirty Balokole, including William Nagenda, the brother-in-law of Nsibambi, were expelled from Mukono for refusing to obey the warden. They would not desist from imposing their ceaseless preaching on other students at all times of day and night. 'Expelled' is probably a misrepresentation, however, having more to do with rumours circulated by revivalists than with the gentle reasonableness of the warden. John Jones had, in fact, made the trouble-makers a generous offer which they rejected. Clearly there was another dimension to all this. Something else was driving the Balokole campaign, which John Jones and even his most vociferous opponents themselves failed fully to appreciate. Although the movement was initially inspired by the need for genuine renewal in the church, John Taylor became convinced that the revivalists in their enthusiasm failed to recognize honestly their own anti-European feeling. Naturally, this lack of self-awareness made their enthusiasm all the more dangerous. They enjoyed using the Revival as a means of bringing Europeans to their knees.

After a spate of disruptive 4 a.m. prayer meetings, followed by preaching to their fellow students, John Jones finally intervened. Calling the enthusiasts together, he pointed out that there are essential rules in any community. For the good order of the college, and out of care and concern for other students, they must stop this early morning preaching. He made no attempt to stop their meetings, but they must not disrupt the routine of others so early. The leaders refused. 'We must obey God rather than man' became their war-cry. In this emotionally charged atmosphere, they made this slogan their sole issue, so that John Jones finally felt obliged to put it to them that they must keep the simple rules of the college community or go. They opted to leave. A few came back, asked to be re-admitted, promised to keep the rules, and stayed. They were met, in other words, with magnanimity at every turn, but John Jones was not dealing with trustworthy opponents. The word was put around that he was against the Revival and that anyone associated with it would be expelled. They made his life hell.[10]

While the Bishop of Uganda supported John Jones, he also did his best to reconcile the Balokole and avoid total schism. It was a situation of great delicacy and deep hurt. For many Christians the arrogant denunciations of worldliness by the young revivalists were deeply shocking. One old clergyman who had been through Mwanga's persecution testified in synod to how hard it was to have a lifetime's faith so cursorily dismissed. Everything was viewed by the young in simple black and white absolutes. They had all the answers and nothing to learn.

Africanization

Although it may be hard to recognize at first glance, the Balokole do in a strange way represent one form of Africanization. They stressed separation where others stressed inclusivity. The revivalists were protesting at one inclusivist model of Africanization and imposing another. Radical cleansing is, after all, as much a recognizable phenomenon within African religion as retentiveness. The Revival was both a huge protest against one form of Africanization of Christianity and itself a major wave of Africanization. It really constituted an appropriation of Christianity not through hierarchy or school but through a very typically African cultural reality, a decentralized association unified by its singing and certain basic forms of behaviour.[11] The Revival undoubtedly created within the missionary church a community in which its members could feel at home.

From his position of oversight at some distance, Max Warren, General Secretary of CMS, made some acute observations about what was taking place in Africa. As one of the principal influences on John Taylor, on whose achievements John Taylor was to build, Max Warren uses a tone of voice and evinces that same sympathetic and generous attitude that would be John Taylor's own. For years to come this would characterize the visionary CMS policy on relationships with younger Churches and diverse cultures.

> I am so puzzled about the revival. It has done some wonderful things for the Africans. But its effect on the Europeans is much less happy. I don't doubt for one moment that it has been used to bless them and that many have got a deepened vision of God and their own sinfulness. I do not doubt that some even may have experienced a long overdue conversion. I am sure that some have come into a far deeper spiritual life, and that all are in a far healthier relationship with the Africans than they were before. All this is glorious and a positive gain. What I find so lacking in the movement is any awareness of the range of Christian living and thinking, any apprehension of the complexity of life's problems once you get beyond man to man relationships, any awareness of the place of thought, of theology, of the discipline of order and the place of pattern in life. I am not asking for intellectualism. I'm asking for awareness. All one gets is the exasperating iteration of pious formulae, which one must not allow to exasperate one because they obviously correspond to some genuine experience. But one just longs to say – 'Hallelujah, brother, but do try and enlarge your vocabulary'. But if you hint at this you are obscuring the simplicity of the truth. Who was the fool who used the phrase 'the simple truth' for the first time? Truth is not a proposition. Truth is to be found only in a Person and in personal relationships, if it is to be saving as distinct from purely scientific truth. And the Truth which is personal is as deep and profound and complex as the very Being of God, even though in his mercy he may reveal himself in simpler guise. But the Incarnation is not simple whatever else it may be.

I am quite sure that the European leaders of the revival are running a serious danger for themselves and the Africans of escaping from the discipline of thinking. Unless the movement grows in stature it will be bogged in emotionalism and infantilism, and from that it will break away into sects. But, of course, to grow is dangerous. Pray God that the revival may not become a 'Peter Pan' which will not grow up.[12]

John Taylor would endorse every word. But if Max Warren and John Taylor were gifted with exceptional insight into the real significance of the Revival, John Jones should not be underestimated. He is described by one who followed him on the staff at Mukono as 'a very able and delightful man',[13] and by others as a 'great man'.[14] John Taylor acknowledges him as a superb scholar of rather more catholic background than himself, coming as he did from the disestablished Church in Wales which had been more uniformly influenced by the Oxford Movement and the Catholic Revival than the Church of England. For all his churchmanship differences, he was nevertheless quite devoted to CMS.

John Taylor plays down his own reputation as the reconciler in this situation, his own success where John Jones failed.[15] Nevertheless, it is undeniable that things had broken down, relationships had failed, and somehow the situation seems to have got beyond John Jones's control. It is an almost impossible situation when all that is taught comes under relentless questioning and constant challenges to authority become the order of the day. This was the situation in which the ringleaders were sent home, and after a time John Jones went home as well. Probably it was the only solution.

Although he says he arrived when the situation was much better, John Taylor undoubtedly inherited this legacy – division, hurt, resentment, combined with bitter memories of John Jones asserting his authority and his need to take control. The fact that John Taylor was able to work at all creatively in this atmosphere is a remarkable achievement. He brought healing for hurt, encouraged a generous spirit in place of narrowness and judgementalism, managed to be courteously patient with those who could be deeply irritating, and was able to see and reverence the good in what was also potentially destructive of community life.

To the Revival, nothing traditionally African was acceptable, and this was characteristic also of the older African clergy. Anything apart from a strict diet of Prayer Book, Authorized Version of the Bible and *Hymns Ancient and Modern* was selling them short, palming them off with second best. Everything traditional in African religion and culture was viewed as dangerously unredeemed. The fact that John Taylor was able to surmount such fear sufficiently to carry through his own programme speaks volumes for the kind of man he is.[16] Thanks to him, the drums could sound again and spirituals be sung in chapel worship. Indeed, the Word could become incarnate in drama, and 'the college and settlement became areas of peace, growth and renewal'.

Reconciler

This happy outcome should not, however, suggest that all was plain sailing, that relationships with the revivalists miraculously became easy. Neither should it be taken to indicate that John Taylor's sensitivity was somehow soft or weak or his generosity unprincipled. The situation remained delicate right through his wardenship, and beyond. One staff member recalls countless occasions when John would introduce something new in chapel, perhaps himself singing a spiritual – as he could do most beautifully.[17] Afterwards, little huddles immediately formed, followed by students coming to see staff members, wanting to 'walk in the light' over it.[18] There seemed to be no escaping this rather tedious scenario, demanding endless patience. After John Taylor returned to England and his African successor, Dunstan Nsubuga, became warden, an attempt was made to stage the Passion play once more, but the holy huddles immediately formed and Dunstan had to back down. The whole project was cancelled.[19]

In a letter to Max Warren of March 1947, John Taylor writes:

> When I described the work of the Spirit which brought about so many conversions in the College during the first part of last year, I also mentioned that the members of the 'Abalokole' revival movement who were in College have been most co-operative, and had been the nucleus of the weekly meeting which was held for Christian fellowship and the building up of the young converts. About half-way through the second term there was a change. Influence was brought to bear upon some of our students by members of the movement outside. There is no reason to believe any mischief-making was intended, but the sequel was a new attitude of suspicion on the part of members of the movement in the College, and one or two acts of disobedience to normal College rules. We on the staff were agreed that plain-speaking and firmness were the right policy, and we made it quite clear that while we were whole-heartedly at one with those in College who wanted to witness to the saving power of Christ, yet we were not going to permit activities that would disrupt the essential fellowship of the College or destroy the inherent discipline of our ordered community. I still believe that our decision was right, though looking back I think our demeanour was a little too unsympathetic; but at that time we were deeply afraid that the enemy of souls was using this development to lead astray the young Christians who had so recently entered the new life, and the tragic memories of 1941 aggravated our fears.[20]

This is a telling admission. The enemy of souls knows well that the enemy of faith is never doubt, but always fear, that the opposite of faith is certainty.

> Fear is never a trustworthy guide to the will of God, and although the trouble was soon over we found that we had lost the old spirit of confidence;

the keen Christians allowed the incident to divert them from their task of witness, and some of the others who were hesitating on the threshold of the Kingdom found in it an excuse for turning back.[21]

Suspicion and fear, loss of self-confidence, partially paralysed John Taylor and his staff because it created a climate for failure rather than a creative flowering of gifts. 'It has been a sad experience, but I believe the damage has been repaired and redeemed.' This, of course, is hindsight masking some of the personal pain, playing down the immediate danger of division and disintegration.

Two qualities central to John Taylor's personality seem to have appealed to Africans. One was having no sense of time whatever, with the tendency to get caught up in what he was doing to the exclusion of everything and everyone else, or to act on brilliant ideas immediately, dropping everything to do so. His spontaneity irritated Europeans, but delighted Africans.[22] Max Warren talks of John Taylor 'moving through life spontaneously without planning anything' as part of his artistic and poetic temperament.[23] This, obviously, is not to be taken too literally, and John Taylor would in any case argue that it is always a matter of *response*, a matter of our need to freely respond to acts and attitudes rather than prescribe everything in advance. In this sense John Taylor is a great improviser, who knows that everything is provisional and uses what is given to him, assembling disparate pieces and unconnected ideas into something new. He is certainly intuitive and creative. 'He had a great perceptive depth of sensitivity. It was *feel* as much as anything. He naturally had a sense of what would be the right thing in that particular situation.'[24]

The second quality was his disarming sense of humour. It is said that we are nearest to God when we laugh because laughter pricks the bubble of pomposity and pride, freeing us of self-absorption and deadly earnestness. John Taylor had this saving gift abundantly in his own life, making it available to others in real need of it. So it is not at all surprising to find in an annual report to CMS, after long paragraphs describing the Lent evangelistic programme, that, in order to avoid 'the danger of false intensity', the warden organized a concert in Holy Week! 'I am sure this helped to steady the ship.'[25] Clearly, too, hospitality and laughter in his own home were important in making friends of his staff. John Taylor as accomplished mimic, musician, humorist and actor, as well as listener and pastor, human being among human beings who all had ordinary human needs for affection and relaxation, helped everyone escape their demanding roles. He encouraged 'evenings when we could let our hair down and just enjoy ourselves'.[26]

Humour was also at hand to defuse more delicate situations. During the first years of his wardenship those revivalists who remained in college kept a very low profile – so much so that John Taylor hardly even realized they were there. By the time the outside leaders of the Revival decided they didn't like what they heard about the college under his care, he was already on such good terms with those inside that he was fairly safe. Ironically, these good personal relationships led the revivalist students to take courage. 'Could we start meeting again?' John Taylor's reaction was 'Why not?' 'We thought perhaps the college didn't want us.' John Taylor said, 'Of course we want you; you're all very good members of the college, and you don't want to break away do you?' Assured that they did not, permission was given. This required some humbling on the part of the warden himself and a willingness to take risks, for such permission inevitably included questioning the authority of the teaching establishment.

This would happen in almost ritualized form. John Taylor would preach in the chapel, and after the service, unrobed, he would walk back up the hill to his house. Two of the youngsters from the teacher-training college would come and join him and walk alongside. They would speak about the sermon, praising God and saying they thought it really was the message from God. 'But', one of them would say, 'we felt that while you were speaking you yourself were actually rather *cold*.' 'Cold' meant you were not at the top of your form spiritually. And for a moment John Taylor would think, 'Really! the impudence! Talking like that, that's not what you say to a preacher.' But then, mercifully, by the grace of God, he had second thoughts and was able to say, 'Well, why shouldn't they, they're doing it out of love, they were not trying to get my comeuppance or anything like that.' So he was able to say, 'thank you for telling me that'. Honest enough and humble enough to admit to himself that one of the reasons for his anger was that the criticism was partly true, he was able to avoid taking offence. So he learned to take it at face value, absorb the irritation and the hurt, and read the situation generously. It was, after all, part of the culture – a very different culture from England with its elaborate code of reserve and understatement, where subtlety was valued and courtesy cloaked criticism.[27]

So it was that a new and more self-authenticating authority began to emerge in the mutuality of relationship between principal and students, in the give and take of engagement. This was rather ahead of its time in the more formal 1950s, and rather eccentric in colonial East Africa. Nevertheless, it was worth the effort, for if some honour was given and respect shown, then you won the right to say something to the students. And John Taylor used his newly earned authority, making it clear that such a free style of relationship between staff and students opens up a two-way street.

> So I said, 'Look, it's all very well you talking about Bible study, but do you realize what you always do? You read a whole passage, perhaps ten verses, and then somebody starts off and says "I have felt such and such a verse is speaking to me", and the rest of the time you all fasten on one phrase, and you keep on repeating what it means to each of you, and it's always the

same. You're really not letting the word of God speak to you, you're echoing one another like a little group of monkeys.' And they laughed when I said about the monkeys. So it's give and take.[28]

Other difficulties faced by the warden included financial struggles. The cost of living had increased dramatically while income from the government for the teacher-training college and from the Church of Uganda for the theological college remained static. Consequently, John Taylor found himself presiding over a substantial debt. This preyed on his mind to such an extent that he found himself on one occasion adding up the numbers on the chapel hymn board! Worry over money was dispiriting. So too were changes in staff which threatened harmony in working relationships and unity of mind and approach. There was also a housing shortage, with staff sharing homes for various periods. The frustration sometimes shows. 'We have at present four houses for five missionaries with their families and a sixth arrives in a month's time.' Adding to all these cares, sickness could strike at most inopportune moments – jaundice, malaria, blackwater fever, as well as less glamorous maladies.

Fortunately, for all these trials there were also triumphs to be counted. A mission by ten teams in ten local villages brought blessings. Groups of students had also been teaching villagers to read. 'The whole venture was undertaken as a witness to the Lord of all life, and as a sequel to our evangelistic mission.' Here is the authentic John Taylor voice and vision. The Lord of all life is celebrated for being so much greater than the Lord of the Church, let alone the Lord of individual Christian souls. There is no trace of dualism here. God, surprisingly, turns out to be not very religious, only wanting us to be human together. Body and soul are intertwined and not to be separated, flesh and spirit are to be saved as one, and there can be no escape into some form of spiritualism. Incarnation is integral to the divine image, stamped on all reality, becoming the invariable pattern of God-with-us even to the close of the age. Christian mission, in this understanding, demands social holiness, for holiness includes wholeness and health. The mission of God in Christ reaches into situations as well as souls, involving the exercise of that authority over evil spirits which Jesus linked so closely with his command to evangelize. The arena of anyone's salvation is not only their inner life, but also the outward institutions and structures of society which make us who we are.[29] All this contradicts decisively the narrowness of the Revival's 'vertical' religion.

Symbolizing this radically different sense of 'communal' or 'horizontal' faith working itself out in the real world, John Taylor offers a story, an acted parable. Astonishingly, a blood transfusion scheme proved successful in a culture where blood is almost magical – the vital stream which flows through each individual out of the past and into the future. The students spent their pastoralia class discussing it, and in that period 'the terrific, silent bombardment of the Spirit began to have its effect'.[30] At the end, one of the lay readers stood up and said: 'If our Lord Jesus was ready to give his whole life for me, I think I cannot refuse to give only a part of my life for others.' Before the day was over, 55 students had volunteered to give their blood. 'There is no doubt that those men had understood and had accepted the highway of the Cross.'[31]

In addition to the teaching of ordinands and lay readers in their own language, there was now a small English ordination class. Simultaneously, a programme began for bringing deacons back into college for two terms in preparation for their ordination to the priesthood. This was an arena in which more personal tutoring could be introduced and this group began to open up the library resources. Each candidate for priesthood was allotted a small church and district within four miles of Mukono where he worked under supervision, pioneering a form of field education far in advance of the rest of the Anglican Communion. The breaking down of the seminary model of training for priesthood has since proceeded steadily, giving way almost everywhere to theology by reflection on pastoral experience. This is yet another instance of John Taylor taking facts seriously, and insisting that Christian mission is always incarnational because God is always becoming incarnate.

Experiential theology

At Bishop Tucker College, John Taylor taught biblical studies and systematic theology. Initially, he was saved by J. C. Jones, who passed over his lecture notes, 'which mercifully had English and Luganda on opposite sides, and then his wonderful marginal notes'.[32] From these notes John Jones largely dictated, because they would be the students' theological textbooks for the rest of their ministry. There was very little else available in print.

> So I started off reading his notes in Luganda, realizing what I was saying, and then I would spend the early part of the evening writing my own notes and my own commentaries. I had had a crash course in Luganda with an elderly woman professor at Colchester, but I forgot a lot on the ship out to Africa. I really learnt it by doing this work and dictating, and reading in the Luganda Bible, so that I was able to discuss theological questions in Luganda before I could go into the shops and order the food I wanted. I learnt it the wrong way around![33]

Unlike English, Luganda is entirely devoid of abstract terminology. What John Taylor calls the 'intractable concreteness of Luganda' made him ask himself at every turn what he really meant by a theological term. 'This exercise instilled in me the realization that every abstract idea, including our idea of God, is derived from experience, and all revelation is given through things that happen. True theology has to be Incarnational.'[34]

This was a crucial learning experience for an evangelical of Taylor's background and education, and, without fully realizing the profundity of the change taking place within, he was gradually adding the Catholic dimension of the Christian view of things to his Protestant heritage. In 1953 he still described himself as 'a deeply convinced evangelical', but in the same breath he acknowledges that 'under God the Anglican Church is called to a special responsibility as a bridge church embracing and drawing into unity the reformed and the catholic heritages'.[35] The Church, he now knew, is itself part of the gospel it proclaims. The individual's experience of the presence of Christ needs to be embodied in the community and communion of the Church. Truly, he could see, the medium *is* the message. Traditional Protestant emphasis on conversion as a psychological act of trust, or even a strictly individualistic emotional crisis, should never be set over against the traditional Catholic emphasis on conversion as incorporation of the candidate into the visible Body of Christ. These are not competing truths, but complementary truths. To set them up in opposition, as Protestant-Catholic polemic traditionally does, is damaging and unreal.

In any case, it was clear in Uganda that the missionary role was not to evangelize, but to service and enliven the existing church. The evangelization of untouched people has always been carried forward mainly by indigenous Christians in the context of Church renewal, rather than by expatriates. Taylor recognized the *preparatio evangelii* that has preceded the planting of every local Church. Before ever the first Christian witnesses arrived, the sociological and psychological foundations of the future church were already laid, and only if that church when it was built conformed to those foundations would it be strong. His task, therefore, was to make sure the local indigenous church was not kept longer than necessary in missionary leading-strings, or shaped too rigidly to some universal model, so that it related responsively and responsibly to its own encompassing situation.

Though he had not consciously identified them at the time, these two principles – grounding all concepts in experience, and embodying the gospel in the life of the Church – induced John Taylor to concentrate on three spheres of experiment in training men for the ministry at Bishop Tucker College.

Community

The first experiment he called *Community*. A village of twelve separate houses was built for the married ordinands and their families, and gradually more and more of the formal curriculum was related to daily life, to the relationships and tensions of that small theocracy. What was understood to be God's method of teaching theology to God's ancient people Israel seemed a good model for training spiritual leaders for African rural communities.

> At Mukono the purely academic must give place to a more 'experimental' theology; the truth of our doctrine must become incarnate in the quality of our common life. Our task is not merely to prepare our pupils for the profession they are to follow in the future, but even more to live with them, here and now, in every daily experience, the life of the Spirit. That is why, more and more, the 'village' of the Women's Training Centre is becoming the centre of all the theological training, as the Christian home becomes the unit for which we are planning. It is why we are including in the time-table regular periods of work in the food-gardens, why we are preparing to start a small herd of cattle, why we shall attempt to raise our new hostels by building them ourselves.[36]

It all sounds very Benedictine, this interweaving of prayer and work, of intellectual study and physical labour. It also begins to sound as if the plan simply went from strength to strength, fuelled by its own momentum. In reality, it was neither so easy nor so straightforward. By September 1951, warden and staff were experiencing 'the strain of an operation in realignment'.

> By the end of last year several of us had become convinced that in the village where the ordinands live with their families, the men and women were being made too dependent upon the planning and help of the staff, and especially upon the woman missionary-in-charge of the wives' training. It seemed to us that this was not the best training for men and women who were the future leaders of a church that was more and more to 'work out its own salvation' without foreign leadership or initiative. The helplessness and poverty of the families was inciting us all to acts of patronage rather than partnership.
>
> We attempted at the beginning of this year to train the members of that Village Community in a greater sense of responsibility for themselves and their community life as the best means of training them for real village leadership in the future.
>
> We inaugurated a weekly Village Council, when the Village Community and the staff should meet together to give thanks for what had been done or given during the past week, to bring forward present needs, both physical and social, and finally after quiet to plan immediate action to meet those needs.
>
> Looking back, I can see that we again made our usual mistake of thinking too fast and taking it for granted that our thoughts could quickly be understood by others. The result was a deeply entrenched resistance to the new ideas; first of all just because they were new, and later because of having become gradually aware of how firmly the patriarchal conception of the missionary's status and function had been implanted in their minds. 'But

you are our father', was their constant retort. 'We are not disobedient; we will build or dig if you order us. But you must tell us what you want us to do; we will not have these groups.' And if we have a need, we will come to your house and tell *you*; we will not deal with one another's needs.

We realised after a while that we were facing a far deeper resistance than we had anticipated, and God gave us the needed humility and patience to apologise for our impetuosity and to deal more sympathetically with the reluctances of the students. Slowly a loving firmness won the day by the grace of God, and the new methods of community living were adopted one by one. We have a long way to go. There are still occasional outbursts of bad temper or sulks. But at least they have all seen that, though the missionary refuses to be their father, he is genuinely anxious to become their brother. It is being very worth while. But if this is what is meant by realignment, then it is going to be very, very hard work.[37]

Moving from the patriarchal model of dependence to one of 'mutual responsibility and inter-dependence in the Body of Christ' is necessarily slow work.[38] Clericalism is so ingrained in Christian tradition that even the tremendous shock wave of the sixteenth-century Reformation failed to dislodge it. Centuries in which a clerical caste became expert in dis-empowering the people of God are not dismissed overnight, and even when time is allowed for new ideas to take root, intellectual assent has still to grasp the heart and the emotions.

This initiative of John Taylor's tells us a great deal about the man and about his theology, for humility, gentleness, patience, and weakness are central to his doctrine of God. At the heart of everything is a kenotic, self-emptying, self-giving, self-sacrificing, Christlike God, who always prefers persuasion to overpowering.

It is all here in embryo in this early experiment – John Taylor's impetuosity, his thinking too fast, taking for granted that his thoughts will quickly be understood by others, his almost naive confidence that a good idea will be welcomed and will carry the day. Time and again we will see these same characteristics informing his ministry as General Secretary of CMS and later as Bishop of Winchester. Time and again they will cause upset and provoke resistance. Some people are not interested in ideas, many simply want to be left undisturbed, others have no imagination to envisage what can be in place of what already is, and then there are those who genuinely disagree and cannot embrace the vision. Dependency is more comfortable than responsibility. Being the child of a father is easy compared to being adult sisters and brothers. Making real decisions involves making real mistakes and this entails failure and living with the consequences.

If, however, we see John Taylor's quick mind in all this, his rare ability for analysis of the current situation and imaginative ability to picture something better, we are also taken to the heart of the man in his innate humility. He is able to step back sufficiently from his own scheme to see where he has gone wrong, to admit that he himself makes mistakes. He is also able to be firm when necessary and to win the day, but slowly and lovingly. He doesn't absolve himself and put the blame on the students, becoming angry and impatient. On the contrary, he is able to make haste slowly, being patient enough to allow time for resistance to be overcome, loving the students into something rather than insisting they embrace change solely at an intellectual level. 'At least they have all seen that, though the missionary refuses to be their father, he is genuinely anxious to become their brother.' No wonder realignment is 'very, very hard work'! This kind of humility is both risky and exhausting, and it is the fruit of walking by faith, involving terribly difficult sustained inner struggle, self-doubt, disappointment and pain.

Creativity

The second sphere of experiment was the whole area of *Creativity* – the development of drama, indigenous music and other art forms. The gospel cannot be merely verbal. Imagination and emotions must be engaged.[39]

> Those who have been educated to imitate, whose thought is second-hand and who speak in clichés, whose skill consists in repeating the movements and the processes of others, may attain a high proficiency and usefulness as professional technicians, but as persons they remain deeply unfulfilled and resentful.[40]

What was needed was unprejudiced, experimental fostering of existing African art-forms, rather than forcing Africans to copy European models. The task of the teacher in Africa should be to assist in the creative evolution of an indigenous drama as rich as any the world has seen.[41] For teachers to achieve this approach, some knowledge of history is required, both the history of Africa and of drama, together with a special humility and sensitivity, sympathy and patience.[42] With the willingness to let go the security of tight control over the drama, and the encouragement of creativity rather than imitation, the producer may well be surprised by natural talent. In cultural terms, the choice for the missionary lies between destruction or development.[43]

The wholeness of life lived in the village found its focus and expression in the worship of the chapel. Morning Prayer and Evening Prayer gave a steady daily routine, with a voluntary thirty-minute noon service of recollection – a time for silent meditation. Inevitably, steadily, the rather stark Word-centred chapel worship of a traditionally evangelical college was becoming more sacramental, but in freshly imaginative and historically non-controversial ways.

At the coming of the rains we bring a great pitcher of water into the sanctuary, and we offer to God soil and seeds and hoes before our planting begins. And such worship flows outwards into the little things of life; the lighting of a lamp in the home, the drawing of water from the bore-hole, each is made the occasion for a tiny act of devotion by some who are learning this way of life.[44]

Gradually and gently the John Taylor revolution was taking place, winning hearts and heads, for all life belongs to God, not just some isolated 'spiritual' dimension.

In a word, we are seeking to make this college into a creative community wherein the future leaders of the Church, men and women, should live together the Christian life in its total application to a daily round of work and study and worship and leisure, carried through in a close fellowship of common devotion to Christ the centre.[45]

Again, it sounds very Benedictine, this balanced diet of labour and prayer, exploration and rest.

One of John Taylor's unique achievements at Mukono was the staging of parable plays in the normal course of the liturgical year, and on several occasions a Passion play as integral to the Holy Week worship of the college. In the face of strenuous opposition from the revivalists, who distrusted all things African being mixed with Christianity, he managed to draw on the African gift for spontaneous and powerful dramatization, devising a truly African preaching of the cross capable of speaking powerfully to Ugandans. Significantly, the play was staged in the chapel, but the chapel was not turned into a stage. The action of the drama was always subordinate to the worship, an integral part of one co-ordinated presentation of a theme. There was need for refinement and discipline of a God-given skill, but the aim was not to obscure simple African ways with stagy, European effects. The aim was always to keep it natural. There was, tellingly, no written script.

It is natural for a people who look back over four centuries of printed books to think a play must first be written before it can be acted. But to an African, who is still far more at home with the spoken than the written word and who therefore retains a spontaneous flow of vivid speech which we have lost, it seems more natural that the acting of the story should precede and give birth to the dialogue.

It was the producer's custom to gather the players together in a classroom, and, after a period of prayer and quiet, to tell them the story of the parable with all the vividness he could command, emphasising the mental reactions of the characters. Then, as soon as he saw that their imaginations were beginning to kindle, he allotted the parts and told them to act the story. Desks were pushed aside, and there and then on the bare classroom floor, without properties or costume, the parable came to life.

Dialogue flowed strongly back and forth, character was realised and expressed, the incomparable story was told with a vigour and directness that the Author Himself would surely have approved.

Afterwards we discussed it; important omissions were noted for correction, new emphases were suggested, mostly by the players themselves; then they did it again. So it was repeated many times, while slowly the details of gesture and grouping were perfected. After the sixth or seventh run-through the words had become fixed, and thereafter were as invariable as if a script had been prepared in advance. Yet there was no conscious memorising, and therefore none of the forced or stilted acting that comes from dividing the attention between word and expression. The only thing that was learnt by heart was the total dramatic situation from which both the spoken word and the bodily movement spontaneously arose. For the Passion Play the same method was followed. Only the words of Christ, which were almost entirely taken from the Gospels, were previously prepared and had to be learnt. But in this case almost every player was already so familiar with them that memorising them was largely a matter of revision. All other speech was allowed to flow naturally from the development of the story, and from a careful study of the dialogues of the Upper Room.

The outstanding merit of the African way of dramatisation lay in its directness and sincerity, and anything that suggested artificiality seemed to strike a discordant note. The same principle of sincerity guided us in the smaller questions of costume and music. In the end we devised simplified biblical dresses, all based on the *kanzu*, the plain, ankle-length robe that the Arabs introduced in the nineteenth century, and which has become the normal man's dress of Uganda. We used Negro spirituals, which our African choirs sing with great understanding, and these were perfectly in keeping with the spirit of the whole presentation.[46]

Above all, however, this drama was conceived within the drama of Christian liturgy.

We never tried to disguise the fact that we were in the chapel. Our chapel existed for the showing forth of the very story that we were trying to tell; indeed we were simply making visible the drama that had been constantly unfolded there every time the creeds were recited, every time the Gospel was proclaimed and set forth in the Word and the Sacraments. So now, standing in the sanctuary, the Lord brake bread and gave it to his disciples; on that same spot the Cross of Calvary was set up; and there he stood in the glory of the Resurrection to greet his friends and to give them peace. On the following day when we came there for our Easter Communion, there was not one for whom that place had not become more deeply significant and precious as a house of prayer and communion than ever before. The play derived from the chapel and was part of its worship.[47]

Given the background of suspicion and division in the college, there is little doubt that one effect of these plays was to bring the actors together in a common cause, establishing relationships of trust, building a new sense of community. This comes through forcefully in John Taylor's memory of one particular performance. Everyone who had taken part in the play knew that they had passed through an unforgettable experience. During the days of preparation it was evident that each one of the players was living at a higher level than normal, was attaining a stature greater than his usual self, was in some degree transfigured by the glory they were trying to enter into together and portray. It was apparent in the classroom, in the vegetable plots, indeed in every sphere of daily routine. On the day of the performance the producer stressed the importance of every player and every singer remaining absolutely quiet in their places at the end of the play, until the congregation had left the chapel. This direction was carefully observed. Then, after a word of thanks and a short prayer, the choir was dismissed and the producer went up the aisle expecting to see the players standing and waiting on the other side of the curtain, elated with the excitement that always follows a performance. Instead, he found them kneeling together in the sanctuary as one after another poured out his thanksgiving and adoration.

> The stream of prayer flowed pure and unbroken for fifteen minutes more, and then all remained kneeling in silence. And in that stillness such a dedication was made as could not be framed in words. Then, one by one, they slipped out of the chapel; there was no formal dismissal that night.[48]

All this, says John Taylor, was, on the human side, entirely the fruit of prayer.[49] This is true only if the presence and ministry of John Taylor is appreciated as an integral expression of that prayer. Always there is need for the mediator, for the priest, a particular personality to enable and set free the creativity of others, orchestrating individual players in harmony. Characteristically, this is how God works, through us and with us rather than independently of us, operating mediatorially rather than magically. This is how the only true God answers prayer.

Consciousness

The third area of experiment, introduced towards the end of John Taylor's ten-year term as principal of the college at Mukono, as Uganda entered the final run-up towards national independence, was that of political *consciousness*. Given the background of the intensely apolitical Revival, we may doubt that this required only a more deliberate reference to current affairs in the routine study of the Hebrew prophets and the background to the gospels.[50]

Transformation of society as necessary to salvation is far more demanding than separation from all that soils or pollutes the pure individual Christian soul. 'In retrospect it appears that this last experiment was initiated at least ten years too late to be of any use in equipping the Church of Uganda for what was to come.'[51] John Taylor's own estimate is that this particular experiment missed the bus, but they still had to make the attempt because ideas are unreal unless they are grounded in experience. 'If people feel that God cares nothing for the things which vitally affect their daily lives and stir their deepest emotions they will not easily be persuaded that such a God loves them in any sense at all.'[52]

This struggle with the place of social and political action as integral to the Christian mission is a constant in John Taylor's missionary pilgrimage, particularly after leaving Uganda and working with the International Missionary Council and, later still, with the World Council of Churches. His belief is that our world cannot be abandoned to the devil or secular processes, that we shall not build the Kingdom of God in this world, but that God will nevertheless give it to us. He is convinced that

> all our planning and patience, our fighting and faithfulness, our longing and loss, will be related to the coming of His Kingdom, not as a builder's effort is related to the finished cathedral, but as the caterpillar's struggle for existence is related to the butterfly.[53]

Early in his time at Mukono, John Taylor recognized 'the need for at least some clergy capable of reading the signs of the times and becoming interpreters and prophets to a bewildered people'. The need was for a church 'capable and prepared to speak the truth, to counter with truth and moderation the rising tide of rumours and suspicion and terror-mongering, and to rebuke with the truth, where necessary, the injustice which masks itself under specious high-sounding phrases'.[54]

The personal cost to someone as sensitive as John Taylor in the situation of Mukono and the Church of Uganda was bound to be great. In a fascinatingly unguarded passage in his Annual Letter to CMS for 1951, John Taylor admits to being physically sick from one remark.

> I expect you remember the occasional acts of selfishness or pride that hit one like a physical blow, so great is the disappointment. It sounds ridiculous but I know it is no more than the truth to say that I had to go into hospital for a fortnight, earlier this year, because a group of students had said: 'What will you pay us if we do this?' At such times there does suddenly come an overwhelming darkness and misery, and physical nausea, when one clings to the Lord with something like desperation. These moments, of course, go hand in hand with acts or attitudes 'so full of glory' that one is transfigured, inspired, filled with strange vigour. Desolation and transfiguration, perhaps, cannot be had apart from each other, but prayer is needed 'that we may be saved from self-pity or cynicism or condescension, or any other damnable form of pride'.[55]

Other issues were pressing in the Church of which Bishop Tucker Theological College and its warden were a part. In an unusual report to headquarters, John Taylor apologizes for writing about the wood when CMS supporters would rather hear about the trees. 'One gets little chance of considering the wood as a rule … here at Mukono there are lots of nice trees I could have written about, and it might have made a more cheerful letter.'

It is here, however, in *not* writing to amuse the troops and prise open the cheque books, that a window is opened for us into a particular moment in the life of the Church of Uganda.

> Do you know what there is behind the statistics, and behind the stories of glorious individual victories? As one goes on growing closer to people one hears more and more, and sees more, and at times it seems to pile up like the clouds before the thunder breaks. An afternoon's visiting during which out of ten Christians visited only one was living in Christian marriage – of communicants turned away from the communion rail because the bread had run out and the parson hadn't time to send to the vestry where he knew there was more – a marriage party kept waiting in the church porch until the bridegroom had given the priest a large enough present to satisfy him – a vicar, whose wife was away, living with a young girl for two months but, when she was pregnant, sending her out to sleep with his house-boy so that he himself should not be accused – children refused confirmation because they could not pay a fee of ten shillings – the great majority of vicars refusing ever to read the lessons in church because this is normally done by lay-readers and so is beneath their dignity – church services in the holidays when compulsory school attendance is no longer possible beginning with a congregation of three old women, with perhaps ten more people drifting in just before the sermon, and that in a church that musters four hundred during term time. The thing that hurts is not such facts in themselves, but the attitude of taking them for granted, of expecting nothing better from one's clergy or one's Church.[56]

Here we begin to see and feel something of what this Church was really like. It was a church in which there was a sacramental famine,[57] in which priest and eucharist were anything but the norm. But this was also strangely advantageous, for it was also a Church where 80 per cent of Anglicans were excommunicated![58] If the leader of the local congregation had been a priest and the principal form of worship eucharistic, this would have been disastrously exclusive. In what sounds like a complete contradiction in terms, the absence of priests actually kept the congregation together as one for almost all their worship.

Central to this picture of the wider Church in the rural villages, then, is the catechist or lay reader, who was frequently catechist-schoolteacher. He was the Church's one local man. It was the catechist and no one else who ensured that the vast number of Christians that multiplied during the first half of the twentieth century became, most of them, Catholics, Anglicans, or Presbyterians and not members of an independent church or millenarian cult. In the context of innumerable villages the catechists continued to represent *Ecclesia Catholica*, the universal community and communion of Christians, as well as literacy. They represented what Adrian Hastings calls 'the three Rs: Reading, Writing and Religion'.[59] Catechists were not entirely local. They might be moved. They might even have a bicycle. Almost unpaid by the church, they often supported themselves by trade unless they were doubling as teachers paid by the state. A few would be promoted. To us they may stand for no more than the local community. To their people, and even to themselves, they stood for and were linked with a world of religious and secular power, the world of the bishop, a cathedral, even the Archbishop of Canterbury or the Pope. They were far-flung outposts in a new ecclesiastical geography growing up around them. They visited their diocesan headquarters from time to time, and the way things were there was the way things should be in the village too. Protestantism or Catholicism, biblicism or papalism, the catechist had somehow to represent these great things to his fellow villagers, standing for values, ideas and powers whose authority he could sense but whose meaning he could hardly begin to apprehend.[60]

The extraordinarily high number of excommunicated Christians of all persuasions was, of course, a failure of indigenization, a failure effectively to Africanize a culturally captive European Church. The points in dispute were moral and theological. Traditional initiation ceremonies such as circumcision were attacked or forbidden by missionaries. The Churches also frowned on associations and societies largely concerned with identity and status in the community, for these also included religious elements considered pagan and dangerous. Only dreams as revelatory or vocational were on the whole approved, for Scripture is so full of dreams as to make them almost exempt from missionary suspicion.

Most problems, however, had to do with marriage. Polygamy was condemned. For most this attacked symbol rather than reality. Chiefly polygamy was not for the poor man anyway. 'One wife for a teacher, but a chief should have more.' Christian matrimony, known as 'ring marriage', was highly regarded but might be impossible or, if possible, too expensive. Many just didn't get around to it. 'Over polygamy', says Adrian Hastings, 'few Africans were ever convinced by the missionary case and hardly surprisingly. It was not an obviously strong one.'[61] In any case, the tension was largely over the *enactment* of marriage. Nothing but church marriage would be accepted by the missionaries, whereas customary marriage continued to constitute marriage in the eyes of society and the state. For almost all Christians, at least those not in church employ, customary marriage was essential, with marriage in church an attractive extra which it would be nice to have sooner or later. But marriage according to Christian tradition could be difficult and expensive, something which in many countries involved travelling a considerable distance to the principal mission church because it could not be performed in the village. Equipment could be difficult and expensive: a ring, a white dress, bridesmaids, the hired lorry to take them all to church. People were not opposed to all this, many may have actively coveted it, but they often just did not get round to it. Moreover, if you were Catholic and marrying a Protestant, it would not be possible anyway. So a monogamous marriage between two Christians, not by the church and incurring lifelong excommunication, was a quite common phenomenon; customary requirements had been fulfilled and no African doubted that it was a valid marriage.[62] This appalling indictment of missionaries represents an astonishing failure of imagination and will on the part of bishops and other Church leaders. Had John Taylor remained longer in Africa, as was his expectation and hope, he might have helped solve some of these problems. Certainly, he could have supplied some much-needed imagination.

Perhaps the last word on Bishop Tucker College at Mukono should open an even wider view, albeit one that some will call romantic, but which others will recognize simply as love. John Taylor gives an essentially priestly insight into the whole enterprise, for the priest stands close to God and is caught up in the passion and the suffering of God, as well as in the sheer joy of the patient miracle-worker.[63] And no priest is really priest until the heart is broken. Only wounded hands can bless.

> We, Africans and Europeans, who work on its staff consider that we are among the luckiest of God's children who live in these puzzling and portentous days, for we are convinced there is no place for fear or doubt in a world where God is so evidently at work. There is nothing in life so completely humbling, nor so intensely exciting, as to be allowed to stand, as it were, at the Potter's elbow and watch Him mould the clay; to be persuaded with absolute certainty that one can commit oneself, together with all those others with whom one is bound in the bundle of life, into those same Hands. For we have not yet seen the limits of this patient miracle of the Eternal Grace, which lays hold upon the dusty, ignorant young goatherd, the merest unknown ragamuffin on the fringes of the Church, and draws him into the Household of Faith, and makes him to become a leader and a shepherd of the sheep.[64]

CHAPTER FOUR

Way of the Cross

Breaking

T HE JOURNEY through preparation for his own ordination, his work as a priest in two English parishes, and his ten years teaching seminarians in Uganda all contributed to breaking down the romantic image of the missionary for John Taylor. What he calls 'small heaps of unreality' were, one after another, simply swept away.[1] The final breaking of the image only occurred, however, with breaking from Uganda itself. 'I had loved Uganda and expected to spend my working life there: I thought that was what good missionaries did.'[2] As events unfolded, it could not be. Their older daughter was at boarding school in neighbouring Kenya, there being no suitable school in Uganda. The younger children, Peter and Veronica, were still at home. The perceptive headmistress of St Andrew's School alerted the Taylors to the fact that Joanna was showing signs that she was accustomed to seeing, signs that the child desperately wanted to be living at home for longer periods. The headmistress wrote, saying, 'I can see these signs; at present she's still very happy, but in another year she could be getting into all sorts of trouble.' John and Peggy felt they had no option other than to honour this perception, even though it meant sacrificing their work in Africa and returning to England. In their minds, there could be no question of sacrificing the well-being of their daughter, or chancing that all would be well.

In routine recitals of John Taylor's career dates little or nothing of this formative crisis is revealed. Writing the preface to *Christ is the Kingdom*, John Taylor's centenary lectures for Wycliffe College, Toronto, what the Principal says is true so far as it goes:

> After studies in Cambridge and at Oxford, followed by pastoral work in England, he entered a long period of missionary service in Africa. He then joined the staff of the International Missionary Council in 1955, became the Africa Secretary for the CMS in 1959, and its General Secretary in 1963. He became Bishop of Winchester in 1974, is a member of the House of Lords, and Prelate of the Most Noble Order of the Garter.[3]

A seamless robe, so it would appear, or at least a steady and predictable progression, an effortless rise to eminence, gathering various honours –

among which the Principal is careful to mention the Wycliffe College Doctorate in Divinity! – along the way.

It was not quite so smooth a ride. There are mysteries and unresolved questions, particularly about 1954–5. Things did not just fall painlessly into place. Crisis, gaps with nothing congenial or useful to do, loss of direction, doubt and darkness fill the days between resignation as Warden of Mukono and extended research work for the International Missionary Council. That year was a time of danger for the whole family, living in genteel poverty in an expensive part of London, and of intense inner misery for John Taylor himself. Apart from such shattering experiences, of course, John Taylor would not be the John Taylor we know. Suffering this prolonged trauma forged and fused personality and theology, creating something intensely real and lastingly attractive.

Back in England, CMS naturally used him for deputation work. After all, he was still on the pay-roll. This meant adding to his feelings of emptiness and waste the agony of encouraging others to go where he could not, to serve people he knew and loved so well. These early months at home in England were filled by such deputations, and they intensified his grief. Looking back, John Taylor probably needed this length of time really to begin to emerge from the ten intensely rewarding Mukono years. No doubt every ounce of this time was required in order to leave his work in other hands, in order really to let go. At the time, however, all he knew was anxiety about surviving the present and about what the future might hold. No real work emerged for him. No new doors seemed to be opening and he could see nothing clearly.[4]

With no new task in sight and the obligation to address audiences continually for CMS about a calling that was no longer his, John Taylor was now forced to face the fact that his childish vision of the missionary as first-class Christian was mistaken. The missionary as Christian hero had been an illusion. In his current depression, he saw this fantasy as his perennial idol, worshipped faithfully and served energetically all these years. His brutal awakening opened windows of self-awareness which lasted a lifetime. 'From that time, whenever I have caught myself trying to be the stuff of which heroes are made, I have known what is going on.'[5] But how could it be that God, who had prepared him for nothing else than missionary work in Uganda, seemed now so cruelly and devastatingly to abandon him? He had given his heart and his heart had been broken. All those years of going out of himself into the mysteries of a foreign culture, embracing the primal vision, all his striving to enrich the Church of Uganda through forming its next generation of leaders, all the hard-won theology of experience – was this to be wasted? What on earth had it all been for? What could his mission now be?

This was a crisis in faith of major proportions for a man just reaching the most creative and fruitful years of his life.[6] The disappointment and bewilderment might have stultified his creativity, resentment might have turned to bitterness, poisoning any future ministry. The lightness of touch in John Taylor's later references to this dark night of the soul belies the seriousness of the challenge. The breaking of idols shook the foundations, calling everything he had taken for granted into question, demanding that he build afresh from the ground up.

Depression and hurt, disappointment and fear, began to surface as intense anger. It took John Taylor a long time to identify the real object of his anger. With no new work and too much time to think, he began to ask himself what these feelings meant. 'Why do I feel so hurt?' 'Why am I so angry?' 'Who am I angry with?' At first, his anger took the form of resentment of CMS, but he soon realized that this was no more than an easy target. His real anger was not directed at God's representative, but directly at God. He was frightened to find himself so angry with God.[7] Was this not proof that his faith was weak? Surely, to rail against God was the ultimate human betrayal? Yet had not God done the betraying? He was cast aside, feeling completely lost, like a frightened child. Just as he seemed to be reaching the top of his form in Uganda and doing his best work, it was all taken away.

Only when the anger was faced, admitted to himself and to trusted friends, was he able to transcend it. Only after naming his anger honestly for what it really was could he begin to move forward. New thoughts now began to arise. Was the timing right, perhaps, in some way he could not see? Much as he hated to think so, was his real work already done? Is this just rationalizing after the event, a way of coming to terms with what cannot be changed, or are these new thoughts pointers to truth? There is, of course, no way of telling. Even now, forty years later, it is impossible to be sure.

> It's very difficult to know. Would I, after ten years, begin to be a bit self-satisfied and stuck? I just don't know. Or did I need that traumatic removal, and then return, in order to be able to see? I don't know.[8]

Of one thing, however, John Taylor is certain.

> All those years I still had been nursing the very childish, romantic view of missionaries in the magic forest. I still wanted to be top Christian, and there was a lot of pride in being a missionary. But God had said – rather harshly – 'Thank you, but you can forget all that, that's not what it's about.' And I think it all came right when at last it came to a sort of climax, quite quietly when I was by myself, and I told Peggy I'd been nursing this quite false image, really of self-importance, and she was the one who paid for it. She had never got that sort of vocation. So it was a very hard lesson to learn, very painful.[9]

Who, we may ask, were the ministering angels in this pain?

Strangely, he was not much helped by Max Warren. 'I think he probably did understand, I don't remember talking to him, he was very busy.'[10] Undoubtedly, Max Warren would have understood. After all, he had been through a dark night of the soul himself when his own missionary work was unceremoniously cut short. Undoubtedly, he *was* very busy. But the excuses offered late in life somehow don't ring quite true. Was John Taylor ashamed to talk with Max Warren, ashamed of his own frustration and anger? Did he go on blaming CMS – not so much for leaving Africa as for making him enthuse about it to others – more than he dared admit?

One ministering angel was the rather academic vicar of the small church in Chelsea where John and Peggy worshipped, and where he became a sort of curate. He also worked on a few radio dramas for the BBC, telling some of the parables, and this work helped. Here was a fresh opportunity to use his theological and artistic expertise. Douglas Webster, later Canon of St Paul's but at that time with the CMS education department, asked him to write a volume for a new series of books. He wrote *Man in the Midst*, and found he really liked the experience of writing.[11]

> Only by learning our purpose can we understand our nature. Heirs of the earth and of time, yet open towards heaven and attuned to eternity, made of the dust yet made for God, we are creatures of the borderland, men of many worlds. We stand at the point of intersection, of many planes; from this fact derives our destiny and our danger, our tensions and our tragedies.[12]

The theologian and the poet emerge clearly between the covers of this first book, and most of the theological themes characteristic of his mature work are already to be found here in embryo. Not that new ideas and new dimensions did not come with experience, but it is extraordinary to see how far back the seeds of some of his ideas go.[13]

Next came a request from Penguin. They wanted a paperback on Christianity and Africa, would he do that? Drawing on all his recent first-hand experience of the great continent, as well as his developing theological convictions, he wrote *Christianity and Politics in Africa*.[14]

Happy hours reading and writing in the Chelsea Library proved immensely therapeutic. The gloom was slowly lifting. Here was an unexpected opening, a new start, a really fresh beginning. Writing was something he discovered he was good at. He was acquiring a new skill and a new satisfaction, a new form of creativity. Above all, perhaps, a rather depressed and disoriented John Taylor was encouraged to learn that he could do something else besides being a missionary, besides teaching ordinands. 'It was really a life-line.'[15]

From a distance, indeed from beyond the grave, another angel reached out to take John Taylor by the hand. This was the German pastor martyred by the Nazis, Dietrich Bonhoeffer.

Reading Dietrich Bonhoeffer's recently published *Letters and Papers from Prison* in his own very different imprisonment was wonderfully liberating and stimulating.[16] To discover such an unexpected soul friend, bridging their very different worlds of background and life experience, kindled afresh the fire of faith which had been burning so dimly. Here was another lifeline to sanity, a renewing of trust in the divine purpose. Lit up by Dietrich Bonhoeffer's vision, energized by his profoundly passionate and completely rational commitment, John Taylor eagerly embraced 'religion-less' Christianity. Bonhoeffer gave him a name for what he had already discovered to be true in Africa. No lesser stage than the whole wide world is the arena of the divine Spirit's concern and creativity, and now this was confirmed and celebrated from an entirely different and unlikely direction. The secular world is the place where the Word is continually made flesh, where the Incarnation reveals that incarnation is the order of the day – every day and everywhere, at all times. Learning to trust his own experience, John Taylor discovered that this theology made sense, indeed, that it was radically orthodox. It also fitted well, of course, with Max Warren's persistent emphasis on taking all human history with full serious-ness as the only locus of salvation history.

At about the same time as he was reading Bonhoeffer, John Taylor met and sat at the feet of Hendrik Kraemer and Walter Freytag, both of whom became strong influences. In particular, they taught him to keep his eyes fixed on God, putting the Church with its pretensions and claims permanently in proper perspective. They reinforced in him the truth that God is always greater than the Church: that the Church depends on God, but that God does not depend on the Church. They also helped him draw out the implications of the crucial insight that humankind is capable of using everything, even religion, against God. The routine and ritual of religion domesticate and tame what is so dangerous, helping us escape the terrifying presence and demand of God.[17] This Barthian influence helped John Taylor to go on living in a larger room than any ecclesiastical structure can provide, helping him to take lightly the in-house squabbles which consumed others. Such theology goes hand in hand with his shrewd assessment of the narrowness of many Christian concerns, and the Church's preoccupation with ordering its own internal life. As Karl Barth himself says, religion is unbelief, for it is easier to fall to our knees in prayer than to stand on our feet in responsible action.[18]

For all his attraction to Karl Barth, however, it is the martyred Dietrich Bonhoeffer who lives most powerfully in John Taylor, and we must detour a little in order to understand why.

Theologia crucis

It is said that the uses to which the theology of Dietrich Bonhoeffer has been put tell us more about his disciples than about the master.

> Psychologists rejoice in Bonhoeffer's emphasis on maturity, secular sociologists at his pungent opposition to clericalism. Barthians see his work,

despite a few pot shots at 'revelation positivism', as an application of the master's critique of religion begun in his *Epistle to the Romans*. Tillichians find the 'world come of age' another symbol for the truly 'theonomous culture'. Dietrich Bonhoeffer has become a wide-open pastime, for he wrote just enough, but not too much, to make room for nearly everyone.[19]

If this observation is true, we must ask what Bonhoeffer was really saying, or we will have no chance of seeing why he became so important to John Taylor. Indeed, we must ask if John Taylor heard Bonhoeffer's true voice or not. Was his reading of Bonhoeffer just wishful thinking, just another invention, yet another distortion?

On one level at least it seems that John Taylor heard the authentic voice of the martyr. Perhaps such acute listening was possible only because of his own brokenness, because Bonhoeffer spoke to him precisely at that moment in his life when he could hear, when the seed really would fall into the ground and die into life. For the Spirit does not give itself in glib encounters, where we exchange second-hand thoughts. 'Our defences must be down, broken either by intense joy or by despair. One way or another we must have come to the end of ourselves.'[20] Prior to the moment when he had to abandon his work in Uganda, life for John Taylor moved forward in a fairly predictable pattern and the will of God seemed plain enough. Home, school, university, theological college, ordination, pastoral experience in two very different English parish settings – all this was preparation for his life's work as an overseas missionary. He would exemplify in his own life the quintessential characteristic of Christianity, namely its missionary nature. Suddenly, this whole world-view with all its predictability had crumbled. Now there was no clear vision for his future and he had no status or proper place in the scheme of things. Now he was daily struggling to make some sense of his unexpected predicament. He was adrift, doing theology in darkness and pain, depressed as he had never been before. In powerlessness, in helplessness, he connected easily with the powerless, helpless Bonhoeffer. If it is true that Bonhoeffer's life is the hermeneutical clue to his thought,[21] that he enacted his own theology with absolute seriousness in his resistance to the Nazi regime, paying the ultimate price,[22] we should not be surprised by his ability to connect with others counting the cost of discipleship. It has been said that 'he provides an example of Christ-centred thinking, costly discipleship, and worldly faith'.[23] It is little wonder that this man's *theologia crucis* resonated so profoundly and lastingly in the suffering John Taylor. This was cross speaking to cross. For both Dietrich Bonhoeffer and John Taylor thought as theologians, and the heart of their theology is always christology.[24]

It is, of course, a well rehearsed truism to say that the heart of any Christian theology must be christology. For Dietrich Bonhoeffer, however, following in the footsteps of Karl Barth, this is anything but a routine suggestion. It may be that Bonhoeffer even took Barth at his word with more seriousness than Barth himself. Barth claimed that 'It is in Him and Him alone that the Father is revealed. It is He and He alone whom the Holy Spirit reveals. Therefore dogmatics must actually be Christology and only Christology.'[25] But whereas Barth did not really work consistently from this premise, Bonhoeffer tried to do so. He grounds all his reflection solely upon the concrete actuality of God revealed in Christ, over against philosophical theology and existentialist 'pre-understanding'. From *Sanctorum Communio*[26] to *Letters and Papers from Prison* his theology is entirely determined by the biblical witness to Jesus Christ. In all this he attempts to be more faithful to Barth's theological task than he believed Barth was himself: to expound the biblical witness to Christ intelligibly and in the fullness of its revolutionary implications.[27] It is in this spirit that Bonhoeffer is bold enough to reject the traditional god of Western theism and explicitly refuse the god who could literally do anything in or about this world. Bonhoeffer did not believe in God characterized as unambiguously omnipotent, the prime mover, the first cause, the ground of all being, absolute in glory, supreme in power. By this definition, Bonhoeffer was an atheist, insisting that all Christians should join him in his atheism, indeed that all people should repudiate the image of God he repudiated. Over the course of a lifetime, John Taylor has joined him in this as in so much else, devoting all his creative energies to exploration of the Christlike God. The Christlike God stands in judgement on all idols, not least those with respectable theological pedigrees. John Taylor agrees with Bonhoeffer that the actions and sufferings of the man Jesus, his words and wounds, are nothing less than the actions and sufferings, the words and wounds, of God. The being of the man Jesus is the meaning of the world. This figure of the gospels whose being is entirely gift, this man who lives in humiliation and weakness and rejection, is all in the world we know of the only true God.[28]

For Dietrich Bonhoeffer this one true God is powerful only in weakness. God is weak and helpless and suffering, not omnipotent in any usual sense of the word. Knowing so much about weakness, helplessness and suffering himself, Bonhoeffer felt the attraction of what this God could accomplish in weakness. Unlike most Christian theologians, he took at face value the centrality of the cross of Christ, believing that the cross is the only true picture of God that the world has ever seen. What we learn about the content of the word 'God' must be learned entirely from Jesus. We shall not talk properly of God unless we have first learned to speak of Jesus, not the reverse.[29] Jesus must displace God and take priority over God in any theologizing which stands a chance of being authentically Christian. Shifting ontological priority from God to Christ means taking Barth an important step further, but it also confronts the bulk of Christian tradition or at least radically questions its underlying assumptions by recalling it to its genesis. One particular human being, a man who lived and died in a particular place at a particular time in a particular way becomes the sole key to unlocking the mystery of God's being and nature. Jesus speaks in this particular way about the particular God, matching his preaching with his living and dying. In the Jewish imagination of Jesus and in the Hebrew imagination of Jesus's ancestors, God is a personal figure with a definite character. 'The character of this God, who loved righteousness like an Amos, agonized over the folly of his people like a Jeremiah, and loved like a Hosea, becomes central to the image of man for those informed by that story.'[30] The pattern of the living and dying of Jesus refines and confirms the image we have of the invisible One he calls *Abba*, his own dear Father.

It is inevitable that christologies worked 'from above' give priority to God the Father, fitting Jesus into the picture as best they can. For Bonhoeffer, Karl Barth was the most powerful contemporary exemplar of this venerable tradition. But is this where Christianity begins, or must christology now be done 'from below'? Doing christology from above is routinely flawed, and Barth's christology is no exception. 'Behind it lies the idea of the Father as really more God than the Son, as antecedently God, and as the real cause of all things.'[31] But if God has a human face, if Jesus is the human face of God, how can we begin anywhere else? If all we know of God is to be found in Christ, then all we learn elsewhere of God is to be measured against this incarnate way, truth and life.[32]

Bonhoeffer did not begin his theological quest by asking what selection of biblical treasures or ecclesiastical concepts we can still offer the modern world. Contrary to popular opinion, he was no reductionist. He did not ask how to communicate better the message Christianity possesses. He was not a salesman to have-nots. Always his question was the same question: What *is* the message? He became an evangelist only in asking 'Who are You?' In other words, Christ is not the problem, we are. Christ is there, and we must answer him. This means that christology is always an open and unfinished task, for we are living new responses each day to the One who calls us, responding anew to our encounter with Christ in the world.

So far as Bonhoeffer is concerned, Jesus Christ is the centre of humanity, nature, and history. 'The one who is present in Word, sacrament and community is in the centre of human existence, history and nature. It is part of the structure of his person that he stands in the centre.'[33] Bonhoeffer thus conceptualizes the whole of reality christologically. Reality, it can be said, has a christocratic structure. Christ is not absolute reality *added* to worldly reality. In the Incarnation, Christ takes up the world into himself, so that we can say that he establishes an 'ontological coherence' of God's reality with the world's reality. And this unity of all reality in Christ is not synthetic or artificial, but real and valid in Christ the redeemer and reconciler, Christ the vicarious deputy.[34]

In Jesus Christ the reality of God entered into the reality of the world. The place where the answer is given, both to the question concerning the reality of God and to the question concerning the reality of the world, is designated solely and alone by the name of Jesus Christ. God and the world are comprised in this name. In Him all things consist (Col. 1:7). Henceforward one can speak neither of God nor of the world without speaking of Jesus Christ. All concepts of reality which do not take account of Him are abstractions.[35]

Whoever sees Jesus Christ does indeed see God and the world in one. He can no longer see God without the world or the world without God.[36]

One immediate and welcome consequence of this theology is that all dualism is done away with at a stroke. The supernatural is found only in the natural, the holy only in the profane, the revelational only in the rational, the Christian only in the worldly, the spiritual only in the bodily. In other words, all things are reconciled to God in Christ.[37] The crucified Lord is the triumphant centre, and the triumphant one is the crucified. Consequently, only Christ, who has so intensely united the divine and the human, can finally lead us beyond our own folly and vanity, whether it be that of other-worldly piety or this-worldly atheism, to true religion and genuine faith.[38] In this, Bonhoeffer is deeply indebted to Barth, who insists that there cannot be two levels of reality existing side by side. The Incarnation makes this impossible. Nothing and no one can stand outside the revelation in Christ, who has reconciled all things to God by the blood of his cross. There is only one reality, the reconciliation of all being in Christ.[39]

For all its freshness, Bonhoeffer's cosmic Christ in whom all reality is found is at the same time unmistakably the Christ of the Catholic creeds, just as he is recognizably the Christ of the traditional Lutheran theology of the cross, the *theologia crucis*. Bonhoeffer's espousal of a kenotic christology, a christology of condescension or humbling, is set firmly within orthodox Christian tradition.[40] His christology always maintains its roots in the classical notions of the patristic age, aligned with the consistent teaching of the Fathers of the Church. In worship, confession, apologetics, teaching and everyday conversation we find him using the wide range of christological titles found in the New Testament and the Fathers. He worships Christ with the ecumenical formulae of the great liturgies and with the personal pietistic and subjective names for Jesus found in his German hymn book. In this fashion he prays to Christ to the end of his life, whether in pew or prison.[41] Always for him, and increasingly as he enters resolutely into his destiny in time of war, the whole fullness of God is found precisely in the humble, earthly, human life of Jesus. In a word, infinitude is emptied into finitude.

We have the Exalted One only as the Crucified, the Sinless One only as the one laden with guilt, the Risen One only as the Humiliated One. Were this not so, the *pro nobis* would be done away with, there would be no faith. Even the resurrection is not a penetration of the incognito. Even the resurrection is ambiguous. It is only believed in where the stumbling block of Jesus has not been removed. Only the disciples who followed Jesus saw the resurrection. Only blind faith sees here.[42]

It is evident from this language that the Risen One as the Humiliated One is Dietrich Bonhoeffer's Christ. Jesus is the beggar among beggars, the one laden with guilt who bears it to the end, the powerless one helpless on the cross, the despised and forsaken and suffering one, the crucified one. The single visible sign of God in the world is the cross. God's way in the world is the way of the cross. God knows no other way. There is no escaping this truth, this essential Christian insight into the nature of reality, this clue to the way the grain of the world runs.

> Our God is a suffering God. Suffering forms man into the image of God. The suffering man is in the likeness of God ... Whenever a man is in a position of weakness, is aware of his existence with God and his likeness to God, he shares God's life.[43]

This theme of the *theologia crucis* is constant through all Bonhoeffer's writings. There is never any deviation from the centrality of the cross. The cross stands for the way of suffering, paradoxically manifesting God's power most clearly in weakness. The cross exemplifies the full emptying of God in the Incarnation, God's complete and unreserved identification with us, God's self-sacrifice for us. To be Christian is to be a human being, but what makes one human is 'participation in the sufferings of God in the secular life'.[44] In Jesus Christ, the Lord of the cosmos, all created things have their origin, essence and goal. Through the command of the cosmic Christ all creation is set free to fulfil its own laws, to fulfil its own destiny, to be genuinely itself, to be, in other words, genuinely worldly.[45] The atoning cross sets human beings free for life before God in a godless world. The cross 'sets men free for life in genuine worldliness'.[46]

Bonhoeffer's theology never lets go this defining vision of kenotic christology. When John Taylor came upon the *Letters and Papers from Prison*, he found that Bonhoeffer had coined his own christological title in addition to all the traditional titles. In the prison cell at Tegel in suburban Berlin, Bonhoeffer began to spell out further his earlier insight in terms of Christ as the man-for-others. It is a typical attempt at non-religious interpretation, pregnant with the theological base and ethical outcome of Bonhoeffer's participation in the German resistance movement. This longing to speak intelligibly to his own generation arises out of his willingness to share in the guilt of those plotting the assassination of Hitler. The title springs directly from his understanding of the essence of Christ's person, revealing the essence of the Trinitarian God whose whole life consists in 'being-for', whose life is characterized in the movement of gift giving.

> Christ is not Christ as Christ in himself, but in his relation to me. His being Christ is his being *pro me*. This being *pro me* is in turn not meant to be understood as an effect which emanates from him, or as an accident; it is

meant to be understood as the essence, as the being of the person himself. This personal nucleus itself is the *pro me*. That Christ is *pro me* is not an historical or an ontical statement, but an ontological one. That is, Christ can never be thought of in his being in himself, but only in his relationship to me. That in turn means that Christ can only be conceived of existentially, viz. in the community ... It is not only useless to meditate on Christ in himself, but even godless.[47]

This powerful, absolute statement, so apparently harsh at its end, Bonhoeffer never tires of proclaiming boldly in one form or another. 'He is the centre in three ways; in being-there for men, in being-there for history, and in being-there for nature.'[48] Or, again, 'the form of humiliation is the form of the *Christus pro nobis*. In this form Christ means and wills to be for us in freedom.'[49]

Being there for others, then, is the very essence of being Christ. To conceive of Christ in any other way is godless delusion. It is to think as Peter thought when, speaking for the company of the twelve disciples, he rejected the possibility that Jesus should suffer and die in fulfilling his mission. To conceive of Christ other than in terms of the suffering servant of God becomes positively satanic, the ultimate lie.[50] True confession of the identity of Jesus can never be separated from the cross. Because the essence of Christ is his being the man-for-others and because Christ is the only fully human being, it follows that the essence of true humanity must necessarily be found in being-there-for-others. Our true identity is only located in the self–other relationship. It is only the self turned outward toward others that finds fulfilment. Turned in upon itself, the self is bound, trapped, enclosed, imprisoned. Only as we turn to others do we experience transcendence. Thus, the person in community is the only person possible. It follows that the other who is distinct and different from me is always the form in which the divine is experienced. According to the Lutheran formula *finitum capax infiniti*, the finite bears the infinite. Bonhoeffer's favourite quotation is 'corporeality is the end of God's path'.[51] Because Christ is in and with and under human sociality, we only find ourselves, experiencing self-fulfilment, or achieving self-formation, in being with and for others. Being with and for others is how we are formed in Christ.

Authentic selfhood, then, turns naturally on love of neighbour. 'This is my body which is *for* you.' Responding to the presence and claim of another is in fact, whether we recognize it or not, response to the presence and claim of God. 'The transcendental is not infinite and unattainable tasks, but the neighbour who is within reach in any given situation. God in human form ... the man-for-others, and therefore the Crucified, the man who lives out of the transcendent.'[52]

If the essence of individuality for Christ and for us is being-for-others, then the same is true of the Church as a whole. 'The only way in which the Church can defend her own territory is by fighting not for it but for the salvation of the world.'[53] 'The Church is the Church only when it is there for others.'[54] No wonder Bonhoeffer judged the state Lutheran Church and even the Confessing Church so harshly, for neither could resist compromise with an evil government to preserve its own privilege and influence. Neither church was prepared to take risks for the sake of the persecuted, neither risked speaking for the voiceless, both were timid and afraid. Like the intelligent, educated, reflective men of the resistance, church leaders were too slow to take action, too scrupulous over motive and means.[55]

Right to the end Bonhoeffer maintained this unity in his christology, ecclesiology and anthropology. Those who see little ecclesiology in Bonhoeffer's prison letters fail to appreciate the fact that he never detached his thinking about the Church from his thinking about Christ. Christology without ecclesiology ends in abstraction. There are always persons, visibly gathered and drawn into the fate of Christ. Being-there-for-others is the ground of reality itself. His christological title is faithful to the tradition, non-speculative, relational, and central to all being and to all reality. There is continuity with the past, and it is theological, existential and ethical. Furthermore, it is as simple as it is profound, as understandable as it is sophisticated, as anthropological as it is theological.[56]

> Jesus is there only for others. His 'being there for others' is the experience of transcendence. It is only this 'being there for others', maintained till death, that is the ground of his omnipotence, omniscience, and omnipresence. Faith is participation in this being of Jesus (Incarnation, cross, and resurrection). Our relation to God is not a 'religious' relationship to the highest, most powerful, and best Being imaginable – that is not authentic transcendence – but our relation to God is a new life in 'existence for others', through participation in the being of Jesus.[57]

This thoroughly consistent christology of the *theologia crucis* may be firmly grounded in Lutheran tradition, but it also moves beyond it. Bonhoeffer's vision is that of the *Christus Pantocrator*. With this vision of the enveloping sovereign Christ embracing the whole creation, he develops a theology of the cross which expresses a christocratic understanding of all reality.[58] This is his reading of reality, of things as they actually are in the world. It is his reading, as John Taylor would say, of the facts. This opens up the way for his glad collaboration with people who do not name the name of Christ at all, but who nevertheless perceive reality in the same way he does. Just as action in accordance with Christ must be in accordance with reality, action which accords with reality must accord with Christ. It follows that the primary difference between moral and immoral action corresponds naturally and directly to the degree of con-*form*-ity or non-con-*form*-ity to the *form* that Christ takes in the world.[59] Another way of putting the matter is to say that the Christian asks 'How is Christ taking form in the world?' and 'How can I conform to Christ's form in the world', while the non-Christian asks 'What is real?' and 'How can I conform to reality?' In Christ, God's reality and the world's reality cohere. Reality itself is endowed with christological character.

> It is with the Christ who is persecuted and who suffers in His Church that justice, truth, humanity and freedom now seek refuge; it is with the Christ who found no shelter in the world, the Christ who was cast out from the world, the Christ of the crib and of the cross, under whose protection they now seek sanctuary, and who thereby for the first time displays the full extent of His power. The cross of Christ makes both sayings true: 'He that is not with me is against me' and 'He that is not against us is for us'.[60]

The movement in Bonhoeffer's christology can be charted in this way: if *The Cost of Discipleship* is a commentary on Matthew 12.30, 'He that is not with me is against me', then *Ethics* and *Letters and Papers from Prison* provide commentary on Mark 9.40, 'He that is not against us is for us'.[61] This is clearly an instance of biography influencing theology, for the development occurs with Bonhoeffer's experience of resistance to the Nazi regime, working alongside those who shared his passion for justice, but without his devotion to Christ. Finding his collaborators in the resistance to be true and faithful companions in their common cause forced Bonhoeffer to think more honestly and more generously than before about their place in God's present and God's future. This was, of course, an intensification of his experience within his own family, where people he loved were indifferent or hostile to Christianity and saw the Church as an outmoded institution. In their integrity they were, nevertheless, willing to work and risk their lives in the struggles of human destiny.[62] Indeed, these non-Christians were doing precisely what Christians should have been doing. Bonhoeffer had to account theologically for this truth of his experience, and honesty demanded that he say more than that they were a living judgement on the existing Church and its members.

Bonhoeffer's christology during the time of his imprisonment is not distinctive in terms of the *pattern* of Christ's life as the man-for-others, for this remains constant. What changes is the *place* where this life is lived out. It is not so much that the *way* of Jesus has changed, but the *where*. This follows for the Christian life as well, surely no surprise for a thinker so christocentric as Bonhoeffer.[63]

> The Christian, unlike devotees of the redemption myths, has no last line of escape available from earthly tasks and difficulties into the eternal, but, like Christ himself ('My God, why hast thou forsaken me?'), he must drink the earthly cup to the lees, and only in his doing so is the crucified and risen Lord with him, and he is crucified and risen with Christ. This world must not be prematurely written off; in this the Old and New Testament are one. Redemption myths arise from human boundary-experiences, but Christ takes hold of a man at the centre of his life.[64]

If this christology of suffering-for-others in the 'secular' life is accepted as normative, it follows that Christians should expect to experience such suffering. For when Christ calls someone, he calls them to come and die.[65] 'It is not the religious act that makes the Christian, but participation in the sufferings of God in the secular life.'[66]

> I am still discovering right up to this moment, that it is only by living completely in this world that one learns to have faith. One must completely abandon any attempt to make something of oneself, whether it be a saint, or a converted sinner, or a Churchman (a so-called priestly type!), a righteous man or an unrighteous one, a sick man or a healthy one. By this-worldliness I mean living unreservedly in life's duties, problems, successes and failures, experiences and perplexities. In so doing we throw ourselves completely into the arms of God in the world – watching with Christ in Gethsemane. That I think is faith, that is *metanoia*; and that is how one becomes a man and a Christian.[67]

John Taylor and Dietrich Bonhoeffer have this in common, that wherever they found themselves they sought Christ. What has been said of Bonhoeffer can be said also of his follower: 'If one asks what was the centre of his life and thought, the answer is contained in the name Jesus Christ.'[68] For Bonhoeffer, the pattern and the place of Christ and the Christian life were learned as a prize of war. Jesus Christ was searched for and found in the claims of political life, in all the plotting and deception of resistance. Bonhoeffer was able to show John Taylor that the real question is always existential. This existential question is ever new, for it is always about *today*. 'Who is Christ for us today?'[69] This 'today' refers to the modern world, to the world come of age, to today's world, God's present moment of salvation.

In Bonhoeffer's today and in our own today, religion has declined and human beings are taking control of areas of life previously beyond our control. Talk of the 'world come of age' has fed the enthusiasms of later theologians in a variety of ways, becoming particularly significant for the 'death of God' school of theology.[70] Bonhoeffer's talk of 'religionless Christianity' was meat and drink to those who hoped to abandon all the traditional practices of piety in their quest for 'faith' identified as the struggle for a better world – for social justice, equity and freedom. This, however, is to misinterpret and misrepresent Bonhoeffer, who had no intention of encouraging any notion of action apart from devotion, as his own prayer life to the end plainly testifies. Neither was he naive, or overly optimistic, in talking about a world 'come of age'. It seems likely that he chose this term to avoid talk of the 'secular' world,[71] having come to believe that 'secular' was a typically patronizing term which allowed the Church to dismiss those outside its own borders. The German word *mündig*, with which he avoided talk of the 'secular' world, does not mean moral maturity or completeness or perfection. It refers to 'one who speaks for themselves'.

In other words, the reference is to the passage from adolescence to adulthood. You are no longer a minor, a child, a dependant. You are on your own. In this sense you have 'come of age'. You are now fully responsible for your own actions, accountable for yourself. On their own, Bonhoeffer says, people are self-confident, responsible, strong, exercising their powers. God is to be encountered in the midst of this psychological maturity rather than when we are at our wits' end. If God is located on the periphery and depended on only when human power peters out, then people at their most religious are people at their most exhausted, defeated and self-denigrating, and also at their most self-serving, turned in on themselves. Religious consciousness as the Church has traditionally presented it means that humanity is *less* when it is most with God, and *more* when it is most godless!

The tragedy is that the Church has too much to lose by changing direction, so the Church strongly opposes any rediscovery of Christianity in its non-religious biblical roots, and is the ablest opponent of its own conversion. Clergy go on attempting to claim a place for God by marketing certain questions and problems, particularly those to do with guilt, suffering and death, to which only God supposedly can give any answer. The ploy of church leaders is to relativize the present, reserving for themselves the ultimate questions, which are then used in a fatuous attack on the world's maturity. Religion preserves a place for itself by projecting a bleak prognosis of unhappiness, sin and despair onto the world. This means that the world come of age is closer to confronting the biblical God than religious Christians, for the Church is captive to the God of religion. In stark contrast to his followers, Christ himself regarded a person's life and health and happiness as in themselves blessings, because the whole of human life belongs to his Father's kingdom. If faith means to share the attitudes of Christ, the Christian can do no less. This means that the emerging Church of the future will be more modest, an intense community loyal to Christ, nourished by the arcane disciplines of the liturgical life. It will be a poor, apparently powerless Church experiencing and distributing costly grace.

This deliberate retreat from what might be called a protestantism of negativities and denunciations towards what might be characterized as genuinely biblical evangelical faith obviously appealed to the evangelical John Taylor, opening out to his fertile imagination an attractively *Christian* anthropology. At the heart of any authentically human faith, then, is a reverent agnosticism, for which talk rather than silence must justify itself. Such talk will justify the breach of silence only when it is humble, careful, sparing. It will be sure of what Luther called the utter 'havability' of God in Christ, but modest, reticent and tentative in commending this reality. True apprehension of transcendent reality is relative and fragmentary. Bonhoeffer worries that Christian faith has not gone far enough in accepting religious ignorance viscerally as well as intellectually. This honesty obviously appeals to someone who has spent ten years in Uganda, and knows first-hand that England is as much the mission field as Africa. So pre-eminently a preached faith, Christianity has always believed that it has something to *tell* everyone about God. Preaching makes Christianity garrulous and quarrelsome, a highly conceptualized religion. Preoccupation with the Word has produced a great deal of wordiness, giving birth to poor little talkative Christianity!

It is time for all who preach the gospel to recognize that revelation is to be understood in terms of God's transcendent hiddenness, God's disclosing to us 'the fringes of his ways'. Revelation is a decidedly refracted light, not a pure beam. We are given sufficient guidance to live in obedience to God in the changes and chances, the mysteries and tragedies of life. Indeed, knowledge of God cannot be gained apart from immersion in the stuff of everyday existence, because the world is founded in Christ and this is where we meet Christ in our neighbours. But while we are given hints and clues, we are not given clear, neat answers for immediate reference. God remains elusive, unpredictable, surprising, free both in the teaching and the mysterious person of Christ. It follows that all our humanly inadequate notions about God are continually in process of revision. 'The God of Jesus Christ has nothing to do with what God, as we imagine him, could do and ought to do.'[72] For faith to be authentic it must learn again and again how little it knows, and speak tremblingly out of silence. 'The spoken Word is the inexpressible: that which cannot be spoken is the Word.'[73] Karl Barth pressed such an affirmation so hard that the humanity of Jesus tended to get lost in the sovereignty and power of the triune God, ending in a *theologia gloriae* in order to ensure the *graciousness* of God's action toward us in Christ. In contrast, Bonhoeffer's theology quite evidently is a *theologia crucis* in order to ensure the *costliness* of God's grace in Christ.

> We have seen the exalted one, only as the crucified; the sinless one, only as the guilt-laden; the risen one, only as the humiliated. If it were not so, the *pro nobis* would be destroyed and there would be no faith. Even the resurrection does not break through the incognito.[74]

This truth demands human responsibility. Responsibility is characteristic of the life of Jesus himself and consequently characteristic of any true Christian life in the world. This theme becomes increasingly central in Bonhoeffer's thinking and in the theology of John Taylor after him. It means taking mature responsibility for our own actions regardless of whether at times we act childishly, immaturely, foolishly or irresponsibly. Responsibility is not diminished or cancelled by inevitable lapses of this kind. In this sense, having acquired responsibility involves an irrevocable loss of innocence, for we can no longer return to adolescent dependence. Bonhoeffer's appropriation of the term 'come of age' is lifted from Kant's description of the Enlightenment. 'Immaturity is the incapacity to use one's own intelligence without the guidance of another person.'[75] Using our own autonomous reason, we can and do answer life's questions. We can and do interpret natural and social processes, all without the tutelage of any divinity, without God as a working hypothesis. This is why Bonhoeffer is so sure that God is not to be conceived as a God-of-the-gaps, filling the blank spaces in our knowledge or the blank spaces in our competence. God cannot just be the answer to those questions we still cannot answer, for it is certain that the stop-gap God will gradually be squeezed out of the equation altogether.

> God as a working hypothesis in morals, politics, or science, has been sur-mounted and abolished; and the same thing has happened in philosophy and religion. For the sake of intellectual honesty, that working hypothesis should be dropped, or as far as possible eliminated.[76]

What then of religion? Decay of religion is undoubtedly central to the world's coming of age. By 'religion' Bonhoeffer means a particular way of believing and behaving in a misguided attempt to cope with human weakness and deficiency, combined with an equally misguided attempt to preserve God from extinction. Taking an honest look at his own world, Bonhoeffer realized that it was getting on quite well without the god preached by the Christian Churches. As a matter of intellectual honesty, this god should be dropped. The Churches were simply fighting a losing battle to secure room for religion. Since the Enlightenment the Churches had been trying to offer god as the answer to ultimate human questions – the answer, in other words, to *unanswerable* human questions. This god is gradually squeezed out as, inevitably, we do find answers. In this sense, Christian answers are no better than any other religious answers.

In stark contrast to all this, Jesus, so far as Bonhoeffer could see, did not come to provide answers to ultimate questions. Jesus did not *solve* our questions about suffering and dying – he suffered and died! Where human knowledge runs out there is no Christian revelation waiting, and when human strength runs out there is no *deus ex machina* hovering above. All religion is dismissed if it allows only for the *deus ex machina*, the God of the gaps. Religion is heretical when it is provincial, whenever it refers to a separate religious department of life. It follows that metaphysics, thinking in two distinct realms, the supernatural completing the natural, must be abandoned. Equally, individual inwardness, pietism or other forms of ascetic escape from the world are a distortion of reality and true religious concern.

Religion in any of these senses of the word is not necessarily constitutive of human nature and it flies in the face of the Christlike God who overcomes all dualisms. Growth of human autonomy and decay of religion, therefore, go hand in hand in the world come of age. The result is greater human responsibility, for human destiny falls into human hands in ever greater measure. This means that the Church has to escape its self-centred stagnation and look beyond itself to the world, where many good people are interested in what the Church is about. In a word, Christians must stop pretending that they understand the world better than it understands itself. Humanity is now of age, so people need to be treated like adults. Secularists look to people of faith for solidarity, not tutelage. The transcendent is not the unattainable, the eternal, but the present, given, tangible neighbour. To be Christian is not to be in some specific way religious, but to participate fully in human life, to live as Jesus lives – in God and with God, as though God did not exist.

> The God who lets us live in the world without the working hypothesis of God is the God before whom we stand continually. Before God and with God we live without God. God lets himself be pushed out of the world on to the cross. He is weak and powerless in the world, and that is precisely the way, the only way, in which he is with us and helps us.[77]

This means that the religious act, by definition, is always partial. Faith, by contrast, is something whole, involving the whole of who we are and the whole of life. This is a distinction Bonhoeffer learnt from Luther: religion comes from the flesh, but faith is the gift of the Spirit.[78] 'Jesus calls us, not to a new religion, but to life.'[79] As one commentator has put it, this is to live 'as though God were indeed God, not score-keeper, Band-Aid, bonbon, celestial oracle, Good Humour man'.[80] God with us is God who abandons us – as he did Jesus – forcing us to stand on our own feet, insisting that the world make itself. The only difference between Christian and pagan is that the Christian chooses to stand by God in God's suffering. Humankind is called to come to God's aid, to share God's plight, to take responsibility for alleviating suffering. Jesus' God, who needed all the help he could get, is in his very weakness seen to be Lord of all the earth. Rather than attempt to salvage for God an acre in the secular wilds, we are to claim the whole world as none other than the place where God's kingdom is breaking in, claiming this time, our own time, as the age of Jesus.

This means, naturally, that we will suffer with Jesus. Perhaps the reality and the truth and the implications of this crucial insight emerge only when prose gives way to poetry.

> Men go to God when they are sore bestead,
> Pray to him for succour, for his peace, for bread,
> For mercy for them sick, sinning, or dead;
> All men do so, Christian and unbelieving.
>
> Men go to God when he is sore bestead,
> Find him poor and scorned, without shelter or bread,
> Whelmed under weight of the wicked, the weak, the dead;
> Christians stand by God in his hour of grieving.

God goes to every man when sore bestead,
Feeds body and spirit with his bread;
For Christians, pagans alike he hangs dead,
And both alike forgiving.[81]

All this Bonhoeffer welcomes, because it is clear to him that all this is of God, that this describes the reality of the world God has made and is still making. For him, the world come of age is nothing less than the result of an historical movement centred in the cross. Through the weakness of the cross God is inexorably pushing the world toward responsible adulthood.[82] It is precisely this contemporary outgrowth of the *theologia crucis* which allows the biblical God to appear afresh in place of the god we have ourselves constructed, the god we inevitably invent for ourselves. Now we begin to see, as if for the first time, the God we never knew.[83] The exploration of this Christlike God dwelling in a world of many religions and none becomes the central quest characterizing the theology of Bonhoeffer's disciple, John Taylor. For John Taylor the perennial question is 'What is God like?' Another way of asking the same question is 'Who is Christ for us in this moment?' For anyone who pays serious attention to life within and around them, the question is 'Where is God in this event?'

> Here is the decisive difference between Christianity and all religions. Man's religiosity makes him look in his distress to the power of God in the world: God is the *deus ex machina*. The Bible directs man to God's powerlessness and suffering; only the suffering God can help. To that extent we may say that the development towards the world's coming of age ... which has done away with a false conception of God, opens up a way of seeing the God of the Bible, who wins power and space in the world by his weakness.[84]

In the cross, God takes up all things into God and reconciles them, restoring the lost wholeness of creation. Jesus, the incarnation of the suffering God, the compassionate God enfleshed, drinks the earthly cup to the lees. He lives without religious illusions, without ascetic escapes, without the *deus ex machina*. He denies all privilege. He breaks through the bonds that fetter human beings, freeing us for the dignity and responsibility of being-for-others. Jesus meets others at the centre of their lives, not on the periphery. He calls them 'not to a new religion, but to life'. His concern is that people should be strong, that they should be healed and well, inter-dependent adults rather than dependent children. Jesus calls others to grow up, to come of age, to live as adult daughters and sons of God rather than as infants. In a word, in place of childishness he calls for childlikeness. In the world come of age, we cannot off-load our responsibilities onto God any longer. God's self-disclosure in Jesus has set in motion a movement from religion to life, from other-worldliness to this-worldliness, from using God as a working hypothesis to living before God as if God were not there. Our vocation now is so to trust that we can live before God without God. For Christ does not lead us in a religious flight from this world to other worlds beyond, but rather gives us back the earth which we are to serve as loyal stewards,[85] responsible and creative partners with the Creator.

So far we have concentrated only on the question 'Who is Christ for us *today*?' The other way of asking the question, of course, is 'Who is Christ for *us* today?' In other words, precisely who are we who constitute 'us'? Bonhoeffer's co-conspirators were part of the question and part of the answer. They helped him see Christ as the man for others in the very centre of 'life's duties, problems, successes and failures, experiences and perplexities'. By their passionate commitment to the common cause, without recourse to religion in any form, they forced Bonhoeffer to be honest. Somehow, he had to make theological sense of their unconscious or anonymous Christianity. His prison theology is really his working through his resistance experience for himself. This attempt to make sense of things for himself is classic biographized theology. Never for a single moment is it detached from the events of his own life and the time in which he lived.[86] While his theology made his first political moves possible, his political moves in turn formed the new manner of his theology. The clear result of this biographized theology is a shift from Christ's presence centred in the Church to Christ's presence centred in the world. In other words, Bonhoeffer offers a cosmological christology of the *theologia crucis*. This unfailingly constitutes a *concrete* christology.[87] 'Incarnation, crucifixion, and resurrection are the dynamics of all reality and the forming forces of true selfhood. The *vita Christiana* is a polyphonic life that lives from these dynamics.'[88]

In words intended to challenge Barthian theology, Bonhoeffer asserts that the pattern of reality is that 'God is not free *of* man, but *for* man'.[89] It follows inevitably that being-for-others is the only way to be truly human, as it also follows inevitably that being-for-others is the only true form of Church. If this is the way the grain of the world runs, we must run with it, aligning ourselves deliberately to the form and pattern disclosed in Christ. Christian life, therefore, becomes a freely chosen conformation to cosmic reality. This is what it means to do God's will on earth as it is done in heaven.

Which brings us to the major criticism levelled against Bonhoeffer's christology. If Christian life is a *conscious* conformation, the life-for-others lived by atheists or by people of other faiths is necessarily *unconscious*. Bonhoeffer's brief mention of unconscious Christianity acknowledges that this is indeed the case.[90] Bonhoeffer's christology is an ontology that for him takes in all that is real. The dynamics of the Christ event are the dynamics of reality in general, the dynamics of all reality. God's reality and the world's reality cohere and are fully reconciled in the person of Jesus Christ. Ethically, it is simply assumed and asserted that action which conforms to Christ simultaneously corresponds to reality, and that action conforming to reality simultaneously corresponds to Christ. In the resistance movement Bonhoeffer found a community whose actions corresponded with reality and thereby conformed to Christ's form in the world, but whose perception, understanding and articulation of reality were certainly not christological.

While this equation of reality with Christ appears at first sight attractive, the problem quickly becomes plain. If reality can be known apart from knowing Christ, or even if Christ can be known apart from the Church, then Bonhoeffer's stringent claims about the necessity of the revelation of God as Christlike, with church as the locus for experiencing and understanding this revelation, are sharply called into question. If he maintains his insistence on conscious christology as the only way of perceiving and understanding genuine reality, what are we to make of the suggestion that non-Christians who live for others actually live out a 'religionless Christianity'? If the revelation that God is Christlike is the indispensable clue, how can anyone do without knowledge of this clue?

Bonhoeffer stands unhesitatingly with Barth in insisting that divine self-disclosure creates its own 'contact points', rather than being received by some sort of religious apparatus constitutional to human nature. Divine revelation is quite distinct from natural revelation or natural religion. Divine revelation is God searching for us. Natural revelation or natural religion is our searching for God. For all his longing to claim that any action in correspondence with reality simultaneously conforms to Christ, Bonhoeffer never dissolves his christological ethic into a humanist ethic without Christ. In other words, Bonhoeffer does not anywhere suggest that being-for-others in and of itself is the way that reality is realized. He always insists that the being-for-others of *Jesus*, and our participation in *this* particular being-for-others, is the way that the cosmic reality given in Christ comes to expression in the world. Being-for-others in and of itself is not, and cannot be, Bonhoeffer's ethic. He was too clear-sighted for that. He insists that efficacy of action depends wholly on conforming to the particular being-for-others that we see in Jesus of Nazareth. In other words, there is no faith-free way of being-for-others.

To charge Bonhoeffer with such criticism is, it must be admitted, somewhat unfair. This is not only because it seems impertinent to suggest that a martyr, whose theology was crafted *in extremis* and whose thinking was permanently interrupted by the Gestapo, might have taken greater care to present us with a neater package.[91] In the nature of the case, Bonhoeffer's most challenging, seminal theological statements are fragments, partial insights, rather than components of a well-ordered, carefully systematized totality.[92] To the continually asked question, 'Who are You? Speak!',[93] Bonhoeffer answers by fragments and by his life. He had no theological system as such, having neither the leisure nor the luxury of constructing one. Like John Taylor after him, he is inescapably a theologian of insights, not a systematic thinker. Inevitably too, the questions later systematic theologians read back into Bonhoeffer reflect later attempts to argue for forms of unconscious or anonymous Christianity. This is patently anachronistic. Dietrich Bonhoeffer lived and worked and died at a time when Christianity could still be assumed as integral to European history. Even those who had consciously abandoned what they understood this faith to entail were yet influenced by it and still breathed its air.

To look back on Bonhoeffer from a distance and from a time when this claim can no longer be made is surely to judge him unfairly. For all his prophetic abilities, he remained a man of his time, searching for a worldly, politically viable, life-affirming expression of Christianity.[94] He hinted that his suggestions about 'unconscious Christianity' might be problematic,[95] acknowledging awareness of possible difficulties or objections. Had he lived he would undoubtedly have found this to be so, and possibly offered more than his critics by way of elucidation or solution. It is certainly an area in which his followers, in an increasingly contracting world, the global village of many religions and no religion living side by side, have struggled and continue to struggle. We can see now that the notion of unconscious or anonymous Christianity is a hangover from the era of Christendom, and perhaps we can even begin to face the fact that Christendom itself was an aberration. As Bishop Krister Stendahl has pointed out, all the gospel images of God's reign and rule are minority images – salt, light, yeast.[96] Was Christianity ever meant to dominate? Why should this or that thoroughly secular person be unconsciously Christian? Why should they not be unconsciously Buddhist? The very idea of unconscious Christians seems from our vantage point suspiciously imperialistic in a way that could never have occurred to Dietrich Bonhoeffer fifty years earlier. Nevertheless, for John Taylor, *conscious* apprehension of the essential 'clue' God provides for us in Christ becomes the controlling rationale for Christian mission, the sole motivation for evangelism.[97]

CHAPTER FIVE

Primal vision

'THE 1950s were a good age for the missionary movement' because Protestant decline, Adrian Hastings judges, was not yet too evident and Catholics were going from strength to strength.[1] Max Warren was now principal Protestant strategist, and respected as a scholar of considerable historical and cultural sensitivity.

> Among both Catholics and Protestants probably no other decade in missionary history could lay claim to such intelligent vitality. The rather ponderous, slow-thinking, paternalistically benevolent but heavy-handed note of the inter-war years was giving way to something altogether sharper, more self-critical, more willing to recognise that God had always worked as much outside the Christian Church as in it.[2]

This spirit is found in Geoffrey Parrinder's *West African Religion* (1949), Bengt Sundkler's *Bantu Prophets in South Africa* (1949), Trevor Huddleston's *Naught for Your Comfort* (1956), and John Taylor's *Christianity and Politics in Africa* (1957).

> Doubtless all these books could be criticised, but they and others of the same period collectively show a much more open and immediate recognition of the weight and validity of African human and religious experience as of the political rights of Africans and the missionary responsibility to be critical of colonialism and still more of racialism.[3]

Not until the end of 1955 was John Taylor invited to join the research section of the International Missionary Council to carry out the first in a series of field studies on the processes of growth in local churches, and to undertake the exploratory setting up of further studies. This was an inter-disciplinary task lying in uncharted territory between sociology and theology, and it taught him to value listening rather than speaking. It also resulted in what Hastings considers to be a 'work of major importance', namely his book *The Growth of the Church in Buganda*.[4]

The IMC project was an attempt to get systematic theologians to learn ecclesiology from the experience of young Churches, but the theologians did not want to know. Theological truths were apparently independent of experience and the project was a failure. At least it was a failure in the immediate and short term, for we still have the exquisite writings of John Taylor, in which his ability to 'listen deeply with the inner ear of the heart and the spirit' was revealed. These are *The Growth of the Church in Buganda: An Attempt at Understanding* (1958), *Processes of Growth in an African Church* (1958), *Christians of the Copperbelt: The Growth of the Church in Northern Rhodesia* (with Dorothea Lehmann, 1961), and, finally and decisively, *The Primal Vision: Christian Presence Amid African Religion* (1961). Perhaps only now is the time ripe for the Church to absorb the insights collected in these writings. This ripe time is born of necessity in the multi-cultural and multi-faith environment in which we now find ourselves. It is also a time born of a newly discovered humility as the post-Christendom Church adjusts to its life as one religious minority among many.

John Taylor began this new phase in his ministry by returning to Uganda, where in 1956 he lived for three months in a mud hut in a Ganda village. This was followed by a further three months in three other villages and some special investigations in the life and thought of the African bourgeois intelligentsia in one of the large towns. In this second stage, he had close contact with African government officials, politicians, journalists, school teachers and others, reflecting on his experience and discussing it. In 1958 he would spend ten months in Northern Rhodesia, engaged in a similar study. Once again Peggy, left behind as sole parent of three small children, had a high price to pay in terms of loneliness and poverty. At this distance it is impossible to imagine any organization expecting any family to tolerate such a situation, let alone an international ecumenical office calling itself by the name of Christ.

John Taylor's approach in this extended field work was simply to discover what was there.[5] What is there may not seem very remarkable or startling, indeed it will almost certainly be totally ordinary, but it always deserves to be taken seriously as the arena of God's activity. In this stance we meet again his resolute determination to pay attention to the facts because God is in the facts, mixed up in the detail of any and every situation. The hard and messy given-ness of things is what interests this researcher, for he is concerned that the world in which the Church lives should be conceded its full theological value.[6] The world is infinitely rich and the alert theologian is immersed in this richness. In other words, it's a jungle out there, and theology must mirror ontology. Any theology worthy of the name must take note of what is actually there in lived experience and the given history of revelation, not pretend that life and revelation must mirror whatever the theologian thinks is logical. 'To put it bluntly,' Graeme Garrett says, 'you have to feel your way along the jungle trail and face whatever leaps out at you. Doing theology is more like cutting a path in a swamp than thinking mathematics in a chair.'[7]

As we have noted already, John Taylor belongs to the school of diversifiers in the theological quest, and his speciality is what Garrett calls 'theological ad hockery'. The unifiers are the systematicians, the dogmaticians, the creed writers. They try to map the territory of theological reality comprehensively, logically and inclusively. They offer a vision of wholeness and consistency. They are after the mountain peaks, and the result is elegant and powerful, of fundamental importance to the Church and, perhaps, to the world. The primary example of this kind of theologian is John the Evangelist, whose gospel is an elegant artistic unity presenting the Christ-figure in a series of interlocking images that have a cumulative effect on the hearer – the way, the truth, the life, the light, the water, the bread, the wine, the door, and so on. From there the line continues through Origen, Aquinas, Calvin, Schleiermacher, Rahner, Tillich, Pannenberg and Elizabeth Johnson. Diversifiers, like John Taylor, find all this a bit tedious, abstract, speculative and reductionist. Where's the teeming jungle of real life in it? Diversifiers follow Paul. He doesn't have time for the nicely structured treatise, the elegant and extended formulation of a coherent vision. Paul writes on the run. His followers also have a long and respected pedigree: Tertullian, Augustine, Luther, Julian of Norwich, Kierkegaard, the early Barth, Reinhold Niebuhr, Gustavo Gutierrez, Rosemary Radford Ruether.[8] John Taylor's principal theological mentor, Dietrich Bonhoeffer, was a 'mercurial theological genius of the diversifying type'.[9] Bonhoeffer thought that Paul Tillich sought to understand the world better than it understood itself, and that Karl Barth's theology had become a 'positivism of revelation' that did not take the actual human context seriously enough. 'It thinks it speaks the Word of God universally. But it doesn't.'[10] We live in a pluralist world. God seems to have made it that way. Therefore we need to be more modest, more tentative in our explorations and explanations. In a word, we need to think within a pluralist diversity rather than a universalist unity.

Research in the field is custom-made for any theologian who counts himself a disciple of Bonhoeffer. As he entered into this work, John Taylor attempted to guard against his own 'white blindness' by building up a panel of African consultants and submitting every incipient opinion of his own to the judgement of other Africans. In any case, it was not for him to sit in judgement in any way, shape or form on what he was experiencing. He needed to set aside all his natural inclinations to do so and resist all the temptation for an unusually sensitive person to react and respond critically. Not only could he not risk pronouncing on what seemed to him right, but he could certainly not point out wrongs or make any proposals about the present or future. This exercise, then, was a totally different experience to being in a position of authority as Warden of Mukono. Having no office to fulfil, no programme to execute, no position of influence, no defined role, he had simply to rely on being himself. Now he was simply one human being living among other human beings, cut off from all his usual supports in terms of emotional health and spiritual affinity, entirely immersed in a foreign culture. This ministry of presence was one of weakness and dependency, of patient listening, of watching and contemplating, of simply allowing himself to experience the full reality of small village life. The strangeness of his situation brought its own special trials and there was no escape, no relief. Contact with the outside world was difficult. The post was slow and the sense of isolation could be silently oppressive. In this passive, patient life he absorbed whatever gifts of friendship might be offered, welcoming whatever insight came his way.

Not surprisingly, the whole experience of going back to Uganda to do this more sociological study and research work was in some ways an even more formative influence on John Taylor than his years at Bishop Tucker College. He began to realize how, during the time he was in office at Mukono, he had talked too much. Even though he searched deliberately for African idioms, searching out African ways to express theological ideas, especially in the form of drama and song, he was still always the talker, teaching, giving out. He could never be other than the one with responsibility and the one in control. Even when he wanted desperately to be simply a brother, he could never escape being the father. Actually living in a village, not being a missionary, really listening, and not letting himself make quick assessments of what was being told to him – only this made him aware of how much evangelism must always, in every single situation, begin with listening. The need is for silence and attention, actively resisting the temptation to respond too soon. It is a matter of the missionary saying to herself, 'Wait a minute, what sort of language is he using when he says that?' It involves being sufficiently secure and sufficiently sensitive to stop and ask 'What is *not* being said here that is more important than the words used?' Inevitably, Bishop Tucker College had, all unawares, been something of an 'ivory castle' insulating its warden from what he now experienced and discovered. Sharing in the day-to-day life and concerns of the people, he began to see things very differently. He realized, little by little, how astonishingly ignorant he was, and was really ashamed to find how much was news to him.[11]

> I was invited to celebration dances and funeral wakes, took my paddle with a crew of boatmen for a night's fishing on the lake, talked interminable politics with local Congress leaders and saw the grip of drink and magic upon individuals whom I knew as friends. People became real and lovable as I began to realise the daily life of the village in my blood and along my nerves.[12]

In the beginning of the Christian mission, Paul was so sure, so convinced of the truth of the gospel that he was able to write, 'to the weak I became weak, to the Greeks I became Greek'.[13] John Taylor takes this Pauline claim with utter seriousness. It is the lordship of Christ which is in question here. Either he is Lord of all possible worlds and all human cultures, or he is Lord of one world and one culture only. Either we must think of the Christian mission in terms of bringing the Muslim, the Hindu, the Animist into Christendom, or we must go with Christ as he stands in the midst of Islam, Hinduism, Buddhism, the primal world view, or even into the world of atheism and unbelief, 'and watch with him, fearfully and wonderingly, as he becomes – dare we say it? – Muslim or Hindu or Animist, as once he became Man, and a Jew'.[14] Too often Christ has been represented as the answer to the questions white men ask, the solution to the needs the Western world feels, the Saviour of the world of the European world-view, the object of adoration and prayer of historic Christendom.

> But if Christ were to appear as the answer to the questions that Africans are asking, what would he look like? If he came into the world of African cosmology to redeem Man as Africans understand him, would he be recognizable to the rest of the Church Universal? And if Africa offered him the praises and petitions of her total, uninhibited humanity, would they be acceptable?[15]

Here in a few brief questions John Taylor focuses the fear that actually cripples Christian mission. There is too much to lose in asking such questions, so we stick with the well-worn interrogation, retailing second-hand questions and answers with which we are familiar and comfortable. Asking such questions as John Taylor asks exposes us to the reality of not having any answers, the danger of not knowing, for all we know for sure is that Christ is going on ahead of us and we are called faithfully to follow.

Becoming African or Indonesian or Japanese or Australian or American is the imperative for the contemporary Christian missionary, the equivalent for the Church of today of the early Church becoming Greek.[16] In central Africa our Lady is altogether black, just as in central Australia her Son is Aboriginal, or the Incarnation really means nothing at all.

> We shall one day give birth to our Christ,
> A Christ made flesh of our flesh,
> Our dark flesh of the black people.
>
> On that day when we are wholly yours,
> Our Lady of the Black World,
> All the rhythm of our songs,
> All the rhythm of our bodies –
> O Lady of the Black World –
> Yes, all the rhythm of our dances,
> Exulting in the Spirit
> And in Our Lady who is altogether black,
> Will be as the rhythm of eternity.[17]

Because such total immersion is always the desire and destination of God, this is also the natural home of every Christian. Mission happens here, or nowhere. Obviously, there is no easy route to reach this desirable destination, and no short-cuts are available when Christ is the way as well as the truth and the life. Rushing in where angels fear to tread is only a sign of our own insecurity. Real greatness consists in *not* talking about forgiveness of sins or employing any of the usual Christian rhetoric, until you hear from the people themselves what they think sin is or where their hopes and fears might actually lie. This is a matter of respect, of reverence for the God who is there before us, active in these people and in this strange culture, really present in a religious tradition in ways which elude us. This is what Max Warren meant by saying that the first task of the Christian missionary is taking off one's shoes because we stand on holy ground. Our first resolve must be a determination to trample no one's dreams.[18] In medical terms, first do no harm.

> Because, in an odd sort of way, while sin as a generalisation is commonplace to us all, the way in which it's experienced may actually be *very* different. It's not to say that later they may come to include in their category of sin things they hadn't thought of before, we all do that, but otherwise we are talking in two categories all the time.[19]

So the missionary movement is a two-way street, where dialogue leads inevitably to insight and engagement entails revelation.

There was something very special and precious, John Taylor discovered, about his new situation that made it possible for the people to trust him with truth. But he also discovered that the work of paying attention was incredibly hard. Indeed, the impact of paying sustained attention in this special way turned out to be deeply traumatic.[20] The discipline of keeping one's mouth shut and listening intently was amazingly disorienting, for it involved leaving behind all the comforts and consolations of routine thoughts and attitudes and allowing all assumptions to be seriously challenged. This entailed forcing himself to be open, stifling disappointment, staying with the story even when it sounded like a horror movie or a musical comedy script.[21] The stress and strain of refusing to contaminate the authenticity of the tale by his own too-quick reactions or responses was costly but essential. Much as he longed to interrogate his companions, he knew only too well that inappropriate questions pushed his informers away so that they would not talk so freely in future. 'Only the silence, only the practice of the presence of God, in sacrament and meditation, in a steady painful flowering of sensitivity to all presences, can restore and integrate so that given-ness can be maintained.'[22] Here we hear the voice of long experience, rare and precious experience painfully acquired. Compassion, *com*-passion, literally suffering with – this alone is the proper name for 'the listening, responsive, agonising receptivity of the prophet and the poet.'[23]

John Taylor the poet, alert and attentive, really present, exercises an artist's eye and listens with the ears of the heart, 'the inner ear of the heart and spirit'.[24] The results are hauntingly memorable in their authenticity. It may be true that John Taylor's painfully acquired 'priceless knowledge of people' can never be communicated by words in all its three-dimensional totality,[25] but he manages to come remarkably close in his best writing, bringing to life his own experience for his readers to share.

A girl in a gentian blue frock broke away from the rest and came across the path towards my hut. I bent over the shirt on the table and a moment later there was a tap on the door. During the exchange of salutations on the threshold she remained half hidden behind the doorpost, but when I had invited her to come in, she slipped past me and in one flowing, silent movement was seated on the mat in the corner of the little room, her legs tucked sideways out of sight under her blue dress. As I gave her the formal indoor greeting, cool finger-tips brushed mine with the devouring curiosity of a child. Then the eyes were downcast, the slender hands lay still in her lap, and she leaned one shoulder against the lime-washed wall, as relaxed as a young antelope asleep in the sun.

She looked about twelve years old. I was often to see her racing with the other children on the school field, climbing with long strides to the stony top of the ridge, sweating with her hoe under the early morning sun; yet she never lost that extraordinary quality of stillness many African women seem to possess.

Incongruously I thought of Keats.

> *Thou still unravished bride of quietness,*
> *Thou foster child of silence and slow time ...*

I went on with my ironing.

It was one of those models which work with paraffin and a pressure pump. It makes a continuous small hiss, a comfortable purring sound, and after a few minutes I noticed that my visitor's eyes were following my hand to and fro with puzzled fascination. Then she caught sight of the little blue flame of burning vapour inside the shoe of the iron, leant forward to make certain she had seen aright, and a long drawn Haa of wonderment escaped her lips. She glanced up, saw that I was watching her, and embarrassment wrestled with curiosity across her face.

'Do you see the fire?' I asked.

'Yes. It is a marvel.'

'It burns with paraffin like a small primus stove.'

Her face lit up and she laughed for the joy of comprehension. Then she relaxed again into her former position, no longer shy but quiescent and companionable. It is an unfailing wonder and delight, this tranquillity of human relationships in Africa. Whether it be child or adult makes no difference; one can enjoy the other's presence without fuss or pressure, in conversation or in silence as the mood dictates. Whether the task in hand may be continued or must be left depends upon a score of fine distinctions which the stranger must slowly learn; but one thing is certain – a visitor is never an interruption.

'Thank you for working', she murmured.

'I'm working. But now I am near to finish.'

'That is good.'

I asked her what class she was in. She told me Primary 2. It seemed very low for a girl her age but I knew there could be many reasons for that. 'Where do you live?' I asked her then.

She looked surprised. 'Don't you know me?' She laughed again, richly enjoying the moment, for now she had the advantage of me. Then quickly she was demure again and gentle. 'I live at Wambogwe.'

I had been there several times but no chord of memory stirred. 'I am ashamed. I don't remember your face. What is your name?'

'Nantume.'

Still no light. I cursed myself for a boor and a fool as I had done so often and was so often to do again.

She stood up and moved towards the door.

'I have seen you, Sir. I must go back to school.' And with that she was gone.

I glanced out of the window towards the school where I could see the children at their desks through the open classroom doors. In the evening they would go home. The neat coloured frocks, the smart white shirts and khaki shorts, would come off, not thrown untidily on the bedroom floor as an English child's might be, but folded away in a small wooden suitcase.

And the children would emerge from the huts dressed in the drab, tattered garments of home. Down they would go to the valley with pitchers and paraffin tins to draw the household water; or off to the banana grove behind the house to dig till sunset; or up to the cool winds of the ridge to bring the goats and cattle in from grazing. And if I met them there, these shabby unkempt children, I might not know them, being acquainted only with their groomed and schoolroom selves.

This might well be the most terrible failure of the whole Church in Africa – that it meets people only in their best clothes. Those who can see the children only in their uniforms, the clergy only in their robes, the ordinary people only in some 'Christian' context, are unlikely to plan or preach or legislate with much wisdom or relevancy. Such Christianity becomes something to be put on at certain times and in particular circumstances, and has nothing to do with other areas of life.[26]

The Primal Vision was epoch-making, published at just the right time. Romantic and evocative, sacramental and poetic, it was startlingly original in a Church where there were, and still are, more sermons than symbols.[27] Commending it in what was almost his last *CMS Newsletter*, with its author already designated as his successor, Max Warren was not alone in praising its insights. In Kenneth Cragg's view, it is 'a book which forces the critic to his knees'.[28] In the view of one indigenous African it was 'the book we ought to have written'.[29]

It is immeasurably the most exciting piece of writing about Africa that I have yet come across from the pen of a white man. 'The pen of a white man' – yes, with all the limitations inherent in the fact that the pen was held in a hand that was white. No-one could possibly be more aware of those limitations than John Taylor. But, there are a great many things about the African which only a European who has *listened* to the African can interpret to other Europeans who have never had that opportunity, or perhaps have been afraid to take it. That is an important fact about communication. It is a widespread fallacy that the native of a country is necessarily, by virtue of his 'nativeness', the best interpreter of his own people to the natives of another country! You have to be able to *listen* to both parties if you are to interpret them to each other. And what a listener John Taylor has been ... There are a great many ways of listening, and this book suggests that John Taylor has explored most of them.[30]

White arrogance tends to look down on African religion as primitive, but John Taylor opens eyes to see that it is not primitive, but *primal*. 'Primal in the sense of fundamental, primal in the sense of belonging to the eternal wisdom.'[31]

In a way it was the same sort of study, exposing oneself to the facts, but this time a much more difficult exercise: stretching oneself, compelling oneself to listen and to take in, shedding all one's Christian pre-suppositions in order to enter into another world-view; a world-view which was strange, sometimes shocking, sometimes abhorrent when one first met it. And yet one that had to be taken seriously because it was the world of the dreams of a great many people, of their inner search and their feeling after God, their recognition of God. And I tried to enter into that world, and in *The Primal Vision* I attempted to describe something of that experience. And strangely enough, discovering in this *totally* different world view, how uniquely Christ is the Lord of that world as well as of ours.

I learnt we do not have to pose our European questions in order to find Christ's answers, we do not have to expose our European sins in order to find his salvation. We can actually start from a totally different position, where the questions are different, and the sense of sin is different, the whole world view is different. So one begins by wondering, 'well, where on earth does Christ come into all of this?' But if you can cross over, then, in an astonishing way you discover that there is going to be, there *could* be, a totally African Christianity, a Christianity that came into being through discovering the Christ of their world, not importing the Christ of ours.

But unhappily, Christians are very loath to do that crossing over. It's a bit too painful, it demands shedding too much and learning too much, it demands listening too much. So we prefer to stick within our own boundary lines, and do a certain amount of dictating to other people. But basically it comes back to this business of do we trust the facts? Are we willing to expose ourselves to the facts, as well as to the packaged theologies that we carry around with us?[32]

John Taylor's reflections on this extended exposure to the data, to 'what is there', begin with God. The content of the word 'God' for the great majority of those who called themselves Christian and who had been baptized seemed to be largely the same as in African traditional religion. They used the same terms for the God and Father of Jesus Christ as they used for their Balubaale hero gods. Syncretism seemed to be the common result of the Christian mission, with those who sold charms and even some spirit-mediums and users of malignant fetishes coming to Church on Sundays. Tellingly, however, they were sure that the Christian God does not get angry![33] Is this the beginning, or one of many beginnings, of John Taylor's life-long preoccupation with the nature of God, eventually maturing in *The Christlike God*?

> The Christians in my first village are marked by syncretism, much drunkenness, almost universal failure to keep the Church's standard in marriage, very weak public worship and a strong dislike of being in any way set apart from the rest of the community.[34]

What John Taylor calls 'these tumble-down half-Christians'[35] call out his compassion. They deserve proper care – supervision, teaching, sensitive application of Church discipline. The so-called nominal Christianity of these villagers he compares to the fig tree in the gospel parable: it requires a reprieve for dressing and dunging! He comes strongly to believe that the Anglican Church of Uganda, traditionally strongly evangelical and Protestant in its ethos, needs to make up its mind whether or not it is going to be true also to the pastoral and catholic insights of Anglicanism.[36] God, through the processes of history, seems to have brought the Church into being in much the same gradualist, largely political ways God used in many countries of Western Europe. 'No doubt it is an unspiritual and disreputable beginning – but one which God appears not to despise as much as we do.'[37] It is fascinating to observe John Taylor moving away so decisively from non-sacramental, non-incarnational Protestantism for two reasons. First, it is demonstrably inadequate in providing a satisfactory spiritual home for the people in its care. Secondly – and far more fundamentally important, for all pastoral care ultimately depends on getting this right – it is insufficiently Christian. In other words, this word-centred individualism fails to take seriously the revelation of God in Christ. At base, it is untrue to the Incarnate Word, and this means that it serves some other god.

> It demands slow growth, patient nurture of weak, half-Christians, plenty of prolonged supervision, plenty of pastors, the small, intimate 'parish'; a sacramental life in a liturgical framework; faith in the generations yet to come, and so an especial concern for incorporating and training the children; a discipline so geared to the needs of low-level Christians as not to exclude the majority from the means of grace and the full fellowship of the Church. There is overwhelming evidence of the need for some form of the confessional in the ministrations of this Church. The common

occurrence of spirit-possession of a New Testament variety seems to require that some form of exorcism should be available in the name of Christ, in addition to a more general ministry of spiritual healing. Worship needs to be set free from the inhibiting fear of all 'outward and visible signs', in order that a sense of seriousness and awe may be discovered.[38]

Significantly, the experience of Africa, albeit within the strait-jacket of an austere Church, is nevertheless for John Taylor a sacramental, bodily, materialistic experience. The Church building must become more than another classroom. Divorce between head and heart cannot be tolerated. Healthy religion involves all the bodily senses and connects in more obvious ways with the realities of everyday life. The 'seriousness and awe' to be discovered in the open air will then enter the sacred space, and the sacred space will open eyes to the reality that all space is sacred. He envisages a more gentle church discipline, where the weak are nurtured, with an emphasis on ways of inclusion rather than exclusion. His perception of the need for 'some form of the confessional' opens up the way for spiritual direction and welcomes the need for soul-friends on the spiritual journey. There is here in this particular missionary an extra-ordinary openness to whatever may best serve the needs of the people, together with a refusal to be stifled by historical prejudice in supplying the deficiencies of his own tradition. We can be sure that neither the Church of Uganda nor the Church Missionary Society found these proposals congenial. John Taylor knows that honesty demands that he say all the wrong things, and he seems himself to be as surprised as anyone. The fact is, however, that he can do no other. This attitude is rare indeed. It is imaginative and courageous, great-hearted in its inclusive vision and authentic in its pastoral concern. In a word, it is truly visionary. All this and more is required, if the Church is to offer bread, not a stone.

CHAPTER SIX

All the world

When we cross over the water,
We'll leave all our faults behind,
We'll become just what we oughter,
All wise and humble and kind.

We'll pray much longer and harder,
We'll read our Bibles much more,
We'll discover a holy ardour
We never noticed before.

When we go we'll clearly show
A faith that's burning and bold;
You think it's queer that we don't burn here,
Well, it's just that the weather's so cold.

But as we cross over the water,
Our friends will certainly see
Our shortcomings growing shorter
As we cross over the sea.

Pastors sigh and analysts pry,
They can't find me in their books.
I'm not a case, I don't need grace,
I just need a ticket from Cooks.

So when I set foot on the gangway,
'Twill be a Jacob's ladder for me.
Look for me among the angels,
When I cross over the sea.[1]

In 1959 a man of clear theological vision with an acute wit and a sparkling sense of humour was called to the headquarters staff of the Church Missionary Society, where he worked for the next fifteen years, first as Africa Secretary and then as General Secretary. This work meant continual exposure at every level, international, local and everything between, to the Christian mission experience.

It was a period when one country after another in Africa and Asia was achieving independence, as Britain shed her Empire. Again and again, high hopes were torn to shreds by civil war – in the Sudan, Zaire, Nigeria, Vietnam, Burma, Angola, Mozambique. All this was in some way related to the cold war between the two great world powers, the United States of America and the Union of Soviet Socialist Republics. At the same time new dioceses – Anglican, Roman Catholic and Lutheran – proliferated. Almost all would soon be in the care of indigenous bishops. Anglican mission Churches formerly within the jurisdiction of the Archbishop of Canterbury became, one by one, with Canterbury's active encouragement, autonomous provinces of the world-wide Anglican Communion. Except in India, Pakistan and the Pacific, burgeoning schemes of Church union were aborted, and blocs such as the Anglican Communion and the Lutheran World Federation became more self-aware and significant.

At the same time as the old empire was melting down, tensions at home were undermining old certainties. The new religious pluralism of English society brought other pressing questions. How to dispel insular prejudices? How to help the Churches to recognize and aid sister and brother God-fearers in a consumer culture? How to interpret the familiar concepts of mission in the light of unfamiliar experiences of people of other faiths? Academic snobs, those theologians who had previously ignored missiology as strictly extra-curricular, suddenly became confident experts in the field. John Taylor's opinion of them is made plain when he comments that the only people whose guidance he trusted were those who had enjoyed years of close friendship with Jews, Muslims, Hindus or Buddhists.

From spiritual proximity the missionaries had been warned off comparative religion. They learned not to compare systems and dogmas, but to discover what these things mean in actual life, in the experience of real people living out their faith. In dialogue, people of different faiths rejoice to find much common ground, but are also perplexed and troubled to confront an impenetrable *otherness*. At this point, each can only bear witness to that face of God to which their own religion bears its most characteristic witness. The Christian has to affirm that, whatever else God may be, God is Christlike – and that is a statement that stands or falls according to the lifestyle of the speaker. 'In this day of pluralism the testimony of one faith to another is more than ever dependent upon the conduct of its adherents as a community.'[2]

If God is Christlike, then the ministering and missioning Christian must also be Christlike, so it will not do for this or that exceptional individual, parish, religious community or missionary society to be Christlike in this way and in these circumstances. The whole of God's Church must be Christlike also. Too often, John Taylor has said, dialogue is

> set up as an encounter of representatives in a contest of comparisons or, worse still, a contest of courtesies. And those who argue the theoretical pros and cons of dialogue as a missionary method seem unable to imagine that the adherents of different faiths can simply meet as friends. But unless it

grows out of the gentle delving and slow maturing of friendship, dialogue is only an exercise in indifference, the very antithesis of love.[3]

Consequently, the real thing does not happen in the study or the classroom, but in the home and the bazaar, on the pilgrimage and in the temple. Genuine dialogue is just as interested in the other's unbelief as in the other's belief, in what the other person regards as secular as in what they regard as sacred, and it involves delight in people and the places where they live. 'After all, it is rogues and saints, not Christianity or Hinduism, that are the object of a truly religious concern.'[4] John Taylor writes like this because it is true to his experience. He has absorbed the insights and intuitions of missionaries and missiologists from the whole Catholic spectrum, but, more importantly, he is himself one who delights in human diversity. His own interest is in rogues and saints. This is essential to his own life as human being, as priest, and as missionary.

History

To an outsider, it is suggested, CMS looks as near as anything in the Church of England could look to the Society of Jesus.

> Both are committed specifically to the vigorous advance of the Kingdom of God. Both have cultivated a characteristic spirituality, in which the name of Jesus is central and the source of power. Both command loyalty and obedience of a high order, so enabling the ready deployment of members to precise points of need. Both entrust enormous responsibility to the central authority who is, in effect, one man, whether the General Secretary or the General.[5]

This is a view from outside, but what of the inside picture? What sort of animal is CMS? What is its temper, its mood? How does it think of itself? Where does its energy come from, and how does it work?

The society was founded in 1799 under the inspired leadership of John Venn. That great leader of the evangelical revival in the Church of England, Charles Simeon, contributed to its development in the early nineteenth century. Henry Venn, General Secretary in the middle of the nineteenth century, was a man of exceptional wisdom and far-sighted statesmanship who encouraged the establishment and growth of native Churches under native leadership. A third era roughly coincided with the half century from 1900 to the time Max Warren took over from Wilson Cash. In this phase, there was remarkable development of institutional life in the mission areas – diocesan organizations, hospitals, colleges and schools, some of which were self-governing.

Wilson Cash became General Secretary in 1926 and resigned when he was appointed Bishop of Worcester in 1941, after sixteen years of leadership. It was his achievement to keep the society in the mainstream of the Church's life. Tensions between conservative and liberal evangelicals then, as now, were powerful. CMS had always represented the evangelical wing of the Church of England, and for over a century had been sending out missionaries of evangelical persuasion, but had never required strict tests of doctrinal orthodoxy.

After the First World War, this began to change. Some conservatives now demanded assent to the doctrine of the verbal inspiration of the Scriptures, and to a particular interpretation or model for understanding the atoning work of Christ on the cross. The doctrine of 'substitutionary atonement' was declared to be the sole acceptable model for describing this mystery.[6] The Anglican Church had never committed itself to any such doctrinal strait-jacket. It always allowed that the mystery of redemption could be grasped only via the interplay of various theories and models. Could the society maintain its comprehensiveness in the face of these pressures towards a limiting orthodoxy? If it caved in on such a crucial matter, would it even remain Anglican?

The Church of England's much-vaunted comprehensiveness is wide enough and generous enough to embrace a range of theologies and liturgical practices, precisely because it has never been a confessional church tied to any particular declaration of faith. Even in the highly charged years after the initial break with Rome at the Reformation, Anglican apologists maintained that it was the church of the English people – catholic, apostolic, protestant and reformed. It maintains that it has no doctrine of its own. If you want to know what Anglicans believe you should look at *The Book of Common Prayer*, the Ordinal, and the Articles of Religion. Doctrines embraced by conservative evangelicals may be *permissible* within the Anglican spectrum of theological opinion, but they may not be demanded. To insist seems by definition to lie right outside Anglican ethos and traditional practice.

In the event, the tensions between the two groups could not be contained and a painful split resulted. From 1922, the CMS had a rival in the Bible Churchman's Missionary Society. When Wilson Cash took over in 1926, the rivalry was still intense, the situation delicate. He took his stand on the intention of the founders to form 'a Church society whose special emphasis and message should be evangelical', not an 'evangelical party missionary society'.[7]

For sixteen years Wilson Cash held this line, maintaining the distinction between a society belonging to the whole Church over against sectarianism. Controversy continued. It was a time of many partings of ways between friends. Much of Cash's time and energy was used up in this struggle, this unhappy theological controversy, but 'he never allowed controversy to dirty his soul'.[8]

Bilious comment he always refused to respond to with bile. This was the gentleness not of a weak man but of a very strong one. From Dr Cash I learnt that it is possible to disagree without bitterness even about the most deeply held convictions: to disagree and yet to remain in spiritual fellowship.[9]

Here we have achievement rare indeed, displaying real generosity of spirit. It was, none the less, personally very costly.

Predecessor and mentor: Max Warren

On 1 June 1942, an event took place which would shape John Taylor's life, ministry and theology at almost every point. It is impossible to over-estimate the impact of this event on John Taylor's future. On this date Max Warren took over the General Secretaryship at CMS House, Salisbury Square, close to St Paul's Cathedral in the City of London. He would be John Taylor's loved mentor, image and guide.[10]

As himself the child of CMS missionaries and a former member of the Executive Committee while he was Vicar of Holy Trinity, Cambridge, Max Warren suffered both the advantages and disadvantages of being known to the old guard. His father had worked from an office not far from what was now his own. Older staff could remember the boy visiting the father. Furthermore, Max Warren came to office with a deep respect for his predecessor, having watched his work at close quarters.

One of the challenges, he knew, was the relationship between the General Secretary and the departmental Secretaries. The CMS Executive Committee, in Max Warren's opinion, was very 'independent minded'!

> Leadership of a Committee of laymen and clergy, all men and women of experience in their own fields, and all equally committed to the welfare of the Society as they saw it, calls for adroitness and an awareness that victories in argument can be Pyrrhic, that defeat is not disaster, that *reculer pour mieux sauter* is not only a practical policy on the battlefield, but often the key to arrival at that kind of consensus which makes committee work a satisfying exercise in co-operation.[11]

To claim that he learnt this from watching Dr Cash is easy, and makes this style of leadership sound easy. The fact of the matter, of course, is that Max Warren found it a continuing struggle. Again and again he was saved by his sense of humour and a great deal of personal support.

> As to my immediate colleagues, I was *primus inter pares*, a position in which the *primus* must gain consent from a team of *pares* who were in this case, in terms of experience, far more my superiors than equals – a delicate situation.[12]

So he was first among equals, where the equals were more than equal! Nevertheless, and inescapably, he had to be the chief interpreter of the society to the Church at home and to the Church overseas. Henry Venn had also insisted that it was the prerogative of the Chief Secretary to communicate with the Archbishop of Canterbury and with bishops generally. Also, to circles which knew little or nothing about mission, the General Secretary was accepted as the spokesman of the society.[13]

Another way of talking about this would be to say that Max Warren assumed a position of *episcope*, of spiritual oversight. Indeed, he tells us that at this precise moment he was reading in the Apostolic Fathers and copied into his diary a passage from St Ignatius advising St Polycarp how to be a good bishop![14] In a word, this young General Secretary, in his thirty-eighth year, needed vision – clear vision of the Church and of the Church's mission in the world, and he needed to communicate this vision to his colleagues and missionaries. 'At all times it was my responsibility to be scanning the horizon, marking the direction of events in the world and their bearing on our enterprise, and in broad outline indicating what it must mean for the Society.'[15]

'It is hard now to imagine a more daunting task in Christian leadership for any man to have been called to undertake at that particular time.'[16] It was possibly the most critical juncture in the history of CMS itself, and the world was embroiled in the nightmare of the Second World War. By its very nature the Society was an association, a fellowship, a world-wide family in which some members were at headquarters in London, some were banded together in parochial groups in England, Ireland, Australia, New Zealand and South Africa, while others were working as missionaries in Asia and Africa.[17] Communication was difficult even at home, while those serving overseas found it impossible or dangerous to return. Recruitment was almost at a standstill. There were more than a thousand CMS missionaries scattered over Africa and the East, some in prison camps, many cut off from regular contact with headquarters, many uncertain about the possibilities of war in their own territory. In addition there was widespread disruption among those parishes in England that supported CMS, and the financial outlook was precarious. Air raids on London were making work in the city, where CMS headquarters was situated, dangerous and exhausting for the society's staff. Yet Max Warren had little hesitation in responding to the call to responsibility for the society whose members had been a supportive community for him since childhood and in whose particular function in the calling of God he firmly believed.[18]

One characteristic of Max Warren's vision is the intensely personal style of leadership he offered. 'Strategic wisdom was his honey; people were his flowers – people in person, people in letters, people in their books. Max, like others of his generation and his quality, had far more faith in a coterie than in a committee.'[19] After only a few short months in office he wrote in his diary,

I have no sort of doubt that a primary obligation laid upon me is to make and keep the work of the Society personalized, and to count the achievement of real personal contacts with the Missionaries a first call on my time.[20]

Membership, a living sense of personal membership, by every member of the society – this was his goal. They all needed to feel they belonged, each needed to know that they shared in a great enterprise. The society must be one family in Christ, knowing that they laboured alongside many sisters and brothers, supporters and co-workers.

After Max Warren's death, John Taylor remembered a typical expression of this concern.

> The wife of a new missionary, a few weeks after her arrival in the strange land which was to be her home for the next nine years, received through the post a heavy, glossy catalogue of dress fabrics and fashion designs. The war had just ended and, to one who had come straight out of the austerities of Britain, the brilliant American colour-printing was exhilaratingly beautiful. But the greatest astonishment of the gift was that it came from the General Secretary of their missionary society who had been barely four years in office. The accompanying note, so far as I remember, ran: 'As a mere male I can't pretend to appreciate these things as I am sure you will do, but I hope this will cheer you with its gaiety. Max.'[21]

This incident, according to John Taylor, epitomizes many of the characteristics which added up to greatness.

> Here was that originality of mind which never ceased to see value or significance in something that lay right outside the accepted categories of spiritual concern. Here was the humorous, but perfectly sincere, self-depreciation, and the imaginative interest in individuals with never a thought of their comparative 'importance'. Here was the defiance of normal bureaucratic consideration: four only of the glossy catalogues had come his way and there were four hundred missionary wives, but he understood that the economy of God – a favourite phrase of his – was personal, arbitrary and uninhibited by tidy principle. So he was free to exercise his most characteristic gift of all, the light but intimate gesture of recognition, the hand momentarily laid upon a particular shoulder, which endeared him to countless people because it was the unaffected offer of a totally trustworthy friendship.[22]

How did John Taylor know of this incident, unless the catalogue was sent to a newly arrived missionary's wife in Uganda named Peggy Taylor? Max Warren was unconsciously modelling a style of leadership for his successor, some eighteen years early! Max Warren not only survived by his sense of humour and the support of staff and colleagues, but by imagination, by his conviction that God acts outside Church structures as well as within, by his distrust of 'salvation history' if it is reduced to Church history, and by his relentless insistence on the God of *all* history. One of his abiding convictions was that God is not preoccupied with ecclesiastical politics, that God is not interested in reading the rubrics. God is never the God of this or that particular history, for God is perfectly capable of embracing any inconsistency and quite able to elect to gather more than one chosen people. There can be no question that salvation history includes *all* history.

In the same diary entry, a foundational principle which Max Warren would defend all through his time with CMS is already being articulated.

> I believe that 'Membership' in meaning and implication represents one of the lines along which I've got to work hard because it is so decisive for the preservation of the Voluntary Association principle in our Church's life not least in order to enable the Church to make an effective impact on secular society. I believe Martin Buber's 'Thou and I' [sic] must be translated into a philosophy of society and it can only be done in terms of voluntary associations.[23]

Max Warren never believed in a Church structured only in terms of nation, province, diocese, archdeaconry, deanery, parish, or that the Church as a body should be governed by bishops and their subordinates alone. A deep conviction about the priesthood of all believers and the importance of all the baptized made him naturally sympathetic to synodical government by representatives of all the people of God, clerical and lay together in partnership. But his view was also wider than this. Room must be found, in any and every circumstance, for extra-diocesan and extra-parochial societies and orders, communities and fellowships and associations of the like-minded and the like-motivated, which could combine relative autonomy with loyal service within the episcopally ordered whole. Diversity and freedom, in his view, were not threats to unity, but one essential and energetic expression of it.

His own CMS was one such 'order', and he had been chosen as its leader. This notion of CMS as a religious order like the Benedictines or Franciscans, with himself as superior, was birthed by Max Warren and cultivated by his two immediate successors, although it was always used more in terms of metaphor than as description of actual or potential fact.

Obviously, it is unreal to push the image too far. The work of CMS is clearly the same as that undertaken by many religious orders, but even when supporters of CMS were encouraged to think of themselves as members, the reality was and is that they do not live in community under life vows. They are not, and cannot be, a religious order in the formal sense. Nevertheless, Max Warren found the metaphor attractive and useful, as did his two immediate successors. It also appealed to many CMS missionaries and supporters. They formed a *societas* or fraternity, they were an obedient nucleus of the whole company of Christ, remembrancers of the unfinished task to those churches to which they go as much as to those from which they come, living reminders recalling the Church as a whole to the frontiers in its midst.[24] But was there perhaps in this image also an element of surprise, even of shock to the evangelical ethos of CMS, shock value which Max Warren intended and enjoyed? One element in leadership is the ability to say what is not expected, to produce the startling, disturbing or provocative image, and to do so forcefully and persuasively, but also with some lightness of touch, some gentle humour.

Max Warren 'feared centralisation and bureaucratisation and institutionalism and standardisation'.[25] He cried out for flexibility, mobility, individual initiatives and personal relationships. Typically, he focused his concern in the brilliant symbolic title given to a pamphlet he wrote. The choice lay between Rome and Iona, between two types of Christianity, northern and southern. The second of these types, the Celtic type, has a genius for tolerating, even enjoying, diverse networks of authority. The Roman type tends toward central control. Should the Church be its own missionary society, no longer needing to entrust its missions to individual missionary societies? Should not the whole baptized Body of Christ be engaged in the one mission of God in the world? Yes, of course it should, but when is the reality ever thus? Max Warren was clear that pushing this as the norm was little more than day-dreaming. The historian in him was certain that such seductive theory simply did not work. It never had. It was precisely because nothing was being done that individual societies formed in the first place. They were born of revivals of one sort or another in slumbering or complacent churches. Furthermore, they were personal, depending on friendships between enthusiasts, and they were lay initiatives. Such 'evangelistic spearheads' would always be necessary. They would always mean ecclesiastical untidiness, but efforts to control and contain tend always to be counter-productive. Somehow, apart from this untidiness, this incompleteness, enthusiasm seems to be quenched. Exercise of the wrong kind of authority is the touch of a dead hand. Authentic, secure, unthreatened authority rejoices in unfettered diversity.

Max Warren stood for 'two-ness' – tension, dialectic between the whole Body and its societies. What is needed is complementarity. There must be order, but order leavened with spontaneity and responsiveness. 'It was for the health of the whole body that evangelical and evangelistic societies should continue to express their devotion through praying, through giving, and through offers of lifelong missionary service.'[26] Or, in Max Warren's own words, 'the greatest need of the Church is for decentralisation of effort, not centralisation of power'.[27] The priesthood of all believers has been mentioned, with its inevitable consequence, the democratic principle in the life of the Church. Max Warren was not just historian and pragmatist, but theologian. About the theological foundations of the voluntary association he was quite clear.

The theological principles involved here derive from the doctrine of the Holy Spirit which sees him as ever seeking fresh initiatives in the life of mankind, and never confining himself or his activities to the institutional life of his Church. This further carries with it a high doctrine of the laity which sees the ordinary man and woman as being always potential means by which the Holy Spirit takes some of his initiatives. This understanding of the work of the Holy Spirit lies at the very heart of any theological appraisal of the significance of the Voluntary Association as a principle, whether in Church or State. Somewhere here is to be found the theological rationale for democracy as it has been developed in the West under the inspiration of the gospel. That is certainly to understate my own conviction. There are not very many theological insights which have at once an appeal to my mind and to my heart. This is one of them. And for this one I am prepared to do battle anywhere and at any time.[28]

And he did battle, not least with friends in the ecumenical movement who were determined to merge the International Missionary Council with the World Council of Churches. This step looked neat and logical on paper. It appeared to be the sensible, rational way. To Max Warren, however, it was sheer foolishness, but he was a voice crying in the wilderness. The streamliners could not see that there was as much danger from centralized bureaucracy in Geneva as in Rome.

He feared the gradual replacement of the spirit of expectant evangelism, characteristic of a relatively small autonomous society, by grandiose programmes and verbal directives characteristic of all too many large international organisations. The ethos of IMC was one of mutual consultation and the sharing of thoughts, not that of a hierarchal structure and centralised constraint.[29]

In this, John Taylor was absolutely in agreement. He too feared monolithic structures, huge assemblies, bureaucratic paralysis, loss of spontaneity in responding to the unpredictability of the Holy Spirit.

It was a battle they both lost. The majority had their way and the IMC became a department of the WCC. But not without protest! Neither Max Warren nor John Taylor were persuaded. They remained champions of the voluntary principle. As John Taylor would write much later in quite another context,

I do not put my faith in the big battalions. I distrust the pedlars of an overall strategy and I despair of the busy housemaids of the church endlessly tidying up its inconsistencies. The great ecclesiastical centralizers, like King Saul of old, put their trust in heavy accoutrements and expensive weapons. He could not bear to see the shepherd boy going unarmed into the contest with Goliath, and almost smothered him in an excess of equipment. But David knew better.[30]

The voluntary organization is not an end in itself. It exists to be a channel for the initiative of those who compose it. If it ceases to express this initiative it will die. Insofar as it is responsible and Christian it will have intimate, though not necessarily constitutional, links with a Christian church, either denominationally or ecumenically organized. This is a fundamental principle of community. To see this and to make provision for it is one of the best ways of safeguarding the structures of society from being exploited by power-drunk individuals or power-obsessed bureaucracies. This, he continued to argue, has been the discovery of democracy at its best. Part of the ecclesiological basis for this view is the recognition that the Church really is a mixed society. It is not a community of saints and dedicated persons, but a society of sinners who represent every variety of spiritual development and deformation.

When a bishop at the IMC/WCC Joint Committee meeting in 1956 interpreted the missionary theory of the Episcopal Church as being that every member of the church is a member of the missionary society, he was really saying that 'baptism makes the individual a missionary'. This sounds theologically correct, but the facts give it the lie. Manifestly, baptism does not automatically create missionaries. What baptism does do is make individual members of a missionary community precisely in proportion as this community has a spiritual vanguard which is really *committed* to mission. It does not help towards strengthening this vanguard to pretend that every member of the church is already part of it. To have a unified missionary organization actually obscures the real situation, and prevents the average person ever making any progress at all towards becoming one of the vanguard.

> This is best achieved by voluntary organisations consisting of persons who have joined together on some agreed basis to pursue an agreed aim by agreed methods. If one believes this with all one's heart one is of necessity opposed to the creation of monolithic structures.[31]

Newsletter theology

One way in which Max Warren's intensely personal form of leadership crystallized was in the *CMS Newsletter*. Founded by Dr Cash, Max Warren took the tradition of the *Newsletter* over after only 31 issues. The next 232 letters were his own. This was his pulpit. Here he addressed missionaries in the field as well as home supporters, attempting to keep the connection and encouraging growth in both groups.

Whatever their background, there was always the expectation that missionaries would broaden in outlook, that their theology and practice would alter in dialogue with the people, culture and religious situation where they lived and worked. Those at home who supported them prayerfully and financially tended to remain static in their perceptions of the demands of the gospel, or simply stay narrow in their human sympathies. The *Newsletter* had to help bridge this gulf. Soon it became more than an internal administrative matter, a cheap form of communication within the society itself. Through the monthly *Newsletter* the General Secretary addressed not only the very diverse members of the society. He also addressed the Church – the Church of England, the independent provinces of the Anglican Communion, and the missionary churches. Indeed, more and more members of other Churches were attracted by the quality of the reflections offered. This happened as Max Warren shifted the focus from CMS domestic matters [32] to what he called 'a theology of attention'. This was a genuine attempt to come to terms with the real context within which the Christian mission had to operate.

Always, the *Newsletter* remained the General Secretary's distinctive contribution and responsibility: he did not commit his colleagues or CMS to the views expressed, and he made sure his successors held to this understanding. He wrote to John Taylor refusing his invitation to contribute to a *CMS Newsletter* after he retired. His words reveal a firm conviction.

> I remain impenitently of the conviction that taking the longest and broadest of views, the *CMS News-Letter* represents one of the most important things that the Society is doing. It probably does more to create an image of the Society as regards its thinking than anything else the Society produces – and as you well know its wide circulation exercises an influence amongst many people who know virtually nothing about CMS. I do really doubt whether it ought ever to pass out of your hands as General Secretary. [33]

Exactly the same point was made to Simon Barrington-Ward by both Max Warren and John Taylor.

The character of the *Newsletter* lay for Max Warren precisely in the fact that it is a personal communication from the General Secretary. [34] Apart from the obvious advantage of being able to disclaim any intention of committing the society as a whole to an idea, proposition or action, Max Warren meant what he said. He was assisted in producing the *CMS Newsletter* by a succession of research assistants, sometimes sketching plans for them a year in advance of needing the material, but he never recommended a book he had not first read himself. In his biographer's opinion, he could have become an outstanding journalist, and the same can certainly be said of John Taylor. [35]

Max Warren was always looking for the signs of God's presence: whatever the immediate appearances might be, he believed that it was possible to discern, however imperfectly, the working out of God's purposes. He claimed no monopoly in the ability to read such signs but gladly recognized that writers about other kinds of experience than his own could wittingly or unwittingly bear witness to the divine factor operative in the world's history. [36] He once remarked, 'I have often discovered more truth, more genuine, if unconscious, theological insight in books by economists, sociologists, politicians, travellers, historians and scientists, than I have discerned in much so-called theological writing'.[37] With John Taylor the temper is the same, but to this list he is careful to add poets, playwrights and artists.

What has been said of Max Warren's *CMS Newsletter* can equally be said of John Taylor's. Gradually, not only CMS supporters but also a wider body of missionary sympathizers recognized that here was a balanced, informed, far-sighted commentary on what was happening in the world, based on careful reading of up-to-date books and on a constant flow of letters coming in from different parts of the mission field. There was nothing else quite like it. Every issue was carefully planned, sometimes months ahead, and every issue dealt with an important feature affecting the spread of the gospel. Often events proved that Max Warren's insights regarding likely developments were better informed than those of politicians or journalists. Yet he had no desire to establish himself as an authority on world affairs. Like John XXIII, he was unafraid of the spirit of the age and wanted simply to discern the signs of the times and summon those obeying the missionary commission to face the realities of the movements of peoples, working out appropriate policies accordingly. Max Warren the historian knew that no individual can survive in a closed shop, secular or sacred. 'We are all subject to the influences that surround us, social, economic, cultural and religious.'[38]

What Max Warren called a 'theology of attention' and 'the real context in which the Christian mission operates', John Taylor called 'paying attention to the facts' and 'reverence for the facts'. From Joe Fison, Max Warren and his experience in Uganda he learned to 'keep both roads open' – the theological and biblical road, the road of religious study, but also the road that is wide open to life, the road where poets and artists and scientists are travelling companions.[39]

> And not just poetry, not just literature, but experience of the facts. After all a poet is somebody who is essentially aware of the facts, sometimes intensely hurt by them, but he presents life as it is, he presents experience in truth, and to keep that road open is just as important as knowing your theology. To be aware of what actually is, for theology means reflecting on *things as they are* in the light of the bible – all the beauty, all the pain, all the ugliness, all the glory. You can't be alive towards God unless you are alive towards everything else – all the glory and all the pain and all the people.[40]

Years before in Uganda, John Taylor read the diaries and journals of one of the great pioneer missionaries, Alexander McKay, a trained engineer. It was from Alexander McKay that John Taylor learnt that 'truth is one'. Truth is one as mind is one and God is one.

> So there can be but one method of arriving at spiritual truth, namely an unbiased examination of facts, and the resolve to learn from these as they

are, instead of fanciful supposition as to what ought to be. As metaphysics may be called the pure mathematics of theology, so missions are its practical application, and are destined to play as important a part in connecting the vagaries of theologians as practical engineering has done in the domain of theoretical mechanics.[41]

General Secretary John Taylor

Max Warren announced to the President of CMS in 1961 his intention to resign as General Secretary in 1963, and did so on 31 August 1963. It must have been hard for a disciple to step into the master's shoes, and particularly difficult to move along the corridor from the office of Africa Secretary to that of General Secretary. If the challenges in assuming a new role were great within the institution, it was hard on John Taylor also that Max Warren was to remain so close at hand as a Canon of Westminster. He may have been Max Warren's chosen successor, but it might be hard to be fully and freely himself in his new role if he must live always in his predecessor's shadow.

There was also a difficulty of quite another kind altogether. It is reported that when Max Warren received news of the death of the American missionary leader John Mott, he wrote in his diary, 'It is not unfair to link him with St Paul, Xavier and Carey as one of the few men who have caught the imagination of the Christian world from the point of view of the missionary enterprise'. His biographer dared to think that Max Warren himself should be accorded the fifth place in that succession. But Dillistone goes further.

> I regard him as the greatest all-round Christian leader of my own generation. To write about him has been what a recent biographer of Gladstone described as 'an act of homage'. I have often heard warnings about the perils of hagiography. I can only say that this man came nearer to my own conception of what constitutes a saint than any other I have known.[42]

To follow a giant is one thing, to follow a saint is quite another.[43] John Taylor's task was to walk in the way of this sanctity, but to bring to it his own distinctive graciousness and wholeness. If he could not pretend to Max Warren's personal innocence, he could certainly offer the strengths emerging from his own woundedness, his own hard-won insights and humanity.

John Taylor's period of office coincided with an unprecedented time of radical social, political and ecclesiastical reappraisal. It included major missionary gatherings – the Commission on World Mission and Evangelism, and the World Council of Churches Uppsala assembly in 1968.[44] It overlapped with what John Taylor called 'the shameful and futile Vietnam war', and with the Cultural Revolution in Mao's China. The place and function of the missionary, already questioned in Max Warren's time, remained wide open questions. Like his predecessor, John Taylor was anxious to remind the churches of the wider context of God's activity in the world.[45]

> The greatest single issue facing the Church in East Africa, as in the rest of the world, is the acceptance of the fact that God is active outside the structures of the Church and is calling the Church to be ready to abandon, if necessary, its entrenched position in its own institutions and become involved more effectively in the life of the world. The Church is in danger of becoming a spectator, watching from the touchline the main arena in which the life of the world is being lived and where history is being made.[46]

Absolutely everything is to be lived in the context of mission. Those who say the Church is primarily constituted not for witness but for worship set up a false dichotomy, a false alternative.[47] 'To share in Christ's mission is to let the world overhear our praises.' Little wonder, then, that John Taylor has a clear vision of worship and liturgy as central to evangelism, and that within months of taking up the reins as General Secretary of CMS he should be writing in a *Newsletter* of signs and symbols, space and architecture as servants of God's purpose, knowing that we who shape buildings are in turn shaped by them, for every building tells a story.

Change of address

On October 24, 1966 new CMS headquarters were opened in Waterloo Road south of the Thames by the Queen and the Archbishop of Canterbury, representing nation and Church. Typically, in John Taylor's mind this was not 'to gild our occasion with reflected glory', but to make a theological point: nothing is ultimately secular, God is in everything, nations as well as churches serve in salvation history.

> We believe that Mission is something which God is doing. By the call of Christ and the outpouring of the Holy Spirit, God involves his Church in what he himself is doing for the world. But God acts for mankind through nations as well as through Churches. The 'secular' is as much the arena of his redemption as the 'sacred'. Under his hand a nation has its mission just as a Church has.[48]

The decision to move from the hallowed Salisbury Square location was actually taken in Max Warren's time, but it fell to John Taylor to guide the ship from familiar waters into a new era of uncertainty. For this sea-change he realized that he had to prepare not only himself and the headquarters staff, but also supporters of CMS in the Church of England, and missionaries overseas for whom the offices at Salisbury Square represented a rock, a symbol of security and continuity in the fluctuating circumstances of their lives. Perhaps it is those who actually have left everything to follow Christ who are most tempted to invest too much in such symbols.

> It is going to take us all a long time to remember that our address is no longer Salisbury Square and it will take an even longer time and much prayer and faithfulness in the unfamiliar surroundings, before we shall feel about Waterloo Road as we certainly do about this small corner of the City, that it is not only a familiar but also a fitting home.[49]

John Taylor was, of course, well aware that CMS had had several homes already, and this appreciation of the past helped him distance himself from too close an attachment to any particular 'holy' place. For himself, however, and no doubt touching the emotions of many others, he speaks of one of the sources of his own inspiration and sense of belonging to a great society, a great movement, a great family. 'Ever since I knew of it, it has been an inspiration to me to remember that the sanctuary of our present House-chapel is on the very spot where the committee meetings of that first headquarters were held.'[50] Such associations are precious, even sacred and sanctifying. But John Taylor's sense of history, like Max Warren's before him, is deeply unsentimental. History is God's arena where, in people and places, events and circumstances, we can see the invisible creator Spirit at work, shaping, calling. As the move from the City of London to the very different environment of South London drew near, he recalled aborted plans from 1912 to move from Salisbury Square to Westminster. That scheme represented a desire to be aligned with government and Church, close to the political and ecclesiastical establishment. By the first decade of the twentieth century Salisbury Square was dominated by newspaper offices. A commentator at the time claimed that 'the whole neighbourhood was changed, the CMS was almost buried in great newspaper printing offices and Salisbury Square was no longer a natural centre for a religious Society as at one time it had been'.[51]

Naturally, John Taylor is quick to highlight the fallacy here, the unfaithfulness of hankering after a 'religious' setting and the seductive desire for power and influence. God, surely, had a different idea of a missionary headquarters' natural habitat.

> Far from being an inappropriate home for our Society, this cradle of the British Press was surely, under the good hand of God, the most fitting and the most helpful neighbourhood that could possibly have been chosen for us; and this has become more and more apparent as the national press grew to its full stature and power. For our giant neighbours may have played a greater part than we care to admit in reminding successive Secretaries of CMS that those who would proclaim the kingdom of God must watch to see what is happening in the kingdoms of this world.[52]

Like it or not, the world always sets the agenda for theology.[53]

Typically, such convictions have firm biblical roots. For John Taylor it is no accident that Israel lies between the rival civilizations of Egypt and Mesopotamia, that God's chosen people live in a precarious home on a trade-route. The Hebrew prophets heard God's voice 'as they watched the traffic go by'.

> I think it is not fanciful to believe that it was for precisely the same reason that God gave our Society its home alongside the main route between the Guildhall and St Stephen's Hall, Westminster. Fleet Street has for many centuries been the line of communication and tension between Commerce and Government, a tension which assumed special significance during the period of British expansion overseas [when missionary churches were being planted in British colonies]. Half-way along that line of polarity stood two arbiters – two prophets, one might say – each with an independent mandate by which to judge the issues: the law with the independence of the judiciary, and the press with its freedom of comment. These were the protagonists into the midst of whom God introduced the young CMS as an apprentice prophet come to learn his trade; young and discredited indeed, but with a mandate more august and absolute than any other.[54]

But the misplaced disappointment of 1912 had surfaced more recently too. Before the site in Waterloo Road was found, another attempt to move to Westminster – ironically enough to the same Smith Square considered so desirable years earlier – had been frustrated. Acknowledging that many still crave 'a niche at Westminster, within the capital of the ecclesiastical establishment', John Taylor declares that he personally rejoices 'that God is placing us again in a more secular environment'.[55] The neighbourhood of Waterloo Road has no religious pedigree worth claiming; indeed, it 'appears to have been shockingly devoid of any religious history at all!' The area between Lambeth Palace and Southwark was originally an undrained marsh, home to the poor who worked on the river and to gypsies. With the opening of Westminster Bridge it became a place of pleasure gardens and entertainment, and with the coming of the railway it was heavily industrialized. 'Does it, I wonder, mean anything that we are moving from a setting of great newspaper offices to a centre of drama and of music?'[56] John Taylor is never simply historian, but always visionary, dreamer, imaginative theologian. So now he dreams for CMS, assuaging the sense of loss common to the whole society by setting before them a vision of potential gains and benefits and opportunities.

> For us, it appears to be a change from the world of the printed word to the world of the arts. Maybe, under God, this is no accident. Perhaps our new neighbours, like our old, have something to teach us for the sake of Mission.[57]

In the City of London members of CMS were forced to remember the importance of the world of affairs. On the South Bank they will be alert to their need to learn of the inward world of human emotions and dreams.

In Salisbury Square they moved among the masters of one kind of communication, whose skill had a good deal to teach the society about the communication of God's good news. Across the river there are new opportunities for fresh associations with the masters of a different kind of communication. 'I fancy that we shall need to learn a good deal more of their vocabulary of symbols and parables if we want to get through to the secular man of our day.'[58] Behind this statement we glimpse the young theological student, fresh from reading English literature at Cambridge, setting out his new theological books on his shelves at Wycliffe Hall. He is told by Joe Fison to 'keep both roads open', to welcome divine revelation in art – indeed, from anywhere – as well as in specifically Christian or Jewish tradition. This is an injunction that will stay with John Taylor all his life. Informing this too is experience as an African theological college principal who himself found catholic sacramentalism being added to his evangelical inheritance. Here is the General Secretary of a missionary agency distinguished by its protestant ethos sowing seeds of a broader and more inclusive vision, but a vision which is attuned and responsive to contemporary culture, a very practical vision, a dream with its feet on the ground.

So history is important, and knowledge of the *details* of history is important, for study of history reassures us that what is happening is in God's hands and that it is God who goes before us. 'But we still have to move. We still have to pull up our roots.'[59] And faith does not magic away the usual human consequences.

> However great our faith, this will certainly have a deep psychological effect. Our crossing of the river is bound to impress us as a symbol of the spiritual pilgrimage, the death of so much that is familiar, the movement into the unknown, which characterises the age we live in.

History and familiarity provide a sense of identity.

> Without a sense of identity, without an assurance of what we are meant to be, we become paralysed and totally unable to go forward into the unknown. And this is a very common malaise of these days.[60]

It is, as John Taylor knows well, but does not actually spell out, just as commonplace even in the supposedly faithful and trusting community of the Church, even in a particularly deeply committed manifestation of this Church such as CMS. The call to pull up roots is also the perennial call of God to take up the cross, to loosen our grip so that our hands can open out to receive the next gift.

For himself and for all those in his care, John Taylor gives two images to hold on to in the swirling waters of change: one biblical and traditional, the other contemporary and secular. The first is the supernatural rock gushing drinking water in the desert for the pilgrim people of God. The second pictures a trapeze artist in the circus who must let go in order to grasp afresh.

> The idea of the marching rock is not, after all, so weird to anyone who has motored across the plains of South India or Eastern Uganda and seen how one isolated crag seems to stay with the traveller hour after hour. This is an apt and evocative image of that which is permanent and reliable in the midst of change, an image of Christ himself, but also of the unchanging call of Christ and of that identity which obedience to the call gives us. God is the Rock but he is the Rock which journeys on.[61]

And then there is the trapeze artist who must let go her safe hold on the past and reach out for a firm grasp on something new, 'depending for a breathless interval on a relatedness between the past and the future'. Moses, called to pilgrimage, cries anxiously: 'Who am I?' and is answered: 'Certainly I will be with you.' But when he asks: 'What is your name?', God answers: 'I will be what I will be.'[62]

All this will somehow find embodiment in the architecture of the new headquarters, and particularly in the new chapel – free of the rich associations of the past and pointing to the future.

> To know Christ is to live looking forward, believing in an ultimate encounter to which all symbols point, while accepting the 'not yet' which makes them necessary. For, as has been finely said, 'all truths are shadows except the last'.[63]

Living fully in the present moment, lovingly appreciative of the past but with eyes open expectantly to the future, could be John Taylor's motto and sums up his perennial stance. And the present is devoid of past glory. Christendom has come and gone, and will not come again. This is one of John Taylor's themes at CMS, as it will be in Winchester. It is a truth the Church doesn't want to hear. Nostalgia is easier than facing reality, but John Taylor's passion is to draw the fearful Church out from behind locked doors to 'an intense reverence for the facts', to 'the excitement of discovering the facts, and of insisting on truth, of exposing oneself to things as they really are, and having done with pretensions and half-truths'.[64] For all their reverence for history, Christians are not museum keepers, and the Church cannot spend its energy clinging to an ascendancy that no longer exists.

Chapel of the Living Water

Quoting Peter Hammond's *Liturgy and Architecture* in his third *Newsletter* – unusually, we may think, for the new General Secretary of a great missionary society – John Taylor fastens on these words: 'The cathedral typified wealth and power and esteem, if not downright human pride ...

It was the fortress of faith, the stronghold of religion, the rhetorical assertion of the temporal triumph of Christendom.'[65] Modern churches, or the best of them, are by contrast marked by austerity and humility. They are of modest proportions and honest about their own construction in raw concrete or unrendered stone.

> Such a return to humility and realism will help the Church to face the fact that to a vast number of people today her words and her symbols are dead. A Church which is not content to speak only to its own narrowing circle must strip away all the uncomprehended symbols – the monograms, the emblems of forgotten legends and all the antiquarian points of ritual. There are a few fundamental things we should be saying, and even they will not be heard unless we offer them in the simplest integrity. It is, using Peter Hammond's phrase, better to come before God – or man – naked than in period costume.[66]

The key to unlock the meaning and significance of liturgical worship, for John Taylor as for the whole modern liturgical movement, is that Christian worship, like Jewish worship before it, is not about looking or even listening, but people doing something together. In other words, it is active, not passive, and corporate rather than individual. The first Christians had no church building and when, later, they adapted the Roman basilica it was not for its grandeur or symbolism but simply because it provided the simplest form of shelter for a company gathered around the Table of their Lord, led by their spiritual father.

> But, alas, there followed what a Roman Catholic theologian has called 'the slow but continuous disintegration of sound liturgical thinking which took place during the Middle Ages'. The corporate action of the whole company became the remote and mysterious prerogative of the spiritual fathers, while the People of God were turned into a passive audience whose sole function was with meek heart and due reverence to watch and listen.[67]

And just as the mass was a ceremony to be observed, so the church building became an object-lesson to impress the beholder with soaring arches, storied glass and the long vista through screen and choir to the far-off Presence.

The sixteenth-century Reformation brought a return to the primitive understanding of worship through the open bible, the restored communion and the direct access of every believer. But the church buildings did not reflect the change, other than causing the layman to hear sermons instead of observing masses.

> The inspiration of all that is vital in new church architecture today is the desire once again to provide a house for the Lord's company gathered around His Table to read the Word and share in the Breaking of Bread, a

house that will shelter them but never shut them away from the world which is their proper milieu.[68]

These ideas, these theological understandings, this Christian stance where witness and worship go hand in hand, will be expressed in bricks and mortar in the building of Partnership House in the Waterloo Road.

Standing on a great thoroughfare, it must speak to those who cannot understand the traditional symbols by being honestly what it is meant to be – a block of offices, a place of meeting and consultation, and a place of prayer and spiritual renewal.[69]

The architect's way of expressing this three-fold function with integrity was by allocating a separate building to each. But the long, six-storey office block, in plan like a Z that has been pulled out almost flat, curves through the whole lay-out, binding it all in one. Lying on a second axis at right-angles to this are the chapel above the main entrance portico in front, the committee room wing at the back and the staircase hall of the office block between them. The chapel, standing forward of the receding office block, is visibly of central importance but it is austere and of no style that could bind it to one culture or period more than another. It is simply an upper room. The passer-by might wonder what it is for. That at least is a better introduction than something plainly labelled and at once discounted. A second look will show one large window of modern stained glass, expressing the theme of mission – the spreading light, perhaps, or the outflow of inexhaustible waters. Visible from the main staircase and the committee rooms, the window will be lit at dusk and shine out into Waterloo Road.

Inside, what was wanted was a place of stillness, silence, and humility. The altar was to be almost central, with seating on three sides on a sloping floor. 'This will give a more intense sense of concentration, and remind us of the God who humbled himself into the midst of our human arena.'[70] The vision included an 'east' wall inclined inwards, overhanging like a great cliff of undressed concrete blocks. On it a great wooden cross, and below the cross, at the foot of the wall behind the Table, a stone font whose water is always running, trickling over its rim and down into the base-pedestal. This is the Chapel of the Living Water. Occasionally it may be used as a baptistery, but the flowing font is not primarily intended for the celebration of the foundation Christian sacrament. It is there for those who seek the still centre and source from which all that we try to be, all that we have to offer, flows out in ever-widening circles to the world. The distinctive sensibility of John Taylor in this whole enterprise could hardly be more to the fore. Indeed, the whole design of the chapel was handed over to him, and he designed it as nearly as he could to what he had visualized it might be in a dream. As he told his compatriots, the whole concept had come to him unbidden, quite literally as a gift by night.[71]

The emphasis on the font, and on 'living' or running water as a central Christian symbol, is both ancient and before its time. Fonts in old churches are usually waterless, lidded, a home for silverfish, a repository for old hymn books or a handy stand to support floral decorations. In new churches it may be hard to identify the font, and rarely do such fonts actually function as fountains. When the new chapel was being designed ecumenical appreciations of baptism as *the* accepted sacrament of unity across all ecclesiastical divisions was still in its infancy. After all, the Second Vatican Council had barely ended, with its new teaching that catholicity subsists in the Roman Catholic Church but is not confined to it, and baptism was still largely restricted to infants and considered a private or family matter of no immediate importance or interest to the gathered congregation of Christ.

In his choices, John Taylor is also busy ensuring that two cul-de-sacs of Christian history are avoided. First, there is no place in the scheme of this chapel for the static presence of Christ in the reserved sacrament, always a divisive issue between catholic and evangelical Anglicans and unacceptable to the constituency traditionally represented by CMS.[72] The flowing font is anything but static in its symbolism, and historically has not caused any division. Secondly, the alternative of a crucifix or a plain empty cross is side-stepped by the great rough-hewn wooden cross with its three prominent wrought iron nails. Unlike most empty crosses, cleaned up, polished, and even bejewelled, it is clear that this cross has been used. Clearly, resurrection is not some fairy-tale happy ending. The cross is central. It remains the principal Christian symbol, not the empty tomb. God's strength is perfected in weakness, in divine κενωσις (*kenosis*), the humbling or divesting entailed by incarnation.

At a later stage, as the chapel was coming to completion, John Taylor offered more details of his vision in a *Newsletter* which brings together reflections on society and world, church and mission, symbol and art in proclamation of the gospel.

> If, as Bonhoeffer suggested, our Christian affirmations, cheapened by too much shallow use, must be purged by a period of silence, it may be that the non-representational arts, abstract design, music, dance movement and, supremely architecture, have to speak as never before. Since we, perforce, must hold our peace, let the stones cry out.[73]

And it is worth noting that the new CMS headquarters was coming to completion precisely at the time the splendid new National Theatre was rising on the river bank nearby. It too would prove controversial for those without much imagination. Did John Taylor see here a parable hidden from less sensitive eyes, detecting a beauty in two buildings destined to be immediately criticized as ugly and utilitarian? The apologia is striking, and in some ways serves for one as much as the other. It also spells out in an uncommon way the particular kind of theologizing which always characterizes John Taylor's perception and reflection. Always, he seems to be striving to make connections, to hold together in Christ sacred and secular, nature and grace, body and spirit, transcendence and immanence. Our mission is God's mission, and God's mission is reconciliation, the mission of the Beyond here and now.

> The honest, unpretentious use of raw materials, the expanse of windows looking out to the world, will, I hope, say something. At the heart of our activity the chapel will be a pool of silence, as far as the architect can make it. Visually it is not cut off from the rest of the building, and from most points one can look right into it. It is important also that from inside the chapel one can look right out of it, not only back into the corridors and committee rooms, but, more importantly, down into the ceaseless traffic of the Waterloo Road. 'Glory to God in the High Street'! We are, I believe, only on the threshold of a new theology of the horizontal 'here-and-now-ness'. Yet we must not simply opt for that alone, and those who too readily abandon the vertical of God's transcendence are robbing us of an essential dimension. Now I understand why the angle between the east wall and the floor of our chapel had, from the beginning, been so crucial in my thought that I had asked for the floor to slope downwards and the wall inwards, as if to intensify that that point of intersection was the place for the overflowing font. It might be that the architect must suffer an unresolved conflict between the two foci of attention as the only honest symbol of a reality we are still groping to express.
>
> Modern drama is wrestling with the same theological issue. For three centuries we have had directional theatre, the picture stage presenting that 'other' reality over there, until its clichés became irremediably banal, and dramatists demanded the theatre in the round, with all the immediacy of audience-participation. But experiment showed that to abandon the picture-stage entirely was to throw away precious gains of perspective. And so a solution has been found which retains the picture stage while thrusting out from it an apron stage on which the players can perform in the very midst of the auditorium. This suggested to our architect the resolution of the dilemma. The great east wall sweeps down past the cross and the flowing water to the floor where, in an unbroken movement, it thrusts out into the body of the chapel the sanctuary-dais on which the Holy Table stands. It is a fine diagrammatic symbol of 'the Beyond in the midst'.[74]

CHAPTER SEVEN

Theology come of age

Folded the cope at the foot of the bed,
Mitre still crowns the episcopal head.
Hush! hush! whisper who dares,
Bishop John Robinson's saying his prayers.

'Ground of our being' – that's right I know,
For my image of God has got to go.
That beard's too big and that heaven's too high,
I can't say my prayers to a man in the sky.

If I study my Tillich a little bit more
I can doubt all the things I believed before,
And I'll emulate Bonhoeffer, page by page,
A religionless man who's come of age.

I'll say to the kids on their weekend trip
Just cherish an I–thou relationship;
Take your leather-clad girl on your motor-bike,
If you love her enough you can do what you like.

I've written a book, and wasn't it fun,
And *Honest to God*'s had a wonderful run.
Now what was that prayer I'd pray if I could?
Oh, – 'God bless my royalties, make them good.'

Folded the cope at the foot of the bed,
Mitre still crowns the episcopal head.
Hush! hush! marvel who dares,
Bishop John Robinson's saying his prayers.[1]

So-called 'South Bank religion', symbolized by Bishop John Robinson's best-selling paperback *Honest to God*, came as a shock to almost everyone in the Church of England, from the Archbishop of Canterbury down.[2] Most responsible ecclesiastical authorities seem to have taken fright, with the notable exceptions of Max Warren and John Taylor.[3] While all the nasty insinuations quoted in these verses were being employed in Church circles to discredit John Robinson, John Taylor was sufficiently relaxed with the secular God and unperturbed by the nervous and bitchy world of ecclesiastical politics to sing about it and teach others to do likewise. He knew that all the abuse hurled at John Robinson was untrue and respected his biblical scholarship and pastoral concern. He also knew that there was nothing novel here, that the bishop's book was simply popularizing ideas of Dietrich Bonhoeffer and Paul Tillich. It is equally significant that John Taylor was accustomed to treating Christ's disciples as adults who can think for themselves, rather than impressionable children to be protected from dangerous ideas. The widespread alarm about potential damage to those of 'simple' faith was not shared in the CMS General Secretary's office because it was based on ignorance, insecurity and fear. Archbishop Michael Ramsey, after an unusually insensitive and clumsy initial reaction, came to see *Honest to God* and its aftermath as symptomatic of the contemporary crisis of faith. John Taylor seems to have understood this instinctively from the first.

No theology springs new-born out of nothing. All theology grows out of human experience, and all theology matures in response to actual events and encounters with people, developing from provocations of some sort or another. In the 1960s John Taylor's participation in World Council of Churches meetings and assemblies, together with his constant travels, stimulated his interest in the 'secular' school of theology. This development in his thinking was helped by reading other theologians, principally Gibson Winter, Harvey Cox and Masao Takenawa, although it is, of course, traceable directly to his immersion in the work of Dietrich Bonhoeffer. We can plot the contours of his emerging reflections in the *CMS Newsletter* of this period.

Very early in his time as General Secretary, John Taylor is writing about Christ in the world, doing his work of salvation wherever women and men are becoming more human, more alive. No stretches of the world are beyond Christ's concern, and the redemptive Spirit is active everywhere – in a prison in Uganda, Alcoholics Anonymous meetings, through the therapy of a hospital clinic, in the battle for decent housing or for desegregation. These are battles not for abstract justice, but for restoration of individual personalities. In all these ways, men and women are being made more human, helped to be more alive. 'This is the Lord's doing. It is difficult for a Christian not to feel that he recognises his Master's hand in this.'[4]

For some, recognition of this kind comes naturally, and John Taylor is such a one. 'Keep both roads open', Joe Fison told the novice theological student, and reading Dietrich Bonhoeffer only reinforced that advice.[5] For others, of course, any such acknowledgement or recognition presents considerable theological difficulty. Some say the identification cannot be made at all. Reconciliation in Christ, they argue, is first and always with God, for Christ's redemption is primarily from sin. They concede that God may work *providentially* through the thought and organization of any or all aspects of the 'secular' world, but they claim that God works *redemptively* only through the Church's proclamation of the divine work in Christ's incarnation and crucifixion and resurrection. Others reply that all God's action is redemptive, that our relationship with God cannot be artificially isolated from all our other relationships, that the arena of our salvation is always here and now, where humankind is subject to the principalities and powers of this present world. These people argue that we can only experience God's gifts of forgiveness and reconciliation, repentance and faith, in the ordinariness of daily living.

This battle is not confined to international ecumenical gatherings, but rages in the CMS and, indeed, at least some of the time in John Taylor himself. It is said that every preacher preaches only one sermon – and always to themselves. In his theology John Taylor knowingly talks to himself first of all, allowing others to overhear his inner conversation. It just so happened that in the case of the *CMS Newsletter*, he was overheard by some 18,000 people monthly! Many of these found it difficult to recognize the Master's saving hand in sociological rather than psychological terms.

Unlike many Christians, some of them theologians and bishops, John Taylor had the advantage in that he began by welcoming secular theology. Beginning with the simple conviction that we are to love the world as God does, it presented no threat to him. This is, after all, God's world, indeed the only world of God that we know.[6] Nothing could be more firmly rooted in biblical revelation than the conviction that God made the world and finds it very good, but 'our Lord continues to embarrass us all because his love is so undiscriminating and his grace so frequently anonymous'.[7] Indeed, God seems unbelievably naive in lavishing love on undeserving places and people. Our difficulties arise, in John Taylor's view, because this foolishness of the God of the cross has rarely been taken seriously by the Church, let alone become truly and operatively central in Christian thought, worship, ministry and mission.

So he starts not from any fearful, defensive or embattled position, but from the security of faith. There is no residue in him of Calvinist disdain for the corrupt, sinful world, so marred by human disobedience that almost nothing good remains. Secularization is actually seen to be neutral. It is simply a fact of life. We are not to combat secularism, or form an army with other religious people to do so. Instead of 'clasping hands across the bridge of a common hypocrisy', Christian missioners have the responsibility and the opportunity to interpret to people of other faiths this strange child of Christianity, for 'secularism ... so far from being essentially the enemy of the Church, is, at least historically, its child'.[8]

In a word, then, John Taylor begins with better facts than many other Christians. He is careful to look at history and reflect on things as they actually are, rather than firing automatic and misdirected shots from the hip. 'The technocratic era, though it is not the Kingdom of God, is not the Kingdom of Satan either; it is a phase of history in which the Lord and Satan are both at work.' This refreshingly cool and unruffled language is welcome in the Church, where the dispassionate language of thoughtful observers with no particular axe to grind too often gets lost in the ignorant clamour of hysterics. John Taylor calls Christians to stop thinking negatively and defensively, insisting that they do so as intelligent and careful 'bible students'.[9]

This, however, is only the preliminary skirmish leading into a full-blown embrace of secularization. Secularization, he will boldly and unambiguously assert, is actually the Lord's doing.

> Mankind is being led into secularisation by the Lord of history. Its promises are his promises and its dangers are the risk which God is taking, as so often before in his purpose for Man. That is the staggering re-orientation we are being called to make. We are to accept the secularisation of Man.[10]

We are to accept and welcome what God is doing, and work *with* God rather than *against* God.

Although John Taylor does not make it explicit, there is here a clear debt to Judaism in terms of seeing humankind as partner and co-worker with the Creator. Indeed, in this whole debate the realism of Jewish theology, its this-world focus, is never far away, and this encourages us to think that Christianity may be rediscovering its roots in the parent faith more authentically than it ever did in Greek philosophy and Hellenistic dualism.

Science and technology can be celebrated as having set us free from dependency. 'The secular spirit is essentially the spirit of responsibility.' This is what made Israel 'secular' in comparison with the surrounding religions of the ancient Near East. This is what made Jesus 'secular' in the eyes of his contemporaries.

> Life is not something which the priests can run for you, nor can the questions it poses for you be answered by anyone else. There is no more magic of any kind, and no more oracles. Man is out on his own in the world with history in his hands. His salvation is to add the words 'under God'. But unless that affirmation also means 'in Christ', it can sustain little meaning at all against the drift and drag of godlessness. For the world is a place in which it is 'easy to forget' – and one cannot come out of the world in order to remember.[11]

Reflecting Bonhoeffer's characteristic language, at this point John Taylor comes up with one of his own characteristically memorable images. 'Man has come of age and his Father's birthday present was a do-it-yourself kit.'[12] So there is no more Christendom, no special areas of the globe or of any human life, no holy of holies, no religious zone into which we may retire to lick our wounds, to be religious, or out of which we can advance – batteries recharged – to face the 'secular' world. 'Secularisation represents the collapse of ecclesiastical totalitarianism.'[13] This demolishing of the medieval *Corpus Christianum* represents – as it also anticipates – the doing away with every *corpus religiosum*, just as the destruction of the

Temple at Jerusalem signifies that all our temples are, in principle, abolished. 'There is no way back, but there is a way ahead.'[14]

This way ahead is not some attempt to rechristianize the world, swamping secularization and swallowing up other religions. If there was ever a place for such a scheme, it is in the past. The way ahead is proclamation of the human need for salvation here and now. The future commits us to struggle for interdependence over against self-interest, for meaning and dignity in place of chaos and disillusionment. This is the human struggle to be responsibly in control of our destiny, in which we need a God who gives the divine self to enable us to be truly human. Here we are presented with no facile humanism. The gospel must remain the gospel in all its challenge to human assumptions and in all its reversal of human wisdom, but the gospel is for our salvation in *this* world. Following Christ is not a highway out of this world into some other world beyond, an escape from the turmoil of earth to the tranquillity of heaven. Central to this theology is the conviction that 'there is no salvation for the hereafter which is not first salvation for the here and now'.[15]

One consequence of the 'staggering reorientation' to which Christians are called is that the Church can no longer accept the role of a 'department of religion' in human life. If God is at work in God's world, leading humankind out into greater liberation and power and danger, restoring and fulfilling individual lives – often quite independently of the Church – then to co-operate with God is not necessarily a 'religious' activity at all. The worship of the Church is not so much to be understood as our service of God, in the sense that we speak of 'services' of worship. We have been taught to expect to find God in word and sacrament, in doxologies and creeds in the life of the Church, 'when all the meaning and glory of his Name is to be found in the family budget'! The worship of the Church is specifically designed for re-entering the myth, enabling our contact and communion with the Truth. It is for 'nerving'[16] us with a sense of meaning and ultimate forgiveness, a sense that God is with us and for us in our secular responsibility. Liturgy is all about opening our eyes to find the God of the broken bread in all brokenness, in other words in everything and everyone.

Another direct consequence of the revolution in which we are engaged is the ministry of the whole people of God, the whole λαος (*laos*), the actual exercise here and now of the royal priesthood of all believers. The Church, and the whole Church rather than just the clergy as representative, is servant of the world. This means, ironically, that in this 'secular' age ordinary Christians will need to know more theology than ever before.[17] The whole body of Christ needs to be theologically literate and intelligent, engaging in theological reflection on their everyday experiences, learning to think about their occupation in a Christian way and learning to choose in a Christian way. Ordinary men and women 'who have to keep the faith and to survive in the grey world of business negotiations, trade union loyalties, party caucuses, popular journalism, competitive television', will be learning to think and choose in a Christian way, interpreting the hand of God, actively reaching out to take God's hand.[18]

If the ecumenical debate over secularization surfaced and became a central issue at the meeting of the Commission on World Mission and Evangelism of the World Council of Churches in Mexico City in December 1963, the division between theological psychologists and theological sociologists was at its most naked only at the Uppsala Assembly in 1968, causing John Taylor to remark that he felt he had been all his life travelling to Uppsala![19]

What emerged here was a quarrel about grace and the gospel. It was, of course, a very polite quarrel – 'since we belong to a generation that dreads a row more than death itself'.[20] The delegates lacked the courage to clash. They had no idea about how to fight like Christians. They could not even begin to get past the stiff refusal to listen to one another, so entrenched positions were painfully restated in place of genuine dialogue. There was also an absence of any adequate theology to undergird social action, linking the human quest for peace and justice with the human quest for truth. 'The champions of the two sides battled for the inclusion of any phrase that might safeguard their own position, but they rarely listened to each other. There was no real meeting.'[21]

Someone, however, seems to have been listening quite hard, listening very carefully, forcing himself not to shut out the voices he disagreed with, drinking in the remarks that irritated him most. And this same someone was capable of doing the necessary theology, or needing only the stimulus of this frustrating and dangerous deadlock to provoke his further reflection. For this was not just a question of immediate ecclesiastical politics. The failure to meet one another on this territory had the potential to cripple the work of the Church in its service of God's world for years to come.

John Taylor began to offer a way through and a way forward in the Assembly itself, particularly in the session when he was asked to introduce the discussion on 'Renewal in Mission'. He likened the deliberations of the Assembly to the temptations of Jesus in the wilderness. Whatever the decision to emerge from their time of testing, he is clear about one thing: the answer God gives is not likely to be self-evident and will win almost nobody's approval. 'The traditionalists will accuse us of perverting the people, while the greatest of the prophets will ask: are you the one we were led to expect, or should we look for another?'[22] And he tried to reach them by drawing deeply on the biblical foundation of their common faith, and by humour – recalling the parable of the Good Samaritan.

> I am haunted by a new version of the parable, in which the priest and the Levite and the Samaritan travel again down the road from Jerusalem to Jericho. This time all three notice the fellow half-dead at the roadside. The priest sees a frightened man facing death and in the Name of Christ tries

to bring him the things that transcend death. The Levite sees a confused and bewildered man and in the Name of Christ tries to explain what is happening to him so that he can find some meaning and take a grip on the situation. And the good Samaritan sees a typical victim and, while binding up his wounds, begins planning in the Name of Christ a campaign to clean up the police force. And, because each of them claims priority and the greatest relevance, they tear the poor man apart. They tear him apart, body or mind or spirit, individual or incorporate, because none of them sees all of these as a single whole, none of them sees Man.[23]

Typically, the story encapsulates John Taylor's theological reflection on the facts of the situation. In embryo, his later and fuller treatment of this tragic splitting up of what is all of a piece is already present. Typically too for such a christocentric theologian,[24] John Taylor begins with Jesus who – shockingly – is too easily overlooked in ecclesiastical debate. Re-running the dominical parable is a smart ploy – deliberately appealing to the emotions, to imagination, consciously attempting to go behind the exchange of stale slogans. Characteristically, he also plays down his contribution as simply an invitation to look for a new synthesis. Whatever the circumstances, Christians do well to start with 'a humble and very open mind, at that point which is the irreducible and ... indestructible minimum of Christian Faith, namely the magnetic impact which the person of Jesus made upon his first disciples and makes upon us'.[25] That, after all, is where it all began, and when all the foundations are being shaken that is all that may be left to us.

This biblical approach, however, is never fundamentalist or literalist in approach, ignoring the findings of modern biblical criticism.[26] Like Max Warren before him, John Taylor takes his chances with history, acknowledging the risks involved.

> Granted that between me and that human life there will always hang a curtain of Christian explanation and worship, yet it is not entirely opaque. Through its gauzy folds we can make out a consistent stance, a style, a quality, that is at once stranger to us than the span of twenty centuries can account for and more familiar than any other in the Yes it elicits from people of all Churches and all periods.[27]

He offers the Assembly theology, not politics, but is nevertheless very politically astute in so doing. Significantly, also, he offers only whole theology, for John Taylor will not accept any ontological divide between the pre-Easter and the post-Easter Jesus, between the Jesus of history and the Christ of faith. What is irreducible and indestructible is the living Word, for the creator Spirit does not simply point us to the cosmic Christ of the Church's faith, but takes Mary's Son who was dead and is alive, making him our contemporary. 'It is the sight of those still human, wounded hands that makes us cry: "My Lord and my God!".'[28]

From this conviction, many crucial beliefs follow. The commands of Jesus are never generalizations. The faith Jesus looks for is always earthed in some specific act of obedience. So let us not waste too much time on general principles, attempting to codify and contain. The ecumenical Church is as prone as any local parish to waste its energy tidying up the messy world, while God confronts us with particular questions and situations demanding action. Faith consists in such responsive action. Faith is not so much belief in propositions as it is a relationship of loving trust in a person. No one is saved by acknowledging a doctrine, by giving inward or intellectual assent to some credal formula. Jesus knows no such thing as 'saving faith', as it were, in the abstract. He is spontaneous and almost casual in saving women and men, so we may search but we will search in vain for any systematic doctrine of salvation in the gospels.

> In his vocabulary no distinction is made between the healing of a body and the saving of a soul, and in his eyes faith is equally faith whether it be the instinct of a foreign army officer to take him at his word or the commitment which he prays that Peter will not lose in his hour of temptation.[29]

Not surprisingly, Dietrich Bonhoeffer comes to mind.

> Only he who believes is obedient, and only he who is obedient believes. It is quite unbiblical to hold the first proposition without the second ... If we are to believe we must obey a concrete command. Without this preliminary step of obedience, our faith will only be pious humbug, and lead us to the grace which is not costly.[30]

If we think we can do business with God in some private tête-à-tête, this is nothing but cheap grace. If we think we can do business in generalities with the world's agenda, this is nothing but cheap charity! If Jesus insists on anything it is that we must be concrete and specific.

> The language of salvation – sin and judgement, repentance and faith, reconciliation and new birth – is not meant to describe events and relationships in a separate or inner world of 'spiritual realities' any more than the language of psychiatry is meant to describe happenings in a world of dreams. Both are simply ways of diagnosing what happens to a human being in the ordinary developments and relationships of the life of this world. The dreaming self, and the self that experiences God, and the self that works and worries and quarrels and belongs in the here and now, are not separate selves but one indivisible person. That person is continually responding to others, growing more human or less human, turning towards life or towards death, being shaped for salvation or for damnation, through everyday choices and decisions, his own and other peoples', any one of which may have ultimate significance.[31]

In the words of Rosemary Haughton, 'salvation – the life with God that Christ offers – is going on all the time. All the great words of the gospel are seen to be a diagnosis, a blue-print, of something that actually happens in real life.'[32]

That we Christians have to seek conscious allegiance to Jesus Christ is not because there are no degrees of healing without it. It is not because Jesus is greedy for the credit, but in order that every part of human being and human becoming, including our understanding of ourselves, may be made true and whole. Since humankind is a creature of many facets, many dimensions, each aspect of our life is a sacrament of other aspects. This demands the corporate mission of the Church, rather than individual Christian missioners, for no individual will ever be able to minister to all human need, or be the agent of all human renewal. It is not for nothing that Jesus sent out the first missionaries two by two: this is a symbol of the Church. In the living and serving Body of Christ in today's world, 'it is high time for the eye of the prophet to stop saying to the ear of the pietist "I have no need of thee", and for the foot of the missionary to cease despising the hand of the servant'.[33]

As we have already noted, this passion for conscious personal allegiance to the Christ becomes for John Taylor *the* motive for mission. In other words, mission has principally to do with being and becoming *adult* daughters and sons of God. It is all about human maturity and human responsibility. If it is true that the perfect sonship of Jesus himself could not be complete without the cross, then it follows that this perfection cannot be available for anyone else until we become cross-bearers. The world thinks of salvation as healing and restoration of harmony. Suppose, however, that human beings are so constituted that we are only functioning properly when bearing one another's burdens. If this clue to full humanity is accurate, then someone set free by technology, someone whom science and sociology have left without a care in the world, has not yet in fact been made whole.

Our driving motivation for speaking to others of Christ is simply this need and this hope. It is not that we believe that the mercy of God is ultimately limited to those who are within the ark of the visible Church. We can leave the eternal destiny of individuals in the hands of One who was slain from before the foundation of the world – pierced, wounded, bleeding hands. We can acknowledge these same hands at work anonymously in every redeeming event and action through which basic humanity is being saved and brought to its full stature. Yet unless we are to be guilty of the ultimate arrogance and paternalism, we must covet for everyone what, in our moments of highest aspiration, we covet for ourselves: the privilege of walking *consciously* in the steps and in the grace and power of the crucified. 'For in a universe of which he is the Maker and the Lord, the fullness of life cannot mean less than that.'[34] It matters desperately that everyone should know that this name is the name of *their* redeemer. More than anything else, in hearing his name they meet, not someone who has acted for other people, an act in which they are now invited to share as some sort of afterthought, but rather, someone who has done something *for them* – and fully as much for them as for anyone else.[35]

Mutual responsibility and interdependence

Bishop Lesslie Newbigin coined the phrase 'mutual responsibility and interdependence in the body of Christ', which became the watchword for the Churches of the Anglican Communion at the Toronto Congress in August 1963. In a sense, the Toronto Congress marks the birth of the Anglican Communion, for it is a turning point in Anglican awareness of themselves as an international network or family of independent partner churches. There was first the change from a church in the British Isles to a family of churches all over the world, the result of British imperialism and trading. But in this family some churches were clearly 'mother', while others were 'missionary' or 'dependent' or 'younger'. Coming to think of all these churches as equal in authority and responsibility was a slow process. The idea that 'missionary' applies just as much to someone sent out from an African or Asian church to work in America, Australia or Scotland as to someone sent out from England took even longer. It was hard to get past the untruth that mission is something some people give to other people out of their abundance, the 'lady bountiful' view, the Christian West to the pagan rest, stronger helping weaker, older helping younger, superior helping inferior.[36]

> Mission is something that the Church is and does towards the world, and … the Anglican Communion ought to be a partnership of independent churches, planning together and pooling their resources, each helping the others and each receiving according to its need, in order that all together may be a better instrument of the Gospel.[37]

At Toronto the spontaneous conviction of the representatives of the various autonomous Anglican provinces was that Anglican churches belong together at a much deeper and more mature level than any of this, and that they must learn more realistically how to bear one another's burdens. This implied an enhancement of Anglican cohesion and awareness, and such growing unity would strengthen rather than hinder Anglican contributions to the ecumenical movement.

> Strong in their own convictions the Anglican churches will serve the cause of unity believing that their own tradition is not an historical accident or a piece of English-ism or a confessional position but a tradition of scriptural Catholic Christianity, a way wherein Christians can be Catholic without being Papal and reformed without involvement in any of the Reformation systems.[38]

In John Taylor's words, the more Anglicans are able to develop a spirit of 'mature mutuality' among themselves, the better will Anglican churches be equipped to explore similar mutuality outside their own communion. 'As churches learn to become free partners in a household of faith, the ecumenical initiative will be put where it belongs, squarely in the hands of the responsible leadership of each church.'[39]

Mutual Responsibility and Interdependence in the Body of Christ is a deceptively brief and simple document. It is addressed by the primates and metropolitans of the Anglican Communion to their churches – a manifesto, a summons, a challenge, proposing a way forward. Perhaps the most radical notion in initiating this process of reformation is that some aspects of Anglicanism will need to die to facilitate greater unity of purpose and mission.

Sounding this note, rather than appealing for funds for specific programmes, or telling anybody what to do, was perplexing. It is easier, after all, to be asked to do something specific for one's own church, or to do something for another church, than to be asked to be born again. This is a far less negotiable proposition![40] But this way of mutual responsibility, bearing one another's burdens, is Christ's own way, a victorious way, the only way.[41] So every Anglican church was called to examine its own obedience and ask afresh what that obedience requires.

Those who had grown suspicious of the separate autonomy of missionary societies in England, traditionally competitors separated by different ecclesiologies and churchmanship, used the MRI manifesto as ammunition. Obedience would certainly involve the death of these bodies and rebirth would take the form of merger into one central board of mission of the Church of England. No time was wasted. Heads of missionary agencies were called to a London meeting on 25 September, 1963. One agency instead of many would save money, would send a powerful message of the Church's unity of purpose to the parishes, and would be an imaginative response to Toronto. It was urged that the Church of England, of all the churches of the Anglican Communion, was more divided and least able to respond to the Toronto manifesto.

John Taylor seems to have been the voice crying in the wilderness against this push. In this, of course, he was the faithful disciple of his mentor and true to himself. As we have seen, Max Warren disliked centralization and bureaucracy in church as well as state and, for the sake of the voluntary principle, fought against centralization all his life.[42] John Taylor was as convinced as any that the times called for a new spirit of co-operation rather than competition and a new measure of co-ordination. He did not believe, however, that creating one umbrella organization was the way ahead. His reasons were good ones, but nobody wanted to hear them.

First, he pointed out that one organization would not be practical. The many missionary agencies within England and the many diocesan missionary associations overseas could be absorbed as suggested, but this would be an unacceptable infringement of the liberty of people at home and of diocesan bishops abroad. 'It is this tendency of any centralised body to demand a monopoly of the field which most alarms me.'[43] There is also, with the missionary work of religious orders (Community of the Resurrection, Oxford and Cambridge Missions, Church Army, Mothers Union, and so on), a natural and right jealousy over independent status, although they do often operate closely together.

Diocese-to-diocese giving was also likely to increase as a direct result of Toronto, just as there would be growing interest in adopting specific projects due to relationships formed between bishops and other church leaders. 'Even if we wished to we could not absorb this diversity in one central voluntary organisation; the only way is by setting up better machinery for consultation and co-operation between all the different agencies.'[44]

Anglican instruments for this purpose must clearly be ecumenical, but if non-Anglican agencies are also to be incorporated into one agency, how big will this body be? Size and centralization do not make for adaptability and quick response to need. We want greater, not less, adaptability. Spontaneity and enthusiasm will be lost in the proposed cumbersome new system, superficially attractive and efficient though a merger may seem to be on paper. Unity in diversity is the pattern of Anglicanism, and one gift we should bring to the ecumenical Church. Anglicans should know better than to be calling for unification. Rather, we should be advocates for unity at a round table. Unlike some of the romantic visionaries gathered at the September meeting, the romantic visionary John Taylor had done his homework. He talked about the facts of life. If his first point had to do with impracticality, his second was that this was a top-down initiative. Thirdly, the argument from economic rationalism would not stand up to examination. He pointed out that there is no demand for centralization from the strongest supporters of the various missionary agencies. The arguments of the economic rationalists will not hold. Already staff are stretched to the full, the same work cannot be done by fewer people, proposed savings are illusory, savings will actually be minimal. There is no need for the chauffeur to do the cooking!

Fourthly, there is the argument from religious identity, the distinctive ethos of the missionary community. In all this, John Taylor is plainly concerned that the distinctive witness of CMS and the other agencies should not be lost. CMS is primarily concerned for the evangelism of the world. This is not just a matter of church to church. Building up the local church is always a means to an end, never an end in itself. It is done always with an eye on the world beyond the Church, the world that God loves and the Church is called to serve. New nations in Africa and Asia demand lay and non-professional missionaries to work in trade unions, commerce, university faculties, and government departments. Sending persons to persons is primary. CMS cannot surrender its right to send people wherever they may be asked for – and neither should the other agencies.

CMS believes it is called to be a *societas* – a fraternity of people committed to one overruling concern. It exists as a distinctive fellowship to keep alive in isolated members working on strange frontiers a concern for the frontier, an invisible bond of membership in a community committed to evangelism. 'This will involve a discipline tougher and at times more inward than any regulations because it will have to be capable of great flexibility.'[45] Training is understood mainly as initiation into this particular community, rather than simply as preparation for service overseas.

John Taylor's views were greeted with hostility. The good sense of his arguments would not be recognized until years later. For the moment they were greeted with irritation. Pencil comments in the margins of Archbishop Michael Ramsey's copy of the minutes of the London meeting, no doubt made by a chaplain, go so far as to suggest that John Taylor was 'quenching the Spirit'! This is harsh criticism. He is dismissed as self-interested, his views regarded as special pleading. But if there is quenching of the spirit, which spirit needs to be quenched here? John Taylor himself felt he was at war against the spirit of Leviathan, and with the gift of hindsight it is hard to think him wrong.[46] Nevertheless, hostility is frequently good provocation for the theologian. The pain of rejection forces prolonged inner argument, healthy and honest self-doubt, re-examination of the arguments in the light of responses or lack of response. It is not surprising to find John Taylor doing his subsequent theology in terms of a biblical picture.

> One of the best parables of the missionary relationship is the miracle of the great catch of fish which proved too much for Peter and Andrew and their crew to handle alone. So, Luke tells us, they beckoned to their partners in the other boat that they should come and help. When the second boat arrived on the scene, James and John didn't, I imagine, take charge of the operation. It was Peter's catch and, under Christ, Peter was the man to give the orders. But neither did they abandon their own boat and try to scramble into Peter's. That would have sunk the whole effort. Nor can we see Peter and Andrew and James and John all diving out of their separate boats into the perfect oneness of the waves.[47]

Partnership in mission does not mean the surrender of identity, but the submission of identity in the cause of particular operations. And this is all the more necessary when the fishing involves not just two boats, but a whole flotilla.

The Cadbury Lectures

In 1966 the senate and council of the University of Birmingham invited John Taylor to give the eight annual Edward Cadbury Lectures in Theology early in the following year.

It was Max Warren who suggested the theme of the Holy Spirit in the Christian mission. He also suggested some sub-headings around which to think. Particularly intriguing and surprising was his question 'What was the Holy Spirit doing at Calvary?' John Taylor took up these suggestions, partly because he already had some material on the Holy Spirit which he had used with some success in retreats and quiet days with clergy and other ministers. In a busy life it is good not to have to begin from scratch. This was an opportunity to further refine his thoughts, to sharpen and deepen these meditations.

He was at this time living with the suggestive idea that the Christian Church had, in its two millennia, passed through a time of devotion to God the Father and moved on to focus on Christ, but that it was now moving into an era of the Spirit. In the phase of concentrating on God the Father, the Church lived under the severe gaze of a majestic cosmic king and judge, sovereign in will and ways, inscrutable, intangible, immutable, omnipotent, the great god of Greek philosophical thought. Christ, by association and participation in the life of this god, was remote and daunting, a plenipotentiary figure, the Christ Pantocrator of Byzantine icon and mosaic, dominating the domes of Orthodox Churches, domi-nating the imagination of most believers. Naturally there was a reaction to this, a move away into an era of Christ, with a great focusing on the humanity of Jesus and his gentle mother. This brought a softening of attitudes, a gentling of the Church's discipline, a warmth towards people, an emphasis on salvation, mercy, redemption. Now there were many signs that the neglected, elusive, shadowy figure of the Spirit was coming into the foreground. John Taylor had been living with these ideas since his last days in Uganda.

It also seemed to him that concentration on the person and work of the Holy Spirit was called for if Christians were to deal creatively with their encounter with other faiths, and in any meeting and dialogue between people of different faiths. All his missionary experience pointed to this.

The lectures were duly written and delivered. They were quite good, and they were well received. After all, he had been re-working this material for at least ten years, so he knew what he wanted to say. He worked around the themes of 'Spirit of Truth, Spirit of Life, Spirit of Love' – all very conventional and orthodox. Because he, along with most clergy, was living in the word 'outreach' just at this time, all his familiar material was shaped in connection with that image of mission.

So there absolutely must be a chapter on the Creator Spirit. This must be followed by a chapter on the Spirit who speaks through the prophets, the Spirit who speaks in all the tension between what is and what might be in any given situation, the actual and the potential, for the Holy Spirit is the creator of that situation and that tension, holding it in awareness. The Spirit is the One who pushes creatures towards the necessity of choosing, insisting that we choose and grow. Because John Taylor has always been a very christocentric theologian, it follows that these chapters had to be followed by a major study of the Spirit-filled man of Nazareth and Jerusalem, fully human like us in all things, divine because he is brim-full of the Spirit, because there is nothing about him that is not Spirit-inspired and Spirit-filled. And then a special chapter about what the Holy Spirit was doing at Calvary – which seems such an obvious question to ask once it is asked, although it seems not to have been asked much, if at all, in the history of Christian thinking. How typical that it was the extraordinarily perceptive Max Warren who asked it. The study could then be rounded off with a section about the activity of the Spirit in the Church, the extension of the Incarnation and the fruit of Easter, and the Spirit of prayer and life in God's world.

Publication of the Cadbury Lectures was part of the contract, but, although his work was applauded, John Taylor remained sufficiently dissatisfied with his own material to ask for a stay of execution. There was something lacking. He felt he still hadn't really broken through to the heart of the matter, that something crucial had been missed, but he didn't know what it could be. There was nothing actually wrong with the material as it stood, but there was no spark to ignite the flame, nothing seemed to bring it to life. 'I had written Hamlet without the Prince, and I had no idea what else there was to say.'[48]

So he did nothing more about it, got on with his life and ministry, and waited – no doubt with growing anxiety! The flattering reactions to the lectures disturbed him because he knew the material was good but not good enough, not as good as it should be. He couldn't see how to shape a book from the lectures to his own satisfaction.

Then events took over. He experienced three deaths, and these three deaths began silently to play their part.

First came the death of his old friend and mentor from Wycliffe Hall days, Joe Fison, Bishop of Salisbury. John Taylor looked again at Joe Fison's books on the Holy Spirit, books that had stimulated his own theology and already informed his Cadbury Lectures at every point. But this travelling over well-known ground and along well-worn tracks simply disturbed him further. There was something that needed to be discovered, and Joe Fison's death left John Taylor feeling that he had inherited the task of discovery, that there was unfinished work here for him to complete. This conviction was inescapable and it made him very uneasy.

Then came another death, this one a great deal more traumatic.

> Someone who at one time had been very closely attached to me, and then the attachment was broken, years later wanted to re-establish the attachment, and it was out of the question. I may have handled it clumsily, but she committed suicide.[49]

Guilt over the past became guilt in the present, an inner struggle between the givenness of love on the one hand and the rightness or wrongness of our enjoyment of the gift on the other. There was pain over what might have been and what now could never be, and this lingering pain was suddenly denied any resolution. Living with our own frailty and failure can be deeply traumatic. Feeling responsibility for the irretrievable loss of a life may lead to breakdown. Peggy Taylor, fortunately, was alert to the signs – distraction, silences, overwork – and insisted that something be done. John Taylor went to a psychiatrist 'kicking and screaming'.[50] He was very frightened. Was he coming apart at the seams? Were his life and ministry collapsing? He didn't like the clinical experience and didn't persist with psychotherapy. But, in spite of his resistance, something cathartic happened and some sort of healing process began. Something was unlocked, something was released. His brittle exterior had been pierced and his emotions were able to surface. After the second session he met Peggy and 'talked and talked for about two hours as I hadn't talked before'.[51]

So perhaps it isn't altogether surprising, though I didn't see the connection at the time, that only about two weeks later, when I was taking a journey back from Oxford in the evening that the thing happened which actually underlay the whole book.

I was reading at the time a little paperback by Norman Pittenger called *God in Process*. It was an application of process philosophy to the Christian gospel. I didn't get very far with the book. I can't remember a great deal about it, but I've still got it because on the two blank pages at the end I scribbled the thoughts which suddenly came bursting out of me like a volcano.

It was one of those incredibly beautiful English evenings, the sun was low, there were long shadows from all the corn stooks over the stubble fields and from the trees and the hedges. There was a flaming English sunset in the west, and after this my eyes just dwelt on that scene as the train travelled through the Berkshire countryside, and my thoughts went to what I was experiencing. And I found myself wondering about this experience which was a very common one to me, which I could remember from childhood days, of an extraordinary feeling of being in communion, communication, with a scene, with beauty, as though there was a kind of current between myself and what I was looking at. And I think, probably for the first time in my life, I actually asked the question, 'what creates this feeling of being addressed by what I'm looking at?'

And then I started to scribble. And I'm reading to you now from those two back pages of the little paperback. It's almost illegible, I was writing so fast.

'The source of any profound human response is not the responding person but the presence to which one responds. That is what creates the experience. Awareness and recognition towards a beautiful thing, or towards a truth. I don't work it out, think it out. I have a sense rather of waiting for it, waiting for a disclosure. It is already there, ungrasped. I must relax, be still, to catch it. *Attendre, attention, attendant, en attendance* – all these words seem to suggest that tension of listening, waiting to be spoken to, waiting for something that is going to be said. But what brings these acts? What brings me and that truth together? What makes that beauty present to me? What makes me attentive to it? As soon as being becomes presence, as soon as those things out there, outside, become present to me, they have already become part of me, part of that to which they are present. What we call the *object* of our response is really the subject, it is the activator of the whole experience. And yet not so.

There is a third party between that out there and me within, there is a ground of our presence toward one another, a third party in every encounter who effects the introduction, makes two beings mutually aware, turns being into presence. The chorus-ending from Euripides, yes! Browning has it. Romeo and Juliet encountering across the room, palm to palm. Adam *knew* Eve his wife. *Knew* – the *hagia sophia*, the wisdom, the awareness, that is the heart of all understanding. An element in which two are intimately one, like water. Contact of bodies when swimming are so extraordinarily intimate: think of skin-diving or embracing somebody under the water. Life in the womb is water-life, and then we are born into air-life which gives us our separateness from each other, and yet we constantly discover a spiritual umbilical taking us back through recognition and awareness. Water and the Spirit. The most profoundly simple conversation in literature. So the Holy Spirit is he who makes one aware of the other, who gives one to the other. Pay attention.'

That's where it ended in the little book, and that's where the bigger book began.[52]

All the material of the Birmingham lectures was relevant, but it needed a new introduction and to be lit up all the way through with what to John Taylor was this totally new insight. The book needed to be lit up all through with this experience which is so common to human beings, which is not peculiar to Christians, which is not even religious. The Holy Spirit is the Lord, the Giver of Life, touching all people, bringing them to life, making them aware, giving aliveness and awareness. Every single experience of this comes from God the Spirit. A lot of it, of course, makes havoc of people's lives: we fall in love with the wrong people, we make the wrong decisions. Our aliveness, our alertness, does need something more – some discipline, some shape, some purpose. And John Taylor knows this from his own experience, not second-hand. But the life, the strength, the vigour is there for us all. Here is the creative Spirit. And this is attributed uniquely to the Spirit in Scripture, in that prayer we know as 'the Grace', which speaks of the most distinctive characteristics of the three persons of the Trinity.[53] Love is the principal characteristic of the Father. Grace, or givenness, is the great characteristic of Jesus Christ. And what might we expect next – the power of the Holy Spirit, the light, the guidance or the purity of the Holy Spirit? Significantly, it turns out to be none of these. Instead, the text speaks of the *communion* of the Holy Spirit. It speaks thus because there is no power in the Holy Spirit except the extraordinary power that comes to us from being made aware, the power of being lit up, the power of awareness and of real presence. This is the powerful moment of disclosure, of revelation, of epiphany, that magic moment when the ice breaks, the penny drops, when we truly see. It is powerful only in this sense, and redemptive in this sense, for divine enlightenment means that things suddenly start falling into place and the world is transfigured.

And then there was a third death, the death of Dr James Welsh, who had been the Director of Religious Broadcasting at the BBC and was then teaching philosophy at Surrey University in Guildford. When he died John Taylor was asked to take his funeral. One of the readings was from Martin Buber's classic *I and Thou*. Strangely, it was new to John Taylor. He had, of course, heard of the book, but never read it. Now he found this Jewish thinker saying all the things he wanted to say. So he took some time off and went away quietly to read the whole of *I and Thou*, with some other of Buber's writings. And there, as it happened, he also heard a tape-recording of a talk by Metropolitan Anthony Bloom in which the bishop described how he had helped a woman to learn to pray simply by sitting quietly in her room and being aware – aware of the trees outside, aware of the comfort of her little room, aware of the clicking of her knitting needles against the arm of her chair.[54]

> Because you can't be alive towards God unless you are alive towards everything else, all the glory and all the pain and all the people. And it all came pouring into my mind, and somehow in a way I don't understand those three deaths fertilised my dried-up self. I nearly dedicated the book to them, but it was just a bit too intimate.[55]

If the Holy Spirit is dangerous, making us fall in love with the wrong people, it is equally true that the danger of the Holy Spirit consists in making us fall in love with the right people and things.

> We are falling in love at every turn of the road, with a fold in the hills, the mist over the lake, the stars tangled in the bare branches, the yellow chair in the sunlight, an old song at the peasant's fireside, a new thought flashing from the pages of a book, a lined face on a hospital pillow, a hair-ribbon from Ur of the Chaldees.[56]

'A flash of recognition has higher voltage than a flash of lightning', but it may take us a long time living with a new insight, experiencing the new view, before we can put our learning into words.[57] So it is with the most intriguing question of all those with which John Taylor wrestled in the Cadbury Lectures. His answer to the question about what the Holy Spirit is doing at Calvary is, frankly, disappointing. Indeed, he barely pauses long enough to look it in the face. He seems intent on rushing on to the Resurrection and what the Spirit is doing there, inadvertently identifying himself with a tendency all too common among Christ's disciples. Even by the time the lectures are published some five years later, little more than a paragraph is offered and he retreats too easily into what amounts to an evasion, claiming that this is a mystery we cannot plumb, a mystery that must for ever lie infinitely beyond our understanding.[58] On one level, of course, no one can quarrel with that, but the same truth applies to all human words about the Word, to all our feeble attempts at loving God with finite minds.

All John Taylor manages to say is that at the cross the Holy Spirit is holding Father and Son 'each in awareness of the other, in an agony and bliss of love'.[59] This is a start, but only a very small one. We are forced to rely on what John Taylor has insisted from the start, namely that 'all is imagery … all is experience which only images can adequately convey'.[60] We are thrown back on the art works in the book, which 'say it all better than I can hope to do'.[61] We can only take 'the agony and bliss of love' with us into the art gallery and look on the obscure and not very helpful fifteenth-century Austrian school painting of The Trinity and William Blake's wonderfully dynamic and suggestive charcoal sketch of The Trinity.

Evidently it was too soon to answer the question, or to attempt an adequately Christian answer. The time was not ripe. Perhaps John Taylor's life experience was not yet full enough in terms of his own sufferings and brokenness to initiate any distinctively Christian insight. Only years later is something fuller offered which begins to satisfy, as John Taylor starts to open for us a way into the unfathomable mystery.

> On the cross we see the ultimate reversal of the old idea of providence. The anguished and all too natural prayer was offered, 'If it be possible …', and it was not possible. There was no intervention, only the terrible silence and a gazing into darkness. And on either side of that silence there was pain – the human suffering and the divine as God and Jesus held firm to the intention that had been there before the foundation of the world: Love bent on creating the possibility of an answering love. So we do not see God averting evil to protect his human child; we see him absorbing evil, letting it come upon him in the person of his human child, and so turning the evil into overwhelming good. This is the essence of forgiveness, the forgiveness of men and women by God, and, dare I say it, the forgiveness of God by men and women – God reconciling the world to himself.[62]

How natural it is that the go-between-ness of the Spirit's work – the plus in the equation where one and one is more than two, always so self-effacing, creating awareness in an agony and bliss of love, sustaining that love in the searing pain and the absolute weakness, is in this passage unnamed.[63] For it is the nature of the spark, the current, the secret to remain hidden, to make visible without making itself visible.[64]

Conversation and conversion

Bishop Krister Stendahl defines *the* urgent question facing Christians as 'how to sing our love song to Jesus without telling dirty stories about the rest'.[65]

During his years at CMS headquarters, John Taylor distilled his own approach to dialogue between people of faith, learning how Christians may sing their love-song with passion and conviction, but also with reverence for the dreams of others. He was sure that evangelists who are not themselves changed in the process of evangelism, failing to learn more of Jesus Christ, were not engaged in evangelism. Rather, they were in the business of propagating Christianity, which is something quite different. Influenced by Max Warren and Kenneth Cragg, and stimulated by his time as a missionary in Africa and his international travels as General Secretary, John Taylor began to spell out a way forward in his *CMS Newsletters* and in two major books of enduring importance, as well as in various addresses and sermons.[66]

For sixteen centuries of the Church's life 'mission' was used exclusively of the Holy Trinity. This fact provides the clue to where all our thinking and praying and talking about faith conversations and inter-faith dialogue must begin: namely, with the being and nature of God as disclosed in Christ Jesus. If we start with ourselves, the conversation is over before it begins. We find ourselves in totalitarian faith communities, separated from each other by irreducible differences in culture, outlook and belief.[67] Comparative religion may be informative, but apart from increasing our knowledge about various religious households, comparing religions tends to lock us more firmly into our own. We soon find ourselves in a sterile impasse.[68]

Discussions of this kind operate at the wrong level, with too static an idea of what a religion actually is in itself. They suggest that what shapes human lives is truth *about* God, whereas in fact it is the truth *of* God to which the various religions are responses. Religion is not the system of doctrine and practice fabricated by priests and theologians. Rather, it is a people's tradition of response to the reality the Holy Spirit has set before their eyes, albeit shaped by the peculiar sensitiveness and courage of prophets and reformers and saints.[69] God's self-revelation and self-giving are consistent for all, but different peoples have responded differently.[70] All religions point beyond themselves to the 'uncontainable unattained'.[71]

Naturally, then, John Taylor is careful not to say that any particular religion is *the* truth disclosed by the Spirit, nor even that it contains this truth. All we can say without presumption is that this is how *this* particular people have responded and taught others to respond to that of which the Spirit made them aware. Religions are 'the history of a particular answer, or series of answers, to the call and claim of him who lies beyond all religions' – including Christianity.[72] This, no doubt, comes as a surprise or shock to many followers of Christ, but it is integral to John Taylor's vision and understanding. Christ judges and saves and converts Christianity just as much as he judges and saves and converts every other religion.

This Barthian idea, alive and well in the teaching of Hendrick Kraemer, is one way to avoid the arrogance of affirming the superiority and exclusive truth of Christianity over against all other religions. All religions, including Christianity, are essentially human constructs. As such they are forms of human self-assertion against God. 'The main thing about all religions', says Kraemer, 'the heart and soul of them … is that they are a fleeing from God.' They are, 'in their ultimate and essential meaning and significance, erroneous'.[73] Both Kraemer and Barth rightly insist that Christianity as a religion needs continually to be criticized in the light of Christ. John Taylor would follow them this far, but not when they seem to go an extra step and assume that there is access to Christ in total independence of Christianity. The medium *is* the message. John Taylor discovered this in a deeply personal way in Africa. The gospel comes to us through the living tradition of Christianity as a religion. The Bible is the book of the Church, even if the living Word stands always over any words, however inspired, hallowed and sanctified. It has been said that Kraemer and Barth are clinging to the myth of a unique, exclusive, once-for-all revelation, still making the premature assumption of the superiority of Christianity.[74] I do not think the same can be said of John Taylor's more nuanced view.

Religion is a tradition of response, and for John Taylor, both words are of equal importance.[75] A religion is *traditional* in the sense that it maintains a continuity of convictions and attitudes. As such, it is innately conservative. At the same time, it is *responsive* because 'it reflects even while it transmutes whatever movement of ideas is in the air'.[76] This means that the test of any religion's vitality at a particular time is to ask not only how strongly its traditional convictions and patterns of life are maintained, but also how creatively it is responding to current influences and tensions in the real world where those convictions are proclaimed and those patterns lived.[77] How is this religion answering the call of God now? How is it coping with the tension between conservation and development, the tension between past and future? How is past obedience dwelling with present response?

So we begin with the God who is beyond all religion and immediately discover that what is mutually exclusive for us appears in an altogether other light for God. Startlingly, in the divine vocabulary the words 'unique' and 'universal' turn out to have exactly the same meaning. What we thought was our monopoly turns out to belong to everybody. Whatever the Holy Spirit touches is turned inside out. The favourite joke of God is 'to whisper an especial secret behind closed doors and then shout it from the housetops'.[78] Having taught a particular tribe that it is God's chosen people, they go on to discover that others have a similar tutoring and experience of a like salvation history.

Like Max Warren before him, John Taylor enjoys quoting forgotten biblical texts. 'Are not you Israelites like Cushites to me? says the Lord. Did I not bring Israel up from Egypt, the Philistines from Caphtor, the Aramaeans from Kir?'[79] Exodus, the experience of election and rescue, is peculiar to the Hebrews, but also not. The Spirit comes on the gathered disciples on the Day of Pentecost in such a way that they are compelled to confess that until then it had not been given, but also in such a way that this Spirit-possession simultaneously establishes its continuity with the past. The Spirit's fire falls on them alone, and yet fulfils the promise of a gift poured out on all flesh.[80]

> What is given to us alone lays upon us a responsibility and commitment we can never feel for what is common; and the discovery of what we share brings out a strength of fellow-feeling and openness we can never find in our separate identities. Both the particular and the general are necessary for us and the contrast between them will last as long as time and space. But for the Spirit what is here is everywhere, yet would be nowhere were it not here first.[81]

Basically, this means that any theology of the Spirit is bound to be schizophrenic![82]

In all his thinking and teaching about Christian faith in relation to other great faiths, John Taylor has made much of the mystery of the pre-incarnate Christ, the λογος (logos). The logos is the Word and Wisdom and Reason of God, the Light of all people and things, the Lamb slain from before the foundation of the world.[83] The logos exists before everything, and all things are held together in the logos. If Christ had come down from the cross, all things would have been instantly undone and unmade, the whole universe would instantly have disintegrated, for time itself would have been unborn.[84] From the beginning, the universe is held in existence by the death of its Redeemer, held secure in the pierced hands of its loving Creator.

> The creeds of the Church have not sufficiently recognised that the death and resurrection of Jesus brought a radical change to the Hebrew doctrine of creation. For the patterns of the gospel experience are the patterns of the very fabric of life. The free obedience of Jesus, his dying for us all and his rising again, are both history and universal reality. They happened and they are the way things always happen. And man is saved not by relating only to that historical life, death and resurrection in which the pattern was made plain once for all, but by relating also to that true pattern wherever it emerges in the tissue of contemporary experience.[85]

This stance is of crucial importance in John Taylor's theology and there is nothing tentative or hesitant about it. Indeed, it could be said to be his core belief. The incarnation of God in Christ is not, as it is mostly presented, an isolated crossing of the gulf between human and divine, but the establishment of the fact that there is no gulf. When this revelation is taken seriously, everything is transformed, the world is a new creation, and we are God's Easter people.

Jesus of Nazareth, in his birth and life and teaching and dying, and in his being raised by God, offers us the indispensable clue. Without him we would never have guessed that what we see played out before our eyes in his story is the story of the universe itself. Thanks to him we begin to see the same pattern everywhere, the self-same reality. 'He is the same not only in the today of the crucifixion and the today of personal conversion, but in all our yesterdays back to the first morning, and on, tomorrow and tomorrow and tomorrow.' [86]

And if this is so, it means that we are all, without any exceptions at all, citizens of a *forgiven* universe, where 'being-in-Christ' is a more primary and essential and natural condition of our existence than our ignorance of Christ.[87] Every movement of the human mind or spirit that can be called an act of faith is, therefore, an act of faith in Christ, even though Christ is the unknown 'magnetic pole' which draws us. It follows from this that evangelism is really a matter of inviting human beings to become what they already are, inviting people to be real and to really live.[88] Another way of telling the same truth is to say that we are to help one another to believe we are already accepted, forgiven, loved, that long before we can do anything, long before we confess, the Father comes running to meet us. And those who can name Christ now are both saved and not, for we too await the awakening of the whole creation to its freedom which is already won.

The Holy Spirit is universally present through the whole fabric of the world, and uniquely present in Christ. By extension, the Holy Spirit is present now in the communion of the Church. But even this unique presence is not in any sense enclosed, either in Christ or in Christ's Church, because it exists *between* Christ and the other, *between* the Christians and those who meet them. 'The centre is always on the circumference, yet it proves to be the circumference of *that* centre and not another.' [89] The Spirit's witness to the sovereignty and love of Christ is, therefore, itself dialogue, calling all people to respond. 'Like a fifth column' in the heart of every individual, the Spirit itself is responding.[90] It follows that in any faith conversation, in any dialogue between people of faith, the Spirit is speaking in both participants.

Another essentially biblical emphasis, all too often ignored by the Church, is one we have already seen flowing strongly through John Taylor's theology. It is this: Christ is Lord and Saviour of the whole of person, or he is no Saviour at all.

> Because Jesus insisted on seeing men whole, one could never be sure which aspect of a man's needs he would tackle first. Here comes a paralysed man, helpless and obviously sick in body. His friends have brought him hoping for a simple cure, and Jesus talks about the forgiveness of his sins. Here, on the other hand, comes a clear case of spiritual need, an enquirer asking how

to gain eternal life, and Jesus gives him an economic answer, telling him to give away his goods to the poor.[91]

Because ultimately Christ cannot rest content until all a person's needs are fully met, it doesn't matter much to him where he starts on the work of salvation. Because there is no gap between sacred and secular, because there is no gulf fixed between human and divine, the creative work of redemption is as varied and unlikely as the lavishly indiscriminate divine love itself.

In all of this John Taylor insists that we never lose sight of the dynamically personal quality of any faith that people live by. It is widely assumed that if inter-faith dialogue is to make any real progress it will involve one of two moves: an abdication of any claim to truth on the part of one of the religions engaged in the conversation, or else the abandonment of any cognitive content in religious affirmations generally.[92] Objections to inter-faith dialogue, particularly from evangelical Christians, are often fuelled by the claim that such dialogues set little store on truth and by the fear that concessions will be made. The talk is always frightened talk of 'watering down', fear of the dangers of syncretism.

This betrays a falsely static view of religion. Living in the safety of the ghetto, building the walls higher and stopping our ears will not protect us. Those who fear contamination need to see that it is only as we are prepared to talk with one another, taking into account as full a range of human religious experience as possible, that we are in any position to claim to be concerned with truth. Truth is dynamic, and we are being called relentlessly into the fullness of the truth. Naturally, in any conversation of this sort there is risk involved. We must honestly begin from our 'jealousies', offering our real convictions with passion. 'Leave us at least our capacity for categorical assertion,' pleads John Taylor, 'for that is what we have in common.'[93] It is only the dialogue of the committed that really matters.[94] For all that, however, the encounter inevitably changes the participants, for it necessarily alters their view of their own religious landscape. When a Jew and a Christian engage in such exploration, the conversation will be artificial and trivial unless there is as much chance of the Christian becoming Jewish as of the Jew becoming Christian.

John Taylor never loses sight of the fact that, appearances notwithstanding, a religion is never a fixed system. He keeps always in view those who live their lives within the dynamic, historical, evolving structures of meaning which constitute any religion. Dialogue is never a meeting of doctrine with doctrine, truth claim with truth claim, just as theology itself cannot be divorced from the lives of faithful people seeking understanding. Dialogue searches beyond the theological text books into the hearts of practitioners, to discover from within what is actually believed or rejected. Dialogue must probe beyond the glad discovery of what we have in common to the painful recognition of differences that are mutually exclusive. Just as we will celebrate the similarities between us, so we will want to face these divisions honestly, not papering over the cracks or playing down the reality and depth of whatever separates us. And it may well be our experience that the pain is most intense when we find ourselves using the same words to mean completely different things. Just when we thought we were drawing nearer, the roads diverge once more.

Academic theologians sometimes stall at this point, as they face the reality of mutually contradictory religious affirmations. Is it not possible, or even likely, that inter-faith dialogue will quickly reach a point of stalemate? This, says John Taylor, is the worry of the theoretician, who can see problems on the horizon but has not actually participated in inter-faith conversations. Having himself sat where others sit, and having spent long hours over many years listening with the ears of the heart, John Taylor seems to harbour no such fear.

To stop at the disagreements, he says, is to fail to trust the Spirit's gift of communication and communion, losing sight of the connection between conversation and conversion. This point is not merely semantic. To move on from disagreement to mutual understanding and appreciation is the most important step in any dialogue, and the most important act in evangelism.[95] The gulf is indeed too deep for us to bridge, but what is called for is not panic. Faith is what we need. In other words, we need to trust the One who draws us and who draws us together. What is called for is patient and painful preparation for God's miracle. We are to prepare the way of the Lord, and wait expectantly on God. In our helplessness, our weakness and blindness, in our anxiety and frustration, we turn empty-handed to God who alone can throw a bridge across the chasm. The gulf may still yawn before us, but it may no longer be between us. 'The gulf is seen, as it were, in cross section ... I said "cross section"; for it is nothing less than the cross which is now demanding our decision.'[96] The evangelism of the Holy Spirit consists in creating occasions for choice, and the servant of the gospel can do no less, and perhaps need do no more.[97]

Evangelism as presence, then, is not just some new technique, a missionary method worth trying.[98] It is nothing less than the way of God, God's own way. It is the way of the God of the cross. We live in a universe of I and Thou.[99] To be really and totally present, really and totally *in* the present, is for us to be like God. In the Eucharist Christians claim to be centred on the real presence of Christ, but the evidence suggests that we may not often manage to be really present to one another within the gathered community, let alone to the wider community beyond. Presence simply as being with, presence simply as humble reverence for the other that never desires to manipulate or possess or use the other, authentic face-to-face encounter which flourishes in silence – this is very rare.[100] Real presence is too much for us.[101] John Taylor points out time and time again that the trouble with many professional Christians is that they are 'not all there'![102]

To avoid any direct encounter with the living God we relegate God to a separate realm of existence, to a spiritual world disconnected from this world. All forms of dualism, therefore, are naked attempts to escape from God and, simultaneously, from life-giving contact with each other. All forms of dualism strike at the very heart, attacking the very centre of *Christian* faith. For the revelation of God-in-Christ is God-with-us. Emmanuel is the true name of God once-upon-a-time as it is the true name of God always, the name of the one true God who is always and wholly present in every part of creation. God's transcendence is to be found in God's immanence, precisely in the quality of the divine love perceived in God's 'being there for others'. God creates the universe by committing to it utterly, without reserve. It is the divine nature to give itself totally while remaining inexhaustibly itself. The bush burning but not consumed, the widow's inexhaustible cruse of oil, the miraculously multiplying loaves and fishes, the bountiful eucharistic Bread and Wine – these are the true symbols of God's relationship to the created world.[103] And as the rabbis taught, God speaks from a thorn bush to teach us that there is no place where the *shekinah* is not – even in a thorn bush.[104]

The Christian will always say that the cross is the measure of God's self-commitment to the creation. The cross is the price of God's patient, unpossessive friendship towards humankind. 'Its three hours of silence summed up all the long aeons of his watch for Man's return; its loneliness was the desolation of a presence endlessly rebuffed, unrecognised, anonymous; its agony contained his eternal compassion toward the bent world.'[105] The cross affirms that God's forgiveness and acceptance of us is not complacency, for it is the ultimate expression of involvement and responsibility.

> Intense as is his receptivity toward every sin and every pain in every creature, he is present also with vivid awareness towards all beauty, all faith, all achievement. For the joy that is set before him he endures, and his presence is vibrant with triumph and resurrection.
>
> That is the tremendous Presence in the midst of the world from which our first parents hid themselves and from which Cain went forth into loneliness. That is the Presence which Moses knew, eye to eye and face to face, without which the building of the Chosen Community had no significance or attraction. That is the Presence which is promised unto the end of the world to those who go to disciple all the nations. And this alone is ... God's own way of drawing Adam into his embrace and lifting the despoiled and threatened Creation up into his peace[106]

For all this, John Taylor is very clear about the fact that he is not at ease with any view of the encounter between Christianity and other faiths that abandons either of 'the glorious, tattered banners of our long march: "In Christ alone" and "By faith alone"'. As we might expect, however, he puts his own spin on these slogans. Speaking at the CMS Annual School of

Mission in January 1970 he set these two affirmations in a wider context than many who claim to hold to them. The Church has never let 'no salvation outside' stand literally and unmodified. The covenant with Israel is not the only covenant in the Hebrew scriptures. Prior to it we find God's covenant with Noah, embracing all peoples and all creation. God is Lord of every nation's history. The theme of inclusiveness is as much part of the gospel and of church doctrine as exclusiveness.[107] Love's way forward into truth is to trust the convictions of people of faith more than their denials, and always to remember that dialogue belongs to the time of 'not yet'.[108] For 'the name that is above every name is hidden still and Jesus, who never thought equality with God a thing to be grasped, is humbler than his disciple'.[109] Silence and patient waiting have their proper place. The 'fullness of time' may not be yet, and the secret can be kept a little longer if others thereby are more likely to see and love the Christian's gentle Lord.[110] There is a vast difference between proclamation of the gospel and Christian self-assertion. It may well be that 'the more we chatter, the busier we seem, but the farther from God's silence and God's Word'.[111]

> Those who have lost the capacity for listening, who cannot be there for others, are unable even to be truly present to themselves. In their busy self-assertion they never meet themselves; they are distracted, strained, dispersed. Only the silence, only the practice of the presence of God, in sacrament and meditation, in a steady painful flowering of sensitivity to all presences, can restore and integrate so that given-ness can be maintained.[112]

In dialogue, what is called for is 'the listening, responsive, agonising receptivity of the prophet and the poet'.[113] This is, of course, a hard way to travel, much harder than bold and confident assertion of 'the truth'. Nevertheless, it is Christ's own way, and the authentic Christian ambition can be no more and no less than mission in Christ's way and in God's good time.[114] God hastens slowly. When Christians find the grace to persevere in listening openness in obedience to Christ, enchanting new truths come into view. So too do world-views and practices which seem strange, or make no sense, or even revolt our conventional conditioned sensibilities. But if distaste and frustration can be held in check long enough, entry into the real world of another person begins to be possible.

> I shall see past what to me are distasteful rituals, alien symbols and concepts that carry no conviction to the insights they are trying to express. I shall come to appreciate his understanding of what a man is, how he is related to his family, to the dead, to the whole of existence, and to the ultimate reality. And, as a final bestowal, I shall be given access to the dark places of that stranger's world – the things that really make him ashamed or anxious or despairing. And then, at last, I shall see the Saviour and Lord of *that* world, my Lord Jesus, and yet not as I have known him. I shall understand how perfectly he matches all the needs and all the aspirations and all the

insights of that other world – He who is the unique Lord and Saviour of all possible worlds. And I shall worship with a new-found wonder and falteringly start proclaiming him in the new terms which I am just beginning to comprehend.[115]

How painful and disturbing and threatening this will be is only hinted at. John Taylor is always restrained. There is usually a deceptive lightness of touch in his teaching, but we would be unwise to miss the excitement and the passion in the even voice and the measured words.[116] But this is the voice of experience, painfully and patiently acquired, the voice of personal authenticity out of which John Taylor speaks with authority. Authority is about authenticity, as it is about authorship. John Taylor speaks with authority because he authors what he says in personal experience, refusing all pat answers or intellectually and spiritually lazy traditional formulations. He knows in himself that salvation is by revolution, not evolution, that it comes by irruption, by a new creation which is the act of God.[117] It is not so much that Christ is the Word and the Light which have inspired all religious systems, but that Christ is the One who brings each religion to fulfilment through crisis and conversion.[118]

> As the Holy Spirit turns Muslim or Hindu or Marxist eyes towards the living Christ, the half-truths in their traditions of response will be completed, error will be shown up, disobedience condemned, all evasion of God brought to a halt, and his Son crucified afresh.[119]

Out of all this, John Taylor predicts, a new Jesus-centred Hinduism, a new Messiah-centred Islam, a new Christ-directed Communism will be raised up. In case this strikes a false note of imperialism, he insists that in this process a new *Christianized* Christianity will also be born. All in all, John Taylor's clear and confident missionary theology is characterized by an essential humility, a relentless honesty which refuses ever to claim too much. The enemy of faith is always certainty, for certainty is always driven by human fear. Evangelism is never a burden or a chore, and Christ's mission is not another problem besetting the contemporary disciple. In humble confidence we can relax and smile and enjoy our faith.

> A turn of the head bent intent on a task,
> ripple of light, hem of his garment only,
> or lift of the heart suddenly less lonely
> is all the Easter evidence I ask.[120]

Winchester

Look, the kestrels are back on the tower's crest,
not nesting yet but breasting the wafture of air
up the grey cliff, questing remembered bounds
of their green kingdom, sending tenuous
couriers of fear to mark their tribute down.
They ride, glide; a flicker of feathered fire
lifts them higher and still, so still, they mount, they aspire.

Their rock face beckons beneath the changing skies,
milky under the moonrise, scintillant at noontime:
Who shall ascend into the hill of the Lord?
'Climb!' says the stone, 'but first feel with your eyes
the massive weight, the rough male surfaces
hatched and rimpled for joy of the solid fact.
Touch and believe, lay hand to my scars, and climb.'

They who are caught in the lure of the vision of God
endure the lost vision. As they plod
upward, the ridges veil the pure pale summit.
Now the rhythm is all. They hoist and haul
their own dead weight on pinnacles and gullies,
scale the wet shale, cling to the wind-whipped wall
till the iron of the rock be formed in the unsure flesh.

Only then shall the sesame door of grace
show the more excellent way. Enter alone
and see where all was mass now all is space;
no more a mountain, this, but fountains of stone
or files of lifted wings, trecento descants
sprung from a long-sustained gregorian tone.
Let the heart soar through falling flakes of fire,
hover higher and still, so still, mount and aspire.[1]

The kingdom of Wessex was one of the last of the old English states to embrace Christianity. In 635 CE the aged King Cynegils was baptized by Bishop Birinus. At this time the kingdom contained only the regions south of the Thames from the border of Kent as far as the Mendips, covering the modern counties of Oxfordshire and Buckinghamshire. Cynegils at his baptism conferred on the bishop the town of Dorchester-on-Thames, which became the home of the first three bishops of the West Saxons. Coenwalch, the son and successor of Cynegils, learnt Christianity in defeat and exile, but on his restoration he took Birinus as his teacher and brought over his whole kingdom to the faith. At the death of Bishop Birinus in 650 CE, the king invited a Frankish bishop, Agilberct, to succeed him. A few years later the two fell out and the king cut the bishopric of the West Saxons in half, leaving Agilberct at Dorchester and installing one of his own subjects, Wini, at Winchester. This division did not last. Agilberct resigned and left, and Wini was expelled by his master after only three years. Wessex was actually destitute of a bishop when Theodore of Tarsus became Archbishop of Canterbury in 669 CE, and one of his first acts as Primate of All England was to persuade the king to restore Agilberct to his place. This might have happened had not Agilberct already had a better offer, namely the important see of Paris. He refused to return but in his stead sent his nephew Lothere, whom Theodore and Coenwalch consented to receive.

After the death of Coenwalch Wessex fell into decay and disunion for some years. Bishop Hedda of Dorchester moved to Winchester and this remained the seat of the bishops of the West Saxons thereafter. As the years passed two new dioceses were carved out of Winchester, Sherborne and Ramsbury, but after 931 CE the diocesan limits remained fixed for some six hundred years. All through Norman and Plantagenet times the great and wealthy see of Winchester, held by a long series of great prelates, most of whom became chancellors of the realm, preserved the exact limits set in 931.[2]

In 1480 Bishop Rotherham of Lincoln transferred the precincts of Magdalen College, Oxford, to the diocese of Winchester. This transference was confirmed by a Bull of Pope Sixtus IV and the arrangement still subsists. In 1499 the Channel Islands were transferred to Winchester from Salisbury, but the Bishop of Winchester's authority in them seems not to have become fully established until the time of Queen Elizabeth I. In 1845 the Ecclesiastical Commissioners transferred to the See of Canterbury the Surrey parishes of Abingdon and Croydon, and the district of Lambeth Palace. By the same order-in-council the populous regions of South London – including the area near the Priory Church of St Mary Overy in Southwark where the Bishops of Winchester had their London house and their notorious Clink prison – were transferred to the Diocese of London. The dioceses of Southwark and Portsmouth are quite modern creations.

For all this carving up, Winchester remains large, covering Hampshire, West Surrey and the Channel Islands. At the time of Bishop Allison's appointment in 1961, it was estimated that the diocese had a population of three quarters of a million people and 264 benefices. In the Middle Ages Winchester was not only one of the largest but also the wealthiest of English bishoprics. According to a saying attributed to Bishop Edington (1345–66), 'Canterbury had the higher rank, but Winchester had the fuller manger'!

The Bishop of Winchester is traditionally Prelate of the Order of the Garter and one of a small handful of diocesan bishops to have a seat by right in the House of Lords. It is necessary to go a long way back in history to find a bishop actually consecrated for Winchester, as Stephen Gardiner was in 1531 and John Taylor was in 1975, for it is regarded as a see to which bishops who have made their mark elsewhere are translated. According to the biographer of Cyril Garbett, 'it is normally a bishopric in which senior prelates come to rest after more arduous and exacting labours in other dioceses'. Winchester was seen as a reward and something of a rest cure. Even by Garbett's time, however, such comments sound out of date.

> Winchester is a quiet and historic diocese, large in area up to the time of its division in 1927 (and still instinctively retaining something of the sense of being a large diocese), conservative, mainly rural, and, even into Garbett's time, perhaps conspicuously feudal; a diocese with a life and a pattern of its own, upon which it is difficult for a bishop to make any deep personal impression. Although it does not exactly run itself, it does not demand leadership like other dioceses; and Garbett ... being a man of great force of character and tremendous driving power, found this a little baffling.[3]

Until Garbett, Bishops of Winchester had for a thousand years lived far away in Farnham Castle. The bishop was, after all, a great national figure and Farnham was more convenient to London. Bishop Garbett, however, took up residence in the very attractive surviving wing of the palace designed by Sir Christopher Wren for Bishop Morley (1662–4), with its lovely chapel. This house, called Wolvesey, had once been described by Bishop Thorold (1891–5) as 'a residence which it is impossible either to use, repair, or occupy'. To Garbett – who did use, repair and occupy! – the house and garden were a joy, with their proximity to the great cathedral, Winchester College across the street and the beautiful Water Meadows beyond.

Even in 1961, when the Prime Minister's Appointments Secretary wrote to the Archbishop of Canterbury about the vacancy-in-see at Winchester, he thought of it as one of the 'great' dioceses. He echoes Garbett's biographer in stressing that 'Winchester is an extremely conservative place'. It is also 'highly expert at putting up passive resistance to ideas and people it does not like'![4] Although the diocese had made it clear that it wanted another bishop like its present one, both Archbishop Ramsey and the Appointments Secretary favoured seducing the very young Owen Chadwick from a promising academic career into episcopal ministry. The offer was made and, not surprisingly, it took Chadwick the historian some time to decline. Michael Ramsey then decided to sound out Max Warren, notorious for turning down more bishoprics than any man had been offered before.[5] He went out of his way to write him a beguiling letter. This letter reveals a good deal of the Primate's view of the diocese, much of which remained pertinent fifteen years later when John Taylor went to Winchester.

You would have there the pastoral charge of a diocese with very varied needs in town and country, and also the chance of bringing into the leadership of our church at home a closer relation to the Church's whole mission in the world. Could anything be more important than that our church at home should see its mission in this new kind of way?[6]

Max Warren's reply to the archbishop does not survive, but we may assume that he agreed about the need of the Church but did not see himself as the instrument for supplying it, for as usual he declined. So far as Max Warren personally was concerned, something else *was* more important! It would be another fifteen years before a General Secretary of the CMS would move to Winchester and begin to implement something of Archbishop Ramsey's vision.

Nolo episcopari?

When John Taylor was appointed Bishop of Winchester in 1974, he was the first priest to be consecrated for the ancient see in 450 years. Since the English Reformation of the sixteenth century no priest had ever directly become Bishop of Winchester.[7] Every bishop for the previous four centuries had been translated after experience in another diocese, either as diocesan or as suffragan. Winchester is where distinguished episcopal ministries climax, not where they begin. Winchester represents promotion for a bishop who has done well in a less significant place. This fact of history alerts us to something of the stature of John Taylor in the eyes of the Church, and particularly in the judgement of those responsible for making senior episcopal appointments in the Church of England.[8] The point is underlined by the fact that with the appointment of John Taylor's two successors, the centuries-old pattern has reverted to its usual course. The promotion of bishops from diocese to diocese also alerts us to a particularly worldly mind about episcopal sees in England, which traditionally has more to do with historical prestige and national and political significance than with the special needs of any particular diocese.[9]

Historically, the See of Winchester is one of the top five dioceses in rank in the English church – Canterbury, York, London, Durham and Winchester. It is doubtful whether John Taylor would have considered leaving his international missionary post with CMS had he been offered a lesser diocese. Indeed, by the time he accepted Winchester, he had already declined at least two other bishoprics.[10] This, however, is not to suggest that John Taylor himself was ambitious for the purple, or gave much thought to status. It is to suggest that any man accustomed to a position of great influence, able to make a significant contribution to the international mission of the Church in the contemporary world, is not likely to exchange this for a less influential position. It is also to suggest that any man with historical sense (and John Taylor is pre-eminently such a man) and romantic sensibility (and John Taylor is clearly a romantic personality) could not fail to be attracted by the associations of an ancient diocese such as Winchester. A see of saints such as Swithun (852) and Lancelot Andrewes (1619–26), of medieval and renaissance statesmen such as Cardinal Wolsey (1529–30) and Stephen Gardiner (1531–50 and 1553–5) and the see of William of Wykeham (1367–1404), founder of Winchester College and New College Oxford, Winchester in the twentieth century became a training ground for great archbishops – Randall Thomas Davidson, Archbishop of Canterbury, and Cyril Forster Garbett, Archbishop of York. For all this, however, we need to note that the circumstances surrounding John Taylor's acceptance of Winchester are more complex yet. The fact is that he did not move effortlessly from CMS to Winchester. This was no simple promotion, a smart career move. John Taylor had, after all, indicated his intention to resign as General Secretary to the governing body of CMS as early as the start of 1974. His plan was to resign at the end of that year, and this was for him a matter of personal integrity. He felt he had given all he had to give and that he was getting stale. By resigning in this way John Taylor placed himself at considerable risk, trusting that some suitable work would open up but without any guarantee or real idea of what this might be. He was stepping into the unknown future in faith. In many ways this decision involved a return to the uncertainties of the time following his resignation as Warden of Bishop Tucker College. In order for CMS to have time in which to find a suitable replacement the Taylors had to live daily with uncertainty.[11]

Pressure was also on John Taylor not to be a bishop at all. His predecessor's habit of declining bishoprics made any move to a diocese difficult – if not impossible. 'Max was so gloriously resistant to bishoprics', John Taylor remarks wistfully.[12] By continuing as General Secretary for 21 years, Max Warren defined this role as a long-term task of supreme importance for the welfare of the churches. The General Secretary of CMS is in a position of power and influence far greater than almost any individual bishop and, in any case, as a matter of theology and politics, Warren was deeply convinced that the Church should not be governed solely by bishops. The structure of the Church was not to be seen only, even if primarily, in terms of interlocking networks of ecclesiastical provinces.

The Church is not limited to being a collection of dioceses, but is also composed of a loose federation of extra-diocesan and extra-parochial societies, religious orders, communities and fellowships. The CMS international community was undoubtedly one such 'religious order'. Undoubtedly, it is also a significant and strategic one. The call to lead such an order placed the General Secretary in the position of a major religious superior, a position of influence and freedom in the service of the gospel and of the kingdom of God far greater than that enjoyed by any diocesan bishop – even, perhaps, by the Archbishop of Canterbury. Indeed, it has been said that being General Secretary of CMS is the nearest anyone gets in the Church of England to being pope![13] No wonder John Taylor, as Max Warren's chosen successor, felt his own resignation almost as betrayal of an unwritten but generally understood trust.[14] John Taylor felt, although Max Warren gave no hint of it, that his revered predecessor secretly disapproved of him 'succumbing' to a bishopric![15]

Ninety-third bishop

On 14 August 1974 it was announced from 10 Downing Street that Canon John Taylor had been nominated to the Queen as the next Bishop of Winchester. In October a photograph of him appeared in *The Winchester Churchman*, and evidently the editor felt that it called for some explanation: 'Canon Taylor rarely wears the conventional dress of a cleric and at most of the higher councils of the church while others wore their dog collars he wore a soft collar and tie!'

On the day of his appointment John Taylor talked about himself and his plans. Asked how he saw the role of a bishop and what he planned to do in this new ministry, his answer was 'I don't know'. He believed in this answer. It was a true answer, and this true answer was an essential ingredient in his whole approach. How could he know what he might do before learning even the simplest facts about the situation facing him, and discovering for himself something of the style of his immediate predecessor? 'I must begin as a learner. And I hope to remain a learner to the end, because I think that's the only way to stay really alive. It's certainly the best recipe for enjoyment.'

In a church just becoming conversant with the management language of 'setting goals' and 'achievable objectives' and 'five-year strategies', not knowing what to do could be amateurism or worse. But there is an echo of Max Warren here, an echo of his distinctive theology. God is altogether in control of history, but God is altogether beyond human control. God is totally reliable, but God is always doing new and surprising things.[16] Not knowing is central to this particular theological stance. At every moment there must be flexibility, spontaneity, the possibility of free and full response to the Holy Spirit. In any truly Christian form of leadership there must always be openness, space, mobility, room for individual initiatives.

Goals are important, plans and techniques are essential as means to an end, but goals can also bind and trap, hamper and hinder. Goals can give the illusion of progress where there is none, encouraging reliance on human wisdom and trust in human strength. Goal-setting can be a way of quietening our anxiety or feeding our own ambition for success. 'I don't know' is not a casual or unthoughtful remark. It is a deliberate answer, more central to the attitude and action of John Taylor than might immediately be apparent. He must learn the simplest facts about the situation, the diocese, his predecessor and his new colleagues. In other words, and before he attempts anything else, he must begin to 'pay attention to the facts'. There will be no theory from this man independent of the facts. There can be no Christian theology worthy of the name apart from facts. So John Taylor was doing rather more than simply stating the obvious when he said he didn't know what he was going to do as Bishop of Winchester. He was being honest at a much more profound level: 'Disorganisation is the basis of flexibility!'[17]

Ministry, for John Taylor, like discipleship itself, is more about response than control. It involves us in responding as fully as we can to the initiative of God. So it was his policy to respect the abilities of others, to cultivate talent wherever he found it – particularly if it was talent he himself lacked – making friends and asking friends to help him, appointing little bits of himself to work at this or that task. It was his way to 'let the flowers grow' without too much intervention, without forcing – and many flowers *did* grow. 'The Diocese of Winchester didn't fall to pieces because he respected people who could do their job.'[18]

So this initial response was not false humility and not an attempt to avoid the question. Nor did it betray a bland personality, or a timid refusal to express an opinion. Rather more than most, John Taylor, as the son of a bishop and as one who had worked as a colleague of bishops throughout the Anglican world, had obviously thought long and hard about episcopacy. He had his own strong and clear views on what were and what should be the true priorities of bishops in the church. 'One thing's quite clear to me: the first priority and nub of the whole job is to strengthen and encourage the clergy.' This is a revealing way of framing the traditional episcopal role of *pastor pastorum*, pastor to the pastors. Much routine talk by bishops about caring for other priests ignores the fact that the bishop must often be the very last to pastor other pastors, for the simple reason that the bishop has great influence over the future of individual clergy. Power all too often precludes relationships of trust and of vulnerability in the life of the Church. Clergy make their own arrangements for their own care, often outside the system and hierarchy of the Church. To 'strengthen' and to 'encourage' is both more realistic, more urgent and more welcome. Significantly, by the term 'clergy' John Taylor deliberately includes other full-time, professional ministers of the Church. This is now routine, but was by no means fashionable then. 'The moral and spiritual support of all such people will be my first and main care.'[19]

Clearly, this bishop-designate knew at first hand something of the pain, the bewilderment, the hopes and fears experienced by clergy in a rapidly changing church and world. The struggles begin not at his door but in himself, in his own authentic engagement with his society and world. The confidence and zest of young clergy will be his special concern, together with all other ministers, all those baptized men and women who give themselves fully and professionally to Christian ministry and mission.

Those who are not ordained and who work in all sorts of supposedly 'secular' employment are clearly recognized and honoured as pastors and prophets too – vigorous, wise, the hope of the future. Christ is being uplifted, he says, by ordinary people – mothers, social workers, nurses, teachers, farmers, shop stewards, journalists. This truth is acknowledged gratefully, and celebrated.

In his last years at CMS headquarters John Taylor got quite involved with groups of younger clergy and diocesan clergy schools, and was quick to realize how deeply some of them were suffering in a time of rapid transition. Clergy were increasingly working in concert with other professionals – social workers, welfare workers, psychologists and counsellors. For some this involved an identity crisis, involving marginalization and threat of redundancy. Certainly, clergy were experiencing the effects of widespread confusion and uncertainty about their role in a changed situation. Changing expectations from within the Church they served also made leadership in the Christian community increasingly more delicate and difficult. The best priests, in John Taylor's view, were too honest to duck the questions and settle for a glib defence of the status quo. He honoured them in their integrity. 'I would like to be able to share the burden and bewilderment with them and perhaps to help them to recapture, if they have lost it, their confidence in the Gospel and their zest for the mission.'

Worried that he might be sounding too clergy-centred, John Taylor went on to make it absolutely clear that the clergy are *not* the Church. The priest stands at the heart of the Christian company to serve and to equip the Church for the work of service and mission. This, however, is more than a chaplaincy role to those already gathered around the Lord's table. The priest is at the centre of a more generous and inclusive community. Those outside the circle must be drawn in, and this will never happen while we think we know both the questions people are asking and the right answers.

> We need to call artists and playwrights and poets to show us the truth. We must make room for the under-25s in our committees and councils – and that may mean making our agendas relevant enough to claim their attention. We must learn to see how frequently Christ is being uplifted by mothers and social workers, nurses and teachers, farmers and shop stewards and journalists. They are the ones who can help to make the Church a source of strength and a rallying point for action.[20]

All this is seen in the most generous of contexts, indeed in the context of the entire global village.

> I believe that one source of confidence, and certainly of zest, is a knowledge of what is happening in the rest of the world. I have been so incredibly lucky in having so many contacts with the world Church and I hope I can share some of that with the diocese. Christians in Hampshire, East Dorset

and the Channel Islands will be more confident and imaginative if they see themselves as part of the ecumenical world Church engaging in world mission. This doesn't mean keeping our courage up with a success story from some other country. It means learning from tiny hard-pressed Churches how to be a minority without getting depressed about it and how to deal positively with failure.[21]

It was and is still a delicate thing to acknowledge the fact that the established Church of England, the ancient Diocese of Winchester, indeed Christianity itself, is now a religious minority. Christendom is over and will not come again. The issue now is not to live off the glorious past or pretend things will get better, but to learn from tiny hard-pressed churches all over the world how to live as a minority without getting depressed, to find God in our actual circumstances, to experience the power of God in failure. How can the Church pay attention to the facts and live joyfully, courageously and prophetically now? One way will be 'to call artists and playwrights and poets to show us the truth'. The Creator Spirit is not, after all, confined to the Church, inhibited by its hallowed structures or tied only to the traditional channels of grace. The go-between God is making connections in and for those who can name the name of Christ, as well as in those who cannot or dare not. We Christians have no monopoly on truth, no monopoly on the Spirit. We do not have all the answers. We need others, we need artists. Not only the bishop is to be and remain to the end a learner; so must the whole Christian company if it is to stay really alive, if it is to enjoy its mission.

By the turn of the year, with his episcopal ordination still a month away, John Taylor had thought in more detail about his approach. He is well aware that this is the first time in almost four and a half centuries that 'an untried, newly-minted bishop' has been given to Winchester, and the last, Stephen Gardiner, could hardly be considered untried, having 'learned statecraft in Wolsey's court and King Henry's council chamber'. While John Taylor confesses ignorance about the details of being a bishop, coming 'completely untried in the administration of the parochial and synodical structures of our Church', nevertheless the learner is already making some decisions.[22]

The first of these decisions is that he will study with care the minutes of meetings, but will not chair diocesan committees. This is not because he feels incompetent to do so, nor yet because he undervalues administration, but because he believes a bishop must work at a *personal* level with people and have time and energy for this. This may seem a bit simplistic, for careful administration *is* ministry, it does care for people and cannot be avoided without hurting people. He is, nevertheless, sending out clear signals about priorities. Basically, he is more interested in individuals than in committees.

John Taylor expects to move from one environment of collaboration to another and looks forward to working with colleagues, particularly senior staff – assistant bishops, archdeacons and the dean of the cathedral. He says he is thankful that synodical government has reduced solo episcopal decision-making. At a time when all authority is suspect, he shares the general unease about authority, but is ready to exercise it for the good of the Church. 'I don't enjoy that sort of authority, but I have learned to exercise it, when I have to, without fuss, as a way of serving the fellowship.'[23] *Episcope*, after all, is hardly novel for him. At CMS he has been engaged in oversight of this kind for long years. But it will be easier without a heavy pontifical image. To this end, he wants to be 'The Right Reverend the Bishop of Winchester' and to be addressed as 'Bishop', rather than claim the historical prerogative and be the *Lord* Bishop of Winchester. He nurtures no ambition to become anyone's Lord! 'I would like to be thought of as a working shepherd rather than a prince bishop.'[24]

Titles and symbols are important indicators of reality. The new bishop announces that he will be happy to wear whatever liturgical vestments are preferred in a parish, but that a working shepherd looks different to a mitred prelate. As he imagined himself in episcopal rig, John Taylor rightly realized that he was about to become highly conspicuous for the second time in his ministry. In the same way that a newly ordained deacon wearing a clerical collar in public for the first time feels that she is the centre of everyone's attention, new bishops can feel very self-conscious. And it was not the pectoral cross, the episcopal ring and the pastoral staff, or even the purple, which constituted the problem. In terms of symbolic significance, it was the lesser but far more obvious item, namely the hat! This alarming prospect led John Taylor to make one of his most bizarre and well-publicized suggestions. Could his mitre be carried before him rather than worn on his head? Why? Because the whole Church shares in the royal priesthood of Christ.

> I do not deny that it has been perfectly proper and obviously convenient for the Church as a whole to vest this corporate function in the Bishop or in the ordained priesthood. But at certain times it becomes vitally important for the whole fellowship to remind itself of the awesome responsibility for the world which, in Christ, it is called to carry. I am convinced that this is one of those times.[25]

Undoubtedly, his reading of the signs of the times was accurate enough. Again, we have a theology of attention to the state of the world, of attending to the facts, of listening to what the Spirit is saying to the churches. It was not the analysis that was problematic but the application. It was simply not understood. A mitre carried in front of a bishop and placed on the altar as a symbol of 'the cosmic priesthood of Christ' seems ridiculous, and the author of the idea immediately becomes something of a joke. At the very least, this new bishop must be eccentric – which probably made him more interesting! The evidence suggests that John Taylor was well aware of at least the most likely misrepresentation.

Please understand me. This has nothing whatever to do with old ideas of 'high' or 'low' church. But this is peculiarly 'my thing', and I ask you to accept it as an idiosyncrasy, if you like, in the hope that with time it will take on more meaning for all of us.[26]

Some just thought the bishop was a fool. 'Bishop's a bloody fool; wear your hat on your head and nobody notices it, have it carried on a cushion and every idiot sees it', said one typically bluff member of the diocese.[27] Others didn't care, or just thought it all a bit silly. Others again imagined that this genuinely humble man was orchestrating greater attention for himself rather than less. Others again disbelieved his explanation, convinced that he was just another low church Protestant. The folly of the mitre is the earliest example of the new Bishop of Winchester failing to connect with his constituency and seriously expecting ordinary people to be interested in the theological reasoning behind his actions. To his credit, at his enthronement he saw at once the foolishness of his directive, and wore the mitre on his head thereafter. The cushion and its chaplain were never heard of again. Even so, whoever was taking all this in must have concluded that something better than a dull time was to be had with such a man in St Swithun's chair.

Consecration and enthronement

On 6 December 1974 the Dean and General Chapter of Winchester duly elected the Crown's nominee, John Vernon Taylor. He would be consecrated in Westminster Abbey on 31 January 1975, the first bishop consecrated by the newly enthroned 101st Archbishop of Canterbury, his father's old friend Donald Coggan. The preacher was Desmond Tutu, later Bishop of Johannesburg, later still Archbishop of Cape Town and Primate of South Africa. The enthronement in Winchester Cathedral was set for Saturday, 8 February, by the Archdeacon of Canterbury, who has the right of enthroning all bishops in the southern province of the Church of England.

The bishop-designate had naturally been in close contact with the Dean of Winchester about the details of the inauguration of his episcopal ministry. John Taylor had preferences of his own drawn from experience, and these were tempered by sensitivity to local custom. Michael Stancliffe, Dean of Winchester, was just the man to research the history of Winchester enthronement ceremonies, and it was he who reminded the people of the diocese of past customs, warning them to expect some changes. In this he was obviously already a sympathetic collaborator with John Taylor. 'We shall be concerned to make it more obvious than in the past that we are welcoming and setting in his *cathedra* a pastor rather than putting on his throne a prelate.'[28]

This meant there would be a minimum of legal formalities. The bishop would not need to knock on the doors with his crozier, seeking admission.

The new Bishop will not find the Cathedral doors shut in his face and have to bang on them in order to get in. If there is any regret at the dropping of a venerable and picturesque tradition, it should be said that this door-knocking is only of recent origin. It was only at the beginning of this century that it began to be used at the enthronements of English Bishops, and so far as I can discover the rubric requiring it at Winchester appeared for the first time in the Order of Service for the enthronement of Bishop Garbett in 1932.[29]

Dropping the title 'Lord', together with colourful but meaningless customs like the door-knocking, must have seemed radical in 1975. Parish tradition, it is said, usually dates back to the last vicar, and so it can be with dioceses. In an extremely conservative institution like the Church, memory is brief but strong. Thirty and more years after this Winchester enthrone-ment, bishops at their installations commonly continue to knock three times on closed cathedral doors. John Taylor is unusual in always being unafraid to ask 'Why?' Although he loves beauty and pageantry as much as anyone, ritual must always answer this question. What does it mean? What does it signify? What are we saying? Ritual or lack of it always says something, making a statement about attitude and belief. Sacramental, bodily acts tell a story. In doing this or not doing that we express ourselves. The question is always 'Which story shall we tell?'[30]

So it was that Winchester's 93rd bishop came to his cathedral Church.

It was noted that he walked bareheaded in the pale winter sunshine, wearing a simple green cope, carrying a real shepherd's crook in his left hand. One of his chaplains was the Bishop of Namirembe in Uganda and the other was the Asia Secretary of CMS. The new bishop made his way through the nave and choir of the great cathedral – the longest nave of any European cathedral – to kneel in silence and solitude before the high altar. Surrounded by so great a cloud of witnesses, with so many expectations focused on him, John Taylor needed the prayer of every heart. In the dean's words, the ceremony had been arranged to allow the clergy and people of the diocese

> to welcome with warmth and encouragement one who must sit in a somewhat lonely seat and who must carry the vital responsibility of giving them pastoral care and leadership in the years ahead when, under God, the Church is going to need such care and vision to no ordinary degree.[31]

Instead of asking redundant questions about 'Who comes in the name of the Lord?', the dean read words chosen by the new bishop from T. S. Eliot. He read as only Michael Stancliffe could – with so much intensity of feeling and with great quietness.[32]

> If you came this way,
> Taking any route, starting from anywhere,

> At any time or at any season,
> It would always be the same: you would have to put off
> Sense and notion. You are not here to verify,
> Instruct yourself, or inform curiosity
> Or carry report. You are here to kneel
> Where prayer has been valid.[33]

Only at one point in the ceremony which then unfolded was the bishop vested in his ceremonial cope and mitre, and that was for the actual seating in the *cathedra*, his chair as chief pastor and teacher and celebrant of the sacraments in the Diocese of Winchester.

His enthronement sermon, traditionally seen as the new bishop's manifesto, setting the tone and direction of his episcopate, called the Church to uncompromising engagement with the real world. Like Max Warren before him, distinguishing between two types of Christianity as 'Rome' and 'Iona', John Taylor contrasted the Christianity of 'Jerusalem' and 'Galilee'. Faith is to be lived out at 'both ends of the line', at home and at work, in Winchester and in London, in Reading or Southampton.[34] In other words, faith is for Monday through to Saturday as well as for Sunday. Faith is equally essential in 'Galilee' as in 'Jerusalem'. There must be no artificial division between worship and work, liturgy and life. One might meet the crucified and raised Christ anywhere, usually when he is least expected, just when he is most needed.

> Jerusalem is all the traditional centres of our religious observance – the village Churches, this great cathedral, the Eucharist shared Sunday after Sunday, the Christmas carols, the Easter flowers, the confirmation class, the wedding bells, new names on the baptismal roll, old names on the war memorial, the PCC and the vicarage fete, Christian Aid week and the Week of Prayer for Christian Unity. Everything, in fact, that most of us mean by 'the Church'. It has to do with home, and coming home. When we talk about 'our Church' we don't mean the one we can see from the office window. This is one end of the commuter line. At the other we are somewhere else, but shall we also be someone else or Christ's same disciple? Galilee is the secular world, where people are expected to keep religion out of it. What of this Galilee? Many of us who have known and loved our Lord for many years in the Jerusalem of our private religious life are in need of a further and deeper conversion to the Christ of Galilee. The Church as a whole still prefers to meet Jesus Christ behind the closed doors of its own weekend Jerusalem, and does not want to find him alive in the Galilee of the job, of politics and of international affairs.[35]

Those listening were invited to join the bishop in prayer each new day – 'before you go to work or while you are travelling there'. The prayer suggested for this purpose captures all that is vital in John Taylor's spirituality, and connects with Max Warren and the whole tradition of missionary concern represented by the CMS. It is beautiful but plain, lovely without being archaic – a classical John Taylor composition.

> Lord Jesus Christ,
> alive and at large in the world,
> help me to follow and find you there today,
> in the places where I work,
> meet people,
> spend money,
> and make plans.
> Take me as a disciple of your Kingdom,
> to see through your eyes,
> and hear the questions you are asking,
> to welcome all men with your trust and truth,
> and to change the things that contradict God's love
> by the power of the cross
> and the freedom of your spirit.
> Amen.[36]

A new chapter in the life of the Church in the Diocese of Winchester was beginning, one that rejoiced in history and acknowledged past splendour and influence, but had no intention of living there. This stance is firm but gentle. There is also sensitivity to what some in this vast congregation may begin to feel, not least the faithful clergy present who are of necessity more Jerusalem-bound than the people of God they serve and empower for ministry and mission. John Taylor goes out of his way to make sure he is not misunderstood by those he needs as brothers and collaborators. No bishop can work creatively if his clergy fail to catch the vision or refuse to co-operate. Collegiality is of the essence in any healthy diocese. Persuasion is the only way, for the Christian bishop cannot use force.

> In my enthusiasm for the living Christ who is waiting to be encountered at the other end of the line, do I seem to undervalue the traditional role of the parish Churches at this end? That is not at all my intention. It is in our 'Jerusalem' of Sunday worship and local Church fellowship that we re-enact and re-affirm the fundamentals of our faith. In that sense we in our mission, like the Apostles in theirs, must begin at Jerusalem. But in another sense Jerusalem comes into her own as the place for celebrating the things that God has done elsewhere. The prayers and confessions of a Sunday Eucharist take on a new pungency when they make mention of the difficulties or opportunities facing particular members of the congregation in their weekday world. The praise and thanksgiving are far more vivid when the company of friends rejoices over some breakthrough, some miracle of the risen Lord, which one of their number has reported from the difficult world of work.[37]

Little England

The move in 1974 from being General Secretary of the CMS to becoming Bishop of Winchester was for John Taylor actually the reverse of what such an experience would be for most. It was a transition into a smaller world. The prestige of this venerable see in the Church of England was one thing, but what the transition really meant for an international missionary statesman, used to moving on the world stage, accustomed to thinking globally, was that he was now largely confined to the peculiarities and particularities of one diocese. There would, of course, be national work to be done as a member of the House of Bishops, and with the Doctrine Commission, and the occasional missionary conference or international journey, but in future these would be exceptional rather than routine.

The physical differences between CMS headquarters in the heart of London and the beautiful and venerable, but very rural, bishop's palace in Winchester could hardly be more striking. The General Secretary of CMS had an unparalleled vantage point from which to exercise his ministry. London, certainly in Max Warren's day and still to a great extent in John Taylor's, was one of the great centres of world power and the focal point for the British commonwealth of nations. The General Secretary headed one of the most efficiently organized units within the world-wide Anglican Communion of churches. He was first among equals in a closely knit cabinet of colleagues, departmental assistants and advisers, secretaries and typists. He was in easy touch with editors and publishers and free of the statutory duties that have to be performed by holders of an episcopal or parochial charge.

Max Warren 'remained firm in the conviction that his own particular call was to serve as leader of a great missionary band rather than as overseer of a great diocesan institution'. He 'rejoiced in the splendour of this calling and stayed within it until, as he believed, the order came for him to step aside and allow another to take his place'.[38] John Taylor intentionally left all this behind when he accepted appointment to Winchester. He admits to beginning to worry that he could not sustain the demands of CMS much longer, that he was becoming stale and beginning to repeat himself, although there is little or no evidence that such personal questionings were shared by his collaborators.[39] More significantly, perhaps, his mind was made up because he felt the need to put into practice at local level what he had been learning from others around the world and what he had been advocating at home and abroad. Moving to Winchester as diocesan bishop would be the test of credibility for these ideas. He felt he could no longer point others in what he considered to be the right direction without travelling that way himself. It was a matter of integrity, a turning point in the working out of his priestly vocation.

In such an equation the view from London is one thing. What of the realized result, waking up to the tranquil sounds of the Winchester water meadows instead of the dull roar of the metropolis? Obviously, it was all more private and less professional. For the first time in many years, John Taylor found himself working from home, with no staff except a secretary. Gone was his public office, an environment where he was surrounded and stimulated by close colleagues. It would be some time before a Domestic Chaplain was employed. The isolation, the privacy and the quiet must have been startling and baffling. Partnership House near Waterloo Station in south London is home to experts in various fields, all of them committed to a common cause. Some of John Taylor's colleagues were known across many years and some were close personal friends. He was supported and stimulated and encouraged here. His special gifts were valued and set free. He could even be bullied when that became necessary. At his fingertips he had all the resources he needed to think and dream and write – expert staff to administer the organization, a well stocked library, all the latest technology in terms of communication. The fact that his chaplain at Wolvesey had to walk down the road for five minutes to the Diocesan Office to photocopy a document is a good symbol of what John Taylor had given up.[40] Professionalism has been replaced, absurdly, by amateur theatricals.

He was on his own now, left to his own devices and resources. No one told him how to be a bishop. He inherited very little in terms of an efficient or comprehensive archive, and all the appurtenances of his office conspired to isolate him from those best placed to help. The word of the bishop was more likely to close down a conversation, where the word of the general secretary was inclined to provoke debate. There were no old friends here who could tell him he was being stupid. Within a diocese, no one can with impunity criticize or castigate the episcopal monarch. Rather than being first among equals, he now had no equal. The City of Winchester is really a small country town, beautifully sited in rural Hampshire, surrounded by quiet villages. Everywhere the bishop looked was history, a sense of more yesterdays than tomorrows. Often, of course, this past was glorious, moving, inspiring, but how to connect with the present, and how to envisage the future? How did the hallowed stones of his 900-year-old cathedral look from the housing estates and factories of Basingstoke, or the slums of Southampton? Was it just another glorious concert hall to the wealthy London commuter set living in cosy Hampshire villages?

Liturgist, teacher and preacher

It is impossible to think of the history of England, its political and royal history, its ecclesiastical and academic and cultural history, without thinking also of Bishops of Winchester. They have been great statesmen, friends of monarchs, lords spiritual of the realm who wielded immense political power – officiating at coronations, founding colleges and schools, commanding armies, judging and imprisoning, even executing. The

Bishop of Winchester's own Clink prison in south London was once sufficiently notorious for 'clink' to become a generic term for any prison.

An event some months after John Taylor's installation is symbolic of the position in which he now found himself, and shows his imaginative ability to use the past as an opportunity for ministry in the present. In the summer he was welcomed by Winchester College *Ad Portas*, at the gate. Literally, the ceremony took place in the shadow of the gate built by his great predecessor William of Wykeham in the fourteenth century. He was addressed in Latin by the prefect, who referred to him as 'a worthy successor to a long line of famous men'. The bishop replied in Latin. It was all very traditional, but was it the first time a Bishop of Winchester had taken this opportunity to discuss four-letter words?

> The most esoteric of all professionals is, of course, the English gentleman, which is why the sons of English gentlemen have for so long been sent to this College to learn Latin. Even the Devil, it seems, has to be conjured or driven out in Latin, which is natural, seeing he is, according to Milton, the best known of English gentlemen. The evidence of his being an Old Wykehamist is mainly circumstantial and is contested by the heads of some other places of learning.[41]

The bishop went on to compare the use of Latin with 'the barbaric words of the Angles and Saxons', and then set out to explore the use of 'four-letter words'!

> It is also true that only he who possesses a Latin dictionary may discuss without shamelessness certain anatomical processes which coarser Anglo-Saxons describe in shocking four-letter words. They are shocking, of course, because they are *meant* to be shocking. Small boys use them to make someone jump. And every time they do this they are unwittingly re-enacting the diurnal underground movement of the rough Anglo-Saxons against their respectable and urbane rulers. Used in this way, four-letter words are vehicles not of sexuality but of rage. This raises the fascinating question: why do adults use these expletives when they are raging alone; some of them, in fact, such as bishops, only when they are alone? With whom are we angry? We are raging against the nature of things, against the inconvenience of the universe, or, in one word, against God. Indeed, we make the object of our anger quite explicit by combining the shocking Anglo-Saxon words with the names of the Deity. Significantly, we call these words 'oaths', and the use of them we call 'swearing', and to swear an oath means literally to invoke God to witness what we are saying. We are much more angry with God than we dare admit, and we want Him to know it, most of all when we deny His existence. We all resemble the little child who asked his atheist parents: 'Does God know we don't believe in Him?' And it is the peculiar belief of Christians that God has done more with our antagonism than He could ever do with our polite approval. For love and

anger walk hand in hand, and the opposite of love is not hatred, but indifference.

As this quirky beginning may suggest, one of John Taylor's real achievements as bishop was his exceptional ability to get alongside people on the fringe of the Church or right outside, and particularly young people. Sometimes this was to talk simply about life issues rather than anything overtly religious. Here he could touch on profound realities where it could be seen that there is no divide between spiritual and secular. At other times he discovered his chance to name the Name, but doing so in such novel and unexpected ways that hardened sceptics were pleasantly surprised, helping to create the possibility of a hearing for the gospel.[42] Here is an early example of this rare ability among indifferent or hostile adolescents, displaying the confidence and lightness of touch that he longed to encourage in other clergy.

In his own cathedral he was a distinguished preacher among distinguished preachers, as his sermons for the great festivals of the Christian year and other special occasions demonstrate. Carefully prepared and crafted, they are models of the preacher's art, revealing John Taylor's sensitivity to the occasion, his theological insight and poetic sensibility. Such preaching is the diocesan bishop's most public teaching role, when he appears naturally as principal speaker at Christian festivals, civic commemorations and special diocesan, county or national events. Here he must articulate the church's voice as its first and foremost representative. To do so without pomposity, freshly, saying unexpected – and, therefore memorable – things, provoking real thought and reflection in his listeners, is all too rare a gift.

Most of a bishop's preaching and teaching, however, takes place away from the limelight of the cathedral pulpit in other and more humble settings – at ordinary Sunday Eucharists in tiny village churches, or when he administers the sacrament of confirmation to teenagers in parish or school. John Taylor is not sure that he was ever really accepted in the diocese, but the evidence appears to belie this unease.[43] As chief pastor and preacher in parishes, it is clear that he was much loved.[44] If he talked over peoples' heads at times, at least they knew he took them seriously enough not to talk down to them. People were invariably treated as adults, capable of facing the truth and needing to take responsibility for working out their own faith with fear and trembling. They were not fobbed off as infants whose 'simple' faith could be easily unsettled or destroyed. It was clear, too, that he took preaching seriously enough to lavish care and attention on the exercise of this ministry and often the poetry of his language and the passion he brought to the task moved people. It seems that his sermons were often something of a distinctive variation on the classical three-point sermon. First, there was the part written at home in Winchester; second, the part written in the back of the car as he was driven to the church; and

1. John with parents, Irene and Ralph.

2. John aged four with mother and sister Aileen.

3. Marriage, October 1940.

4. Family at Mukono, 1953 or 1954. Clockwise from top right: John, Joanna, Veronica, Peter and Peggy.

5. The warden of Mukono with an ordinand and his family in the training village.

6. Farewell from CMS, late 1974 or early January 1975.

7. Before the Enthronement. Winchester, 8 February 1975.

8. John at his Enthronement.

9. The 93rd Bishop
of Winchester with
one of the flock.

10. Visiting Pope Paul VI. Typically, the Bishop presented the Pope with a recording
by Winchester Cathedral Choir.

11. Parish visit. The Bishop of Winchester with his chaplain, Ron Diss.

12. Pilgrims. John Taylor and chaplain Ron Diss walking from Dorchester to Winchester 1979, 1300 years after Bishop Hedda relocated the See city.

13. Peggy and John with Ugandan priest in Britain.

14. Diamond wedding anniversary, October 2000. From left to right: Peggy, Peter, John, Veronica and Joanna.

third, the bit created on the spur of the moment in the pulpit, in the very act of preaching.[45] Sometimes he enjoyed himself so much in his parish teaching role that he preached more than once on the same occasion, saying a few more words after communion![46] For confirmations John Taylor used the technique of most busy bishops: he had one or two sermons which were used again and again in a variety of settings. He began with an idea which developed and grew as he preached it over and over. Sometimes his chaplain had to tell him it was time for something new – the original idea was fine, but the sermon was now too long.[47] Nevertheless, because the people loved him they forgave him much.

As we have already seen, there was always about John Taylor as teacher what might be called the surprise factor. In 1976 the Synod of the Diocese of Winchester did a typical thing. By overwhelming majority vote it condemned what it called a 'sex film of the life of Christ'. Only after the vote did the bishop express his own views and they cannot have been entirely palatable to his hearers, not only because he agreed with those who preferred to let truth fend for itself, but because of his surprising approach to the questions raised.

> What we should learn from this is that whenever the evil in man proceeds beyond a normal point, it comes to bear upon Christ. And when it comes to bear on Christ, we should not simply leap to the defence but try to learn; to perceive what suffering and shame is saying.[48]

In his view, what the church should be objecting to is not the film, but a sex-obsessed evaluation of human beings in general. Films of this kind are based on the assumption that what is called a sex life is an autonomous life, that it can be isolated from every other aspect of bodily existence. Instead of saying something valuable about human beings, films can blaspheme against the essential sacredness of human beings. 'Perhaps we needed it to come to rest on our Lord before we saw the affront of it wherever it is done.'[49]

There was also unusual candour in John Taylor's willingness to expose his own weaknesses and the imperfection of his own family to help the church think more clearly and Christianly about marriage, divorce and desire. Faith and life negotiate as personal experience struggles with received truth. Christianity traditionally knows two states of life: marriage and celibacy. This bishop, however, refuses to dismiss couples living together before marriage or between marriages as sinful or simply wrong. As a marriage celebrant he knows that many couples who live together before marriage have the best chance of making good marriages. As a father he knows that his divorced son should not marry again just to meet some societal or ecclesiastical measure of respectability. Asked if he has himself been tempted to be unfaithful in the four decades of his own marriage, John Taylor pauses – the report says there was a silence – but he then risks honesty. It is, nevertheless – and no doubt visualizing the possible newspaper headlines! – cautious honesty. At times he has been tempted to be unfaithful, just as this is probably true of all couples. 'I have felt tempted to have at least close physical contact with a woman. I have felt it quite hard to say no, that's not on.' [50] In all this there is concern for those who find themselves in complex and compromising situations, and the free acknowledgement that life is no simpler for him than for anyone else. We can also see clearly in John Taylor how genuine pastoral concern triumphs over the temptation to lay down hard and fast rules designed to keep the ecclesiastical establishment happy. We must never underestimate the subtle pressure on bishops within the purple club to run a tight ship, to hold the line, inevitably giving the safe agreed public answer.

There is not much evidence available about his liturgical leadership. He does seem to have made it his habit to preside at the Eucharist regularly every week in his cathedral Church, and to be regularly present at other celebrations of the liturgy and the divine office. This, together with his private tours of the cathedral for dinner guests and friends, demonstrates the power of this ancient sanctuary for a man of John Taylor's sensibility. His personal and public devotion to the real presence of the living Christ in a place where prayer has been valid for so long is unquestioned. We know that in cathedral and parish Church he conformed, as he promised to do on the day of his appointment, with current liturgical usage. This meant that he could be presiding at Solemn High Mass in full pontificals one day and standing at a simple table in an alb and stole the next. He might be receiving life vows in a convent in Catholic splendour this Sunday and preaching at Evensong in convocation robes in a quiet village church next Sunday. We also know that he did this with the greatest possible integrity. In other words, unlike many Anglican bishops, he didn't simply allow himself to be dressed up or dressed down according to the whim of the vicar. He tried to enter into the spirit of the occasion, struggling to understand in himself why this or that liturgical practice – from the most elaborate to the most bare performance – meant so much to these particular people. Into their experience John Taylor would try to enter in order to worship with them fully in their own way. In some Anglo-Catholic parishes he surprised those who didn't understand his gentle sincerity at all by knowing details like how to bless incense in Latin. [51] He was human enough to enjoy the joke when the self-satisfied and pompous were caught napping.

Just as he was concerned to bring to life the daily and weekly liturgies, it is clear too that he was at pains to make episcopal services live with all their inherent dynamic power. At confirmation he would question each candidate individually and do all he could to connect the ceremony with their actual experience of life, taking endless pains in terms of preparing them for the administration of the sacrament and talking with their parents. [52] Indeed, he was capable of startling parents with his own passionate authority. At Winchester College he once told the parents, 'If your boys do as I have told them they will be like wild birds; in the name of God, do not cage them!'[53] With ordinations his policy was that you would be made deacon or ordained priest in the cathedral by the bishop himself, but usually not both. The suffragan bishops would preside at the other ordination in the parish or school where you were appointed to minister. This kept the diocesan and the cathedral focus on the one hand, living links with the catholicity of the Church, while acknowledging the importance of the local Church and the area bishops on the other.[54] This policy also meant that his assistant bishops were treated as valued episcopal colleagues, given real authority by him, rather than mere purple curates.

Desktop ministry

John Taylor's inherited secretary was one valuable link with his predecessor. Mary Tomsen's career had been devoted to episcopal secretarial work, first at Lambeth Palace and later with Bishop Allison at Wolvesey. Naturally, she was accustomed to particular routines and had clear ideas about how the work of a diocesan bishop should be done. Falkner Allison no doubt fitted her image of what a bishop ought to be rather better than John Taylor. It is sometimes said that Falkner Allison was the last of the prince-bishops, punctilious, generous, scrupulous. By contrast, it turned out that the day-to-day grind of being a bishop simply didn't appeal to John Taylor in the same way.[55] Mary Tomsen expected to work closely with the bishop, dealing in a business-like way with the office work, albeit in the seclusion of his house rather than as the central department of a public diocesan office. She thought the bishop's chaplain was best seen and not heard, regarding any attempt to exercise the role of personal assistant as an intrusion between herself and 'her bishop'. It was the time of the BBC version of *Barchester Towers*, so it comes as little surprise that she christened one chaplain Mr Slope![56] At least there was no chance of Peggy Taylor being cast as Mrs Proudie! In his secretary's opinion, John Taylor 'didn't deal with his correspondence as he ought'.[57] Knowing intimately the ways of the court of an English bishop, Mary Tomsen had worked for bishops who were all establishment figures, institutional men who knew their place and their role in reasonably straightforward terms. This is not the best preparation for finding oneself working for a dreamer, a poet, a temperamental artist, some sort of strange creative genius. John Taylor is a deeply un-institutional man at the heart of the religious establishment, the author of *Enough is Enough* and yet simultaneously at home with the local aristocracy, a man passionately concerned to do things well but responding rather lightly to received routine.

One of the reasons why John Taylor seems not to have been a good administrator at Winchester is surely that like most bishops in the English system he was left too much on his own, too isolated in episcopal splendour, with too many trivial matters finding their way on to his desk. One chaplain has an abiding memory of

> John sitting behind his desk, with a dictaphone in his hand, painstakingly dictating an extraordinarily long letter where a short one would have done, thinking hard about every word, with piles of paper all around him which he wouldn't let me take away and sort out. He had to get really desperate, and be ill, before one could say 'Do you think I might deal with a few of those?' But he wouldn't learn from it. When he was better again he'd go back to the same working method, and one couldn't break that.[58]

The chaplain was, of course, too junior to break the pattern, but for John Taylor there was also a deeply felt pastoral issue at stake. In his view, everyone should be treated carefully and personally by the bishop himself. No one should be fobbed off with a two-liner from the chaplain. It is sad that this dilemma was not better resolved, for it is not impossible to develop sufficient trust in colleagues that they can deal with all sorts of important matters with the bishop's knowledge and expressing the bishop's concern. Those who knew John Taylor best could see even from a distance that this was a besetting sin on his part. Max Warren knew that he had always been bad at devolving work, and his judgement was that 'in a diocese it can very easily destroy the wonderful contribution he has to make'.[59]

Much of his failure as an administrator, however, was really born of frustration that he no longer had leisure to write. John Taylor was never happier than when he was writing, but the life of a bishop turned out to be too fragmented to produce the concentration necessary for sustained work of any value. 'Prophets need empty spaces and empty hours in which to gain their perspectives.'[60] *Episcope* means not just administrative oversight, but the spiritual gift of 'seeing the whole' and relating each of the parts to the whole. 'It is a co-ordinating ministry.'[61] Ironically, episcopal life was so fragmented as to inhibit this essential charism almost entirely, so that the bishop's correspondents sometimes got the letter the bishop needed to write rather than the one they needed to receive! A routine request for someone to be licensed to administer Holy Communion might well be answered with a five-page letter outlining the bishop's current thinking on lay ministry, because he needed to get something on paper. 'He'd sit there with the dictaphone, struggling to write this letter that no one needed to receive, but he needed to write, because he hadn't got time to write a book!'[62]

Even before he left London and CMS, John Taylor hit upon the idea of monthly articles in *The Winchester Churchman* after the pattern of his *CMS Newsletters*. Taking the title from the ruins of London House, city home to the Bishops of Winchester for centuries, they would form a series called 'Rosewindow'. Among the warehouses of Southwark, all that remains of

London House is the wall of the banquet hall, with a rose window long empty of its glass. Here is another example of contemporary reality and historical glory intersecting creatively in the new bishop's mind. The present is a long way from the past, but the two are not completely divorced. How shall a nostalgic Church find ways to live now and to speak the good news now, and not only to itself but to an indifferent world? The rose window is an image of the globe of the world, of the cosmos which is God's creation and care, and it dates from a time when the Church was in no doubt about its universal vocation. As such, it is precisely the symbol the new bishop needs.

From the beginning, then, John Taylor determined to attempt something more substantial in these articles than the usual bishop's letter to the diocese.

> I would like to open a window on the wider world from which we 'little-Church-of-Englanders' have so much to learn. For the past three years I have been living within an easy walk of a small patch of the Diocese of Winchester among the Thames warehouses. All that remains of the medieval bishops' London palace is a gable-end with a glorious rose-window. Globe-shaped and enduring, it has given me the title I was looking for. I only hope I shall be able to live up to it.[63]

Part of the difficulty in living up to his dream was John Taylor's tendency to write at considerable length in an increasingly visual culture where many people do not read serious newspapers or journals. We can only hope he is the first and last bishop whose initial letter to his diocese is seven pages long and all about violence![64] As he moved from London to Winchester, John Taylor was convinced that the world was moving into a turbulent period and was asking himself what the seeds of this violence might be. His answer, characteristically, refuses all simplifications of a difficult and complex issue, attempting a Christian analysis of the present moment and looking prophetically into the likely future. From the start it is clear that this bishop demands of himself and of others hard thinking about contemporary issues in their real everyday world, believing that Christians are given the interpretative framework to find God in the course of events, even in 'the crash of falling masonry and the crackle of flames'.[65] Finding God, we are to lend a hand, taking adult responsibility, becoming ministers of reconciliation rather than unwitting participants in violence. 'If we are not consciously committed to the way of reconciliation, our blindly respectable reactions will be part of the violence.'[66]

The style and appearance of The Winchester Churchman also militated against him from start to finish. A dull, amateurish, churchy publication, it was maintained for the committed, being unlikely to present an attractive face of Christianity to anyone else. For the whole of John Taylor's episcopate The Winchester Churchman was edited as a sideline by well-meaning parish priests who served in an honorary capacity.

The Winchester Churchman was a dreadful publication. It was edited by a charming man who didn't do it very well, and then handed it over to another charming man who did it even less well. It did convey a vast amount of information, but one used to see back copies piled up in the back of Churches, and it never really worked.[67]

At no time did the Church take its public image seriously enough to spend the money necessary to produce something better. The two priests concerned simply lacked the necessary professional expertise and, astonishingly, the bishop did nothing to change this situation.

Subscriptions to *The Winchester Churchman* outside the diocese however soared, while within Winchester itself John Taylor's 'Rosewindow' pieces seem largely to have been ignored. 'Half the diocese couldn't understand, and the other half never bothered to read.'[68] No doubt this comment is too strong, for it is notoriously difficult to judge the influence of ideas accurately. It is also true that many people living in the diocese of Winchester were literate and thoughtful and interested in a bishop who took the trouble to respect their intelligence. Many clergy and lay leaders awaited the appearance of the monthly article with keen anticipation, hoping to be stimulated and encouraged in their ministry, and were not disappointed. But it would seem fair to suggest that 'Rosewindow' just wasn't gossipy or trivial or 'religious' enough to catch the attention of the pew-sitting public, and also that John Taylor's theology was considered very odd, making unusual connections between the tradition and contemporary events, always attempting to probe the heart of issues and writing as if he actually believed people might change their minds![69] 'Human kind cannot bear very much reality', according to T. S. Eliot, but this bishop wanted them to delight in it, welcome it and embrace it daily so that God might be all in all, so that they routinely left 'Jerusalem' behind to go with the raised Christ into 'Galilee'.[70]

Pastor pastorum

For all his thinking ahead and careful planning, in some ways the same chaos theory also determined other aspects of John Taylor's episcopal ministry – both the liturgical and the pastoral. He has been accused of having favourites and not dealing even-handedly with the clergy.[71] 'He did not appear very interested in those he did not like, whereas for those he loved nothing was too much.'[72] This is a very serious charge indeed. And it seems that it was more than just not liking certain individuals very much. John Taylor also needed people to like him. He needed people capable of responding to him, people enthused by him, people on the same wavelength. Indeed, it is not too much to say that he needed their applause in order really to be at his best. To know this need in yourself is not necessarily to love yourself.[73] Playing to the gallery is no doubt an essential part of the performance culture of the priesthood. Preachers are dramatists: they set themselves on fire, it has been said, and others come to watch them burn! Priesthood in its sacramental dimensions demands presence, a sense of occasion, sensitivity to mood and the sort of artistry required on stage. 'The performer is always to some degree a miracle-man, eliciting faith.'[74] This may be necessary for the spiritual health of the people of God. What is essential for the priest's own spiritual health, however, is sufficient self-knowledge to distinguish between performance and reality, an ability not to fall for your own tricks or believe your own publicity.

John Taylor is acutely aware of this danger. It is the same danger besetting any performer who longs for others to share his vision. He is conscious too of his own propensity to fall into the trap of longing for applause. Priest-craft, that artistry which is integral to effective priesthood, is a power as open as any to ordinary human corruption, just as persuasion so easily crosses the line to become manipulation. His self-knowledge in this regard emerges here and there in his preaching and writing, but nowhere more strongly than in his poetry.

> Pitiful blinded ape
> to let them drape that rippling
> drum of muscle and hair
> sporting a surplice down
> to your soft shuffle, and all, poor clown,
> to make the round O gape.
>
> The grubby cotton above
> your dexterous glove beating
> time barely conceals
> that rosary loop of chain;
> your impudent lips invite again
> the laughter that you crave.
>
> You hoot your hideous hymn
> and, as the acclaim explodes,
> hammer your iron bowl
> in frantic self-applause.
> Then the split coconut jaws
> yawn wide and scream, and scream.
>
> Silence sudden as frost
> falls across the ring.
> The crumpled dish drops
> like a discarded prayer.
> One polished paw scrawls on the air,
> God help us, the sign of the cross.[75]

'Invite again the laughter that you crave ... frantic self-applause ... the acclaim explodes.' St Mark tells us that Jesus in his home town of Nazareth could 'do no mighty work there' because the people would not allow him, because they did not believe in him or trust him, even though he laid his hands on some who were sick and managed to cure them![76] Here we have a window into the true humanity of Jesus. In his sensitive self-awareness, John Taylor gives us a glimpse into his own true humanity. He has obvious human needs and weaknesses. He needs people to believe in him, and he knows that he needs people to believe in him. He was never a bishop pretending to be free of ordinary human needs, able to perform on automatic pilot, like clockwork, regardless of the atmosphere.

Somehow, John Taylor needed permission, freedom, encouragement in order to perform great works. This has to do with his own need of love, but it is also about sensitivity to environment. Some have tempered the severity of his attachment to favourites by claiming that these were not so much favourites as disciples.[77] Certainly, this must be part of the truth. He couldn't help having an uneven influence if he depended so much on stimulation and energy from others.[78] Like a lot of very original and exciting and interesting people, he was eclectic. Some felt tremendously affirmed and even flattered by his attention, while others felt crushed because they didn't fit into that world or couldn't respond to it or receive what he offered.[79] This is clear from his own memories of having some very creative people around him. He speaks revealingly of 'some of the younger clergy, who I felt at times were like cheer-leaders, saying "Go on John, do your stuff". It was gorgeous.'[80] Clearly, it was a case of drawing on this reservoir of energy and enthusiasm for his own stimulation and refreshment because their high expectations brought out the best in him. If it is true that he never really felt he was accepted as Bishop of Winchester, it was all the more essential to him that these younger, talented clergy loved him.

Of this group he could be very demanding indeed, but they couldn't do enough for him because they knew he was totally committed to working with them.

> One day I saw him three times: he rang me up early in the morning to produce some work for him, and I took it down to show him about lunch time, and finally delivered it at about 11 o'clock that night. He *expected* that, and the corollary was that he would do the same.[81]

For one priest all this happened at a very personal level.

> It wasn't the bishop, it was John Taylor. If it was the bishop, the bishop could have got the same thing done by the bishop's secretary, or the bishop's chauffeur. John Taylor wanted a friend to do it for him.[82]

Another priest remembers John Taylor ringing late one night to ask him to write something and be ready to hand it to him next morning as the 8 a.m. train stopped at Basingstoke on its way to London. It was exasperating, but also flattering, to be asked because it told you that this brilliantly original bishop – *your* bishop – had confidence in your ability and needed your help.[83] And it was the way John Taylor himself worked, under pressure, up against deadlines, at high speed, through the night if necessary. Here was one way of really encouraging clergy to feel useful and necessary colleagues, trusted to collaborate with their bishop in genuinely collegial ministry. It was certainly a way to get them to do their best work. Encouragement is not just an occasional pat on the head or a polite letter of praise rather than criticism following some parish visit. The kind word letting a priest know that the bishop is impressed is powerful, and even this is rare enough. More powerful, however, because more obviously sincere, is the bishop actually depending on the talent and skill of others. This builds a relationship of mutuality and interdependence in place of indifference and isolationism, strengthening the priestly college rather than fuelling competition among the clergy or encouraging infantile dependence between father and child.

His own capacity for work stimulated others to match his efforts, and this seems to have been characteristic of him at every stage in his ministry. One of his staff at Mukono recalls an occasion when John Taylor needed to make a report to the Theological Board on some college land and its use.

> The day before the meeting John asked me as bursar to get together some figures and facts for him to include in his report. With a full teaching day I eventually took these over to him at about 9.30 pm that evening. John and Peggy were listening to some music which we enjoyed, followed by coffee and chat – no mention of the report. By about 11 pm I took my departure. The next morning he handed me an eight page foolscap report prepared for me to run off on the duplicator. As I read it I was amazed at the grasp and all the detail beautifully put together.[84]

The uneven quality of John Taylor as pastor is dramatically symbolized by the treatment of two priests working in the diocese at the time.[85] One came into the Diocese of Winchester for a second curacy because he admired John Taylor, and left three years later never having met him – something that could never have happened with his predecessor Falkner Allison or his successor Colin James.[86] Another priest actually appointed by John Taylor told the bishop, as he was obliged to do, of his wish to marry. This interview took place on 6 September one year and the marriage took place on 4 April the next year. Between engagement and marriage John Taylor wrote to this priest every day – except for one day when the priest saw him three times! Of Max Warren, John Taylor had said

> the economy of God was personal, arbitrary and uninhibited by tidy principle. So he was free to exercise his most characteristic gift of all, the light but intimate gesture of recognition, the hand laid momentarily upon a particular shoulder, which endeared him to countless people because it was the unaffected offer of a totally trustworthy friendship.[87]

The scandal of particularity is characteristic of John Taylor's ministry too, perhaps even more so.

Poetry and drama

Sometimes the bishop worked in odd and radical ways, surprising some of his sedate charges by his imaginative capacity and, given his evangelical background, his unusually generous sacramentality. He must be the only senior bishop of the Church of England (or the Anglican Communion for that matter) in living memory to have taken several months' leave from his usual episcopal duties in order to direct a Passion play in Winchester Cathedral, the drama *Passion and Resurrection*. This would, of course, have presented no surprise to those familiar with his Uganda ministry, or his editing of two beautiful books of photographs of the Mukono Passion plays. Both in Africa and in England, John Taylor conceived this drama as an act of worship and in the cathedral this aspect was highlighted by the use of the nave altar. There the drama began, with those who were to play the part of the Jewish priests actually clothed in Christian eucharistic vestments. There at the Lord's table the drama also ended, with the altar serving as the empty tomb. The whole enterprise was for John Taylor an expression of his ministry as priest in the Church of God and preacher of the gospel of Jesus Christ. 'The thing that really drives one, the fire in the bones, is the longing somehow or other to make this story more real and credible and valuable to other people.'[88]

On each occasion when the Passion plays were presented in Mukono College chapel and in the great cathedral at Winchester, John Taylor took control of every small detail. 'John would have the visual image exactly; it wasn't anybody else's idea; John knew exactly what he wanted.'[89] This clarity came out of immersion in the gospel narratives, imaginative identification with the characters and events of the story in the sacred text, helped by other sacred texts, the words of poets and song-writers, influenced by the images of great artists. This was all characteristic of a bishop who probably did think it was more important to listen to a string quartet than worry about the diocesan board of finance.[90] It was certainly characteristic of a bishop who himself lived and worked as an accomplished artist.

The Winchester *Passion and Resurrection*, the first Passion opera to be composed since the Middle Ages, brought together more than a hundred and fifty actors, musicians, carpenters and dress-makers from all over the south of England to stage Jonathan Harvey's creation. For all his previous experience in Africa, *Passion and Resurrection* was a new and risky venture for John Taylor, simply because of the enormous scale of the work. In a sense, he was putting his reputation on the line, driven by his desire to tell the Passion story in such a way that its reality gripped people for whom the Christian drama lacked meaning or significance. The music itself was both lyrical and strange, atonal and complex. It was incredibly difficult to sing, making some suggest that Jonathan Harvey had done for music what Hitler did for Coventry! Clearly, this event would be no Christmas pantomime for children, just as this bishop was no amateur prepared to accept low standards of performance as the price to be paid for involving all and sundry. One of the professional soloists clearly expected the worst when he was sounded out for the part of Pilate, only to be instantly enthused on his first meeting with the bishop. As a producer, John Taylor was remarkable in that he was able in a few moments to give the actors and singers his own intellectual appreciation of a part. 'What he first said gave one more to work on than what other producers would have been able to achieve in two weeks of rehearsals.'[91]

John Taylor's whole purpose was to create a liturgy rather than an oratorio, a total action, both visually and musically striking.[92] Into this vision he initiated both professional and amateur performers patiently and carefully. If it was necessary for the producer of *Passion and Resurrection* to enter imaginatively into characters like Pilate and Mary Magdalene, and even the angels at the tomb, it was necessary to attempt something of the same with the central figure, the still point around whom the story moves. We can only say that John Taylor attempted this with bold humility. Knowing that any personal view of Christ tends to tell more about the viewer than about Christ makes for caution. The nature of Christ is, by definition, elusive. The quest for the historical Jesus has proven to be a dead end. All we have is the sacred text as it stands, and the gospels are theology rather than biography, even if we allow that they are biographized theology. Only by sustained study and imaginative meditation on the Scriptures can we enter into the mind and heart of Jesus in the life of prayer, and this John Taylor does faithfully and gently.

With other characters in the passion drama the same constraints are less important, but humility is still valuable. What, after all, shall we say of the relationship between Jesus and the Beloved Disciple who leans against his breast at the Last Supper? If thinking and talking about this love is a delicate matter, so too is that between the Lord and Mary of Magdala. Of Mary Magdalene John Taylor ventured to speak directly in terms of the sexual energy between her and Jesus. He does so as the enemy of insidious dualism he is, sensitively, but plainly.[93] The Scriptures are more robustly honest than many Christians dare to be, but this Christian dares.[94] This speech is classical John Taylor theology – authentically biblical and utterly realistic. Not only is there no division between sacred and profane, spiritual and fleshly, but there is also no distance between past and present. In this reflection we see how deeply visual John Taylor's mind is and how much his reading of the gospel text is influenced by Christian iconography. In particular, he sees in his mind's eye all those great paintings representing the moment when the crucified and raised Christ says to Mary, 'Do not touch me!' These images inform his whole theological meditation on touching, bodiliness, embodiment, incarnation, the marriage of flesh and spirit in us and in God, leading to a celebration of what Charles Williams calls *la carne gloriosa e sancta*, the holy and glorious flesh.[95] All this emerges in condensed form as he talks with the performers in the cold cathedral, and they know that they are being allowed access to his heart where the faith lives fully and richly and powerfully. John Taylor is unafraid of this intimacy, inviting his collaborators to be equally real and direct in their relations with him.

> Mary Magdalene stands rather apart from the other two Marys. She's in a very special relationship with Jesus. I personally think there must have been a lot of straightforward physical love that she felt towards him. She's a person who lives on her emotions, has very straightforward physical feelings, and so her grief is very, very passionate, and this comes out in the music. Say, if you like, that Mary is in love with him. I think we make our definitions much too tight in these days when we talk about love. She had that particular intensity of love for him, and so she wants to hold him and wants to touch him. And yet she now can accept the fact that he says really that there's no need for us to touch, 'we've got it all.' So there's that marvellous space between the hands. They don't need to touch. There's no longer any need.[96]

With the professional tenor Brian Burrows, John Taylor discussed the character of Pontius Pilate in terms of Roman mythology. If Burrows was to capture the essence of Pilate's dilemma, he needed to be aware of Pilate's terrible fear of demi-gods and cosmic spiritual forces, and particularly his fear that he might unwittingly frustrate some divine purpose. With the choir boys chosen to play the angels at the empty tomb, John Taylor was able to connect on a different level, yet never for a moment talking down to them. He also managed to engage their imagination without ever patronizing them in terms of their intelligence or their limited life experience. The world of their experience mattered to him because it was real and important to them and, however strange it may be to a man of his age, his concern was somehow to bridge the gulf and talk with them on their own terms. Furthermore, it was a genuine conversation rather than a monologue, one in which the boys were not afraid to interrupt and contribute their own insights. All this is based in his long-held conviction that a child may be profound as well as an adult, and each in their own way can be inspired.[97] The angels at the Easter tomb, the bishop argued, 'are like something right out of this world, trying to turn into human form'.

> But they are something that actually holds the world together, like gravity. If someone was to make a statue of a person representing the force of gravity, then you'd have something that looked like a man or a boy, but something completely different, something mysterious, inexorable, so that you could

never get around it. Or electricity, some human form that represented electricity. It would probably all be sparkling, like static. Try and think of yourselves, each one of you, as representing one of the terrific forces of nature, the things that God actually used to bring the world together.[98]

All this exploration, however, remains in the direct service of christology. The question is always, who is Jesus Christ? Who shall we say he is?

How can anyone interpret the self-consciousness of Jesus is a very difficult question, and in one sense we must say that we can't possibly. But if we don't try, we don't get anywhere with him. We must, somehow, try to penetrate what this or that meant to him, and what he was trying to communicate to people.[99]

Not surprisingly, this disciple of Bonhoeffer, who warmly welcomed the secular theology of the 60s and 70s, speaks clearly and simply now about the fundamental truth at the heart of any Christian faith.

He was, after all, a man, and if we lose sight of that we turn him into an inaccessible figure. I think that's been our trouble. We must start with his humanity, and that means we have to think of him biographically, and try to see into him.[100]

In other words, our starting point is with the facts as we receive them.

You start with a man and his suffering, which is passion, and it's a very ordinary story, it's happening all the time. And this is where I have tried to bring in today's world. Here and there, particularly in both the scenes which show the trial before Pilate, I've brought on little bits of violence of the kind that happen in police barracks anywhere in the world today. Think of Robben Island, the number of men who have committed suicide mysteriously in police barracks in various parts of the world – El Salvador, Russia, almost anywhere, where violence becomes mindless, organized, institutionalized, like automata, just hitting out because that's their job. In that sense, the passion goes on.[101]

Here we have a wholeness of vision. The ancient world and the contemporary world are both radically different and radically similar; everything changes and nothing changes. The Passion of Jesus is both historic event and current reality. Remembrance, central in telling the story, is no escape into another world. It offers us a deeper penetration of the only world we know.

John Taylor loved the cathedral and found in the Dean of Winchester someone strikingly different from himself, but with precisely the same highly developed sensitivity, someone who shared his aesthetic interests and enthusiasms. It was the beginning of a special friendship, but also a special partnership in ministry – one rare enough in an English cathedral close, where bishop and dean can live as two powerfully independent personalities who courteously tolerate one another if the relationship is not actively hostile. The basic difficulty is that the bishop is always simply a guest in his own cathedral, always at the invitation of the dean, and functioning under the authority of the dean and chapter, so well protected are the rights and freedoms of cathedral churches.

> Michael Stancliffe was the most extraordinary man. He was a hermit really, a beautiful, gentle, and I think a very holy man. About three minutes before a service, you would see him slipping into the cathedral from the deanery. It was almost like seeing a ghost! And after the service slipping back, never talking to anyone. A very, very extraordinary man, so incredibly and profoundly loved by his fellow canons that although the cathedral at one level contributed nothing, at another it was a pulsing heart of prayer and love. The canons all loved each other, and Michael ran it all not so much as a Benedictine but as a Trappist.[102]

A wonderfully happy and creative partnership began, sharing ideas, poetry, drama and music. In a foreword to Michael Stancliffe's first book of sermons, *Symbols and Dances*, John Taylor said that 'all who read this selection will realise what a fortunate bishop I was to have him as a colleague, next-door neighbour and friend'.[103] Preaching at Michael Stancliffe's requiem just a year after *Symbols and Dances* was published, he opened a door on their private world which had such public effect. True soul friends are rare enough, but here both found companionship, respect and love.

> It was typical of Barbara that our first experience of their celestial janitorship should have been in the Deanery rather than the Cathedral. Because the Bishop's house of Wolvesey was in the builder's hands when we first came to Winchester, they opened to us not only their doors but the beginning of a rare friendship. We talked about Church affairs, but much more about travel and books, about pictures and people, and the way God's glory shines through all those things. We came to value Michael's sardonic humour and his fastidiousness, and to recognise the passion beneath the even voice and measured words. At the end of the evening meal we learned to take our turn in the game that was more than a game, dousing the candles one by one with the slender long-handled extinguisher, until Michael, that master of poignant ceremony, put out the last one, before we rose and moved into the next room. It was in little ways like that that he forged unforgettable links of affection and raised other people's eyes to see the door that stood open in heaven.[104]

Apart from their adventures in drama and poetry at a personal level, Michael Stancliffe was also significant for John Taylor politically. In senior staff meetings, the dean would never oppose the bishop or join in the chorus of doubts from others. It seems unlikely that he approved everything John Taylor proposed, but at least he understood. Michael Stancliffe was himself a man of passion, although this may not have presented itself to the casual observer.

> He was a man of very great insight. There was a great intensity, which I echoed; we both had passion; but mostly his support was a silent one – he never joined those who wanted to pull me off a thing.' [105]

It has to be said that John Taylor seems not to have connected very well with other members of his senior staff, both those he inherited and even those he himself appointed. While acknowledging their importance in keeping the show on the road, their devotion to duty and their personal loyalty and friendship, he seems to have cast them in the role of institutional guardians rather more than he himself cared to be or could manage. Was it that they were more 'religious', that they naturally felt more at home in the Church and its structures than he did? Some who say that John Taylor was more a layman's bishop than a clergyman's bishop, just as he could connect with fringe-dwellers rather more than most priests, are perhaps touching something crucial and central to his personality and style. And yet the difficulty is hard to pin-point. Indeed, it is hard to see which ideas or enthusiasms or visions his senior staff actively opposed.

The contrast between the bishop and his staff seems to be most starkly revealed in intimate pastoral matters. John Taylor recalls with satisfaction one particular occasion. A talented homosexual priest, attempting to keep his sexuality hidden in a homophobic church and culture, found himself in trouble with the police. The diocesan senior staff were united in their view that this priest should be sacrificed to safeguard the institution. He must be quietly dismissed or transferred to avoid any possibility of scandal. Standing against this advice, John Taylor naturally felt isolated and fully appreciated the risk he was taking. Here was the lonely place of the bishop which no one else can share. When all the good and bad advice has been weighed, the bishop alone takes the decision. His stance in this instance involves putting person above principle. He is somehow very sure that his attitude and action reflect the mind of Christ. Against all the received wisdom of Scripture as traditionally interpreted, and in the face of common episcopal practice, John Taylor suggested to the priest that he find himself a live-in lover and establish a permanent relationship. With his bishop's express support, and with no further need to cloak his secret shame, the man did so. There was no further scandal, and the priest subsequently became a canon of one of the great cathedrals.[106] John Taylor was capable of sailing close to the wind when he deemed it necessary. He was firm, but merciful, tender-hearted and clear-sighted. To his sheep, he showed himself a shepherd, not a wolf.

Practical visionary

If there is any tendency to set dreams and visions over against reality and practicality, John Taylor's *Towards Full Responsibility* initiative provides the antidote. It is in fact a fine example of his special alchemy, wherein no such polarities make sense. We see him paying attention to the facts and doing theology in the light of things as they are. In this project, so far ahead of its time in the Church of England, John Taylor was unreservedly backed by the diocesan secretary, Graham Phillips.

With Graham Phillips he devised and launched *Towards Full Responsibility*, attempting to change a culture and mind-set by challenging the parishes of his very well-to-do diocese to become totally self-supporting. It was high time that the Church Commissioners took on being the pension fund of the Church of England and stopped keeping the Church afloat financially. The bishop was clear that the contemporary Church must stop living off the dead and pay its own way. The sooner the local church became financially realistic, the healthier the whole Church would be. To this end he worked with his diocesan secretary on a budget for what full responsibility would mean, and then set about selling this all over Hampshire. This involved getting right away from any ideas of a quota and simply saying there are some things for which a parish should be responsible. Obviously, a parish community should be responsible for the total salary of all its clergy, the upkeep of their houses and heating, the upkeep of the church and its repair. But this is not all. TFR had the potential actually to increase parochialism, encouraging a parish to look inward and take pride in meeting its own needs and funding an internal budget. A vision of the wider Church was needed to balance this, and set it in its proper context. Thus, there was to be a proportionate contribution towards the training of more clergy, so that the local church was encouraged to be looking to the future, and making its own contribution to its own future. Why should anybody else? If you expect to have a priest in the future you must be serious about selection and training, so a contribution towards a central ordination scheme becomes essential. There are other things that the diocese is doing for you in the parish and these need to be paid for, so there must be a contribution for diocesan work. Then there are parishes in the diocese which can't possibly be asked to do this, and may never be, so there must be a contribution towards them – to further mission within the diocese. And, finally, the Church at home takes responsibility outside the diocese for those parts of the Church which need its help.

Working with this rationale, the two-horse act began travelling the diocese, saying to the Church, 'Now, there's your budget, can you face up to it?'

> We went around, he and I, and we got two deaneries at a time, all their deanery chapter and representatives of all the parishes came together for

a big service at some central Church, and we had a specially devised service, and he spoke and I preached, and we presented a common theme, *Full Responsibility*, trying to say 'This is a *spiritual matter*', a matter of your response to God and your awareness of what it means to be God's Church, and you can't expect the dead to go on paying for this, it's the living must take it on. The Roman Catholics and the Free Church can do it; so can we. And the amazing thing was the number of parishes where they had their meetings afterwards, who said they would be ashamed not to rise to this. And I had a letter only the other day from Bishop Colin who's just retired from Winchester – a very sweet letter in which he said, 'In the light of what's now happening to the Church Commissioners we thank God for the prophetic move which you and Graham gave to the parishes which has gone on since then.' So Graham was a wonderful colleague to have.[107]

Fifteen years ahead of the rest of the Church of England, the Diocese of Winchester pioneered the way ahead in terms of financial responsibility.

One of John Taylor's stated reasons for leaving CMS to become bishop of a diocese was that he was beginning to feel embarrassed about giving advice about revitalizing church life without himself attempting to put his theories into practice. No doubt this was more difficult for him as a bishop than if he had become a parish priest, but he was nevertheless committed as Bishop of Winchester to attempting to implement his vision at local level. He could at least encourage clergy by his experience of the world Church, and this was all about Christianity recovering its nerve and learning to live authentically as a minority among minorities.

It was natural to John Taylor not only to observe with unusual perception experimental church communities on his travels, but also to read whatever was published about house churches and Christian base communities. He was convinced by experience that the way forward for the Church in an indifferent or hostile world necessitated the tightening of relationships within the rather loose association of individual Christians which constituted the traditional parish. This necessity was God's way of nudging the Church into the future, insisting that we become responsible adults. Hostility or indifference are to be regarded not as a threat but as an opportunity, and an opportunity actually given to us by Christ himself. In company with other thinkers, John Taylor looked into the distance and tried to envisage the Church of the future, probably very different from the Church we have known, but God's catholic and apostolic Church nonetheless. Being a naturally hopeful person, the prospect of stormy weather ahead filled him with exhilaration, for the wind and waves call forth from the ship's crew an extraordinary warmth of fellow-feeling and gladness in being in one another's company.[108]

Fundamental to strengthening the local Church would be small groups for companionship, support, initiation into the Christian mysteries, bearing one another's burdens, safe places of genuine friendship where hearts and minds could be opened and hopes and fears shared. John Taylor is disarmingly honest about the inspiration for this development.

> Many years ago, when a fellow priest asked what I thought he might best do to revitalise his parish, it suddenly came into my head to reply: Call a parish meeting and get them to imagine that they were living in one of those situations where the government has made it illegal for more than twelve people to meet together in one place. Ask them to draw up a plan for keeping their own congregation in good heart and properly ministered to under such conditions. And then put the whole of that plan into practice in your parish, with the wonderful advantage of still having a parish Church to use *as well*. I believe God may be inviting us to do something like that in our parishes in the next few years.[109]

Significantly, this vision was to be called forth in an imaginative exercise from the people themselves, rather than imposed from the top down. Likewise, when he began to open up the vision in his diocese John Taylor drew on the experience of the 1975 Lent study groups on *Ministry Today and Tomorrow*. He sought to stimulate a continuation of discussions already begun, rather than impose solutions. The 'little congregations' he envisages – house churches, factory cells, student groups, and the like – will be the catholic Church in little. In other words there are not just more study groups. They offer genuine experience of Church in terms of nurture, witness, service, and sacramental community.

> I believe these smaller, more informal groups of Christians are going to become the essential sub-structure of Church life that is needed to undergird the larger congregation in the parish Church. There is no need to set the two types of gathering in opposition as though they must be alternatives. Both are necessary and complementary. But I believe the life of congregations as we know them will not long survive without the understructure of smaller groups.
>
> When Christians meet regularly in a small group, with a minimum of traditional ceremony and professional leadership, they cease to be passive adherents of a folk religion and become articulate and capable of passing on their faith to others.
>
> If you want a missionary faith ... get far away from your 'Temple', and its traditional ceremonials and securities, and find your corporate *experience* of faith in people's homes.[110]

The key to this knife-edge for Church growth is *intimacy*, the tight circle in which everyone knows each other, where faith is experienced as an essential ingredient in daily life, and into which seekers can be welcomed. The Body of Christ is a body of people, but it is not their organization or their government that makes them the Body of Christ. They are Christ's Body by virtue of the quality of their relationships, to God, to one another, and to the world. What makes the Church the Church is its possession by the Holy Spirit, and the essential activity of the Spirit is to give mutuality, awareness and communion. If these are absent, all our efforts to fill our churches are like holding a colander under the kitchen tap: we turn the tap on twice as hard, but the water merely finds a lot more holes. The only lasting solution is to block up some of these holes, and the biggest hole of all is our lack of face-to-face caring encounter which is the Church's one unique asset and attraction.[111] In other words, the normal parish congregation is too big and too anonymous to really be the Church. There is a low optimum size for a vital self-propagating Christian community. It lies somewhere between twelve and twenty people. Once that number is exceeded the intimacy cannot be found, nor the therapeutic mutual knowledge and acceptance in which the forgiveness of Christ and the renewal of the Spirit are experienced.[112] The parish, nevertheless, remains essential if these groups are not to fragment, and the parish priest will be the link between groups, exercising *episcope* or oversight, moving from cell to cell, co-ordinating, teaching, seeing the whole, making each group aware of the whole.[113]

John Taylor is not afraid to spell out the essential characteristics of the 'little congregations' he is promoting. As he sees it, there are five features of the true Church –

> **Understanding** faith in the context of life in this world. Helping one another to be clear about what we Christians believe and what this has to say about the world we live in.

> **Sharing** the loving acceptance and mutual honesty which is the special gift of the Holy Spirit to the Church, that intimate knowing which becomes reassurance, healing and inspiration.

> **Prayer** such as silent contemplation, the prayer of healing, as well as informal celebration of the Eucharist.

> **Action** to avoid self-centredness and selfishness, looking beyond the circle in the form of specific service to others in the wider community, planning for this in the group but actually serving at other times. This service involves more than bandaging the wounds of the broken; it invites challenging the reasons for their brokenness.

> **Telling** others what the group members are discovering about the power and love of Christ.

In all this, the priest will act behind the scenes enabling others to offer the sacrifice of praise and thanksgiving in spirit and in truth. The priest is a resource, and anyone who thinks of themselves as an expert and begins to tackle problems directly ceases to be a pastor.[114] The essential apostolic ministry involves representing the catholicity of the Church to each of its local manifestations. True *episcope* involves seeing the whole and relating each of the parts to the whole. It is a co-ordinating ministry.[115]

> If the house-group is to be allowed to play its full part in the experience of the individual Christian and in the life of the Church as a whole, it must be allowed to possess the fullness of the Church as a unit of study, pastoral care, service and witness to the world, and worship. And some of that worship must be sacramental: the Church has to be so organised that the Eucharist can be celebrated regularly in each of these small groups. At present in the Church of England this means immediately that the vicar and his curates, if he has any, run round from group to group celebrating like 'massing priests'; or, in a more truly New Testament pattern, an 'elder' is commissioned by authority in the name of the Church Catholic to preside over the group's meetings, including the celebration of the Lord's Supper.

This parent-figure will naturally emerge over time, and will usually be the host of the household rather than the group leader.[116] Careful increase in the number of people ordained to the priesthood while continuing to earn their living in some other walk of life, together with better enlistment of retired clergy, will become a deliberate policy of the diocese. While John Taylor is clear that the Church should learn to use the expertise of lay Christians without trying to turn them into clergy, he is also clear that the diaconate needs to be revived as a full and equal order of ministry.[117] This revival is demanded by our contemporary need for people who are competent sociologists, counsellors, lawyers, educationalists and are also thoroughly trained to think theologically. The Church will have to recognize a body of professionals on its own pay-roll whose function is to offer specialist advice in specific fields to enable ordinary Christians to make a more effective witness in the world.

In many ways, of course, all this was ahead of its time. Initially, it was a matter of planting seeds, encouraging discussion of ideas and attempting to head off excuses for maintaining the status quo. Fundamentally, John Taylor was asking people to move from an inherited model of church as worship club to the biblical model of church as missionary movement.[118] This call still faces the Church all these years later, and the basic problem is the same. 'The one really important decision each of us has to take is the decision not to be afraid of change, because the Church and its future belongs to our onward-marching God.'[119] Sadly, however, fear is easier than faith, and the predicament of the Church needs to get more desperate yet before we choose to embrace the vision. Rather than focus on human frailty and failure, however, John Taylor's theology encourages us to keep our eyes fixed on the Christlike God who, if necessary, will drag the Church kicking and screaming into the future.

Pilgrim way

On Saturday, 4 August 1979, almost mid-way through his ten-year episco-pate, cheering crowds and buglers of the Royal Green Jackets welcomed the Bishop of Winchester when he arrived in the city after walking 70 miles on pilgrimage from Dorchester-on-Thames. John Taylor and 75 volunteers of all ages were commemorating the move of diocesan headquarters from Dorchester to Winchester 1300 years before. They had left Dorchester the previous Sunday, making six stations along the way to Winchester. For the final eight miles they were joined by 225 more pilgrims.

> After being greeted outside the Great Hall by the Mayor of Winchester, the Bishop, who is 66 next month, announced that he felt 'quite marvellous' although his feet were covered in bandages because of blisters. He said that one day they had walked 22 miles. A similar journey from Dorchester-on-Thames was made by Bishop Hedda when he moved the diocese to the City in 679 AD. He brought with him the body of his predecessor, St Birinus. To commemorate this the modern day pilgrims carried a cross in which was set a piece of stone from the first tomb of St Birinus in the shape of the first cathedral Church.[120]

Like the Passion play, this pilgrimage forged lasting friendships between the bishop and some of his priests and lay people. These relationships formed on the road lasted and were wonderfully fruitful. One who became a very close friend cannot recall when he first met his bishop, but is sure planning and then making the pilgrimage was crucial.

> I remember us walking long distances then and having quite long theo-logical discussions with him. At that time David Attenborough's first series of programmes called *Life on Earth* was coming out, and one reading of nature is it's everything eating everything else, and that's the bit David Attenborough never hides from you. I remember having long conversations with him, mile after mile, about this.[121]

Mile after mile of theological discussions also took place with his chaplain in the back of the episcopal car as they were driven all over the diocese for ordinary parish visits and special events. Indeed, John Taylor is always ready to be distracted by theology, always alert to see how connections can be made, always wondering how experience is to be interpreted, exploring the events of the day in the light of God's self-disclosure in Christ. One of his daughters discovered this at quite an early age, and he naturally gravitates to those who wish to venture with him on such excursions into ultimate reality. 'When our elder daughter was a little girl of five or six, she discovered that at bed-time she could postpone the goodnight kiss and "lights out" by engaging her father in theological discussion.'[122] His chaplain was also secretary of the Doctrine Commission of the Church of England, while John Taylor was chairman. Working with the members of the Doctrine Commission helped keep John Taylor alive theologically during his Winchester years.

National ministry: General Synod and Doctrine Commission

Early in John Taylor's episcopate the Church of England was caught up in serious discussion of the ordination of women to the priesthood, although it would not be able to bring itself to act until twenty years later. His approach to this divisive issue opens a window on his unique ability to go to the heart of the matter, dealing gently but firmly with aspects of the proposal which others failed to see, placing it in a larger context of faith. In two speeches made to the General Synod on the same day, this special gift from John Taylor to the Church is strikingly evident.

In a masterly overview of the theological issues, Kenneth Woolcombe, the Bishop of Oxford, made a strong case for the ordination of women. One after another, he disposed of the objections. This is a development in Christian tradition driven not by feminist concerns, but by theological convictions. It coheres with a rightly understood incarnational and eschatological theology. The Church is not being pressed to come to a hasty decision. After all, the length of time already taken in the debate over the ordination of women matches almost exactly that taken by the Church of the fourth century in discussing the doctrine of the Holy Spirit![123] We must pay attention to the fact that women are quietly insisting that they experience a sense of God calling them to priesthood. The Church cannot keep silent, or temporize, or offer an equivocal reply. Half-hearted measures are insensitive, even cruel, compared to a clear no. As to the ecumenical objection that no part of the Church should act before the whole catholic Church makes up its mind, it is urged that each local church has a primary obligation to bear witness to the truth. If one church believes there are no fundamental objections to the ordination of women to priesthood it has a positive duty to say so to the other churches. This will be a new ingredient in ecumenical debate, a fresh initiative to which other churches must respond. All this is laid out in an exceptionally competent, logical and clear fashion, with courtesy and respect for those who differ.

The difference between Kenneth Woolcombe and John Taylor has nothing to do with debating skills in themselves. John Taylor's presentation is equally fair, honest and reasonable. Nevertheless, there is a qualitative distinction, a sense that the discussion is lifted into new realms which have nothing whatever to do with the usual point-scoring of synodical debate, nor even with winning an argument. It is difficult to put a finger on what precisely characterizes this new voice, but it certainly has to do with a fresh and unusual perspective, an unexpected vision offered to everyone present, with an invitation to obedience. 'Once we have seen that there are positive biblical reasons for this decision, to postpone acting upon it may be the kind of spiritual disobedience which ends in loss of vision.'[124]

John Taylor's contribution to the Church's thinking had to do solely with representative and mediatorial priesthood. 'We are not talking about a Church of England clergyman and whether his job could be done by a woman; we are talking about priesthood.'[125] We should not be asking whether we want to see a woman in sole charge of a parish, but whether we want to see *any* person, male or female, in sole charge of a parish!

> Both the difference and the complementarity of male and female lie far deeper than function. It is not a matter of the division of labour: one for the pulpit, the other for the kitchen stove. Man and woman are different down to the tiniest particles of their being. They are different even when they sit side by side at a concert or when, together, they try to comfort a friend. The contribution of both the complementary elements of human nature is needed in all functions, just as both male and female, each in its distinctness, must contribute to that holiest of all functions, the procreation of life. The responsibility for the life of this world cannot safely be left in purely male hands, for they are too authoritarian, too manipulative and too ready to turn our God-given dominion into raw domination. The male touch needs to be tempered by the female in order that we may move towards 'reverence for life'. And reverence for life is going to be the dominant theme, whether we realise it or not, of more and more of our significant debates in this assembly. It should have been the underlying motif in our discussion earlier this week on abortion; it should affect all that we have to say about euthanasia, the care of the elderly, the rights of minorities, ecology, and so much more. And, in a violently technological world, we shall never preserve reverence for life until we recover a profoundly priestly attitude toward creation.[126]

Here is the clear-sighted, plain-speaking prophet and poet. Here speaks one who is a priest to his fingertips, but is yet vividly aware of his own inadequacy and incompleteness. He knows in his bones that the priesthood of Christ is no perpetuation of the Levitical priesthood. In Christ we experience the restoration of that priesthood common to human beings. We are called to work with the Creator upon the creation – developing, civilizing, bringing all to that perfection which lies hidden in the vision of God. On the other hand, we stand within creation as that part of it which is sufficiently articulate to offer up to God all its yearning and striving toward that same perfection. And the being who is put into this priestly role is created both male and female. Male alone or female alone can only offer defective priesthood. The Church is *pars pro toto*, a royal priesthood on behalf of the whole. And within the Church the ordained are *pars proto toto*, receiving from the ascended Christ gifts for ministry so that the whole people of God may better exercise its priesthood. Seeing this truth means we must act without delay. History shows that the Church does not advance by ideological consensus, but by boldness of action. Perhaps he was remembering the insistence of his mentor, Walter Freytag, that 'they who live in the obedience of faith are part of God's action'.[127] The inclusion of Woman with Man in priestly ministry could be the catalyst that brings about this wider theological enlargement. 'It could be the step of obedience that the Spirit, the Animator, is awaiting before he will bring about a new work in us.'[128]

Sadly, this still, small voice was lost in the wantonly adversarial politics of ecclesiastical government and decision-making.[129] Where people are afraid and where minds are made up in advance, faith and the Spirit have little chance of operation or penetration.

His voice was raised also in the Doctrine Commission of the Church of England, which he chaired in succession to the Regius Professor of Divinity in the University of Oxford.[130] Here too, John Taylor had to struggle to be heard, but this time his adversaries were the philosophers rather than synod representatives or theologians.

In 1987, writing in the preface to the Doctrine Commission report, *We Believe in God*, John Austin Baker, Bishop of Salisbury, his successor as chairman, underlined John Taylor's achievement in the Doctrine Commission chair.

> It is important to emphasise that the Report is unanimous, and that no part of the book carries the name of an individual author. *Believing in the Church* also had the unanimous support of the whole Commission, but final decisions as to the wording of each essay, after it had been carefully reviewed by all the members collectively, rested with the individual author. The entire text, however, of *We Believe in God* has been agreed by the whole panel. This does not mean that individual members would not, left to themselves, have worded this or that differently, but that all are prepared to stand behind every sentence of the text as printed.
>
> This was a very considerable achievement on the part of all concerned, but especially of the Chairman who initiated the project and guided it to completion, John Taylor, till 1985 Bishop of Winchester. To him all of us would wish to pay the most heartfelt tribute of gratitude and admiration. In theological thinking inexhaustibly creative, in love and devotion an inspiring friend and colleague, his leadership has been of decisive significance for the Commission's work. We hope that *We Believe in God* will also be recognised as a worthy memorial of his dedicated service as head of the Commission.[131]

This is rather more than routine acknowledgement or formal courtesy.

The Doctrine Commission of the Church of England had had a chequered history and was arguably at its lowest ebb when John Taylor became chairman – at least in terms of public esteem. It began in 1922, and eventually reported in 1938. It was then resurrected in preparation for the 1968 Lambeth Conference, because the status of the Articles of Religion appended to the Prayer Book was on the international Anglican agenda.

If the autonomous provinces of the Anglican Communion needed to know where they stood in relation to the Articles, the Church of England certainly needed to sort out where it stood. This was, of course, a politically sensitive and contentious exercise because evangelicals tended to look to the Articles as their 'title deeds' and any attempt to revise or abolish them was resisted. After this success, the Commission – then called 'The Archbishop's Commission on Christian Doctrine' – moved on to the vexed question of public liturgical prayer for the dead and after that to eucharistic theology. Eucharistic theology came on to the Commission's agenda when the Liturgical Commission asked its opinion about consecrating more bread and wine when the original provision ran out! It seemed trivial, and in any case the liturgists rejected out of hand the theologians' view. It is, however, important to note that the Commission did these things because it was asked to do so by the Church. It is important to note this because the Commission was perceived by many to waste its time doing little things. Indeed, ironically, it gained the entirely untrue popular reputation of being 'just a group of academics deciding what they wanted to do'![132]

This mixture of fact and fiction is admirably captured in the remark that the Commission 'really got some flak for the report before John took the chair, when they were so divided that all they could do was produce individual essays'.[133] That report was *Christian Believing*, produced by a Commission chaired by Professor Maurice Wiles, and published in 1976. It is not entirely accurate to condemn it as a collection of individual essays, for a joint commission report of 58 pages precedes the essays. Nevertheless, the greater part of the book – 95 pages – is certainly made up of individual members' contributions. This is because the Commission saw it as its duty to respect and respond to the fundamental difficulties many thoughtful people were experiencing in the culture of the time. Within a framework on which Christians right across the ecumenical spectrum might agree, the Commission sought to model the freedom that individuals might rightly enjoy to work out their own faith affirmations with intellectual integrity. This approach was misunderstood in the Church of England, where something more domestically reassuring was preferred. Sadly, it was easier to caricature those responsible for this considerable achievement as 'negative' theologians, and to dismiss what they wrote, than actually to enter the conversation.

Given the state of the Church at the time it is not surprising that membership of the Doctrine Commission was entirely male, and that all but one were dons. The one exception, Michael Green, then rector of the famous evangelical church of St Aldate's, Oxford, can hardly be classified as an ordinary parish priest representing an ordinary parish constituency. It is also true that John Baker, canon of Westminster, was also rector of St Margaret's, but while St Aldate's and St Margaret's may function in more commonplace ways than most would guess, it is still true that they are rather exotic by comparison with a team ministry in Basingstoke.

John Taylor's own assessment of the state of play when he took over the chair of the Doctrine Commission is that 'there was a reaction against their report in the church, and so I came in on the crest of a wave of people wanting something different'.[134] Others suggest that this reaction against the report was quite pronounced: 'It was slated by the church.'[135] Evidently, the Church didn't like looking into the mirror to find itself so divided, particularly because it was true.

The severity of these judgements, including that from John Taylor himself, demonstrate the popular mood in the Church at the time. Regardless of their accuracy, and however distressing they may be to those intimately involved – indeed, precisely because they are so extreme and hurtful – they are noises we need to hear if we are not to underestimate the difficulties facing the Commission.

The place of theology and of theologians in Anglicanism is tenuous. There is always popular fear of doctrine being imposed from above. Perhaps this is part of the no-popery tradition, but whatever its origin, fear is always the antithesis of faith, the mortal enemy of all faith. Even John Taylor is capable of using the word 'academic' in its pejorative sense – the ivory towers of the academy being, by definition, remote from the real world where people laugh and bleed and struggle to be faithful. Was it that the Church rejected a Doctrine Commission which successfully forced it to look in the mirror, or was it that the Church refused to look at all and resented those who encouraged it to do so?

It might be better history to suggest that the Church of the 1970s was in denial about the turbulence of the 1960s, simply refusing to think through the implications of the 'death of God' and *Honest to God* debates.[136] Rather than receive the unwelcome challenge to engage the contemporary questions, and make the effort required to change the currency of Christian proclamation, it was easier to shoot the messenger.

Looking back, it becomes clear that anger in the Church over *Christian Believing* was disproportionate to the provocation. Members of the Doctrine Commission were not removed from the common life of the Church. Indeed, they were of all people most acutely aware of the intellectual challenges to belief, and passionately concerned to help ordinary Christian people to be faithful in engaging with their contemporaries, particularly with fringe-dwellers and those genuinely concerned to explore the possibilities of faith. If they felt it was a hard but exciting time to be Christian, they differed in this from their less secure and less articulate fellow-travellers. They offered adventure and deeper exploration of the mystery which grasps us, where too many in the Church craved reassurance that they were already on the right track and respite from the storm. One symptom of this craving for security is the fact that the standing committee of the General Synod refused to put the report on the synod's agenda. It was never discussed. The Commission was condemned unheard, its words unread. 'But the agenda has not gone away, and the Church of

England has paid dearly for its cowardice in refusing to grapple with basic issues of belief in the last quarter of the 20th century.'[137]

In the face of so much fragmentation, the next three reports of the Doctrine Commission had somehow to express the corporate nature of faith. Significantly, the working title of the first of them, *Believing in the Church*, was, all the way through the process, *Corporate Believing*.[138] It was an important achievement, more important for the Church to produce than for the Church to read. And even if the reports didn't become best-sellers, 'the house-party picture of people who were writing good things, and preaching good things, and who were being stimulated by the shared experience – that was probably more of value to the church than the books they struggled to produce'.[139] These were welcome signs of healing.

How did this reconciliation come about? The answer seems to lie somewhere in John Taylor's personality, for while there is more continuity between the various incarnations of the Doctrine Commission than is sometimes admitted, John Taylor succeeded in building trust between the Church and its theological commission where it did not exist before.

The Doctrine Commission had been used to meeting over a number of days. John Taylor inherited this arrangement and all meetings were residential over several days in different parts of the country. It is said that he ran the Doctrine Commission like a series of house-parties for friends.[140] Within the family he expected you to share not just your ideas but your-self.[141] Living together, praying together and eating together were as important as thinking together. So too was drinking together, and the chairman was careful to provide the bar himself if there was none, or see that there was a convenient pub if they stayed in any teetotal establishment.[142]

All this was considered essential to doing good theology together. Naturally, individuals fought passionately for things in which they believed, and which they thought the Church would lose at its peril. Nevertheless, conviction was pitted against conviction in an attempt to penetrate to deeper levels of truth, and always in a spirit of wanting to reopen questions in order to uncover underlying issues, seeking fresh ways to heal old wounds. The aim was always to reconcile traditional hostilities by really listening to one another, rather than shouting one another down. In some ways, it must be acknowledged, John Taylor's task in all this was easier than that of his predecessors. The membership of the Commission in John Taylor's time was still representative of different schools of thought in the Church of England, but it was nevertheless rather more homo-geneous than before, giving the members greater freedom. There was more basic consensus, and less need to contest precise details of phrasing. The one or two identifiable evangelicals or catholics were certainly loyal to their particular tradition, but open to new ways of expressing it, while most members, including John Taylor himself, were centrist Anglicans. This gave greater scope for John Taylor's natural inclination to expend creative energy on exploring fresh territory rather than revisiting old battlegrounds.

Years later, in prefaces to the reissue of a book which meant a great deal to him and a group report in which he delighted, John Taylor reveals some of the convictions undoubtedly driving his leadership of the Doctrine Commission.[143] For the unusual ecumenical group who produced reflections on 'the complementarity of men and women in ministry' called *A Fearful Symmetry?* John Taylor had high praise.

> Instead of deploying arrogantly rigid certainties, they re-opened the questions to uncover the underlying issues. Instead of winning arguments they have come to recognise and value God's truth in each other. They have not resolved their differences but transcended them through their delight in the unity of spirit which they have discovered.

Writing about the delicate process of inter-faith dialogue, John Taylor expresses beliefs equally essential in intra-faith dialogue, where members of one church may only recognize one another's faith with difficulty.[144] Talking among ourselves can be as difficult as, if not more difficult than, dialogue with peoples of other faiths and none.

> Those who argue the theoretical pros and cons of dialogue as a missionary method seem unable to imagine that the adherents of different faiths can meet simply as friends. But unless it grows out of the gentle delving and slow maturing of friendship, dialogue is only an exercise in indifference, the very antithesis of love. The real thing does not happen mainly in the study or the classroom, but in the home and the bazaar, on the pilgrimage and in the temple. It is just as interested in the other man's unbelief as in his belief, in what he regards as secular as in what he regards as sacred. So a great deal of the value of this exquisite book lies in its uncomplicated delight in people and the places they live in.[145]

In these observations we simply hear a very human voice, albeit the experienced voice of theologian and missionary. Finding such a voice in such circumstances is all too rare.

The motto of the Doctrine Commission under John Taylor's chairmanship could easily have been the word common and vital to both these reflections: *delight*. And yet this may not be quite right.[146] It was hard work, although it was often fun. For John Taylor himself it seems to have been something of an intellectual lifeline, another opportunity for testing his experience and theology in company with some of the best minds in the Church of England. 'It's the discovery of *koinonia* – to live together in community and to wrestle with each other's papers is to discover a common life. That's the mark of John Taylor.'[147]

Farewell

If Jerusalem and Galilee were the place names for a contemporary Christian presence at the beginning of John Taylor's episcopate, by the end of his ten years as Bishop of Winchester, the view had broadened. There is a third place on the map which is just as pivotal – the coast where land and sea meet, where one looks beyond the land to the horizon.

In the gospels, this is the coast of Tyre and Sidon, beyond the land-locked borders of the promised land. In the diocese of Winchester, it is the view of the English Channel, including the Channel Islands which are part of the diocese.

> For the first and only recorded time Jesus stands looking out to the level horizon of the sea. What did it say to him whose whole vocabulary had been of corn fields and sheep folds, vineyards and lakeside fishing nets? Impact there must have been, for he was of all men most responsive to a landscape of small plots enclosed in boundary walls; he had grown up to recognise the frontiers between one demesne and the next, one tribal heritage and another. His landlocked world was a network of barriers.
>
> But here the dark blue Mediterranean stretched without line or marker to the horizon and the galleys ploughed their paths hither and thither with no thought of trespass. Even that straight horizon was no boundary, but only the limit of a man's sight. And down there among the rigging and the bales of the fortified harbour, Greeks and Romans, Phoenicians and Egyptians, and men from any port between Cornwall and Ceylon, the slave and the freeman, the honest and the crook, accepted one another in the tough, salty brotherhood of trade.[148]

John Taylor, also exceptionally sensitive to a landscape or seascape, is convinced that these sights 'stirred in Jesus a subversive thought', just as they do in him. The sea needs to flow into the minds of Christ's disciples now as it did in the beginnings of the Christian movement.

What will this mean at the end of the second Christian millennium and at the beginning of the third? In St Paul's words, it will mean 'welcoming one another as Christ welcomed us'. In ecclesiastical terms it will mean ordinary things like welcoming the joining or amalgamating of parishes. It must include crossing class barriers to welcome people of different backgrounds into the community of the Church. It means welcoming women into roles previously reserved exclusively for men. Socially, it means welcoming people of different races and creeds as neighbours in the same street or city. Nationally, it means welcoming the participation of workers in policy-making decisions once reserved for executives. In conservative Hampshire, it means welcoming the voice of 'Her Majesty's most loyal Opposition in Parliament instead of seeming to deride it'.

This last counsel from the cathedral pulpit is both visionary in the wide sense and practical in specific detail. Perhaps this is also a conscious attempt to rectify previous reticence? Theological principle is notoriously difficult to translate into detailed practice and this translation may best be left to the imagination of individuals who hear the gospel. The preacher must take care not to cultivate dependency by making decisions for the congregation. The call, for preacher and congregation alike, is always to corporate responsibility and individual decision. But what of those with little imagination? And what of our capacity for self-delusion and avoidance of the clear implications of Christian teaching? Where does the task of the preacher begin and end in this equation? 'Perhaps I should have been more insistent, more explicit, in working out those practical implications and consequently more misunderstood and disliked. It seems impossible to judge the point where gentleness becomes cowardice.'[149]

Now, at the end, it is time to take this risk. For the gospel must touch down in the real world. It must connect. Faith must make a difference to the way we live now. Catching the vision of the open sea enables us to turn back and live it out in the narrow land.

At the last

John Taylor died just before midnight on 30 January 2001, the eve of the anniversary of his consecration as bishop. In retirement from active ministry he had remained as active as ever. 'He carried on being the person he had always been: he wrote and thought; he sent those marvellous Christmas poems; he spent time with his family and friends, and travelled, just making God real to lots more people.'[150] In demand as a teacher, preacher and retreat conductor, he continued to share his wisdom generously until the very end of his life. Knowing as much about suffering as he knew about success, he was gladly received as a fellow traveller and explorer, a mystic who understood that there is no way of loving God apart from simultaneously loving neighbour and nature. His vision was always about seeing God's world whole.[151]

In old age, nothing from his long experience was lost, not a single drop. Indeed, it is plain from the work undertaken and the quality of the published material that he was at the top of his form. This continued until very near the end. The central question continued to be addressed: Who is God, what is God really like, how *Christian* is the Christian Church's God?

Much of this was focused in his continuing meditations on at-one-ment, the true meaning of atonement wrought in Christ. It had been impossible to work this out, as he had hoped to do, in an official report of the Doctrine Commission of the Church of England.[152] As a respected bishop, known for his reverence for the categories of biblical thought, who had become a liberal theologian, whom no one could accuse of diluting the revealed faith, he was free to chart such realms. In 1982 he had asked members of the

Doctrine Commission to write papers on the weakness of God and they encouraged him to explore his own intuition that this insight is essential to any credible late twentieth and early twenty-first century theology.[153] In truth, however, the traditional opposition was strong enough to block any breakthrough in the Commission itself. Characteristically, John Taylor pursued the matter for himself, using the material other members supplied and working his ideas out in dialogue with various audiences in his retirement. We can see that he was using parts of this material with the students of his old theological college, Wycliffe Hall in Oxford, in the 1985 Chavasse Lectures. He returned to the theme more fully at the Romess Summer School in Rome in 1990, and again with the Society for Ordained Scientists in 1991, eventually publishing the resulting book as *The Christlike God* in 1992. Atonement, he would argue, is achieved not so much in Christ offering human suffering to the Father in sacrifice, as by offering divine suffering to humankind in love.[154] Calvary, in this daring and compelling vision, is all about the suffering God seeking our forgiveness.[155]

As so often with John Taylor, this is all about seeing and about learning to see in new ways so that what we usually miss comes into view. He whose eyesight was so afflicted helped thousands to see as if for the first time. He who wrote so compellingly of the Holy Spirit as the Giver of life, of awareness, of communication and communion, was himself exemplary as a life-giver.[156] Many will happily testify that parts of themselves were asleep before they met John Taylor.[157]

> I remember ... on the Diocesan Pilgrimage from Dorchester-on-Thames to Winchester in 1979 walking around the edge of the Atomic Research Station at Harwell, and John talked about atomic structure, and how marvellous it is, and quoted the line from Hopkins about the God who puts the veins in violets. He then went on to talk about God's concern with the little and the invisible and how significant that was for our understanding of Jesus, who was also always concerned with the little and with the detail, as well as the whole picture. He seemed able, always, to put experience under the microscope or, conversely, to look at it through a telescope.
>
> There was a connectedness about his thinking which was distinctive. His mind didn't seem to be in compartments, but everything was related to everything else, and above all he had the gift of reflecting on ordinary everyday events, and finding meaning in them. He was always aware of what was going on and what was happening. He didn't stay on the surface. So I learnt from him, as have countless others, that God can be found in everything. John wrote and spoke, but above all he wrote on lives.[158]

There can be no doubting the fact that this writing on lives could be very costly. Grounded in his own childhood, it constituted a pattern of living as self-giving. His children remember their parents filling the house with guests from all over the world. Even Christmas was never a narrowly family affair. Like his father before him, John Taylor was always available for other people and other people's children, but was not always there for his own family.[159] His family had to share him with so many others that retirement presented itself as an opportunity to make some sort of reparation, especially to Peggy, but also to Peter and Joanna and Veronica. It is perhaps not unfair to suggest that by this time the pattern was too well established to be substantially altered, and John Taylor could be painfully aware of this.[160] Retirement did, in theory at least, mean more time with Peggy, more time with adult children and grandchildren, more time with friends. In fact, of course, John Taylor continued to be in demand. Almost as soon as he left Winchester in 1984 he was in Geneva giving Holy Week talks to the staff of the World Council of Churches, resulting in one of his loveliest books, *Weep Not for Me*.[161] After the Chavasse Lectures of 1985 he was leading a Mission to the University of Oxford in 1986, giving a series of talks published later the same year as *A Matter of Life and Death*. *Kingdom Come*, published in 1989, grew out of the Three Hour Devotion on Good Friday 1988 in Westminster Abbey, the Provincial Conference of the Scottish Episcopal Church and the Cantess Summer School in Canterbury that same year, as well as clergy conferences in Chelmsford and Chester in 1989.[162] In 1989 he also published a selection of his poetry.[163] All this thinking and writing and editing for publication, not to mention sermons up and down the land, lectures and retreat addresses, meant that Peggy continued to endure 'a closeted and preoccupied husband' with the kind of love he was always thinking and talking and writing about.[164]

Not surprisingly, his funeral became the climax and celebration of this way of life. Inevitably a very public affair, his family had now to endure the eulogizing by so many who shared a little of their own much more profound sense of loss. To others an inspired teacher, a great priest and prophet, even a saint who made God near and real and believable, for them he was simply husband, father, grandfather. Sharing him in death as in life was a curious mixture of pain and comfort. All the more precious, then, were the quiet moments, particularly at the vigil.

> His coffin, covered with a linen pall and flanked by six tall white candles with a spray of Magdalen lilies laid upon it, was very beautiful. We said some prayers, then sat for a long time in silence, so we were able to have our private time alone with him in the calm of the candlelight. The next day the chapel was filled with sunlight and the glorious sound as of angels.[165]

The humble theologian approached his own death trusting, except in the bad moments of terrible pain and loss of dignity, that personal life goes on beyond death. Typically, he was not prepared to claim too much or pretend to a certainty beyond human reach. Indeed, he felt strongly that our gratitude should not be greedily conditioned by the hope of resurrection, preferring as an ideal a prayer enclosed in a letter to Victor Gollancz from a fellow-student just after the outbreak of the First World War, following their last term together at Oxford. Printed in the order of service, it was the first greeting for those gathered for the funeral that John Taylor had so carefully devised in every detail.

> To have given me self-consciousness but for an hour in a world so breathless with beauty would have been enough. But Thou hast preserved it within me for twenty years now and more, and hast crowned it with the joy of this summer of summers. And so, come what may, whether life or death, and, if death, whether bliss unimaginable or nothingness, I thank Thee and bless Thy name.

To which was added a poem of his own, summing up his whole life's quest, his vision and the revelations of divine love granted him, the words set to music by his friend Jonathan Harvey.

> Should you hear them singing among stars
> or whispering secrets of a wiser world,
> do not imagine ardent fledgling children;
> they are intelligences old as sunrise
> that never learnt right from left, before from after,
> knowing but one direction, into God,
> but one duration, now.
>
> Their melody strides not from bar to bar,
> but, like a painting, hangs there entire,
> one chord of limitless communication.
> You have heard it in the rhythms of the hills,
> the spiralling turn of a dance, the fall of words,
> the touch of fingers at the rare right moment –
> and these were holy, holy.[166]

Later, at the Memorial Service in Winchester Cathedral, there were surprises, pleasant surprises or revelations into the private heart of this very public man.

Nearly blind, John Taylor, for whom vision was so central and so precious, lived his final months in the presence of the famous icon of the Holy Trinity by St Andrei Rublev. At the end, word and image were held together, so that the icon and the text on which it is based had to be provided in the order of service.[167] There too, greeting those gathering in the cathedral that afternoon, were two of the six or seven poems John had in his head from his experience with the icon in his dying. Only these two were written down, the others went with him on his final journey.

These last sermons that John Taylor offered to the world, crafted in pain, show us the sensitive soul still expecting divine revelation through ordinary human experience.[168]

At the last he is still searching patiently, passionately, for the right word – in company with Peggy, his most perceptive encourager, together knowing themselves tangled with God.[169]

Must it be I, then, the wanderer Abraham,
acclaimed for faith in an impossible promise,
who sits now at ease in the shade of the tree
named at the start as the place to make good the blessing?
How shall an immigrant possess the land,
or an inbred sterile clan people it?

Yet miracle it is to sit in the tent door in the heat
of the day and the day's discord.
But why this intrusion of a chosen people,
branded by covenant, tangled with God
from all creation as his partner and mirror-image?
Better the simple universal witness
of the visible world to every soul alike,
whereby we learn to live in the two Realities
of Him who is and all that is becoming,
of the Changeless and the ever-changing,
of the Stillness and the Activity.

How right that, with his ashes so recently buried in the quiet of the
Lady Chapel garden next to the great cathedral he loved so well, John
should then be speaking silently to the hearts of all those gathered inside
to honour him, another Abraham.

Love in its fullness loomed, love
loomed at the tent door in its truth,
not the sole unique truth
reserved for the incomparable God,
but for a love consisting of communion.
I, Abraham, looked for a single
flower; but it has blossomed into a
multiple head, made for sharing.
Love's ultimate reality, gazing at the Son
proclaims 'I AM'.
And He, as love's obedience,
responds 'I will'.
And the Spirit, love's delight,
says 'look and see'.
Their mutuality precedes creation
being Eternal, and offers the only space
in which it can exist.
So the cup of suffering at which they gaze
is the price already paid
for the world's pardon. 'The Lamb
slain before the foundation
of the world.'[170]

CHAPTER NINE

Christlike God

Unlike the maze in an English garden, which is designed to help the explorer get lost, the labyrinth in a gothic cathedral is arranged so that explorers find their way to the centre. Quietly, prayerfully, persistently walking the labyrinth inevitably brings the pilgrim to the heart of the matter. Theological enquiry, of course, is not quite like this. Undoubtedly, there are many false starts and wrong turns along the way. Some highways turn out to be side roads, or even dead ends. Theology can be maze-like for individuals and indeed for whole Christian communities. We assume we have arrived when we are still far from home. John Taylor's relentless pursuit of the *Christian* God, his will to discover and proclaim only the God who is truly Father to Jesus Christ, can be likened to walking the medieval labyrinth. Rather than losing his way, it seems that the direction has become for him steadily more obvious. Taking seriously the revelation of God's nature in Christ, giving it its full weight, allowing it to determine and shape and direct everything, has occupied his attention from his earliest days. There is no stage of his life and ministry when this concern has not been central for him. Indeed, it can be said that his long and intimate experience of the mission and ministry of the Church in the world has served only to deepen his passion, making the quest more urgent for him.

In his earliest book, *Man in the Midst*, he is already writing about Jesus Christ as the hallmark and measure of both divinity and humanity.

> We are accustomed to think that if we want to know what God is like we must look at Jesus Christ, and should our conception of God differ in any way from what we see in Jesus, then our picture of God needs to be adjusted. But it is equally true to say that if we want to know what Man really is we must look at Jesus Christ, for only in Him have we ever seen what Martin Luther called 'the proper Man'.[1]

This has the flavour of an orthodox formula routinely recited, the kind of slogan no Christian theologian would ever question. Strangely, however, very few consciously and energetically put it into practice, pressing it until it defines and shapes the whole fabric of theological exploration. Adjusting our picture of God is too threatening for most of us, too fraught with the danger and risk of heresy, to become a daily preoccupation. We are also too insecure in ourselves to juggle with our own identity, which, as John Taylor knows, is the other side of such theologizing. Jesus Christ is the measure not only of 'the proper God', but also of 'the proper human being'. Yet, for all the 'business as usual' flavour, there is a deceptive seriousness of purpose here. Perhaps it is still in embryo, but it will become the work of a lifetime. Ten years and more in Uganda, experiencing the primal vision at first hand, sifting inherited theological concepts and constructs to see what they really mean, faith seeking understanding so that it can be taught in a new and very concrete language, leaves this particular theologian in an internal state of flux. What does it all add up to? What has he learnt? What is he still learning, as he returns to the West informed by an alien culture? Already, this new author is sure that there is no genuine theology which touches only the heavenly realm while leaving the earthly plane intact. From his study of the Scriptures in the light of the best commentaries of his day, from his readings in the Fathers, from his own experience as priest and pastor in England and Africa, John Taylor is already actively opposed to any tear in the fabric of reality. Already he is sure that the Christian revelation denies all forms of dualism, knitting together in the incarnate Lord all that we split asunder. To look at Jesus is simultaneously to see the face of God and to look into our own eyes. Indeed, the martyr Dietrich Bonhoeffer, whose prison writings are only just beginning to appear in English as John Taylor begins to write, is teaching an already christocentric John Taylor that Christ is in fact the measure not only of God and humankind, but of all things without exception.[2]

In this final chapter we need to look even more closely than we already have at the Jesus who opens a clear view into the heart of God. We need to see through John Taylor's eyes the One whose living and teaching and dying disclose God's Christlikeness distinctively among the great world religions and definitively for all human beings. Using the word 'Christian' as an adjective rather than a noun, we need to chart something of what it means to allow Christ to heal our blindness. What are the consequences for theology, anthropology and mission, when they become genuinely *Christian* theology, *Christian* anthropology and *Christian* mission?

Christian God

The concept or image of God is the central issue.[3] Everything depends on who God really is as God. Faulty apprehension of God as a metaphysical being over and above and outside time and space, who fills gaps in our knowledge and descends to our aid in boundary situations, has fundamental consequences for the way we live here and now. Both Karl Barth and Dietrich Bonhoeffer agreed with Blaise Pascal that the God of the philosophers and of much popular Christianity is not the God of Abraham, Isaac and Jacob, let alone the Father of Jesus Christ. They were agreed that the metaphysical God must die completely in order to make room for the true and living God: Jesus Christ as revealed on the cross and proclaimed and attested in the Scriptures. The human face of God has been obscured and distorted beyond all recognition and must be allowed to turn afresh to us in revelation, in gracious self-disclosure. We are to allow the only true God to look into our eyes and melt our hearts.

John Taylor is clear that we can begin only where God begins, namely with the fact that God acts and has acted in history. Jesus Christ is God's event, and always the primary event for the Christian. Revelation is personal and allegiance is personal. 'I am a devotee of Jesus before I am a believer in Christianity.'[4] To start with the man Jesus is to start where the disciples started. They felt his magnetism, his hold over them, the enchantment of his personality and presence, his disturbance of their complacency and challenge to their ideas. They loved him long before they began asking who he was.[5]

> Out of the Bible and in the Church God comes, as it were, striding to meet us in our contemporary situation; and in that meeting we find an absolute demand to do His will in His way, and a devouring conviction as to what that will and that way really are.[6]

We are not handed a set of moral principles or religious ideals. We are given insights into truth resulting from personal encounter with a particular kind of God and through faith in this particular kind of God. This encounter leads to praise, to theology as rhapsody, to theology as doxology.[7]

> Jesus was so intensely alive that seen against that glowing vitality other men seemed like candle-flames in the sun. He was so real that His gaze never flickered or swerved with the self-deception that is habitual to us, but he 'saw himself steadily and saw it whole'. Yet never did He guard himself from the impact of sin and suffering. We throw around ourselves the hard protective shell of indifference, and, beyond the small circle of our personal sympathies, ward off the woe of the world with the high walls of our individualism. But Jesus, because He was wide open to God, was wide open to men, for it is impossible to be one without the other. The vicarious suffering of Christ was not, as it has sometimes been represented, a sort of legal fiction; 'in all their afflictions he was afflicted' was quite literally true through the imaginative sensitiveness of His perfect Manhood. In a limitless compassion He Himself knew what was in Man. He groped in the darkness of Bartimaeus, and was filled with the self-loathing of the leper; His soul was sick with the Magdalen's sin, and was lost in the tortuous suspicions of Judas. As true Man He felt to the full His involvement with All-Man, and carried the world in His heart.[8]

But John Taylor is no romantic if this means being without a sure foothold in the real world. He knows that history must be capable of sustaining such praise, otherwise his theologizing will be little more than wishful thinking. Is it possible or not, for instance, to say that Jesus's humanity was perfect, that he of all people was imaginatively sensitive to some inordinate degree? Is this in any way verifiable, or is this simply Christian devotion built on previous Christian devotion? Honesty compels us to acknowledge that the faith of the Church is terrifyingly vulnerable, since God chooses to put revelation completely at risk in the flux of human history. It is of its very nature an extremely precarious experiment, open to misperception and misunderstanding, not to mention possible or even probable failure. John Taylor believes that twentieth-century biblical scholarship affirms that in the documents of the New Testament we are dealing with remarkably trustworthy material, although we must confess that all the writers arrange their material as theology rather than biography and that all of it comes to us interpreted and shaped by the earliest Christian communities. Nevertheless, of the person who is the central figure in the story, we can say: 'This was no-one's invention. This strange yet consistent character is the Jesus who started it all.' Indeed, while the evangelists themselves could not grasp his truth fully, so that the Church had to include four gospels rather than one in the New Testament canon, so also later doctors or saints, however brilliant or holy, have been unable to do so. The truth is that he grasps us, while we never grasp him.[9]

It is no surprise then, that from first to last, theology for John Taylor turns out to be christology, or that his christology is consistently pursued 'from below'. Always he begins with the facts, something he learned as a missionary in Africa. In other words, he begins nowhere else than where the first disciples began, with the evidence of Jesus himself. The fact of this historical man Jesus is the criterion for christology. The historical Jesus is the locus where we learn to speak of God, Jesus as a genuine individual whose life is open to scrutiny like any other life. In other words, you cannot begin christology with a fully developed concept of God already in place and then specify how much divine being can be brought within the limits of human existence. On the contrary, it is only in Christ's full and true humanity that we see all we can see of the divine nature and reality, so that the pre-Easter Jesus and the post-Easter Jesus are one and the same. The risen Christ is the same one who died on the cross. The five wounds survive in eternity. The resurrection adds no new revelation to what is already given. God is known to us in the complete human obedience of Christ perfected in suffering. The historic life of Jesus is the characteristic action of God. The εχενωσεν, the *kenosis* of Christ, that self-emptying involved in his self-giving and self-oblation, is not some dimming-down of the divine nature, a curtailment of it, but a positive expression of it.[10]

The first Christians began with Jesus the man, with someone they knew to be *totus in nobis*, entirely one of us. They quickly recognized in him something exceptional, but whatever he did and whatever he was, they had no doubt that he did it and was it as a man, as a fellow human being. From his intimate communion with God sprang an unusual authority, out of which he attempted to imitate God in all his relationships. He made God near and real and believable in a new way.[11] So much so that his followers were finding it impossible to think of God apart from this man, as he coloured all their impressions of God.[12] Being in his presence was habituating them to see God in a new light.[13] He was also evoking in them new convictions concerning God.[14] To be with him was to have your religious experience enlarged and transformed.[15] He was like a ladder reaching up from earth to heaven.[16] When they called him κυριος (*kurios*), the Lord, it was a title open to higher and higher gradations of meaning, ranging from the profound respect due to a prophet through to the reverence which is due to God alone.[17]

> Because he knew God to be gracious and forgiving he consorted with those who most needed compassion and forgiveness. Because he knew God to be just he denounced the hard-hearted and self-righteous. Because he knew the nearness of God in experience he announced the immanence of God's intervention to take control, lived as one already within the coming kingdom, and dared others to do so with him.[18]

Inevitably, living out what he understood to be God's nature in such uncompromising fashion brought Jesus to grief, to a cross between two thieves, to the place where God has always been.[19] In other words, there is nothing new or novel here. It's just that we see the reality for the first time. Helplessness and execution were never optional; they are integral to this way. Astonishingly, however, it was precisely in this disastrous, God-forsaken debacle that the truth of Jesus was experienced.

> Once again the earth was waste and void, once again the darkness was upon the face of the abyss, once again there was absolute chaos because it looked as if love had been defeated. And once again the Spirit moved upon the face of the waters of death in a new act of creation, and God said, 'Let there be light'.[20]

Here we hear the distinctive voice of the prophet and poet.

> Their certainty of his exaltation by God, which was also a certainty of his presence in their midst, convinced them that his knowledge of God as Father had been true, his representation of the Father in his words and behaviour had been true, his message that the new age of God's rule was about to break in and be fulfilled, his defiance in setting himself above certain customs and his disturbing acceptance of outsiders and outcasts was confirmed, and even his decision to let himself be handed over to helplessness, apparent failure and death was truly vindicated. By raising him from death into glory God had acknowledged it all. The one who had called people to believe had become the object of faith, and to decide for or against God's rule was identical with a decision for or against Jesus.[21]

Yet for all their certainty about Jesus' matchless intimacy with God, his disciples instinctively avoided naming him God as such. They did not compromise their Jewish monotheistic faith, because they were at pains to safeguard the distinction between the risen Lord and the God who raised him, between Jesus and his God and Father, between the one who was sent and the One who sent him.[22] It was the later attempt to embed the Christian faith into the very foundations of European thought which enriched the Church with concepts it could not have hit upon in any other way, but also lumbered it with fixed ideas it has still to unlearn.[23] It is hard to avoid the impression that John Taylor's acknowledgement that Christian theology has been enriched by philosophical concepts from a culture foreign to that in which it was born is little more than paying lip service. His heart isn't really in such affirmation, for the down side of the bargain is that so many of these philosophical concepts have proved lethal to the flowering of authentic Christianity. There is, in the mind of John Taylor, an inevitability about the unlearning that will happen in the continuing dialogue between the gospel and culture, but he also recognizes the strength of the resistance movement. In the past four centuries, and especially in the twentieth century, analysis of what is meant by 'to be' and 'to know' has exploded many of the basic assumptions of the classical and medieval philosophy that has been underpinning theology, and this must have its effect. Nevertheless, John Taylor's urgent need to help the process along is plain, for 'the battle drags on around each of the four bastions of the older theistic philosophy like a military pageant staged amid castle ruins'.[24]

In order to escape our fixed ideas about God and allow Jesus of Nazareth to revise the content of the word 'God' for us, an extensive demolition operation is required. A lifetime of preaching and teaching convinced John Taylor that it is insufficient simply to present the gospel. Alongside this consistent and patient presentation, active attack on persistent distortions is demanded. The propensity for human beings to invent God in our own image seems to be so perennial that this two-pronged approach to the problem becomes necessary. To put the matter bluntly, European philosophy presents us with a god who is inaccessible, splendid in isolation, unchangeable and unaffected by the world. On the face of it, this schema appears to contradict the gospel in every basic essential. It seems to present a flat denial of God's decisive revelation. In Jesus we meet God who draws near to us, God whose being and nature is overflowing Love, God who is full of surprises and new initiatives, God who suffers with us and for us. Disastrously, in the face of this experience, the Church has avoided drawing the inevitable conclusions, expending its energy in attempting to make the gospel intellectually respectable by forcing it into the classical philosophical strait-jacket. Jesus is worked into an already existing picture of God rather than allowing Jesus to critique and reconstruct all existing images of God. The theological bracketing off of the incarnate Christ makes him inadmissible as evidence of the essential nature of God.[25] John Taylor's abiding passion is so to set the gospel free of this entanglement with

Western philosophy that we may meet Jesus 'again for the first time'.[26] The contention of this study is that his attempt to do so is convincing, and the radical orthodoxy he offers in place of traditional orthodoxy is attractive in a world of many religions and none.

The earliest Christian attempts to reconcile God's absolute difference and beyondness with accessibility and relatedness to the world simply reinforced the supposed chasm between God and the world. The Absolute stood over against the creation, uninvolved and untouchable. They could not see that, infinite as the difference must be between God and all that is, yet the very creatures who recognize this have in themselves something that belongs to the same order as God. Far from needing the divine Logos to bridge the gap between divinity and humanity in a spectacularly uncharacteristic gesture, human beings are the common ground on which finite and infinite meet.

> This must mean that the immanent God preserves his incognito. Like the potentiality of things, God's presence within them is strictly undetectable. If you ask what is actually there beside the physical facts you must answer 'Not a thing'. And if something in the way things are alerts you to the 'more', then receive that 'more' by faith, for it leaves no trace by which you can convince others. For God in his involvement in the world *is* the transcendent One, the Beyond. The truth of God transcendent and of God immanent, his mystery and his availability, must be held together as a single reality, dialectical to human thought but indivisible in itself. This is not poetical paradox but the dialectical truth forced upon us by the fact that the transcendence of God consists in an inexhaustible self-giving.[27]

So, not surprisingly, John Taylor quotes approvingly the second-century apologist St Justin:

> I know that the Immovable comes down;
> I know that the Invisible appears to me;
> I know that he who is far outside the whole creation
> Takes me into himself and hides me in his arms.[28]

The Christian experience of God as triune is precisely this – it is human experience. It is not, in other words, merely some dogmatic formula which must be fitted somehow into the assumption that God is indivisibly and simply one.

> Had Christianity been free to witness to its experience of the saving potency of Jesus and the inner process of prayer without resorting to metaphysical definitions it need never have turned God into an object of logical definition, nor taken up a position so incompatible with simple monotheism.[29]

Sadly, however, it was soon forgotten that the words Father, Son and Spirit are all metaphors, as the doctrine of the Trinity was tragically formulated so as to become incomprehensible to ordinary Christians and an affront to other monotheists.[30] Had it been otherwise, the course of religious history might have been quite different, not least because the rise of Islam seems in part to have been reaction against Christianity's perceived perversion of pure monotheism. Yet Christians began to speak of God in trinitarian terms only because they were forced to do so in order to be true to their experience – their personal experience of God above and beyond them, of God alongside them and of God within them. If we look for analogies to speak of God, they will inevitably be completely inadequate human analogies which yet point reliably to the truth. For example, when we look within to our own fragmentary experience of love, we are compelled to speak of God as Love in more than static terms.

> If the One that is before and beyond and within all is self-giving, self-abandoning love, there must be within that love a ceaseless reciprocity between that which is ever anew pouring forth love from its inexhaustible fullness, that which ever receives and recognises and responds with love, and that which, in love with love, as it were, delights in the very goodness of that mutual exchange.[31]

The doctrine of God's changelessness has to do, then, not so much with what the philosophers supposed was self-sufficiency in God, as with God being always true to the divine nature.[32] It is about God being always God, faithful, true, stable, reliable.[33] This, John Taylor argues, does not prevent God doing new things by way of self-expression or self-disclosure, for 'God's sameness is not monotony'.[34]

> The very Word of God was being spoken, God the Son was present in their midst, yet what was heard and seen was nothing but human. The 'becoming' was complete. As with the divine immanence in all creation so now with the Incarnation, his being 'here' does not exhaust his being both everywhere and beyond all place. And again, as with the immanent presence so with the incarnate, there was no extra 'substance', no additional element of divinity alongside the human fact. The human and divine aspects of Jesus are distinct only as two equally true ways of understanding this human being whom God has become. He eludes the grasp of biography, and the silence of his solitude when he withdraws for prayer, walks ahead on the road or hangs from the cross, is wrapped in a cloud of unknowing. Kierkegaard called it 'the most profound incognito', but in fact it was not a concealment but a revelation. Precisely by becoming nothing but man God disclosed the whole truth of himself, all we shall ever see ...[35]

If it is true to say that theology is always christology, it is equally true to claim that christology is always soteriology. In any serious attempt to rethink christological belief, the primacy of soteriology must be recognized. The sense that the story of Jesus Christ provides the clue we need, the key to life, the answer to our moral idealism, is the driving force within any christology worthy of the name, the energy behind any worthwhile theology. Above all, this story expresses God's involvement in the suffering and evil of human experience and demonstrates God's commitment to redeeming the creation, or it is not worth the paper it is written on.[36] This brings us to the heart of John Taylor's attempt to revise the doctrine of God, to seek an authentically *Christian* doctrine of God, allowing the Christlike God to step forward, leaving the idols behind.

When he insists that theology is always christology and christology is always soteriology, John Taylor is saying in unison with Luther and Bonhoeffer that the cross lies at the heart of it all. The most effective way to strike a death-blow to the philosophers' God, making space for the real God, is to fasten on the philosophical insistence that God is untouched by creation, unaffected by suffering, high above all the heart-breaking beauty and the equally heart-breaking brutality of life as we know it. Christianity's embracing of a god reigning in isolated, untouched splendour stems from two Greek metaphysical concepts: apathy (απαθεια – *apatheia*) and sufficiency or contentment (αυταρκεια – *autarkeia*). Apathy indicates insensibility to passion or feeling. For Aristotle, immateriality and pure reason characterize God's nature. God, therefore, experiences neither passion nor feeling. Experiencing passion would indicate that God is affected from without. Divine contentment, sufficiency or autonomy also supports the Greek conviction that no external being affects or moves God. Aristotle's God is not deficient or insufficient in any way and has no potential for change. God has no need of me and cannot move. God is the still point of the turning world, entirely passive.[37] God is immutable.[38] Any god who is subject to suffering like all other beings cannot possibly be God. Greek philosophers like Plato, Aristotle, Parmenides and the Stoics developed an understanding of God as the absolute monad, One who is self-sufficient, immutable, impassible and static.

The adoption of Greek philosophical categories by Christianity, characterizing the patristic, medieval and modern periods – the whole of Christian history, in fact – undoubtedly falsified God's nature as revealed and attested biblically. The hellenistic Jewish theologian Philo prepared the way by adopting *apatheia* as a prominent figure in his understanding of the God of Israel, and virtually all the Fathers of the Church simply took this for granted.[39] Although Ignatius and Irenaeus occasionally link Christ's Passion with God's Passion, they deny suffering as a legitimate divine attribute.[40] Ingeniously, they manage to insert a *cordon sanitaire* between God the Father and God the Son.[41] They subscribe to the paradoxical assertion that God cannot suffer except in Christ. God as God is undoubtedly impassible, yet in Christ God undoubtedly suffers! God is the Timeless, the Unseen, the One who is beyond touch or passion, who yet becomes subject to suffering, the incomprehensible made comprehensible, emotionless except in the incarnate Word.[42] No attempt is made to explain this paradox, an idea which occurs nowhere in the New Testament but which is simply introduced as a logical necessity into the doctrine of the incarnation.[43]

Like all of us, including Jesus himself, the Fathers were children of their own time and place and could not be immune from whatever ideas were in the air. An attempt to break through the Greek axiom was made in the second century, but the two key thinkers, Noetus and Praxeas, solved the problem by arguing that God the Father appears in Christ in person, that the Father is born of Mary, suffers and dies. The Catholic Church condemned this as the heresy of Patripassianism – the heresy, literally, of the suffering Father.[44] Tertullian, Clement of Alexandria, and Origen all fought furiously against any idea that God as God could suffer, or even that the divine nature in Christ might be capable of experiencing pleasure or pain. The Father is, by definition, invisible and unapproachable and placid. Tertullian actually spells it out in so many words: 'God the Father is, so to speak, the God of the philosophers.'[45] The doctrine of impassibility conquered and was considered as axiomatic in early Christian theology. Both Arius and Athanasius asserted confidently that it is only the human nature in Christ which suffers, for the divine nature is to endure in uninterrupted happiness. 'Because the impassible Word was in the passible body of Jesus, it destroyed the body's weaknesses in order to do away with them in us and to invest us with what was his, that is, immortality.'[46] Gregory of Nazianzus, likewise, resorted to paradox: 'by the sufferings of Him who could not suffer, we were taken up and saved'.[47] This impassibility tradition, a basic presupposition of all christological doctrine, was consistently upheld by Hilary of Poitiers, Augustine and later by the scholastic theologians, none of whom were able to break away from the language and conception of immutability derived from philosophical and Christian traditions. St Hilary really gives the game away when he writes, 'passibility denotes a nature that is weak'.[48] Such weakness, he reasons, cannot by definition be applied to the perfect Son of God. 'The person of the Word had no infirmity or passibility. And so when he suffered his nature remained immutable, because like his Father, his person is of an impassible essence.'[49]

Augustine's influence was so strong that he provided the framework for Western Christianity within which all future discussion of the immutability and impassibility of God is held. Anselm, for one, in order to preserve the Aristotelian idea of divine impassivity, had to deny any real feelings of love and compassion in God, maintaining that although we experienced God as compassionate, there is really no compassion in God as God. 'Thou art compassionate in terms of our experience, but not compassionate in terms of thy being.'[50] So as not to stray from accepted orthodoxy, these theologians tie themselves in knots, making pure nonsense of the gospel. So it is that St Thomas Aquinas upholds the tradition. God is *actus purus*, the 'passive *potentia* is wholly absent from Him, for *passio* is to be attributed to something only in respect of its deficiencies and imperfections.' Consequently, it cannot exist in God.[51]

Theologians of the sixteenth-century Reformation, except for Martin Luther, did not manage to bring about any break with the ancient and medieval theologies. As John Calvin writes, 'Surely God does not have blood, does not suffer, cannot be touched with hands.'[52] Only in Luther's thought does St Cyril's distinction between the proper nature of the Word and the body which the Word assumes begin to vanish.[53] For Luther, there can be no distance between the two natures of Christ: if Christ suffered, God also suffered. God suffered and died by virtue of the hypostatic union confessed in the Catholic creeds.[54] For all his formal orthodoxy in accepting the creeds and councils, Luther was bold in refusing to define the person of Christ by any prior doctrine of God, namely the Greek idea of divine *apatheia*. The suffering of Jesus as God's own suffering, for Luther, lies in the unity of the personal identity – Jesus the God-man *in toto*.

It follows that Luther's *theologia crucis* is a theology of revelation, not any a priori doctrine of God. God is the God revealed in Jesus Christ, the living Word attested by the written word in the Bible. Who God is in essence is beyond human speech, and those who seek the absolute, uncovered God are, according to Luther, speculative dreamers, simply theologians of glory. To be Christian is to humble oneself before God in God's chosen self-disclosure as attested in Scripture. This means that a Christian theologian has no choice but to be a theologian of the cross. 'We know God in the Scriptures ... where He is revealed to us, and we ought to know about this God alone and withstand all adversaries.'[55] The Scriptures are the swaddling clothes and the manger in which Christ lies. 'Simple and little are the swaddling clothes, but dear is the treasure, Christ, that lies in them.'[56] The Word of God is not words; the Word is Christ.[57] Tellingly, in contrast to the scholastic emphasis on being, the basic category for Luther's exegesis is deed.[58] This is truly evangelical, in the pure sense of being true to the evangel as it is presented in both the Jewish and the Christian Scriptures. To be concerned with God's being is inevitably to engage in human speculation. To concern oneself with God's deeds, on the other hand, is to be concerned with God's revelation. We are to rely solely on God's self-disclosure as experienced in God's redeeming work. We must prefer fact to theory, and this involves the theologian in a proper humility in the face of mysteries too great for human comprehension.

In a typically direct and colourful remark, Luther says:

> Begin where Christ began – in the Virgin's womb, in the manger, and at his mother's breasts. For this purpose he came down, was born, lived among men, was crucified and died, so that in every possible way He might present himself to our sight. He wanted to fix the gaze of our hearts upon himself and thus prevent us from clambering into heaven and speculating about the Divine majesty.[59]

No wonder Luther was determined that the Bible must be liberated from captivity to hellenized or any other a priori theological formulations. The Bible precedes any a priori notions of divine impassibility or passibility.

Biblical language about the Passion of God must be taken seriously – as it was not by the majority of the early Church Fathers since the time of Clement of Alexandria. So *theologia crucis* has to do with theological method, with the way one does theology from the ground up and in its entirety, not with one doctrine such as atonement set alongside others. The cross is 'not only the subject of theology; it is the distinctive mark of all theology'.[60] More precisely, Luther's *theologia crucis* is a dialectical principle linked to his theology of faith. 'The correlative to *crux sola* is *sola fide*, for it is through faith, and through faith alone, that the true significance of the cross is perceived.'[61] The theologian of glory expects God to be revealed in glory, majesty and strength, so, naturally, it is impossible that God is really present in the cross of Christ. The scene of dereliction is rejected out of hand as the self-revelation of the eternal nature of God. By contrast, the theologian of the cross accepts reality as it is. The theologian of the cross calls a thing by its true name, declaring that it is God incarnate who suffers death, even death on the cross for the sake of humanity's salvation. Only in the shame and humility of the cross can we find the true and gracious God. God has spoken, and therefore we are able to speak of God. The theology of the cross opposes the theology of the medieval Church which attempts to ascend to God by speculative, ethical and mystical means. In the cross of Christ God says a definitive 'No' to all human efforts to discern God's being in itself and so to achieve salvation apart from Christ.

The true theologian, for Luther, is one who beholds not the invisible but the visible God. 'Christology is the subject of theology.'[62] Luther argues that the only God he knows is God incarnate in Jesus Christ. As Luther sees it, Jesus Christ is presented in the New Testament – and presents himself – as both human and divine. The chasm between humanity and divinity is, therefore, non-existent in Christ. Luther rejects all philosophical attempts to explain this mystery. He does not for one moment pretend to know how Jesus can be both God and human, or how the divine and human natures can be one, but he accepts both simply because he is faced with the evidence that Jesus enacts both the divine and human life. The ecumenical creeds and councils of the Church must only ever be read in the light of Scripture. For Luther the basic christological question is settled at Chalcedon in 451 CE, asserting the unity of the two natures in Christ. Divinity and humanity are to be held together. Christ's humanity is 'the holy ladder to his divinity'.[63] God will, and may, only be found through Christ's humanity. Knowledge of God from above is, therefore, by definition impossible. 'One must begin from below and rise up.'[64] Luther holds to the principle, *finitum capax infiniti*: it is precisely in the finite human person that the infinite God dwells. This leads to bold statements intended to shock complacent Christians awake – as necessary at the end of the twentieth century as in the sixteenth. 'These two natures are so united that there is only one God and one Lord, that Mary suckles God with her breasts, bathes God, rocks him, and carries him … Pilate and Herod crucified and killed God.'[65] Christ's humanity is no curtain behind which an impersonal and immobile God continues to hide, for such humanity would be no humanity. Christ's humanity is the genuine article, for in itself it actually expresses God's heart, the innermost essence of God. This understanding constitutes a revolution in the conception of God in the history of the Church. Luther stands as a 'dei-passionist': God is the personal and living One who is present in the man Jesus and really shares in his human suffering. In this theology, like is known by unlike, utterly reversing all human concepts of God imported from outside. However venerable the theological tradition, however impeccable the philosophical pedigree, all other views are unequivocally declared heretical.

As one commentator says –

> Luther's *theologia crucis* breaks through the whole system of metaphysical theology. He tries consistently to see, not the cross in light of a philosophical concept of God, but God in the light of the cross. For Luther, the hidden God is the God hidden in the suffering and the cross. We should not try to penetrate the mysteries of God's majesty, but should be content with the God of the cross. We cannot find God except in Christ; anyone who tries to find him outside of Christ will find the devil.[66]

In other words, for Luther the movement within the God-man flows in both directions: the divinity informs the humanity, but the humanity also and equally informs the divinity. Before the Incarnation, as Luther understands it, God could not and did not suffer. Since the Incarnation, as Luther understands it, God can and does suffer. Philosophy deals with God in abstract, and therefore God cannot be said to suffer. Christian theology, however, deals with God *in concreto*, and thus God must be said to suffer. In Christ, God suffers, but God's suffering remains an incomprehensible mystery.[67] Jesus, the God-man, the crucified One, gives to the predicate 'God' its substantial content, revealing the true identity of God. The meaning of the word God is provided, not by philosophy, but by its reference to the person of Jesus Christ. This means that Christianity must necessarily think about God only in connection with the crucified Christ. God is revealed as passible in the Incarnation. In the Incarnation God suffers not only in the humanity of the Son but also as God the eternal Son, because 'God's Son and Mary's Son is only one Person' or 'one Son'.[68] Suffering is therefore ontologically constitutive of the being of God and of the eternal Son of God. God's heavenly divinity cannot be protected from the taint of human suffering. God's involvement shows scant respect for those definitions of God which put God opposite us, defining divinity in opposition to humanity, so that God is most God by negating the terms of the human condition.[69] The identity of God is none other than God as self-disclosed in the cross. The identity of God is regulated by the content of the divine as revealed in Jesus. The Greek idea of divine impassibility has obscured the biblical revelation. The suffering of Christ as God's own suffering is established in the concrete unity of Christ's personal identity, which is to be explained according to the old doctrine of *communicatio idiomatum*. Luther understood the person of Jesus Christ primarily in terms of what he does *pro nobis* as our redeemer. The fundamental truth of the Christian faith consists in the fact that God in the passion history of Jesus Christ has suffered the curse of death and the misery of infinite suffering, and eventually suffered them into defeat. In the light of this expiatory suffering it becomes clear that God is nothing but love through and through.

John Taylor, so powerfully influenced by Luther through his reading of Dietrich Bonhoeffer, is compelled to go a crucial step further than Luther in claiming that what we see in the wood of the cradle and the wood of the cross dates not just from the historical moment of incarnation. Such a notion inevitably collapses into two distinct gods, leading directly to devaluation of God's self-disclosure to the Hebrew people, and even to anti-Judaism. Luther, as we know, could be virulently anti-semitic. The Son of God and Son of Mary is Jewish. What we see in Jesus the Jew, according to John Taylor, discloses not some newly minted God, radically transformed by recent human experience. What we see is nothing else but God as God is eternally, always and everywhere. The Incarnation is not exceptional, but typical. God cannot be untrue to God's own nature. God's freedom does not consist in being able to do simply anything, to bring about an infinite choice of possibilities, but in being able to turn everything to the service of the one purpose that God wills to bring about.[70] In other words, God's hands are tied by love.[71] Humility and the form of a servant are not disguises of God or unnatural to God. These are of God's very essence, meaning that God cannot draw near as a prince or even a professor, but only in some lowly and obscure form.[72]

Noting the endless ingenuity with which theologians have identified a saving disconnection at some point along the line from the Crucified to the Almighty, to relieve them of having to draw the terrifying logical conclusion, we must also go on to register that in doing so they have simply been rather perversely reflecting the *sensus fidelium*.[73] For the plain truth is that the Christlike God is not the god most of us want most of the time, and the Christlike God is not the god some of us want at any time. When we are hard-pressed, the god we really want, the god we believe we need, is the god of human fantasy offering magic solutions to all our problems. Possessing the quick fix, any god who intervenes in moments of darkness and distress to soothe and solve, rescue and release, is more attractive than God the suffering companion on the way.

It is necessary to quote John Taylor at some length if we are to appreciate not simply his intellectual commitment to revising the received doctrine of God so that it becomes distinctively Christian, but also his passion and sense of urgency.

We human beings are physically puny in a world of brute force. From our childhood we long for greater power and more perfect control. We admire the strongest, the victor, the one who outsmarts the others. So, with our gift for fantasy, we project those images of domination out into the skies and call it God.

God is imaged as the super-potentate among the emperors, the master-mind over all the clever controllers. God (unlike us) can do exactly as God wants at any moment. God (like our secret wishes) fixes everything. Get him on your side and you can't lose. And what human psychology brought to pass, the philosophers were quick to rationalise.

If Jesus is Lord in that sense then the thirty years of Incarnation were like an exceptional assignment he had to undertake involving a disguise and some temporary hardship and humiliation. His radical reassessment of authority ... presumably was meant for the duration only. And the victim on the cross was enduring merely the last bad patch before the climax when he could throw off his disguise, mission accomplished, and get back on the throne of the universe. The helplessness and pain tell us nothing new about God.

That is how the Church has too often presented the story. But that is not the only way of saying 'Jesus is Lord'. It can be announced as a reversal of all our assumptions and expectations. *Jesus* is Lord. His unconditional acceptance of all and sundry is the ultimate power. His patient, suffering, non-assertive love will have the last word. His inexhaustible endurance will outlast every defeat. That is what the ruler of the universe is like.

John Austin Baker ... 'The crucified Jesus is the only accurate picture of God the world has ever seen.' C. E. Rolt ... 'The only omnipotence known to God is the Almighty Power of suffering love.'

Theologians and poets have delighted to play with the paradox of the Incarnation: 'Our God contracted to a span.' But their endless conceits have served to muffle the outrageously unbalanced and unbalancing corrective which the Incarnation makes known. This is more than paradox. In the tug-of-war contrast between human and divine the tension has slackened because the concept of *God* has been shifted. If God was in Christ we have to come to terms with a God to whom it is natural to be humble, frustrated and at risk.[74]

If this is true, then the coming of Jesus was a prodigious revelation that turned previous ideas of God on their head. If we take it as true that God in Christ is revelation – epiphany, self-disclosure, showing, the opening of a window into the very heart of reality – then we must be willing to have our picture of God corrected, even revolutionized, by what we see here. And what we learn about God in Jesus Christ includes both the inexhaustible activity of Galilee, redemptive and life-giving, *and* the silent passivity of the Passion, hands tied and at the disposal of others.[75] To suggest, however, that the Son is now safely back on the throne of the universe, exercising plenipotentiary power as usual, ignores one essential element of Christian orthodoxy. It has always been part of the Christian confession of faith that the Son's humanity is incorporated into the nature of God.

> That much of the 'adventure' still goes on within the being of God; not the flawed and incomplete thing we are familiar with, but humanity fulfilled as God intended it, the common ground of transcending self-abandonment which we all potentially share with God.[76]

If, then, the incarnate Word is truly God's self-disclosure we must begin to give full weight to the newness and the discontinuity in our understanding of God which the gospel conveys. The God Jesus called *Abba* was certainly the God of Hebrew revelation, but his relationship to this God and the events that issued from it amount to a radical redefinition of divine sovereignty.[77] This is the secret at the heart of Christian revelation, if revelation it is, and therein lies both its continuity with the past and its staggering novelty. [78]

For all this, however, there is only so much that can be stated with logical precision. In the nature of things, the passion and the power of God's weakness as the theologian experiences it can only be evoked in the human heart, which is why in the final analysis only the poet can be the theologian we need. For it is the poet who uses words sacramentally as well as descriptively, so that they point or beckon beyond themselves to that which they cannot possibly contain. This is a rare kind of knowing and loving, a knowledge and love which pass human understanding.

It is said of Charles Williams, who influenced John Taylor so much in later years, that he was not a systematic thinker. 'A coherent thinker, yes, but not in the sense that he defined his terms and proceeded stepwise through a logical argument. He is certainly not illogical, but his logic is imaginative rather than linear.'[79] It is not hard to see how the two became soul-friends. 'You are the only author since Dante', W. H. Auden told Charles Williams, 'who has found out how to make poetry out of theology and history.' The reference is to Charles Williams' verse, but in his prose he is a poet of similar achievement. 'The poetry he makes of theology and history ... will have its effect, as good poetry always does, on mind and feeling at once.'[80] These words could with equal justice have been written of John Taylor the poet, so W. H. Auden's assessment stands in need of some revision in order to make room for another in this great tradition.[81] Whether in verse or prose, John Taylor is the skilled and searching wordsmith who always writes theology as the love-song it is and must be.

> They say it was her innocence drew him
> down from the high places and the heath land.
> Or was it the magnet of his intent
> approach that brought her barefoot

to the meeting among the moonlit trees?
It was he, the chalky blur on the blackness
beyond the clearing, watching her
at ease on the sawn stump. Then the glance
of light off that long lance
tossed in salute as he dared and
crossed the impassable bright space.
Alien and fathomless his eyes
probed hers for mutual meaning,
till she saw the fine-drawn tear-drains
lining the pierrot mask and breathed
his acrid animal heat.
The brittle ivory of his limbs at last
folded to her feet and the sharp
imperious crest lay pressed
like a beam aslant her shoulder.
Sleeking the warm buckram of his ears,
she chanted as one in a dream:

> *Stay, love, with me*
> *till we shall see*
> *all that is yet to be.*

They came upon them there, the hunters,
in the dark time when the moon had set.
Because he was rare and mysterious
or because her embrace affronted them
or because they knew the going price
of the horn, but mostly because
it was a monstrosity, against nature,
to be one where always were two,
distinct and apart, they killed him.
Staunching the warm blood of his heart
she chanted as one in a dream:

> *Stay, love, with me*
> *till we shall see*
> *all that is yet to be.*[82]

Christian anthropology

Everything depends on who God is as God. God is not an abstraction
without practical or everyday implications. If we cannot live on bread
alone, it is also true that we cannot live on ideas alone.[83] The way we live
in the world now depends on the identity of God. When the connection
goes unnoticed, or even when it is actively repudiated, who God is
nevertheless determines the shape of reality, for 'the structure of the world

images the nature of its Creator'.[84] Any anthropology deserving of the name Christian is ultimately about the way 'the grain of the world' runs. In other words, it is about authenticity and integrity, about how things really are in themselves, about human being and human becoming, about how to live truly human lives. Any truly Christian doctrine of God is so intimately bound up with a truly Christian doctrine of humanity that the two become inseparable. The 'ordinary' is so charged with divine glory that the Holy Spirit can be said to open our eyes to boiled potatoes as much as to Jesus Christ, and although we routinely miss the point, looking for greater wonders, this is the real miracle.[85] It is little surprise that John Taylor's theology is thoroughly humanistic. Our real doctrine of God emerges into daylight depending on whether we see this humanism as high praise or devastating criticism! In John Taylor's hands, the uniqueness or distinctiveness of Jesus is never aggressive, always enlightening, always revelatory, always inviting, never threatening.

> Let not my humble presence affront and stumble
> your hardened hearts that have not known my ways
> nor seen my tracks converge to this uniqueness.
> Mine is the strength of the hills that endure and crumble,
> bleeding slow fertile dust to the valley floor.
> I am the fire in the leaf that crisps and falls
> and rots into the roots of the rioting trees.
> I am the mystery, rising, surfacing
> out of the seas into these infant eyes
> that offer openness only and the unfocusing
> search for an answering gaze. O recognize,
> I am the undefeated heart of weakness.
> Kneel and adore, fall down to pour your praise:
> you cannot lie so low as I have been always.[86]

If the only true God is the God we see in Jesus of Nazareth, the 'undefeated heart of weakness' enfleshed, then Christianity is the most materialistic of all the great world religions.[87] In Jesus we see that matter matters, that all dualism is overcome, that reality is all of one piece, a seamless robe. 'Unlike John the Baptist, who chose the way of separation from the world, Jesus came eating and drinking, and scandalised the religious leaders by being so normal.'[88] The principal consequence of the doctrine of the Incarnation is that there is no division between sacred and secular, that the walls we build to distinguish one arena from another do not reach up to heaven. The revelation of God in Christ is resolutely opposed to any kind of dualism and the Scriptures as a whole witness to this.[89] It follows that an essential part of the ministry and mission of the Christian company, both communally and individually, involves aligning ourselves with God in this struggle for truth with all its immediate practical consequences for the way we live. Any genuine christology, meaning any christology which takes seriously the real humanity of Jesus rather than seeing him as God temporarily disguised as a human being, has far-reaching implications for the way we understand ourselves and treat each other. 'Christian thought ... should move from the direct knowledge of the nature of God to proposals for action within the social and political sphere.'[90]

It seems strange, but fair, to say that traditional doctrine has rarely faced up to the obvious fact that Jesus is one of us. Traditional christology worked within a supernaturalist framework; popular religion expressed this mythologically, while professional theology expressed it metaphysically. In this schema, God the Son comes down to earth, is born, lives and dies within this world as a man. From 'out there' enters one who does not belong here, who nevertheless lives genuinely and completely for a time within the human realm. The central christological question becomes 'How?' – How can Jesus be fully God and fully human? Commonly, this has amounted to little more than a question about how oil and water can be combined. When divinity and humanity are thought of as opposites, it is impossible successfully to create any real integrated being. Almost always, for all the protests to the contrary, christology has actually been some form of docetism in which Jesus was not really human at all. Rather, 'he was God in human form, full of supernatural knowledge and miraculous power, very much like the Olympian gods were supposed to be when they visited earth in disguise'.[91] Incarnation has been presented as the divine substance being plunged into flesh – like chocolate coating or silver plating.[92] John Taylor sees as clearly as John Robinson that this whole picture of a supernatural Being coming down from heaven to save humankind, 'in the way that a man might put his finger into a glass of water to rescue a struggling insect, is frankly incredible'.[93]

As followers of Dietrich Bonhoeffer, both theologians are inevitably attracted to kenotic christology as the only way of understanding at all satisfactorily the divine and human in Christ. This is why the nineteenth-century trickle of interest in kenoticism becomes a flood in the twentieth century.[94] The problem with so much modern kenotic christology is that it tries to work within traditional christological categories, assuming that it is his omnipotence, his omniscience, all that makes him superhuman, of which the incarnate Christ divests himself.[95] The mistake of the kenoticists has been to propose that such stripping or shedding of divinity is what is needed in order to become truly human, a process of reduction or refinement to see how much of the divine being can be brought within the limits of human existence.[96] But what if *kenosis* is not the dimming down of the divine nature in an atypical act of condescension?[97] What if, as John Robinson asserts, 'it is as he empties himself not of his Godhead but of himself, of any desire to focus attention on himself, of any craving to be "on an equality with God", that he reveals God'?[98] If it is in making himself nothing, emptying himself of ego, in his utter surrender of himself to others in love and in loving-service, that Jesus discloses and lays bare the ground of God's being and of human being as love, then this turns all human notions about what is fitting for God on their head. This is the paradox of personal existence, that the one who utterly emptied himself, Jesus Christ, is precisely the one who permits us to glimpse that utter fullness that we call divine. In other words, *kenosis* and *plerosis* are one and the same.[99] In his kenotic christology, John Taylor, along with John Macquarrie and others, is saying that in God this self-giving is eternal reality, that it is the very essence of the divine nature, which is none other than patient, persuasive, self-sacrificing, longing and hoping, suffering love.

For those created in the divine image it follows that real human life is likewise about giving ourselves away. Real human life necessitates self-emptying, self-giving, self-limiting in order to be freely available. Indeed, there can be no chauvinism here, for this is the pattern of the whole creation and of all creaturely life. The Incarnation is *typical* of God, always and everywhere. Incarnation supplies the essential clue apart from which we might not see how the cosmos holds together.[100] In other words, there is a universal principle of life-through-death, of individual self-immolation in the interests of a larger claim, which is at variance with the universal principle of self-preservation. Only so is our evolution explicable. How could the law of the jungle lead us out of the jungle? How could an inherent ruthlessness lift us into sensitivity? Ruthlessness is not the last word. It was not the Word that was made flesh at Bethlehem.

The immanent Creator must have been of another temper. And in the humility of Jesus, his pureness of heart, his forgiveness, his courage and sacrifice, his infinite concern for all … persisting even in the throes of death, we meet the eternal, persuasive love which through the countless aeons has been striving, suffering, going under, yet ever rising to new life, within the fabric of his universe.[101]

> I see his blood upon the rose …
> His crown of thorns is twined with every thorn
> His cross is every tree.[102]

When Jesus rises from the table of the Last Supper and without a word pulls off the seamless robe, girds himself with a towel, pours water into a basin, and begins to wash the disciples' feet, this is 'the last veil' being drawn aside so that his followers can behold the only true God.

> When the Son of God took the form of a household slave he lost nothing of his godlikeness, for that is God's role. Every woman who turns back to the kitchen when the guests have left to begin the washing up is most like God at that moment, especially when the thought is farthest from her mind. The cleaners who wake in the small hours and walk the empty streets to clear up yesterday's mess in schools and offices have more of God in their action than the head teacher or the managing director. Like the patient seas

in Keats' poem, 'the moving waters at their priestlike task of pure ablution round earth's human shores', our Creator has been cleaning up the mess, in ceaseless serving love, from the beginning of time, for there is no one else who can do it … God is he who gives himself in love. God is he who pours himself out in service to his world. God is he who is wounded for our healing, broken for our forgiving. God is he who shares himself in an eternal exchange of life for life, a ceaseless interflow of love and belonging.[103]

On this reading of the gospel, the living and dying of Jesus is the only turning point in human history.

Up to that point history ran straight on. But the man-for-others reversed the old law of 'each for himself', and revealed the deeper principle which from the beginning was always at work in the midst: that in order to continue to be one must be a gift, an offering.[104]

As Dietrich Bonhoeffer suggests, we have to range ourselves with God in God's suffering if creation is to move toward its goal. Only so will divinization, *theosis*, ever be realized as the ultimate destiny of the universe.[105] Truly, Christ humbles himself to share in our humanity that we may share in Christ's divinity.

If it is true that Dietrich Bonhoeffer enlarged and extended John Taylor's vision of human solidarity as one essential consequence of authentic christology, it is also true that this prison theology, forged *in extremis*, meshed perfectly with what Africa was teaching him. Here John Taylor found himself caught up in the biblical reality of the personal totality of all being, experiencing the monstrosity of isolated Western individualism, while knowing the truth of the confession 'I am because I participate'.[106] Here he learned, in a credal echo, how a person 'was made man' by stages and degrees.[107] This naturally meshed with his appreciation of the real humanity of Jesus, who as much as any one of us had to become truly human by stages and degrees, by the interplay of all the usual influences and inspirations, by the pressures and provocations of the life he shared with other human beings.[108] We all exist because of our involvement, by our belonging to family and community, by sharing in the life of a people.

This, I believe, is the heart of the Gospel for Africa and it was from Africa that I learnt to tell it this way.

'In Adam all …' wrote the Apostle, and Africa understands that better than we. She knows what it means to be in the first ancestor, to live in the organism which is growing out of him, to be him, his blood coursing the living veins, his soul infused in the body, his destiny and disposition working itself out through time. But fundamental to that destiny and disposition is the estrangement, the inability to find or face the all-pervading Presence of God. The terror of the Presence, the 'panic', the dread, compels Man to make a god who is remote, to raise a hierarchy of intermediaries that thrust him still further away … Here is the universal irony of Man's situation, that what seems to be a search for God is in fact a flight. Everyman is in Adam, and Adam is hiding from God.

And so the All-Present himself passed into the closed circle of the human family. Stage by stage he was initiated into it as we are; by birth, by circumcision, by presentation with sacrifice, by instruction, by attendance at the feasts, he was made man – 'made of a woman, made under the law'. He begged for the baptism of repentance, immersing himself into a complete participation in our involvement in one another's sin, and in all the effects of our estrangement from himself.

As true part of the body that was in flight from God, yet he faced the other way, standing his ground against the headlong spate, and lived every moment towards the Presence of God and towards the presence of his brother.[109]

Some consequences of Christ's stance are inescapable. This decisive turning point in human history now demands of us a like turning. This is why the typical New Testament word is μετανοια (*metanoia*), meaning changing direction rather than a change of position. Metanoia means turning about in this world rather than seeking escape into another world. It has to do with a change of the centre, swinging the whole person away from the old direction of self-assertion and independence so as to face God as seen in Christ.[110] 'And the *metanoia*, the miraculous turning, is going on within the original organism of Man, and must go on until the whole universe, all in heaven and on earth, is reconciled to Christ and brought into unity in him.'[111]

The Christ of the primal world-view, which by contrast with the contemporary world-view is also the biblical world-view, demands of us decision but not disengagement. If the word αλληλους (*allelous*) – one another – rings through the pages of the New Testament like a peal of bells,[112] the word responsibility does so in the writings of John Taylor. Both, of course, speak of mutuality, of community and of communion.

> Wash one another's feet ... confess your sins to one another and pray for one another ... forbearing one another and forgiving each other ... teaching and admonishing one another ... comfort one another and build each other up ... love one another as I have loved you.

In John Taylor's first book, written while he was recovering from the traumatic ending of his decade of missionary service in Uganda and just prior to embarking on his field work with the IMC, this emphasis is striking and unavoidable. So also in his second book, where the word 'responsibility' and its derivatives is used twenty-four times in fourteen pages![113] Our responsibility as human beings consists precisely in our ability to respond. 'The greater apes do not wrestle with temptation; the mouse does not blame the hawk, nor the trout reproach the otter; the tape-worm never feels ashamed, nor does the cobra seek to make amends.'[114] We alone know who God would have us be and what God would have us do, and we are constrained until we respond in creative and freely chosen obedience.[115]

John Taylor is in no doubt that Jesus is unique, that he is the God-given archetype of creaturely response to God. Insofar as we can penetrate the mystery of his life, the Church was truly inspired in concluding that in him, in Jesus, God the Son, the eternal Son in the Trinity, was incarnate.

> Which I take to mean that that in God which is eternally dedicated and obedient to God's own self-giving purpose became a man and lived out that divine obedience in the human response to God of Jesus of Nazareth, so bringing about that perfect partnership of the creature with the creator which was God's eternal purpose.[116]

Nevertheless, this uniqueness of Jesus is sterile if it remains unique. It is not just that he gives others who put their faith in him the right to become adult children of God. It is also that he feels the need of partnership, the human need for company, for the pooling of gifts and the energy of ideas and ideals shared. One consequence of our participation in Christ is that the revelation of God in Christ enables us to respond as whole persons, rather than as split personalities.

> Body and soul are parallel and interpenetrating along the whole range of Man's being; his soul is involved in his animal nature no less than his body; the body shares in his spiritual experience as well as the soul. Man battling with the elements, in the grip of sexual passion, or digging desperately for water, is not mere body: soul fights and desires as well. Man wrestling in prayer, burdened with guilt, or caught up into ecstatic communion with God, is not pure soul: body, too, may share the agony, the sickness or the thrill.[117]

In all we are and in all we do, we are involved and responding to the Christlike God in our totality, and we must renounce the blasphemous attempt to put asunder what God has joined together.[118] This commitment is informed by the fact that Christ did not *have* a body, but *was* a body, and that Christ *is* a body still, for the eucharistic assembly of the baptized is his body in the world even now.[119] Our bodies are what connect us with each other. Human sexuality is the sacrament of our involvement with others, and so of our involvement with God.[120] Within us God draws the frontiers of such diverse realms – soul and body, mind and matter, animal and spirit – as if to stretch us by such tensions until God 'can play upon us as on an instrument of well-tuned strings and make the music of heaven to be heard on earth.'[121] So it is that God heals us of dis-ease, calling us from disharmony into wholeness.[122]

Perhaps this essential dialectic of response and responsibility as lived out by ordinary people both christologically and eucharistically is best encapsulated in the words of a sermon by the bishop in his cathedral one Corpus Christi. It is not, of course, that we have arrived, that we ourselves are already what we receive, namely the Body of Christ. 'Like a waterfall, we are there because we are going there.'[123] Here, in the preached word, the living Word of the gospel speaks eloquently, revealingly, so that we touch the incarnate Christ and see into the heart of God.

The beloved Body which is presented and given for the world in the Sacrament is the body that was fashioned in the darkness of the Virgin's womb during the waiting months. The Body of Christ in the Sacrament is the tiny human creature that was laid to sleep in the cattle-trough. It is the body that sweated at the carpenter's bench and ached under the desert sun and slept rough when there was nowhere for him to lay his head. It is the body that shrank in the garden from the coming ordeal, that writhed under the lash and protested, like countless other human bodies, against the outrage of torture. It is the body which, as Second Adam, explored the strange uncharted dimension of resurrection which is God's intention for all human bodies. And this is the body which still exists as a body in the very Being of God, matter itself made divine in a manner beyond our knowing. *'This is my Body which is for you.'*

But that is not the end of the matter. We confront the Body of Christ not only in the Sacrament that perpetuates it and makes it present.

'Lord, when did we see you?' 'I was a hungry man and you gave me food. I was that young man in gaol, remember? I was that creature huddled under the bridge whom you took in that night; and afterwards you felt richer for it, remember? This is my body which is for you. It has the fingerless hands of the leper, and you, Francis, threw your arms around it and found yourself embracing me. My body has brown skin and almond-shaped eyes and when it arrived from its long journey into an alien land there were posters saying: Keep out! But you smiled that day, remember? and made me feel welcome and you were blessed by my coming.

My body lies dying in the gutters of Calcutta. There are so many of me that it is hard to remember I am human; but you, my Sister Teresa, you, my many other sisters, you recognised me and poured out your love to fill my last hours on earth. This is my body which is for you – for you to love and for you to be blessed by my presence.

But stretch forth your hand – your own hand. See the familiar lines in the palm, the shape of its fingers, the little scars. Feel the warmth, the pulse at the wrist, that make it yours. This is my body which is for you, which I formed in my own image to be you and no-one else. Have you learned to love it and reverence it as mine? Or do you fear it, dissociate yourself from it and despise it, trying to put asunder what I have joined together, the body and spirit of Incarnation? Yes I have asked you to present to me yourselves, your souls and bodies, but as a living sacrifice, not a bloody killing. I want your body as mine for I find it harder to heal without touching, and when I bless my children I take them up in my arms.'[124]

With the human face of God turned toward us in love, revealing to us the true shape of the world, showing us the way the grain of reality actually runs, we are set free, liberated to deal with each other gently and care for one another patiently. The christology advanced by John Taylor permits us to live trustingly with the questions rather than grasping for security in premature answers to our dilemmas. 'When people wonder why God does not strike tyrants dead or prosper a virtuous man's business they are actually asking for another universe with a different purpose.'[125] The pattern of creation accurately reflects the nature of the Creator, for God has made a world where love can respond to Love, a world which is unfinished and which must go on making itself. This risky enterprise is exceptionally costly to everyone involved in the experiment, and more costly to God than to any other player. Soteriology, we have said, drives christology, just as christology is the beating heart of any truly Christian theology. Where is God in the mystery and the mess of things? How is God involved in pain and loss? Is God touched by suffering? Where is God in the face of evil? Is the divine Love impotent, or does God's heart break with the pain of it all? Does God bleed with us and for us? Is the crucifixion of Jesus the one, perfect and sufficient sacrifice because crucifixion is always God's lot?

Such questions arise for us at the point of extremity, as we look into the abyss and wonder where God is, as we cry out in agony and find God silent. At such moments there is no place for pretence. Stripped bare, we can offer only who we are. We can give only what we have, what our faith gives us and makes us. There is no place for peddling what we imagine we ought to have by any of the usual standards of Christian orthodoxy. John Taylor allows us a rare glimpse into his hidden ministry, one of those intimate moments when theology infuses priesthood put to the test.

> Some months ago I was asked by a friend to visit a young couple whose two-year old daughter had been found dead in her cot. They were still stunned and haunted by the old question *Why?*, and sometimes *Why her?* I simply could not offer them the conventional reassurance about it all being in God's providence, a mystery now but one day to be seen as part of a loving plan. I said to them instead that their child's death was a tragic accident, an unforeseeable failure in the functioning of the little body; that, so far from being willed or planned by God, it was for him a disaster and a frustration of his will for life and fulfilment, just as it was for them, that God shared their pain and loss and was with them in it. I went on to say that God is not a potentate ordering this or that to happen, but that the world is full of chance and accident and God has let it be so because that is the only sort of world in which freedom, development, responsibility and love could come into being, but that God was committed to this kind of world in love and to each person in it, and was with them in this tragedy, giving himself to them in fortitude and healing and faith to help them through. And their child was held in that same caring, suffering love.[126]

In this moment of crisis, John Taylor finds himself unable to offer a commonplace picture of God which he finds impossible to love.[127] He explicitly rejects the God who has everything under control, whose divine providence governs and guides all things without exception, but whose reasons we cannot fathom. This is a view of God and of God's world which squares with a good deal of biblical material. It is to be found in many books of devotion and pastoral practice, and it has given comfort to some people in great distress. It is rejected, however, because, for all its impeccable scriptural pedigree, for all its theological and philosophical respectability, it is simply not sufficiently *Christian*. Indeed, it is a grotesque attempt to explain the mind of God for which we have no Christian warrant whatever. Part and parcel of the routine answer caring religious people give to the question, why do bad things happen to good people?[128] – it is nothing more than our own speculation. It may be the best shot we human beings have devised at penetrating an impenetrable veil, and left to our own ingenuity this is about the best we can come up with. This is the God we construct for ourselves, but this is emphatically *not* the God Jesus calls *Abba*.

Where, we must always ask, is the cross? If the cross reverses the old idea of providence, this human straining to explain or excuse or justify is no *Christian* response, because it leaves God on the outside, at a distance, watching like an uninvolved spectator.[129] It offers us a god who is all-good and all-powerful, but who nevertheless fails to appear when the crunch comes, a god who does not protect or intervene. This idol, so far as John Taylor can see, bears no resemblance to the God who comes striding to meet us in Christ. The self-giving and the self-givenness of God is not simply extraneous to the Other, so that we are strangers who might become God's special concern from time to time. Charles Williams provided John Taylor late in life with language to tell the good news of the incarnate God whose genuine loving inevitably leads to 'co-inherence' or 'in-othering'.[130] The doctrine of exchange or 'in-othering' is the declared law of the universe, the pattern of our existence in this universe, made – as we are, and as it is – in the divine image.[131] Co-inherence, exchange, in-othering is 'natural fact as well as a supernatural truth'.[132] Regardless of whether we recognize it or not, this is the nature of things because it is the nature of the Trinity, the nature of God as Love: 'the Self-Giver, the Self-Given and the in-othered Spirit'.[133] Since this is the mystery of God's own being it is also the means whereby God saves the world. The incarnation, or the flesh-taking as Charles Williams preferred to call it, is an interpenetration of divine and human being. The atonement is the supreme substitution, God bearing the burden of the Other's self-destruction. The gift of the Holy Spirit is the mutual indwelling of disciples with the Lord. To refuse 'co-inherence' is to separate oneself from the nature of things.[134] God wills and delights in each detail of the universe from within its being. Another way of expressing this is to say that 'God is the Beyond at the heart of the music'.[135] In Africa, John Taylor learned that the symbol of this God is not so much the cross above the orb as the cross within the circle.[136]

In other words, 'co-inherence' is the mode of God's loving, the purpose for which God desires an other. The life of the Trinity overflows, and this overflowing love entails restriction – willingness to embrace the pain of *tsimtsum* self-withdrawal.[137] This is the pain of hazardous letting go, the pain of all the victims of the enterprise which God shares through love's 'in-othering'.[138] As the Father loves the Son by making the Son the free agent of the Father's self-expression, so the blessed Trinity loves the creation by calling it to be the agent of divine action. This principle is consummated in the incarnation whereby the Son, God's Given Self, becomes the human partner through whom the only kind of intervention open to God might be perfectly realized.

> Reflecting the divine strategy, Jesus chose partnership and co-inherence as his model of action, first calling disciples to become what St Paul dared to call 'fellow workers with God' and 'joint heirs with Christ', to share his mission, drink his cup and undergo his baptism, and then gathering the Church to become his own bodily agent animated by the Spirit. Jesus' prayer, 'I in them and thou in me', epitomises the principle of co-inherence as the mode of divine providence.[139]

Because God loves by sharing, it is plain that God wills to act upon the creation, God's other, only in and through the processes of the creation, making it make itself. God's providence depends upon finding a channel, a medium, a partner, and depends equally on the partner's response and co-operation.[140]

> The mystery that is God, the ocean in which all things are sustained and from which they receive their being, the unimaginable Beyond which makes people aware of itself in sudden glimpses of another dimension of glory and meaning in ordinary phenomena and events, this sea of joy which is, within itself, the timeless exchange of love given and received, this self-renouncing Christlike power, in the weakness of self-chosen limitation, is set upon the venture of opening out that love into a relationship with what is not God but a true Other, raised up within God to be the object and heir of that love and joy, returning love for love and sharing the eternal bliss.[141]

In such a world, in such a God, co-workers and partners in salvation are not called to put the world to rights or to answer all its unanswered questions. Three duties are laid on us when we are brought face to face with affliction. First, we are to stay with the victims where the suffering is, without running away. Secondly, we are to see through the confusion and untruth by which evil conceals itself and call it by its proper name, not in order to occupy the moral high ground but because only those who see their own human capacity for evil can take in the miracle of God's unchanging and costly involvement. Thirdly, we are to do everything we possibly can to alleviate the suffering and abolish the conditions that cause it. 'For providence's proper name is Immanuel, God with us.'[142] Every opening of one's whole self towards another, every taking upon oneself the burden and the gift of another, contributes a little to that quiet tide which is flowing back and forth, carrying us with it into the very being of God, sweeping us back with God into the life of the world.[143]

If the cross of Christ shows us so much truth about the pattern of the world, it gives us also a glimpse, just a taste, of the searing pain of the divine love at its heart – a glimpse of 'Love's endeavour, Love's expense'.[144]

> God does know more intimately than any the price his creatures have been paying for his huge adventure of making this universe of accident and freedom and pain as the only environment in which love could one day emerge to receive and delight in and respond to his joyous love. He still believes the outcome will outweigh the immense waste and agony, not least the agony of his seeming indifference and inaction. So, knowing we cannot understand, cannot forgive, what he is doing, God has come among us as a fellow-being and fellow-sufferer to make amends and to win back trust. Through his own abandonment and death that Given Self of our Creator calls us to share his hope as he shares our pain, to believe in his staggering, costly venture even while there is little evidence of it ever succeeding.[145]

One of the most significant features of John Taylor's personality is what we have called practical vision. He is a practical visionary, a dreamer with his feet on the ground. His Christian anthropology would be little more than pious theory unless it included plans for Christian action in the world. If it is to mean anything, this commitment must somehow go beyond easy generalities, for God deals personally rather than generally and sees people with faces and names rather than categories and labels. Who we are determines how we live. Who we understand ourselves to be, created in the divine image, controls how we reflect that image here and now in 'the kingdom of right relationships.'[146] For one so prophetically aware of the politics of present crisis and probable consequence, it is not surprising that in his final years as General Secretary of CMS we find John Taylor becoming concerned with one very concrete way of proclaiming the gospel. It is a deeply incarnational, thoroughly sacramental way, for it involves individual Christians and whole Christian communities living out a pattern of 'light-hearted yet deadly serious protest'.[147] Breaking the impasse of global economic imbalance, and salvation from ecological disaster, calls for a new kind of monastic movement, one in which households and congregations can share.[148] This might become a form of Christian proclamation the modern world can hear when it refuses to hear anything else we say.

> It seems to me highly probable that the form that is finally given to the Hebrew folk-stories about the first man reflects the dream that for so many centuries had dominated the ideals and aspirations of the people and had been embodied in their social laws. Adam, made in the likeness of the creator, male and female in his fullness, is set as God's vicegerent in the

world. That is the point at which he bears the image of God. 'Then God said, *Let us make man in our image and likeness to rule the fish of the sea, the birds of heaven, the cattle, all wild animals on earth, and all reptiles that crawl upon the earth.*' But the quality of his dominion over nature is intended to reflect the quality of God's dominion – loving, cherishing and essentially self-giving. This is how it will be so long as, in all his exercise of power, he is answerable to God, seeing that he is himself a creature. Only in his unbroken awareness of God is man's technological mastery safe. Only in his acceptance of creaturehood can his dominion be prevented from becoming raw domination. 'The Lord God took the man and put him in the garden to till it and care for it.' But enough is enough, and answerability means the acceptance of limits. '*You may eat from every tree in the garden but not from the tree of the knowledge of good and evil.*' Adam can be trusted with so vast a sovereignty so long as he knows how to take no for an answer. The earth and all its resources are for you to exploit and develop *but* there is a time for the earth to re-gather its strength and there are others than yourself to be considered. The days and the weeks are yours to make and build and trade *but* there is a time to stand back and take stock in relation to the needs of the whole, and especially those on whose energies you rely. Yes, all the trees in the garden are yours *but* – enough is enough.[149]

What John Taylor envisages is Christians embodying this biblical theology in their daily lives. This is a counter-cultural *way of life*, as opposed to the consumer culture *way of death*. It is a way of life to be lived out by God's minority for the sake of God's majority.[150] Here is no romantic embracing of poverty in a world where millions are poor, when Christian obedience demands we defeat the causes of poverty. This is about moderation, balance, matching, toning in with the whole, an awareness of how we fit into the jigsaw picture over against ruthless greed. Our enemy is not possessions but excess. Our battle-cry is not *Nothing!* but *Enough!*[151] When we reject responsible daughterhood and sonship we turn into anxiously assertive spoilt children who must at all costs have their own way. Our God-given, essentially non-violent dominion over nature becomes raging domination. 'Technology is safe only in a context of worship, and science should walk hand in hand with sacrifice.'[152] When this occurs the result is what John Taylor likes to call 'equipoise', where excess is not simply prohibited but replaced by a lavish generosity of natural and graceful give and take.[153] So begins the eucharistic life and the cheerful revolution, characterized by overflowing gratitude for the bounty of God. We discover together the fun of defying the blandishments and undermining the assumptions of the consumer society.

> We must try to live by the divine contrariness of Jesus. We need a rapidly increasing minority that is entirely counter-suggestible, a minority that calls the bluff of the trend-setters, is a dead loss to the advertising agencies and poor material for the careers advisers. Our need is for men and women who

are free with the freedom of Christ, free to ask the awkward questions that have occurred to no one else, and free to come up with startling answers that no one else has dared to give.[154]

No one is more aware than John Taylor that this stance could easily be interpreted as religious wowserism, that tight-lipped self-righteousness by which religion too often excuses its holier-than-thou attitude.[155] To guard against this we must avoid self-dramatization and cultivate a strong sense of humour. 'We should not take ourselves too seriously, but should take Christ much more seriously.'[156]

> This was typical of those desert fathers with their comical affairs with lions and scorpions and their absurd pillars. It was most typical of St Francis, who loved to pull the leg of another brother just when he was teaching the most startling and profound truth. Once a poor woman came to the Portiuncula begging for alms. Francis turned to Peter Catani and asked if he had anything they could give her. Peter replied that the only thing in the house was the New Testament from which the lessons were read at matins. *'Give it to her'*, cried Francis, *'that she may sell it for her necessity. For I firmly believe that would please the Lord and the Blessed Virgin more than if we were to read from it.'* How absurdly spontaneous and how penetratingly right for anyone wanting to keep a new movement of the Spirit free from religiosity.[157]

Christian Mission

The story is told of an Indian catechist at the end of the nineteenth century dismissed from the Church for some misdemeanour. Burdened with shame, knowing he would never again dare to preach, the man left the area and went to some far-off village where there was no Christian community at all. There, where he was completely unknown, where malicious Christian gossip could never reach him, he settled down and made his living as a potter. The Church never heard of him again and he died there. Years later it was decided to send a team of evangelists to that very place. They rented a house and began to tell the stories of Christ. They were amazed when the crowd of villagers responded eagerly, 'We know the man you are talking about! He lived here for years!' 'No,' said the preachers, 'you don't understand. We are talking about Jesus Christ.' 'Well,' answered the people, 'he never told us his name. But the man you describe is our potter without a doubt.'[158]

John Taylor's theology is so insistently incarnational that it is no surprise to discover that his principal approach to the Christian mission is not one of assertion or action, but of humble reverence and attentive presence.[159] In this view, the Christian *dimension* with its spontaneous radiation is equally and perhaps even more important than the Christian *intention* with all its deliberate evangelistic activities.[160] Christians who stand in the world in the name of Christ have nothing to offer if they do not offer to be present – really and totally present, really and totally *in* the present.[161] The central act of Christian worship revolves around the real presence of Christ in word and sacrament, but those who gather around the table seem to lose sight of one another, failing to reverence the real presence of one another within the assembly, and neglectful of the real presence of those outside.[162] Typically, John Taylor is quick to spot the funny side of this sad tale. 'The failure of so many "professional" Christians has been that they are "not all there"!'[163]

Presence, then, is not just some new missionary method.[164] It is not simply a more effective way for the Church to market its pre-packaged religious goods.[165] In the last resort, it is about Christ being present in us and the Holy Spirit moving between us.[166] Initially and consistently, however, it is about human relationships, about true friendship without any ulterior motive, an involvement in love with no strings attached. Indeed, it specifically renounces any attempt to manipulate or possess or use the other.[167] If the spirit of conquest tingles within us, so that we want to plant the cross as if it were a flag, we are little different from all those others engaged in exploiting the global village.[168] God is not a product to be sold, as the Church is not a company competing for customers, just another international movement with a localized vocation. We are not delivering a recorded advertising slogan to a passing crowd.[169] Because of the Christian conviction that Jesus is God's gift for all people at all times, it is all too easy for us to see things this way, which is why Christians must be continually open to conversion along with everyone else.[170] Always, we must be striving to hold ourselves open to the God who comes striding to meet us on broken feet.

It follows from all our fundamental convictions about who God is, that Christians are only present because God is present before them.

> That is the tremendous Presence in the midst of the world from which our first parents hid themselves and from which Cain went forth into loneliness. That is the Presence which Moses knew, eye to eye and face to face, without which the building of the Chosen Community had no significance or attraction. That is the Presence which is promised unto the end of the world to those who go to disciple all nations. And this alone is their warrant for believing that the way of presence is not merely a new missionary method, but God's own way of drawing Adam into his embrace and lifting the despoiled and threatened Creation up into his peace.[171]

The first duty of Christian missionaries is to take off their shoes in awe as this divine presence confronts them, for however foreign the territory may seem, they know that they stand on holy ground, and must tread gently so as not to trample other people's dreams.[172]

> Lift the stone and you will find me
> Cleave the wood and I am there.[173]

A more developed theology of presence might spell out even more clearly the true shape of things, the essential nature of reality.

Already in the 1950s when the Christian Presence Series of books was commissioned, Max Warren had clear ideas about the current situation of the Christian mission and was able to sketch the challenges ahead with broad brush strokes. First, the contemporary situation is a new experience. Only once before, at its beginnings, has the Church faced a comparable challenge to its claim to meet all the needs of the human heart and mind. After a thousand years of Christian isolation we are again part of a marketplace of ideologies and beliefs, where dozens of other philosophies of life offer themselves. We must face the fact that there is prolonged psychological trauma in the transition from majority player to being one minority in a sea of minorities. What is involved in such co-existence? Must we, can we, limit the universality of the gospel, compromising so as to live harmoniously with our neighbours of other faiths? Must we be aggressive in prosecuting the Christian mission so as not to lose further ground to our competitors? We fear syncretism, the dilution of truth or its contamination by mixing too closely with those who differ from us. Is the inevitable result of pluralism some sort of watering down of religious claims until we reach an acceptable common indifference?[174] Max Warren was confident and bold enough to set up there and then some Christian markers in these shifting sands. At the beginning of the twenty-first century, these are worth recalling, for they are now part of a tradition of response exemplified in John Taylor.

Strikingly, this response begins by being glad about the new situation, because it means Christian faith becomes distinguishable from its past immersion in Western political, economic and cultural aggression. This great new fact is simultaneously a great new opportunity to witness. This, however, is no attempt at vacuous positive thinking, deluding ourselves that the future looks rosy after all. Max Warren doesn't hesitate to say that our Christian witness will be through suffering. In many ways, the way ahead will be for the Church the way of the cross, the way of humility where we learn again that God is not anywhere without witnesses. The call to embrace such a way – Christ's own way – is not to be rejected or resisted or resented, but knowingly welcomed as a matter of faith, as a God-given invitation to more radical trust. As one minority among others we go out to meet God who is present everywhere, expecting to learn more of God's grace and love by discovering how God is speaking to those of other faiths. We have to ask ourselves what is the authentic religious content in the experience of the Muslim, the Hindu, the Buddhist, the secular scientist? We need to sit where they sit, and enter sympathetically into the pains and griefs and joys of their history. We must resist the faithless desire to retreat into the safety of some Christian ghetto, aiming to draw others in with us until there are enough of us to dominate once more. Instead, we must deliberately engage with our new situation. We must not avoid engaging with the facts of life, learning to be present, really present and attentive, willing participants in what God is doing.[175]

It is impossible not to read the life and teaching of John Taylor as expressing these principles, embodying them in costly and joyous particularity. As missionary priest, as general secretary of a great missionary society and as diocesan bishop, he attempts to live gladly in the world in dialogue with others who differ from him. His life and teaching express a catholic generosity of spirit which characterizes what has been called the mainline Christian model of mission evolving across confessional lines.[176] Central to this practice of mission is genuinely open and even painful dialogue, with the long, patient listening this entails. By definition, dialogue is sustained conversation between parties who are not saying the same things. It involves recognition of the differences and respect for the contradictions and mutual exclusions which divide us. The purpose of dialogue is understanding and appreciation, leading to further reflection on the implications for your own convictions. Sensitivity to the convictions of others necessarily has an unpredictable impact on my own, so dialogue involves me in taking a risky step into the unknown without any guarantee about what will happen to me.

This missionary venture is a more exacting exercise than any of us would wish for, because human beings find it difficult to sustain contradictions and live with them.

> Instinctively we either try to destroy what is opposed to our understanding of truth or we pretend that the antithesis is unreal. The reason for this is, I believe, that we are all naturally frightened by the unresolved opposites in ourselves and find it very painful to include and accept the dark self alongside the light, the destroyer as well as the creator in us, both the male and the female element in our personality, both the child and the parent which we are. We want to be a simple unity but in fact we are a structure of contradictions. It takes a higher degree of maturity to let the opposites co-exist without pretending that they can be made compatible. It takes the same maturity to respect an opinion that conflicts with one's own without itching to bring about a premature and naïve accommodation. I suppose this is what is entailed in loving one's enemies.[177]

If dialogue is a form of loving one's enemies, as John Taylor's personal experience attests, then it involves appreciating the reason for opposition, granting its integrity and dealing honestly with its challenges, without surrendering any of our own integrity or diminishing in any way our own examined convictions. And there will generally have to be a great deal more of this kind of patient and painful loving before we can expect any genuine reconciliation of ideas and beliefs, let alone any real experience of communion. It is not difficult to see the implications of this insight for ecumenical relations, or overestimate its importance. In the wide sense of *oikoumene* as all creatures living together harmoniously and peacefully, or in any of its narrower applications to dialogue between churches or between Christians and other households of faith, John Taylor's approach entails an end to shouting matches and the beginning of listening with the ears of the heart. 'If we all made that effort of imagination it might make us humbler and gentler.' [178] With such humility, God is able to work miracles.

John Taylor defines religion as a people's particular response to the reality which the Holy Spirit of God has set before their eyes.[179] He is careful to avoid suggesting that any religion is the truth which the Spirit has disclosed, or that it contains such truth. It may be misleading to speak of the world religions as revelations of God because it suggests that different parts or aspects of God have been apportioned to this or that people. Is this how a compassionate father loves the various children in his family? It seems closer to the truth to believe that God's self-revelation and self-giving is consistent and impartial, but that different peoples respond differently. This approach is characteristic of John Taylor in attending to the facts, taking seriously all the data, working with what can actually be observed rather than presumptuously theorizing. All we know for sure is that this is how these people in this particular culture at this particular time responded and taught others to respond. In the events of their history, and by the insights of their prophets, God made them aware, demanded their attention, beckoned them, awakened them, nodded in their direction. Looking at the matter this way attempts to do justice to what is God-given or man-made in every religion. It also leaves room for the crucial recognition that every religious tradition includes the response of disobedience as well as the response of obedience. Human beings use religion to escape from God as well as to approach God, so both obedience and disobedience are built into the tradition and passed on to later generations. If these later generations respond more readily to the incessant calls and disclosures of the Spirit, reformation of their tradition results. So every living faith is a continual process of renewal and purification, just as it conserves and transmits the tradition as recognizably the same. There is always the dialectic of past fidelity and present response, both answering to the One who is beyond all religion.

Since every religion is a historically determined tradition of response to what the Spirit of God has forever been setting before human eyes, each religion becomes a self-consistent and closed system of culture and language. Communication between systems of this kind is inevitably fraught with difficulty. Problems of hermeneutics arise, impeding communication. The same word will carry an entirely different cluster of meanings, while quite different words mean the same thing. It is not enough to limit our search to similarities or areas of common ground, although they do exist and will give us deep satisfaction when we find them. After all, there is always something else which is common to us all. John Taylor speaks memorably of the jealousies of different faiths, those points in every religion where believers are inwardly compelled to claim for their own traditional response universal significance and finality.[180] Every profoundly convincing encounter with God is with a jealous God. Having experienced God in a particular way, we feel that no other god will do. Whenever we come up against a brick wall of this kind, our frustration must, paradoxically, include an element of rejoicing, for here we can understand each other at a very basic level. What we have in common is the experience of conviction that by definition precludes the other person's belief, and we cannot with integrity accommodate that foreign belief alongside our own.

> So I plead with those who want to make all the intractable convictions relative and level them down for the sake of a quick reconciliation: leave us at least our capacity for categorical assertion, for that is what we have in common.[181]

Patient dialogue will force us deeper in exploring our experience and may lead to reformulation, to fresh attempts to describe what we know, but it may never reduce or dilute the content of the experience which it interprets or translates. Absolute fidelity is demanded of both partners in dialogue, combined with an extraordinary mixture of humility and boldness.[182]

For the Christian, such absolute fidelity requires that we give an honest answer to Christ's question, 'Who do you say that I am?' No doubt this is a formulation arising in the preaching of some of the earliest Christian communities, but it seems likely that the question of identity actually arose for everyone confronted with the charismatic personality and authoritative words and deeds of Jesus of Nazareth. The developing christologies as we find them in the New Testament documents and as they became more sophisticated in the early Fathers are a response to the overwhelming impact Jesus made and continues to make. What makes the apostolic witnesses so remarkable is that, as they thought out the implications of the response they felt compelled to make to Jesus, they refused to diminish any of the truth as they experienced it even when this began to conflict with all the accepted Jewish ideas about God. The first Christians seem to be astonishingly fearless in pursuing the implications arising from their response to the man Jesus himself. What we see is their prolonged exploration of an original encounter that they are not prepared to deny or modify in any way, and we overhear their attempts to find language adequate for expressing this shatteringly unique experience.

> One might say that they were according Jesus the lordship of their universe long before they dared to say, in so many words, that he was their *Kurios*. They were worshipping God in him long before they ventured to speak of his divinity. They had been saved by him long before they had worked out any theory of salvation. And what we see in St Paul, and in all the later Christian teachers, is a bold experimenting with one metaphor after another

to describe their experience and fit it into their understanding of God and the universe. If the theologians of the early centuries failed – and I think we have to admit that in some of their formulations they did fail – it was because they stuck too rigidly to their previous ideas about God which owed more to a philosophical system than to a living experience. Through most of its history, the Church has gone on trying to maintain belief in the God who can undergo neither change nor suffering; yet, for those who have seen the glory of God in the face of Jesus Christ, that old axiom has had to be abandoned. What we say about Jesus Christ is that, if our idea of God differs in any respect from what we see in him and in his life, death and resurrection, then it is our idea of God that has to be changed; and not because of any prescribed dogma, but because, once we have seen him, we could not find it in us to worship a God who was different.[183]

The distinctively Christian confession is that the impact of Jesus is such that, thereafter, only a *wounded* God will do. This is our contribution to the contemporary human search for meaning, our contribution to the conversation between believers of every persuasion. John Taylor believes that 'contribution' is the key word in a society characterized by religious pluralism. Finding ourselves as one minority among other minorities, learning that in God's eyes were are all minorities, prompts the adherent of any faith to stop pontificating about *everything* so as to concentrate on the *priorities* of their own inheritance. For Christians this means that we must begin where Jesus began, with the Kingdom of his Father. This was not, in his understanding, the heaven of later hymn writers. Its setting was on earth, but at a moment of new beginnings when the axe is poised before swinging to the root of the old tree. At such a time of urgency and confusion, Jesus, with what must strike us as naiveté, had one rule of life. He did what he saw his Father doing and called on his followers to do the same. The Kingdom was the communion or company of the God-like. 'Be merciful as your Father is merciful.' 'Forgive your enemies – so shall you be children of your Father.' We are to look at our relationships with each other, our economic and social policies, our commerce and trading practices, and cry insistently: 'Since God is like that, how *can* we behave like this?' This remains the Christian way of looking at things, and we have no mandate for anything more sophisticated. It all depends, of course, on knowing what God really is like, and this comes only from knowing God as Jesus knows God. Prayer of the kind that Jesus engaged in is the way to know God as surely as this, and the years ahead call for a fusion of prayer and politics no less intense than that which brought Jesus to the cross and is already bringing some Christians to theirs.

This, of course, is another essential element in the Christian vision, the distinctively Christian way of seeing things. Jesus did what he saw his Father doing, and never more completely than when he was lifted up on the cross. In relation to the world and in eternal being, we say God is like *that*.

This must be the Christian's contribution to the loving interchange between the great faiths. Let us gratefully honour their magnificent witness to the unknowable mystery, the unity, the faithfulness or the sovereignty of God, but no less gratefully bring our peculiar witness to God's everlasting self-sacrifice, for we uniquely possess the imagery and vocabulary for saying it.[184]

The Name that is above every name is hidden still and Jesus, who never thought his equality with God a prize to grasp at, is very often humbler than his disciple. The disciple can afford to keep the secret a little longer if, thereby, others are more likely to love the disciple's gentle Lord. Nevertheless, however patient we are in awaiting the right moment, and however sensitive we may be in finding the right words, the Name must be named. Nothing less will do if we are to be true witnesses to the Resurrection. If it is true that the patterns of the gospel experience are the patterns of life itself, then it might be argued that all we should hope is that all people will come to live life to the full in their own way, according to their own lights or the insights of their particular religious tradition. There is more than some truth in this relaxed approach.

> The freedom and the protest of Jesus of Nazareth, his dying for us all and his Resurrection, are *both* history *and* eternal reality. They happened, and they are the way things always happen. And we can be transformed, not only by relating to that past life and death and resurrection, in which the pattern was made plain once and for all, but also by relating to that true pattern wherever it emerges in the tissue of our contemporary experience.[185]

Why, then, should we look for more? Why do we seek conscious allegiance to Jesus Christ rather than let people live by the light they already have? Not, John Taylor answers firmly, because there are no degrees of salvation apart from naming the Name, and certainly not because Christ is greedy for the credit. We seek conscious allegiance in order that everyone may rise to their full stature as adult daughters and sons of God, through attachment to him who was and is and ever shall be the complete or fully human being because he is the perfect Son. And if that perfect sonship could not be complete without the cross, then no one's salvation is complete until they also become cross-bearers. The common approach is to think of salvation as wholeness, healing of infirmity, lifting of burdens, at-one-ment where now there is estrangement, restoration of lost harmony. Suppose, however, that we are so constituted as to only really be human when we are bearing one another's burdens? If this is true, then the happy pagan has not yet, in fact, been made whole. John Taylor quotes D. T. Niles, who says that making love is not enough. One must actually say the words, 'I love you'. Kind deeds are not enough. One must say, 'I forgive you'. To be a Christian within this or that particular furrow is not enough. One must perform the duties and obligations of being an ambass-ador.[186] This is not so that anyone should switch from one religion to another. It is not even that society should more and more reflect Christian ideas. It is that men and women should experience the miraculous newness to be found in Christ and start living here and now as citizens of heaven.[187] John Taylor agrees with Charles Williams that the end and objective of Christian mission is nothing less than the complete regeneration of human-kind. 'The apostles set out to generate mankind anew.'[188]

So this is the driving motivation for speaking to others of Christ. It is not that we believe that the mercy of God is ultimately limited to those who are within the visible Church. We can confidently leave the eternal destiny of our neighbours in the hands of the One who was slain before the foundation of the world – pierced hands, than which there can be none safer. We can acknowledge these same hands at work anonymously in every redeeming event and action through which the basic humanness of people is being saved and brought to its maturity.[189] And yet, unless we are to be guilty of the ultimate arrogance and paternalism, we must covet for all what, in our moments of highest aspiration, we covet for ourselves: the privilege of walking *consciously* in the steps and in the power of the crucified Christ. For in a universe of which he is Maker and Lord, fullness of life cannot mean less than that.[190]

Whatever we say will not be heard, however, if who we are and what we do give the lie to our verbal eloquence. All we say or do without love is ultimately worthless. The Christian mission will only be effectual if the Church becomes more evidently Christian – living sacrificially and joyfully, living eucharistically as the sacrament of Christ's real presence in the world. 'Words and symbols speak only where their truth is being lived.'[191] The primary aim of all Christian mission in all its varied activities is to present the person of Jesus Christ, to make him visible, to lift him up, as he truly was and is, so that he may draw all peoples to himself.[192] It must be possible to see him in his humanity, 'and that can only be in the Christ-likeness of other human beings and in a Church that actually *is* his Body'.[193]

This incarnational witness will be the work of ordinary Christian disciples, of the company of the faithful as a whole living out the faith, rather than the great saints or the great sinners who actually prove very little. At the end of the strange meeting between St Francis of Assisi and Sala'din, the sultan is reported to have said, 'If ever I meet a second Christian like you I would be willing to be baptized, but, sadly, I know there is no danger of that.' Less than three hundred years later a king in Peru said something very similar, yet horribly different, to the Franciscan friar accompanying an expedition of Conquistadores, who was offering vanquished Incas the choice of conversion or death. When their king demurred, his hands were cut off and the appeal was then repeated: 'Be baptized and you will go to heaven.' 'No,' said the king, 'for if I went to heaven I might meet another Christian like you.'[194] Only a Christlike church can really preach the Christlike God. This will not necessarily be a church already conformed in every particular to the God it seeks to serve, but it *will* be a church ready to lower its defences because it is more interested in meeting than in point-scoring.[195] It will be a church which does not pretend to know the outcome of dialogue before it starts, a church which has not already made up its mind that Christianity alone is true, leaving others with no real choice but to see the error of their ways and join us. Rather, this church of the future will be humble enough to know it does not have all the answers, humble enough to admit its need of the companionship and insights contributed by other honest seekers after truth.

Already, the Church knows something of this from its own fragmented and divided state. The quest for Christian unity should grow from the desire for an 'in-othering' which will reflect the Christlike God better, so that the world may believe that *this* God and not any other sends Christians into the world in mission.[196] This insistence on 'co-inherence' is one more facet of the characteristically Christian vision of reality – the mutual dependence of all things. We enter into conversation with other peoples of faith because we know that independence is an idol, because we see that isolation is never splendid and that autonomy is a lie. Dependence is the changeless truth about our relationship to one another and to all creation. The autonomous self-sufficient individual is an illusion. The glory of human nature is to depend on one another *for* everything and to be responsible for one another *in* everything.

> The ever-flowing exchange of support, of ideas, of skills, of physical life and spiritual energy, which sometimes humiliates, is actually the image of God stamped upon our very existence. For in our mutual dependence and responsibility we reflect the eternal giving and receiving of the Three in One ... the pattern of the Trinity.[197]

For those who have faith in Jesus Christ, then, the present is the only tense. We can call in that part of ourselves that dwells in the past with its regrets and resentments and scars. We can call in that part of ourselves that lives in the future amid fears, ambitions and daydreams. Past and future, naturally, affect us, but they affect us today. Actually, they are factors of our present. 'And with us now and only now is the Living One – Life itself giving itself as he did for Lazarus, his friend.'[198] This knowledge and love should protect us from all anxiety as we work with patient faith and wait with joyful hope for the coming of the Kingdom. Like Jesus himself, who was clear-sighted, but not clairvoyant, it is not demanded of us that we see tomorrow, but that we respond rightly to the present.[199] This right response determines what the future brings.[200]

> It seems certain that the next few decades will bring more rapid and more far-reaching change to the whole world than anyone can remember or

visualise. Yet Christ's mandate to his followers still stands, whatever the circumstances. It is, in fact, a mandate which changing conditions, resources and techniques can do little to alter, since the mission to which it commits us is primarily to be the human Presence of Jesus Christ who is the same yesterday, today and forever. Our vocation is corporately to make visible his total response to God's love and truth in the terms of each distinct culture, old or new, so as to affirm, challenge, redeem and fulfil it from within, and to take the consequence of doing so with him.[201]

In a Church expanding more slowly than the population of the world, when there are far more non-Christians alive today than in the time of St Paul, we must beware of identifying the missionary objective (what we are given to do) with the missionary hope (what we look to God to do).[202] As Roland Allen said, 'we seek a revelation', and 'revelation is the unfolding of something that is, not the creation of something that is not'.[203] Because we are heirs of the coming kingdom, and because this kingdom is already alive in us, faith in the God and Father of Jesus Christ brings absolute conviction that the End is in God's hands, and this involves an absolute demand to take the present moment into our own.

John Taylor is clear that we know what we are working for, that we can never be content with any continuing city for we look to that city which is to come. Typically, he calls this 'the view from the cross'.[204] From this vantage point we see more than the gathering of an elect minority. There is much in the Bible to support such a view, but Scripture as a whole looks forward to something more than this partial victory. For that is what it will be at the end of time if, for all but the few, the very few, Christ has died in vain. The restoration wrought in Christ is to be coextensive with the havoc wrought by Adam. The mission of God in the world, the mission of Jesus Christ in the Holy Spirit in which the Church shares, is, after all, nothing less than the wooing of our estranged race, down to the last recalcitrant heart, by the Love which will not let us go. So the missionary view of the world and its future is always the view from the cross, and it can only be seen through a mist of pain and desolation and thirst, endured for the sake of the joy that lies ahead.[205]

For all the humility we learn at the cross of Christ, we know with absolute confidence that the kingdoms of this world shall become the kingdom of God and of God's Christ, but this is never the reason for our allegiance. It is not the certainty of success which makes us servants. What matters to a missionary at the end of the day is neither the task nor the outcome, but the One with whom and for whom we go forward.

Notes

Chapter 1: Christ and religion: theological exploration with John V. Taylor

1. M. A. C. Warren, *The Missionary Movement from Britain in Modern History* (SCM, 1965), p. 100.
2. Lester Kurtz, *Gods in the Global Village* (Pine Forge Press, 1995), pp. 1–2.
3. For a useful overview of the literature on the uniqueness or distinctiveness of Jesus see Scott Cowdell, *Is Jesus Unique? A Study of Recent Christology* (Paulist Press, 1996).
4. J. P. Rajashekar, 'The challenge of religious pluralism to Christian theological reflection', in *Lutheran World Fellowship Report* No. 23, 9–23 January 1988, pp. 10, 12.
5. J. V. Taylor, *CMS Newsletter* 303, April 1967.
6. J. P. Rajashekar, 'The challenge', p. 17.
7. Bishop Kenneth Cragg argues for a theology of cross-reference being integral to Christian fidelity. 'Theology's first task ... is to interrogate this diversity of self-legitimation, its own and that of others, and seek what might establish between us the sort of *bona fide* relationship which does not exempt its own credentials from engagement with the other. There is what might be called a Christian resonance in so much of the inter-thought of which a cross-reference theology becomes aware.' It would be uncharacteristic of Bishop Cragg to labour the point, but in a writer of his sensitivity and experience there is little doubt that this theology of cross-reference deliberately evokes Calvary and the cross of Christ. In other words, his theology of cross-reference is always a theology of Cross-reference. All encounters with 'the faiths' take place in this context and in the light of this definitive revelation of God's love. Kenneth Cragg, *The Christ and the Faiths* (SPCK, 1986), pp. 10–11.
8. Michael Ramsey, 100th Archbishop of Canterbury, coined the phrase 'God is Christlike, and in Him is no unChristlikeness at all', and John Taylor, with the aged Bishop Ramsey's permission, adapted this for the title of his book *The Christlike God* (SCM, 1992).
9. Hendrik Kraemer, *Religion and the Christian Faith* (Lutterworth, 1956), p. 20.
10. This is the title given to a diocesan conference on Christian mission in the multicultural and multifaith City of Melbourne, arranged by the then Archbishop of Melbourne, David Penman. *A Garden of Many Colours: The Report of the Archbishop's Commission on Multicultural Ministry and Mission*, presented to the Synod of the Diocese of Melbourne in March 1985.
11. Bishop John Robinson is just one respected New Testament scholar to demonstrate how these biblical texts are rather more complex than they sound on first hearing. Indeed, some that have been repeated like a mantra by anxious Christians seeking to establish their supremacy demand careful contextualization if they are not to be abused in future, or used as weapons against other peoples of faith. See J. A. T. Robinson, *Truth is Two-Eyed* (SCM, 1979).
12. Edinburgh Conference on World Mission and Evangelism, 1910.
13. It could be argued that Islam is more Christianity's sibling than its cousin, in that

both claim descent from the covenant with Abraham and regard Judaism as their parent faith.

14. Matthew 28.18–end, although there is also a Lukan form in Acts 1.6-8.
15. John 20.19-23.
16. Lesslie Newbigin talks of our need to hold the Johannine 'great commission' in tension with the Matthean 'great commission', so that the Matthean commission does not eclipse the Johannine in the Church's living memory. See his essay 'On being the Church in the world', in Giles Ecclestone (ed.), *The Parish Church* (The Grubb Institute, Mowbrays, 1988), pp. 25–42.
17. J. V. Taylor, 'The place and function of the missionary', in R. K. Orchard (ed.), *The Ghana Assembly of the International Missionary Council*, 28 December, 1957–8 January, 1958 (Edinburgh House Press, 1958), p. 31.
18. Lesslie Newbigin, *Mission in Christ's Way* (WCC Mission Series, 1987).
19. J. V. Taylor, *For All the World: The Christian Mission in the Modern Age* (Hodder & Stoughton, 1966), p. 12.
20. Newbigin, *Mission in Christ's Way*, p. 14.
21. 'The church exists by mission as a fire exists by burning.' Emil Brunner, quoted by J. V. Taylor in *The Go-Between God: The Holy Spirit and the Christian Mission* (SCM, 1972), p. 132.
22. J. V. Taylor, *The Uncancelled Mandate: Four Bible Studies on Christian Mission for the Approaching Millennium* (Church House Publishing, 1998).
23. M. A. C. Warren's preface to the Christian Presence series of books published at his initiative. See Kenneth Cragg, *Sandals at the Mosque: Christian Presence amid Islam* (SCM, 1959).
24. Hendrik Kraemer, *Why Christianity of all Religions?* (Westminster Press, 1962), pp. 27–8.
25. Bishop Taylor points out that the term 'global village' is much too sweet to describe 'the spreading uni-culture resulting from the forces of globalization working to eliminate all other cultures other than the Free Market Economy. Our current reality is one of world domination worthy of the books of Daniel and Revelation. An essential component of Christian mission today, Bishop Taylor argues, is that we dissociate Christianity from this, celebrating human diversity as one of God's greatest gifts, so that Christianity does not leave Islam to challenge the global jungle alone. Wherever the term 'global village' is employed in this book, it is used with this insight and critique in mind. J. V. Taylor, 'Christian mission and the next Millennium', unpublished Partnership in World Mission address to the General Synod of the Church of England at Church House, Westminster, Church House, 19 November 1998, pp. 7–8.
26. Lesslie Newbigin, *Truth to Tell: The Gospel as Public Truth* (Eerdmans, 1991), p. 89.
27. Hans Küng, *On Being a Christian* (Collins, 1978), pp. 334, 335.
28. Hendrik Kraemer, *Why Christianity?*, p. 37.
29. Ibid., p. 110.
30. Ibid., pp. 110, 113, 115.
31. Ibid., p. 116.
32. M. A. C. Warren, Theme Address to the Anglican Congress in E. R. Fairweather (ed.), *Anglican Congress 1963: Report of Proceedings*, Toronto: Anglican Book Centre, 1963, pp. 19–30.
33. Max Warren had less than a year as a missionary in Nigeria before being invalided home to England. See M. A. C. Warren, *Crowded Canvas* (Hodder & Stoughton, 1974), pp. 51–72, and F. W. Dillistone, *Into All the World: A Biography of Max Warren* (Hodder & Stoughton, 1980), pp. 34–44.
34. J. V. Taylor, 'Doing Theology', unpublished lecture to Aston Training Scheme, 1981, p. 4.
35. Ibid.
36. Newbigin, *Truth to Tell*, p. 60.

37. J. V. Taylor. 'My pilgrimage in mission', in *International Bulletin of Missionary Research*, 17, No. 2, April 1993, p. 55.
38. Kenneth Cragg, *Jesus and the Muslim: An Exploration* (George Allen & Unwin, 1985), p. 130.
39. Kenneth Cragg, Preface to *Troubled by Truth* (Pentland Press, 1992).
40. Taylor, *For All the World*, pp. 29–40. See Sarah Cawdell, 'A study of the distinctive theology of mission of John V. Taylor' (unpublished essay for Ridley Hall, Cambridge, 1995), p. 8.
41. J. V. Taylor, *CMS Newsletter* 332, November 1969.
42. J. V. Taylor, 'Easter', *A Christmas Sequence and Other Poems* (Amate Press, 1989), p. 26.
43. *For All the World*, p. 35.
44. Ibid.
45. Newbigin, *Truth to Tell*, pp. 32, 33.
46. Bishop Simon Barrington-Ward, interview, 1995.
47. Gwen Cashmore, Introductory Note to J. V. Taylor, *Weep Not For Me* (WCC Risk Books, 1986), p. vii.
48. 'I think that religions are themselves large poems ... In that unique Divine embodiment for which we reserve the term Incarnation, Jesus lives from the first in a wholeness no mortal artist can sustain; he lives on the level of poetry, and thus shows us the way to that quality of life which he calls the Kingdom. This Kingdom is Jesus's own poem, and He embodies it fully, while revealing it as an aspect of God's poem' (Les Murray, 'Embodiment and Incarnation', in *A Working Forrest*, Duffy & Snellgrove, 1997, pp. 310, 324). See also Bob Ellis, 'Les Murray', in *So It Goes* (Viking, 2000), p. 173.
49. 'Religious language, like religious art, evokes more than it states. None of the disputes ... touch the horizon of mystery towards which faith tends without ever reaching.' P. Hebblethwaite, *Paul VI: The First Modern Pope* (HarperCollins, 1993), p. 342.
50. James M. Phillips, review of *The Go-Between God*, in *Theology Today*, Vol. 37, April 1980, p. 253.
51. Les Murray calls the exclusive sovereignty of daylight reason, championed since the Enlightenment, *Narrowspeak*, whereas religions, like all poetry, deal in *Wholespeak*. This, he says, is why Jesus 'refers his message always to the vision of children, to that integral and naturally poetic vision we all have before reason, the dream and the dance drift apart in us and our perceptions flatten' (Les Murray, 'Embodiment and Incarnation', in *A Working Forrest*, p. 324).
52. One recently published example of this particular genre is Richard Fardon, *Mary Douglas: An Intellectual Biography* (Routledge, 1999). Others include John McGuckin, *St Gregory of Nazianzus: An Intellectual Biography* (St Vladimir's Seminary Press, 2001) and J. Pereiro, *Cardinal Manning: An Intellectual Biography* (Oxford University Press, 1998).
53. Cragg, Preface to *Troubled by Truth*.
54. Davis McCaughey, *Tradition and Dissent* (Melbourne University Press, 1997), p. 203.
55. St Anselm of Canterbury coined the phrase 'fides quaerens intellectum', which translates as 'faith seeking understanding'.
56. E. R. Fairweather (ed.), *Anglican Congress 1963: Report of Proceedings* (Anglican Book Centre, 1963), p. 43.
57. Kenneth Cragg, *Faith and Life Negotiate: A Christian Story-Study* (Canterbury Press, 1994), p. 287.
58. Ibid., p. 1.
59. John Taylor's first book, *Man in the Midst*, was published by Highway Press, London in 1955.
60. J. V. Taylor, *The Primal Vision* (SCM, 1963), p. 118.
61. Ibid., p. 191.
62. Elizabeth Templeton, *The Strangeness of God* (Arthur James, 1993), p. 23.

63. Until the sixteenth century the term was used exclusively with reference to the doctrine of the Trinity, that is, of the sending of the Son by the Father and of the Holy Spirit by the Father and the Son. The Jesuits were first to use it in terms of the spread of Christian faith among people who were not already members of the Roman Catholic Church. In this sense it was intimately associated with the colonial expansion of the western world into what has more recently become known as the Third World or, sometimes, the Two-Thirds World. The term 'mission' presupposes a sender, those to whom one is sent, and an assignment. See David Bosch, *Transforming Mission* (Orbis, 1992), p. 1ff. As John Taylor says, 'It is not the Church that carries on the missionary enterprise. God, the triune God, the Father, the Son, and the Holy Spirit, remains till the last day the one who carries on this mission to the ends of the earth' (*For All the World*, p. 25).

64. Taylor, *The Go-Between God*, p. 15.

65. Ibid.

66. Strangely, there is almost no literature on this methodology and, more strangely, what exists appears to be Protestant rather than Catholic. It might, after all, be expected that catholic sacramentalism, not to mention the cult of the saints, would lend itself naturally to such an approach to truth. See James McClendon, *Biography as Theology: How Life Stories Can Remake Today's Theology* (Abingdon, 1976); Michael Goldberg, *Theology and Narrative: A Critical Introduction* (Abingdon, 1981); James Fowler, Robin Lovin *et al.*, *Trajectories of Faith* (Abingdon, 1980); David Duke, 'Theology and biography: simple questions for a promising field', in *Perspectives in Religious Studies* 13, No. 2, Summer 1986, pp. 137–49. If it is true to say that there is little reflective material on biography as a theological methodology, however, this is not to say that biographies of mind do not exist on both sides of the Catholic–Protestant divide. G. K. Chesterton's studies of St Francis and St Dominic are neither biography nor hagiography, but attempts to explore a theological understanding of what such people mean. Henri Nouwen, the popular pastoral theologian, writes biographically or autobiographically. See G. K. Chesterton, *Saint Francis*, although in the opinion of Morris Bishop in his *St Francis of Assisi* (Little Brown, 1974) this is more revelatory of Chesterton than Francis! See also H. M. Nouwen, *Reaching Out: The Three Movements of the Spiritual Life* (Collins, 1976), and *In Memoriam* (Ave Maria Press, 1980).

67. Duke, 'Theology and biography', p. 138.

68. Cragg, *Faith and Life*, p. 7.

69. Harry Williams CR, *Someday I'll Find You* (Collins, 1990), p. 68.

70. Duke, 'Theology and biography', p. 139.

71. George Stroup, *The Promise of Narrative Theology: Recovering the Gospel in the Church* (John Knox, 1981), p. 40, quoting McClendon, *Biography as Theology: How Life Stories Can Remake Today's Theology*.

72. Fardon, *Mary Douglas*, p. xvi.

73. John Updike, *Self-Consciousness* (Penguin Books, 1989), p. ix.

74. J. V. Taylor, interview, 1997.

75. Ibid.

76. Taylor, *Primal Vision*, p. 7.

77. Taylor, Foreword to *The Go-Between God*.

78. Taylor, Acknowledgements in *The Christlike God* (SCM, 1992). In his first book, what was to become the usual disclaimer comes some way into the text: 'Anyone who has read thus far will have realized that none of the thought in this book is original, and may have grown impatient to find so many people's ideas lying ill-digested in the text. Better writers are more adept at assimilating the aliment they receive from others, and the gastric juices of their minds leave not one footnote or inverted comma to tell the tale of their indebtedness.' Even at this early stage, however, John Taylor is convinced of what he will later, under the influence of Charles Williams, call 'co-inherence'. So he goes on to affirm that 'not one of us

has a mind of his own; we are what we devour. Our souls are bound up in the bundle of the living. We breathe the air of our age and think the thoughts of our own generation. We are moulded by our culture and have history in our veins' (*Man in the Midst*, pp. 23–4).

79. Maurice Wiles, then Regius Professor of Divinity in the University of Oxford, told the Bishop of Coventry that *The Go-Between God* is difficult to grasp: 'It is fragmentary and eclectic.' Bishop Simon Barrington-Ward, interview, 1997.

80. J. V. Taylor, letter, 9 May 1998.

81. Barrington-Ward, interview, 1997.

82. Significantly, considering the profound influence of Dietrich Bonhoeffer on John Taylor, Bonhoeffer's theology has been described as eclectic, fertile, fragmentary, creative, provocative, or partial in its insights. See J. W. Woelfel, *Bonhoeffer's Theology: Classical and Revolutionary* (Abingdon, 1970), p. 11; Ruth Zerner, 'Dietrich Bonhoeffer's views on the state and history', in A. J. Klassen, *A Bonhoeffer Legacy: Essays in Understanding* (Eerdmans, 1981), p. 132; Geoffrey Kelley, *Liberating Faith: Bonhoeffer's Message for Today* (Augsburg, 1984), p. 33; Paul Lehman, 'Faith and worldliness in Bonhoeffer's thought', in *Union Seminary Quarterly Review*, 23, No. 1, Fall 1967, p. 31.

83. Cawdell, 'Theology of mission', pp. 3, 22.

84. Maria Boulding, 'A tapestry, from the wrong side', in Maria Boulding (ed.), *The Touch of God* (DLT, 1988), pp. 27–50.

85. 'Foolish consistency is the hobgoblin of little minds, adored by little statesmen, philosophers and divines', quoted by Davis McCaughey in his eulogy for Frank Macfarlane Burnet in *Tradition and Dissent* (MelbourneUniversity Press, 1997), pp. 210–11.

86. Eberhard Bethge, *Dietrich Bonhoeffer: A Biography* (Collins, 1970), p. xx.

87. *The Go-Between God*, p. 128.

Chapter 2: Setting out

1. John Taylor published some autobiographical reflections in the series 'My pilgrimage in mission', commissioned by the editor of the *International Bulletin of Missionary Research* (17, No. 2, April 1993, pp. 59–61).

2. 'Pilgrimage', p. 59.

3. Ibid.

4. Working for the International Missionary Council for five years between leaving Uganda and beginning as Africa Secretary of CMS, John Taylor had to learn to stop himself rejecting at first sight what seemed strange or impossible and force himself to really listen to what was being said to him, asking himself what it could possibly mean, searching between the lines for what was not said, genuinely paying attention to the facts while resisting every temptation to interpret too soon. J. V. Taylor, interview, 1997.

5. 'Pilgrimage', p. 59.

6. Taylor, interview, 1995.

7. BA (Cantab) 1936, BA (Oxon) 1938, MA (Oxon) 1941.

8. Bishop Bill Ind, interview, 1995.

9. Taylor, interview, 1997.

10. Arthur Foley Winnington-Ingram was Bishop of London 1901–1939. See S. C. Carpenter, *Winnington-Ingram* (Hodder & Stoughton, 1949).

11. Taylor, interview, 1997.

12. Ibid.

13. Robin Woods was later Dean of Windsor and then Bishop of Worcester. All three Woods brothers were at Cambridge with John Taylor – Sam at Wescott House and Frank as chaplain of Trinity College. Sam went on to be Archdeacon of Christ-

church, New Zealand, while Frank became Suffragan Bishop of Middlesbrough, before serving as Archbishop of Melbourne for twenty years and, in the last years of his archiepiscopate, as Primate of Australia.

14. Taylor, interview, 1997.
15. The Bible Churchman's Missionary Society training college.
16. Kenneth Cragg, *Faith and Life Negotiate* (Canterbury Press, 1994), pp. 45, 47.
17. Taylor, interview, 1997.
18. Ibid.
19. Ibid.
20. Ibid.
21. The rubrics of *The Book of Common Prayer* of 1662 assume that the altar or Lord's Table will be placed lengthwise in the chancel at communion time, with the congregation gathered around and the presiding priest at the head. For a time in Elizabethan England this was achieved, but then altars returned to their medieval position against the ecclesiastical east wall of the sanctuary. Obviously, this makes standing at the north end of the table impossible, so instead of moving the altar out and standing behind the table facing the people, evangelical clergy continued to stand at the north end, side on to the congregation! When there were two of them, at north and south ends, the 'book-ends' position was born. Followers of the Oxford Movement stood facing the ecclesiastical east, back to the people, and this became known as the 'eastward' position. Typically, these postures hardened into party symbols, indicating churchmanship – high or low, evangelical or catholic.
22. Cragg, *Faith and Life*, p. 1.
23. J. V. Taylor, 'Max Warren', in *New Fire*, 34, September 1978.
24. J. V. Taylor, 'The place and function of the missionary', in R. K. Orchard (ed.), *The Ghana Assembly of the International Missionary Council* (Edinburgh House Press, 1958), p. 29.
25. Ibid.
26. Ibid.
27. Taylor, interview, 1995.
28. Ibid.
29. Ibid.

Chapter 3: Mukono

1. J. V. Taylor, *Mukono: An African College Community Experimenting in Wholeness of Life* (CMS [no date]), p. 1.
2. Ibid., p. 2.
3. Ibid., pp. 2–3.
4. Ibid., p. 3.
5. J. C. Jones ended his career as Bishop of Bangor.
6. Adrian Hastings, *The Church in Africa 1450–1950* (Clarendon Press, 1994), pp. 592–3.
7. The Keswick Convention is an annual gathering of evangelicals for prayer, Bible study, and inspirational addresses. Begun in Keswick in the Lake District in 1875, it has the atmosphere of a summer camp and the aim of promoting what is termed 'practical holiness'. Its motto is 'All One in Christ Jesus'. It continues to meet for a week each year, attracting many international visitors.
8. Adrian Hastings, *The Church in Africa*, p. 597.
9. This judgement of Adrian Hastings is supported by John Taylor, Ray Bowers, Simon Barrington-Ward and others with first-hand experience of the African Revival and its aftermath.
10. Taylor, interview, 1995.
11. Hastings, *The Church in Africa*, pp. 598–9.
12. F. W. Dillistone, *Into All the World* (Hodder & Stoughton, 1980), p. 159.

13. Revd Ray Bowers, letter, 21 April 1995, p. 1.

14. Barrington-Ward, interview, 1997.

15. Taylor, interview, 1995.

16. Daphne Bowers, interview, 1995.

17. Ibid.

18. Ray Bowers, interview, 1995.

19. Ibid.

20. J. V. Taylor, Annual Letter to Max Warren, General Secretary of the CMS, March 1947, p. 1.

21. Ibid.

22. Ray and Daphne Bowers, interview, 1995. 'He fitted into African ways because he had no sense of time *whatever*. He was absolutely hopeless!'

23. M.A.C. Warren, letters to Pat and Roger Hooker, Letter 421, 30 September 1973.

24. Daphne Bowers, interview, 1995.

25. J. V. Taylor, Annual Letter to CMS, 29 June 1946.

26. Ray Bowers, interview, 1995.

27. Taylor, interview, 1995.

28. Ibid.

29. Taylor, *For All the World*, p. 52.

30. J. V. Taylor, Annual Letter to CMS, March 1947, p. 5.

31. Ibid.

32. Taylor, interview, 1995.

33. Ibid.

34. Taylor, 'Pilgrimage', p. 60.

35. J. V. Taylor, Annual Letter to CMS, 11 September 1953, p. 2.

36. Taylor, *Mukono*, p. 5.

37. J. V. Taylor, Annual Letter to CMS, September 1951.

38. This became the catch-phrase after the Toronto Anglican Conference.

39. J. V. Taylor, Letter to Sarah Cawdell, 30 March 1995.

40. Taylor, 'Pilgrimage', p. 60.

41. J. V. Taylor, 'The development of African drama for education and evangelism', in *International Review of Mission*, xxxix, No. 155, July 1950, p. 292.

42. Ibid., pp. 298, 301.

43. Ibid., p. 300.

44. Taylor, *Mukono*, p. 5.

45. Ibid.

46. J. V. Taylor, *Were You There? An African Presentation of the Passion Story* (Highway Press, 1951), pp. 11, 12, 14.

47. Ibid., p. 17.

48. Ibid., pp. 18–19.

49. Taylor, *Were You There?*, p. 17.

50. Taylor, 'Pilgrimage', p. 60.

51. Ibid.

52. Ibid.

53. Ibid.

54. J. V. Taylor, Annual Letter to CMS, 1951.

55. Ibid.

56. J. V. Taylor, Annual Letter to CMS, 1953.

57. Hastings, *The Church in Africa*, p. 556.

58. J. V. Taylor, *The Growth of the Church in Buganda: An Attempt at Understanding* (SCM, 1958), p. 245.

59. Hastings, *The Church in Africa*, p. 581.

60. Ibid.

61. Ibid., p. 587.

62. Ibid., pp. 588–9.

63. This is no argument for clericalism. Anyone can be close to God and share in the eucharistic order, where heartbreak is simply human and humanizing, not to say divinizing. The point is that all who draw close to God inevitably share in God's disappointments, and priests who bear the people of God in their heart must expect to share intimately in rejection, frustration and disappointment, as well as in deepest joy. The representative nature of priesthood makes such experiences unavoidable.
64. Taylor, *Mukono*, p. 16.

Chapter 4: Way of the Cross

1. Taylor, interview, 1995.
2. Taylor 'Pilgrimage', p. 20.
3. Reginald Stackhouse, Foreword to J. V. Taylor, 'Christ the Kingdom' (Wycliffe College, Toronto, unpublished), p. 3.
4. Taylor, interview, 1995.
5. Taylor, 'Pilgrimage', p. 60.
6. Taylor, interview, 1995.
7. Ibid.
8. Ibid.
9. Ibid.
10. Ibid.
11. J. V. Taylor, *Man in the Midst* (The Highway Press, 1955).
12. Ibid., p. 16.
13. Bishop Taylor made this observation himself after reading a draft of this book. 'What surprises me is to see just how far back some of the ideas go' (Taylor, interview, 1998).
14. J. V. Taylor, *Christianity and Politics in Africa* (Penguin, 1957).
15. Taylor, interview, 1995.
16. Dietrich Bonhoeffer, *Letters and Papers from Prison* (SCM, 1953).
17. It is impossible to deny the innate ambiguity of all religions, for 'in every household of faith it is plain that man uses religion as a way of escaping from God' (see Taylor, *The Go-Between God*, p. 190).
18. J. V. Taylor, 'Is Christ relevant to the non-European?', sermon in Great St Mary's, Cambridge, 29 November 1964.
19. Harvey Cox, 'Using and misusing Bonhoeffer', *Christianity and Crisis* 24 (October 19, 1964), p. 199.
20. Taylor, *The Go-Between God*, p. 128.
21. John Godsey, 'The legacy of Dietrich Bonhoeffer', in A. J. Klassen (ed.), *A Bonhoeffer Legacy: Essays in Understanding* (Eerdmans, 1981), p. 169.
22. L. L. Rasmussen, *Dietrich Bonhoeffer: Reality and Resistance* (Abingdon, 1972), p. 15.
23. Godsey, 'Legacy', p. 169.
24. Rasmussen, *Bonhoeffer*, p. 15.
25. Karl Barth, *Church Dogmatics* 1/2 (T&T Clark), p. 872.
26. Dietrich Bonhoeffer's doctoral thesis on *The Communion of Saints* was first published in English translation by Collins in London in 1963.
27. James Woelfel, *Bonhoeffer's Theology: Classical and Revolutionary* (Abingdon, 1970), p. 102.
28. Attempts to fuse Paul Tillich's and Dietrich Bonhoeffer's christologies fail. 'The fully secular man can understand only the biblical God, the one who lives as a human being and suffers by our side, because the very meaning of "secular" is "de-divinized" or "de-religionized", and therefore humanized. The issue between Bonhoeffer and Tillich is the issue between Luther and Schelling, between biblicistic Christocentricity and metaphysical idealism, between the concretely

human and the ubiquitously divine.' See also Woelfel, *Bonhoeffer's Theology*, p. 118.

29. Paul van Buren, 'Bonhoeffer's paradox: living with God without God', *Union Seminary Quarterly Review*, xxiii, No. 1, Fall 1967, p. 53.

30. Ibid., p. 59.

31. C. C. Richardson, *The Doctrine of the Trinity* (Abingdon, 1958), p. 68.

32. On doing christology from below see J. A. T. Robinson, *The Human Face of God* (SCM, 1973). Bishop Robinson, in many ways himself a disciple of Bonhoeffer and popularizing some of Bonhoeffer's ideas in *Honest to God*, argues that there is no alternative now to doing christology from below. John Taylor would argue that there is *never* any alternative, that all attempts at christology from above lead to distortion, usually to some docetic form of christology which fails to take seriously the true humanity of Jesus and leads inevitably to dualism of one kind or another.

33. Dietrich Bonhoeffer, *Christ the Centre* (Harper & Row, 1966), p. 62.

34. Eberhard Bethge, 'Bonhoeffer's Christology and his religionless Christianity', in *Union Seminary Quarterly Review*, xxiii, No. 1, Fall 1967, p. 74.

35. Dietrich Bonhoeffer, *Ethics* (Macmillan, 1965), p. 194.

36. Ibid., p. 70.

37. Bethge, *A Biography*, p. 298.

38. F. X. Manning, 'Religion and ethics in the theology of Dietrich Bonhoeffer, Bishop John Robinson, and Harvey Cox' (unpublished Doctoral Dissertation, Pontificia Universitas Lateranensis, Academia Alfonsiana, Roma, 1969), p. 449.

39. James Woelfel argues strongly that Bonhoeffer could never have conceived his religionless Christianity in the way he did had he not been the keenest disciple of Barth. Nevertheless, one of the most striking features of Bonhoeffer's advance on Barth is the fact that, beginning exactly where Barth began (with the understanding of all reality solely in terms of revelation), Bonhoeffer saw the urgent necessity of interpreting that vision of reality in radically contemporary terms – something that Barth never felt to be either urgent or necessary. Bonhoeffer's originality is as marked as his indebtedness to Barth. See Woelfel, *Bonhoeffer's Theology*, pp. 90ff.

40. The classic instance of kenotic christology in the New Testament is found in the hymn quoted by Paul in Philippians 2.5-11.

41. Bethge, 'Bonhoeffer's Christology', p. 70.

42. Bonhoeffer, *Christ the Centre*, p. 116.

43. Bonhoeffer, *Letters and Papers*, pp. 360–61.

44. Bonhoeffer, 'Outline for a book', *Letters and Papers*, pp. 188, 190.

45. Bonhoeffer, *Ethics*, p. 298.

46. Ibid., p. 297.

47. Bonhoeffer, *Christ the Centre*, pp. 47–8.

48. Ibid., p. 62.

49. Ibid., p. 114.

50. See Matthew 16.13-23. The construction of this passage by the evangelist, following Mark, suggests that Bonhoeffer has seen to the heart of the matter in declaring that the cross is not so much *the way* to a crown, but that the cross *is* the crown.

51. Bethge, *A Biography*, p. 174.

52. Bonhoeffer, *Letters and Papers*, p. 202.

53. Bonhoeffer, *Ethics*, p. 202.

54. Bonhoeffer, *Letters and Papers*, p. 203.

55. See the fascinating discussion of the failure of Bonhoeffer and the resistance to Hitler in Rasmussen, *Bonhoeffer*, pp. 174–211. What he says about the resistance surely applies also to the Church. They failed 'because nice fellows do not make good revolutionaries'!

56. Bethge 'Bonhoeffer's Christology', p. 74.

57. Bonhoeffer, *Letters and Papers*, pp. 201–2.

58. Rasmussen, *Bonhoeffer*, p. 22.

59. Ibid., p. 23.

60. Bonhoeffer, *Ethics*, p. 59. The sayings are Matthew 13.30 and Mark 9.40 respectively.
61. Rasmussen, *Bonhoeffer*, pp. 35–6.
62. Bethge, 'Bonhoeffer's Christology', pp. 65–6.
63. Rasmussen, *Bonhoeffer*, p. 77.
64. Bonhoeffer, '27 June 1944', *Letters and Papers*, p. 176.
65. Bonhoeffer, *The Cost of Discipleship* (Macmillan, 1966), p. 79.
66. Bonhoeffer, '18 July 1944', *Letters and Papers*, p. 190.
67. Bonhoeffer, '21 July 1944', *Letters and Papers*, p. 193.
68. John Wilcken, 'The ecclesiology of Ethics and the prison writings', in Klassen, *A Bonhoeffer Legacy*, p. 202.
69. Bonhoeffer, '8 June 1944', *Letters and Papers*, p. 170.
70. In the ancient Church a theology of the death of God was put forward towards the end of the second century in the school of thought known as modalism. Praxeas, who we will meet again in Chapter 10, taught that at the Incarnation the Godhead was emptied into the person of Christ without remainder. It was God the Father who came down into the Virgin's womb and was born as Son, proceeding from himself. It was the Father who suffered and died, hence the nickname 'patripassianism'. In the 1960s an extreme form of this theory was put forward by a group of theologians, notably T. J. J. Altizer, who asserted that God died when Christ died on the cross. According to Altizer, Christ's death was really an act of self-annihilation, of total self-emptying (*kenosis*). Christ was not resurrected, ascended or glorified, and hence 'the radical Christian' can rejoice in the death of God because he perceives the forward movement of the Spirit and knows Christ as a secular presence in a world which is now happily rid of the traditional Christian conception of God as almighty Creator, reigning in transcendental glory, a distant king and final judge. The connections with Dietrich Bonhoeffer and John Taylor are obvious, but they no more believed in the actual death of God than did Praxeas or Altizer. As Alan Richardson has commented, there is some significance in the fact that this dead God remains a lively subject of popular interest, if we may judge by the number of books and journal articles devoted to the post-mortem. See T. J. J. Altizer, *The Gospel of Christian Atheism* (1967); T. J. J. Altizer and W. Hamilton, *Radical Theology and the Death of God* (1966); T. W. Ogletree, *The 'Death of God' Controversy* (1966); D. Sölle, *Christ the Representative; An Essay in Theology after the Death of God* (1967); G. Vahanian, *The Death of God* (1961); Alan Richardson (ed.), *A Dictionary of Christian Theology* (SCM, 1969), pp. 88–9.
71. After 1939 Bonhoeffer never again used the term 'secularizing' by which an arrogant Church patronizingly dismissed a whole period of human history. See Bethge, 'Bonhoeffer's Christology', p. 68.
72. Bonhoeffer, '21 August 1944', *Letters and Papers*, p. 391.
73. Bonhoeffer, *The Cost of Discipleship*, p. 27.
74. Bonhoeffer, *Christ the Centre*, p. 112.
75. Bethge, *A Biography*, p. 770, citing Immanuel Kant, *Was ist Aufklaerung?* (1784).
76. Ibid., p. 771.
77. Bonhoeffer, '16 July 1944', *Letters and Papers*, p. 360.
78. Bethge, 'Bonhoeffer's Christology', p. 66.
79. Bonhoeffer, '18 July 1944', *Letters and Papers*, p. 362.
80. Daniel Berrigan, 'The Passion of Dietrich Bonhoeffer' (*Saturday Review*, 30 May 1970), p. 20.
81. Bonhoeffer, 'Christians and pagans', *Letters and Papers*, pp. 348–9.
82. John Godsey, 'Barth and Bonhoeffer: the basic difference', *Quarterly Review* 7, Spring 1987, p. 23.
83. Dietrich Bonhoeffer and John Taylor were forerunners in terms of what would become a major thrust in theology at the end of the second millennium of the Common Era and the beginning of the third, namely the search for the authenti-cally *Christian* God. See Marcus Borg, *The God We Never Knew: Beyond Dogmatic*

Religion to a More Authentic Contemporary Faith (HarperCollins, 1997).

84. Bonhoeffer, '16 July 1944', *Letters and Papers*, p. 361.
85. John Godsey, *Preface to Bonhoeffer* (Fortress, 1965), p. 34.
86. Dr Rasmussen has conclusively demonstrated that interpretations of Bonhoeffer on this point are not correctives so much as confusions. Bonhoeffer's emphasis is always on doing theology contextually. See Rasmussen, *Bonhoeffer*, pp. 92–3.
87. J. A. Phillips, *Christ for Us in the Theology of Dietrich Bonhoeffer* (Harper & Row, 1967), p. 28.
88. Rasmussen, *Bonhoeffer*, p. 90.
89. Dietrich Bonhoeffer, *Act and Being* (Harper & Row, 1962), pp. 90–91. In contrast to Karl Barth, whom he respects, Dietrich Bonhoeffer relentlessly avoids all objective abstraction. God is 'haveable', graspable in the Word in the Church. The difference between this early christology and his later christology is the location of the 'haveable' Christ, 'haveable' in the world as well as in the Christian community.
90. Bonhoeffer, '27 July 1944', *Letters and Papers*, p. 197.
91. Dr Rasmussen admits to feeling uncomfortable in making criticism of Bonhoeffer's christology along these lines, but he does point to a significant deficiency – at least for the world emerging after World War II. It does seem unrealistic and unfair to suggest that Bonhoeffer should have foreseen the problems of a later time, when all his emotional and intellectual energies were consumed in addressing his own time. See Rasmussen, *Bonhoeffer*, pp. 168–73. As John Phillips remarks, 'In Bonhoeffer study, organisation itself cannot escape being interpretation' (*Christ for Us*, p. 21).
92. Ruth Zerner, 'Dietrich Bonhoeffer's vision on the state and history', in Klassen, *A Bonhoeffer Legacy*, p. 132. The similarities between Dietrich Bonhoeffer and John Taylor as theologians can hardly be missed. Both eschew systematized structure, taking the risk of offering provocative insights, inviting others to take up the responsibility of theological exploration for themselves.
93. Bonhoeffer, *Christ the Centre*, p. 30.
94. Eberhard Bethge, 'Bonhoeffer's assertion of religionless Christianity – was he mistaken?', in Klassen, *A Bonhoeffer Legacy*, p. 22.
95. Bonhoeffer, '27 July 1944', *Letters and Papers*, p. 197.
96. Krister Stendahl, unpublished Quiet Day Address, House of the Holy Redeemer, New York City, 26 October 1992.
97. J. V. Taylor 'Christian motivation in dialogue', in *Face to Face: Essays on Inter-Faith Dialogue* (The Highway Press, 1971), pp. 14–15.

Chapter 5: Primal vision

1. Adrian Hastings, *The Church in Africa*, p. 567.
2. Ibid.
3. Ibid.
4. Adrian Hastings, *Mission and Ministry* (SCM, 1971), p. 145.
5. J. V. Taylor, 'The Uganda Church today', *International Review of Mission*, Vol. 46, No. 182, April 1957, p. 136.
6. E. R. Fairweather (ed.), *Anglican Congress 1963* (Ontario, 1963), p. 3.
7. Graeme Garrett, *God Matters: Conversations in Theology* (Liturgical Press, 1999), p. 7.
8. On this whole unifer/diversifier distinction see Garrett, *God Matters*, pp. 1–16.
9. Garrett, *God Matters*, p. 9.
10. Bonhoeffer, *Letters and Papers*, pp. 327–8.
11. 'I take courage from the conviction that one necessary qualification for the stranger who wishes to speak is to know how little he has understood. That, at least, I have learned in many bitter experiences' (Taylor, *The Primal Vision*, p. 7).
12. Taylor, 'The Uganda Church today', p. 138.
13. This is, of course, to paraphrase. Paul actually says 'to those outside the law I

became as one outside the law', and this is integral to becoming 'all things to all people, that I might by all means save some' (1 Corinthians 9.20-22).

14. Taylor, *The Primal Vision*, p. 105.
15. Ibid., p. 16.
16. It should be noted that Bishop Taylor is fully aware of the dangers inherent in this process of inculturation, as we shall see in Chapter 9. When Christianity became Greek there were obvious gains in terms of intellectual categories of thought and communication, but the process also involved surrendering something of the distinctively Christian revelation of God to the god of Greek philosophy. Danger, however, makes for caution and care rather than abandoning this risky but essential task.
17. Gerard Bissainthe, 'Prière de l'homme noir à Notre-Dame du Monde Noir', quoted in Taylor, *The Primal Vision*, p. 16.
18. Warren, *I Believe in the Great Commission*, p. 8.
19. Taylor, interview, 1995.
20. Taylor, letter to Sarah Cawdell, 30 March 1995.
21. Taylor, interview, 1997.
22. Taylor, *The Primal Vision*, p. 191.
23. Ibid.
24. Gwen Cashmore, Introductory Note to J. V. Taylor, *Weep Not For Me* (WCC Risk Books, 1986).
25. Taylor, 'The Uganda Church today', p. 139.
26. Taylor, *The Primal Vision*, pp. 8–12.
27. Ibid., p. 12.
28. Kenneth Cragg review in *The Church Times* quoted on the cover of *The Primal Vision* (fifth impression, 1977).
29. Bishop John Austin Baker, letter, 1 April 1998.
30. M. A. C. Warren, *CMS Newsletter*, No. 258, March 1963, p. 4.
31. Ibid.
32. J. V. Taylor, 'Doing Theology', unpublished lecture to Aston Training Scheme, 1980.
33. Taylor, 'The Uganda Church today', p. 139.
34. Ibid., p. 141.
35. Ibid.
36. Ibid., p. 142.
37. Ibid.
38. Ibid.

Chapter 6: All the world

1. This ditty, composed by John Taylor for 'Southward Bound', the final CMS staff party at Salisbury Square before the move to the new Partnership House in Waterloo Road, South London, encapsulates the relaxed and humble conviction of an experienced missionary, one who would encourage those in his care not to take themselves too seriously or make their urgent task solemn.
2. Taylor, 'The Uganda Church today', p. 61.
3. J. V. Taylor, Introduction to Klaus Klostermaier, *Hindu and Christian in Vrindaban* (SCM, 1969), p. viii.
4. Ibid.
5. Editorial in *Theology*, 77, No. 654, December 1974, p. 617.
6. The doctrine of the atonement or reconciliation of God and humankind is one element in the whole Christian doctrine of salvation. How did Christ effect this change in the relationship? Theologians have answered differently in different ages. Four main theories have presented themselves: 1) the subjective, moral or exemplarist theory; 2) the classic or dramatic theory; 3) the juridical, penal or

substitutionary theory; and 4) the sacrificial theory. No one theory should be allowed to be antagonistic to another. All belong to catholic truth, for each expresses an element of the truth uniquely its own, and no one theory, or any combination of them, is sufficient to contain the fullness of the reality. The judicial, penal or substitutionary theory is particularly associated with St Anselm of Canterbury (1033–1109), who, in an attempt to move away from a long tradition of seeing Christ's death as a ransom paid to the Devil, conceives of Christ paying the debt owed by sinful human beings to God. Jesus is our substitute, who bears the penalty for human sin, offering satisfaction for the sins of the whole world in our stead. One problem with this is that there is no real substitution in the simple sense of the word. Rather, Christ endures for us and on our behalf, though not strictly instead of us, what we can never endure for ourselves. Substitution or penal language is really talking about God's eternal and passionate love, which is willing to endure to the uttermost the terrible consequences of sin which in justice belong to us as sinner and not to God. Unfortunately, the doctrine is often construed crudely so that it speaks of anything but divine love, turning God into a vengeful and cruel monster who gladly devours his obedient Son. See 'Atonement' in Alan Richardson (ed.), *A Dictionary of Christian Theology* (SCM, 1969), pp. 18–24.

7. G. H. G. Hewitt, *The Problems of Success: A History of the CMS 1910–1942* (SCM, 1971/1977), p. 443; F. W. Dillistone, *Into All The World* (Hodder & Stoughton, 1980), p. 31.
8. M. A. C. Warren, *Crowded Canvas* (Hodder & Stoughton, 1974), p. 115.
9. Ibid., pp. 115–16.
10. Taylor, interview, 1997.
11. Warren, *Crowded Canvas*, p. 116.
12. Ibid., p. 117.
13. Ibid.
14. Ibid.
15. Ibid., p. 121.
16. F. W. Dillistone, 'The legacy of Max Warren', *International Bulletin of Missionary Research*, July 1981, p. 114.
17. Dillistone, *Into All The World*, p. 97.
18. Dillistone, 'The legacy of Max Warren', p. 114.
19. J. V. Taylor, 'Max Warren', in *New Fire*, 34, September 1978, p. 7
20. Dillistone, *Into All the World*, p. 76.
21. Taylor, 'Max Warren', p. 4.
22. Ibid. This belief that 'the economy of God is personal, arbitrary and uninhibited by tidy principle' is shared by Max Warren and John Taylor, and is characteristic of their approach to Christian leadership and pastoral ministry. In the case of John Taylor it emerges as one contentious feature of his Winchester episcopate, namely that he had favourites. Regardless of how that particular situation is judged, it is indicative of the intimate relation there always is for him between belief and behaviour, between theology and life.
23. Dillistone, *Into All the World*, p. 76.
24. Taylor, *For All the World*, pp. 68, 74, 77–8.
25. Dillistone, *Into All the World*, p. 113.
26. Ibid., p. 115.
27. M. A. C. Warren, *Towards 1999*, a vision document produced for CMS in 1957.
28. Ibid.
29. Dillistone, *Into All the World*, p. 117.
30. J. V. Taylor, *Enough is Enough* (SCM, 1975), pp. 87–8.
31. Warren, *Crowded Canvas*, p. 158.
32. Dillistone, *Into All the World*, p. 90.
33. Ibid., p. 89.

34. Ibid.
35. Ibid., p. 92.
36. Ibid., p. 93.
37. Quoted by Dillistone, ibid.
38. Dillistone, 'The Legacy of Max Warren', p. 115.
39. Joe Fison was Chaplain at Wycliffe Hall, Oxford, when he first began to exert a strong influence on John Taylor. Later he was Vicar of the University Church, Great St Mary's, Cambridge, then Canon of Rochester, Canon of Truro and finally Bishop of Salisbury.
40. Taylor, 'Doing Theology'.
41. Alexander McKay, quoted by Taylor, ibid.
42. Dillistone, *Into All the World*, p. 6.
43. J. V. Taylor, *CMS Newsletter* 263, September 1963, p. 1.
44. John Taylor contributed to the CWME meetings in Mexico in 1963 and in Bangkok in 1972.
45. Timothy Yates, 'Newsletter theology: CMS Newsletters since Max Warren, 1963–1985', in *International Bulletin of Missionary Research*, January 1988, p. 12.
46. Taylor, *CMS Newsletter* 313, February 1968.
47. *Newsletter* 279, February 1965.
48. *Newsletter* 297, October 1966.
49. *Newsletter* 295, July 1966.
50. Ibid.
51. Eugene Stock, quoted by Taylor in *Newsletter* 295.
52. Ibid.
53. Taylor, 'Doing Theology'.
54. *Newsletter* 295.
55. Ibid.
56. Ibid.
57. Ibid.
58. Ibid.
59. Ibid.
60. Ibid.
61. Ibid.
62. Ibid.
63. Ibid.
64. Taylor, 'Doing Theology'.
65. *Newsletter* 267, March 1964.
66. Ibid.
67. Ibid.
68. Ibid.
69. Ibid.
70. *Chapel of the Living Water*, Partnership House pamphlet.
71. Taylor, interview, 1997.
72. It should be noted that CMS England and CMS Australia are distinct organizations, and CMS Australia is much more conservative than its more liberal English parent. At the time the new headquarters were built, the alternative and more catholic missionary society, the United Society for the Propagation of the Gospel, was located in its own headquarters in Tufton Street, Westminster. Now they share the premises at Partnership House in Waterloo Road and, of course, the chapel. For some comments on the first encounters between the general secretaries of CMS and USPG see Ian Shevill, *Between Two Sees* (Churchman Publishing 1988), pp. 84–7. Bishop Shevill claims that the initiative of bringing together the rivals CMS and USPG was his own, but the process of having the two governing bodies live together for a conference sounds like John Taylor's voice, and the three questions to be considered sound quintessentially Tayloresque

as well: 'Where have the Societies come from?', 'What does each hold dear in the 1970s?', 'What is the way ahead for both of us?'.
73. *Newsletter* 297, October 1966.
74. Ibid.

Chapter 7: Theology come of age

1. J. V. Taylor, 'Vespers', written for 'Southward Bound', the final CMS Staff Party at Salisbury Square before the move to Partnership House in Waterloo Road on the South Bank in 1966. This composition is printed in the script with this disclaimer: 'Every insinuation in this song is so outrageously untrue that it would be impudent to apologize for any line of it to one who is both a great man and a friend. J. V. T.'
2. See Owen Chadwick, *Michael Ramsey: A Life* (Clarendon Press, 1990), pp. 370–2.
3. Max Warren had been a reader of the original manuscript, and had warmly encouraged John Robinson to get the book into print. See F. W. Dillistone, *Into All the World: A Biography of Max Warren*, p. 155.
4. Taylor, *CMS Newsletter* 269, March 1964, p. 1.
5. Taylor, 'Doing theology', p. 1.
6. Mark Gibbs and Ralph Morton, *God's Frozen People* (Collins Fontana, 1964), quoted by Taylor, *Newsletter* 269, p. 7.
7. *Newsletter* 269, p. 2.
8. Ibid., p. 3.
9. Ibid.
10. Ibid., p. 2.
11. Ibid., p. 3.
12. Ibid.
13. Gibson Winter, *The New Creation as Metropolis* (Macmillan, 1963), quoted by Taylor, *Newsletter* 269, p. 4.
14. Arend van Leeuwen, *Christianity in World History* (Edinburgh House Press, 1964), quoted by Taylor, *Newsletter* 269, p. 4.
15. *Newsletter* 269, p. 4.
16. Ibid., p. 5.
17. Winter, *The New Creation*, quoted by Taylor, *Newsletter* 269, p. 7.
18. *Newsletter* 269, p. 8.
19. *Newsletter* 320, October 1968, p. 3.
20. Ibid., p. 4.
21. Ibid., pp. 3, 4.
22. Ibid., p. 4.
23. Ibid., p. 5.
24. Taylor, 'Doing theology'.
25. Taylor, *Newsletter* 320, October 1968, p. 4.
26. John Taylor describes his theology as biblical theology, or at least did so before the term was discredited. By this he means engagement with the sacred text so that there is 'an ever-unfolding perception of the significance of certain crucial events'. See J. V. Taylor, 'Divine revelation through human experience', in Iain MacKenzie (ed.), *Bishops on the Bible* (SPCK, 1994), p. 4.
27. Taylor, *Newsletter* 320, p. 5.
28. Ibid.
29. Ibid.
30. Quoted by Taylor, ibid.
31. Ibid.
32. Rosemary Haughton, *Why be a Christian?* (Geoffrey Chapman, 1968), quoted by Taylor, *Newsletter* 320, pp. 5–6.

33. *Newsletter* 320, p. 7.
34. J. V. Taylor, 'Christian motivation in dialogue', in *Face to Face: Essays on Inter-faith Dialogue* (The Highway Press, 1971), pp. 14–15.
35. Taylor, *For All the World: The Christian Mission in the Modern Age*, p. 28.
36. Ibid., p. 55.
37. J. V. Taylor, 'Missionary responsibility in the Anglican Communion', *International Review of Mission*, lv, No. 218, April 1966, p. 149.
38. Michael Ramsey, Archbishop of Canterbury, Foreword to J. Wilkinson (ed.), *Mutual Responsibility and Interdependence in the Body of Christ* (SPCK, 1963).
39. Taylor, 'Missionary responsibility', p. 148.
40. Stephen Bayne, Introduction to *Mutual Responsibility* (Seabury, 1963), p. 13.
41. Archbishop Ramsey introducing the manifesto to the Congress, *Mutual Responsibility* (SPCK, 1963), p. 13.
42. Douglas Webster, 'Max Alexander Cunningham Warren', *The Dictionary of National Biography 1971–80* (OUP, 1986), pp. 885ff.
43. J. V. Taylor speaking at a meeting of heads of missionary agencies in London, 25 September 1963, in the Michael Ramsey papers in Lambeth Palace Library: Correspondence on *Mutual Responsibility and Interdependence in the Body of Christ*, in *Ramsey Papers* 44, folios 84, 91–4, 161–8.
44. Ibid.
45. Ibid.
46. Taylor, 'Missionary responsibility', p. 154.
47. Ibid., pp. 154, 155.
48. J. V. Taylor, *A Matter of Life and Death* (SCM, 1986), p. 2.
49. Ibid.
50. Ibid.
51. Ibid., p. 3.
52. Although an account of the writing of *The Go-Between God* features in one of the Oxford University Mission talks collected in *A Matter of Life and Death*, a more intimate and more personally revealing account is to be found in the unpublished lecture to ordinands of the Aston Training Scheme in 1981. See Taylor, 'Doing theology'.
53. 2 Corinthians 13.13-14.
54. Taylor, *The Go-Between God*, pp. 18–19; Anthony Bloom, *School of Prayer* (DLT, 1970), pp. 60f.
55. Taylor, 'Doing theology'.
56. Taylor, *The Go-Between God*, p. 9.
57. Ibid., p. 16.
58. Ibid., p. 102.
59. Ibid.
60. Ibid., p. 7.
61. Taylor, Foreword to *The Go-Between God*.
62. J. V. Taylor, *Weep Not for Me: Meditations on the Cross and Resurrection* (WCC Risk Books, 1986), p. 13.
63. Taylor, *The Go-Between God*, pp. 125, 126.
64. Ibid., p. 16.
65. Krister Stendahl, sometime Bishop of Stockholm, Professor of Theology Emeritus at Harvard Divinity School, unpublished Quiet Day Address given at the Retreat House of the Holy Redeemer, New York City, on 26 October 1992.
66. *The Primal Vision*, first published in 1963 by SCM, has gone through many impressions and been in print ever since, as has *The Go-Between God*, first published in 1972 and winner of the Collins Religious Book Prize that year.
67. Taylor, *The Go-Between God*, p. 183.
68. Taylor, 'Christian motivation in dialogue', p. 2.
69. Taylor, *The Go-Between God*, pp. 182, 183.

70. J. V. Taylor, 'The theological basis for inter-faith dialogue', Lambeth Interfaith Lecture, 2 November 1977, published in *Crucible*, January–March 1978, p. 7.
71. Taylor, 'Christian motivation in dialogue', p. 9.
72. Taylor, *The Go-Between God*, p. 182.
73. Hendrick Kraemer quoted in Maurice Wiles, *Christian Theology and Inter-Religious Dialogue* (SCM, 1992), p. 29.
74. Wiles, *Inter-Religious Dialogue*, p. 30.
75. 'Each of the great religions is a culturally-determined tradition of response and disobedience to these varied types of experience whereby the Lord God announces his presence and calls to humanity' (J. V. Taylor, 'Divine revelation through human experience', in *Bishops on the Bible*, p. 8).
76. Taylor, *The Go-Between God*, p. 183.
77. Ibid.
78. Ibid., p. 179.
79. Amos 9.7.
80. Acts 1.1ff.
81. Taylor, *The Go-Between God*, p. 179.
82. Ibid., p. 180.
83. The identification of Jesus with λογος (*logos*) emerges in the gospel according to John as the kernel of all the New Testament sayings that use *logos* in a specific sense; the new thing is the pre-existence of the *logos* and its transition into history. Jesus is presented as the teacher of the *logos*, for he *gives* the *logos* and also *is* the *logos*. In Christ there is unity of speech and action. Pre-existence is also a theme in Paul – Romans 1.4; Philippians 2.5ff; Colossians 1.16; cf. 1 Corinthians 8.6). See Gerhard Kittel and Gerhard Friedrich, *Theological Dictionary of the New Testament* (Eerdmans, 1985).
84. Taylor, *The Go-Between God*, p. 180.
85. Ibid.
86. Ibid.
87. Ibid.
88. Ibid.
89. Ibid., p. 181.
90. Ibid.
91. Taylor, 'Christian motivation in dialogue', p. 5.
92. Wiles, *Inter-Religious Dialogue*, p. 41.
93. Taylor, 'The theological basis of inter-faith dialogue', p. 12.
94. Wiles, *Inter-Religious Dialogue*, p. 32.
95. Taylor, *The Go-Between God*, pp. 186–7.
96. Ibid., p. 187.
97. Ibid., p. 189.
98. Ibid., p. 195.
99. Taylor, *The Primal Vision*, p. 189.
100. Ibid., p. 190.
101. Ibid., p. 192.
102. Ibid., p. 189.
103. Ibid., p. 193.
104. The Shekinah ('that which dwells') in Hebrew theology is the cloud of the divine presence, and functions as a way of bridging the gap between the aloof or transcendent God who cannot be located in any particular place and sinful human beings or the material world. See J. T. Marshall, 'Shekinah', in *A Dictionary of the Bible*, IV (T&T Clark, 1902), pp. 487–9, and C. G. Montefiore and H. Loewe, *A Rabbinic Anthology* (Macmillan, 1938), p. 13.
105. Taylor, *The Primal Vision*, p. 194.
106. Ibid., p. 195.
107. Taylor, 'Christian motivation in dialogue', pp. 1, 2.

108. Ibid., p. 12.
109. Ibid., p. 13.
110. Ibid.
111. Ralph Harper, *The Sleeping Beauty* (Harvill, 1956), p. 111.
112. Taylor, *The Primal Vision*, p. 191.
113. Ibid.
114. Lesslie Newbigin, *Mission in Christ's Way: Bible Studies* (WCC Mission Series, 1987).
115. Taylor, *The Go-Between God*, p. 189.
116. John Taylor speaks thus of Michael Stancliffe, Dean of Winchester, making the real basis of their rare friendship plain, for they shared these very English qualities. See his Foreword to Michael Stancliffe, *Jacob's Ladder*, pp. ix, xii.
117. Taylor, *The Go-Between God*, pp. 191–2.
118. Ibid., p. 190.
119. Ibid., p. 192.
120. J. V. Taylor, 'Easter', in *A Christmas Sequence and Other Poems* (The Amate Press, 1989), p. 26.

Chapter 8: Winchester

1. Taylor, 'Kestrels Returning to Winchester Cathedral', in *A Christmas Sequence and Other Poems*, p. 27.
2. Gordon Crosse (ed.), 'See of Winchester', in *A Dictionary of English Church History* (Mowbray, 1912), pp. 643–7.
3. Charles Smyth, *Cyril Forster Garbett, Archbishop of York* (Hodder & Stoughton, 1959), p. 214.
4. David Stephens to the Archbishop of Canterbury, 1 May 1961, Ramsey Papers, Lambeth Palace Library, 8, p. 250.
5. Early in his 21 years at CMS, Max Warren was, with the full support of both archbishops, offered the ancient northern see of Carlisle, bordering Scotland and the Lake District; later he was repeatedly offered various English dioceses; later still, the Archbishop of Canterbury (Fisher) wished to appoint him Archbishop in Jerusalem, and in 1957 he was unexpectedly elected Archbishop of Melbourne, the second largest metropolitan diocese of the Anglican Church of Australia. All these he declined, feeling no call of God in any particular instance, no inward call *testimonium internim spiritus*. Indeed, Warren's boast was absolute – *nolo episcopari!* See F. W. Dillistone, *Into All the World: A Biography of Max Warren* (Hodder & Stoughton, 1980), pp. 109ff., and Edward Carpenter, *Archbishop Fisher: His Life and Times* (The Canterbury Press, 1991), pp. 602–3.
6. Archbishop Ramsey to Canon M. A. C. Warren, 19 July 1961, Ramsey Papers, Lambeth Palace Library, 9, p. 124.
7. Stephen Gardiner was Bishop of Winchester 1531–50 and, after deprivation of his diocese and imprisonment in the Tower of London under Elizabeth I, was rehabilitated as Bishop of Winchester and Chancellor of England under Mary I, 1553–5.
8. Bishops in the Church of England at this time were still appointed by the Queen on advice from the Prime Minister. In practice, the Prime Minister was advised by the Metropolitan of the Province, in this case the Archbishop of Canterbury, Michael Ramsey. This was just before the reform of this process which resulted in the wider church and the diocese having greater say in the selection. At the time of John Taylor's appointment, there was a Vacancy-in-See committee which gave the Diocese of Winchester some say in the kind of bishop they desired, but the Crown Appointments Commission began work only in 1987. It should, however, be noted that in dioceses of great historic prestige, such as Winchester, the national role of the appointee as a bishop of the Church of England (then with

a seat in the House of Lords) remains a major concern alongside the perceived needs of the individual diocese. The final choice in John Taylor's appointment lay with the Prime Minister of the day, Harold Wilson, in consultation with Archbishop Ramsey of Canterbury (about to retire) and Archbishop Coggan of York (about to be translated to Canterbury). See Bernard Palmer, *High and Mitred: Prime Ministers as Bishop-Makers 1837–1977* (SPCK, 1992).

9. This has certainly been the case until the recent introduction of reforms in the process of episcopal appointments and it remains an important consideration, certainly in regard to the major dioceses. Not only is it considered important to have the right bishop for a particular diocese at a particular point in its history, but essential to have the right people composing the bench of bishops as a whole at any given time, so that the Church of England is governed well and the bishops can make a substantial contribution to national life and leadership through the House of Lords and other avenues of influence open to them.

10. By 26 April 1973, Warren, in private letters to his daughter Pat and son-in-law Roger Hooker, CMS missionaries in India, says that Taylor has already declined two bishoprics, and Warren is 'full of foreboding' that it will not be long before he will leave the CMS for some other bishopric. See Graham Kings, 'Max Warren: candid comments on mission from personal letters', in *International Bulletin of Missionary Research*, 17, No. 2, April 1993, p. 58.

11. Taylor, interview, 1997, and letter, 16 November 2000.

12. Taylor, interview, 1995.

13. Bishop Bill Ind, interview, 1995.

14. Dillistone, *Into All the World*, p. 111.

15. John Taylor admits that Max Warren never so much as hinted that he disapproved, and the evidence from Max Warren's private letters makes it clear that this was not in fact the case. John Taylor was the exception to his rule and he was delighted with the appointment. Indeed, the letters supply evidence of the Prime Minister's office sounding out Max Warren about the appointment of John Taylor to more than one bishopric (M. A. C. Warren, letters, 398b/1, 4 May 1973; 533/2, 8 February 1976; 595/1, 17 April 1977). These unpublished letters remain the private property of Pat and Roger Hooker, Max Warren's daughter and son-in-law, and are held in the CMS Archives at Partnership House London.

16. Dillistone, *Into All The World*, p. 149.

17. Ind, interview, 1995.

18. Ibid.

19. Taylor, *The Winchester Churchman* October 1974, p. iv.

20. Ibid., pp. iv–v.

21. Ibid., p. v.

22. Taylor, *Winchester Churchman* January 1975, p. i.

23. Ibid.

24. Taylor, *Winchester Churchman* October 1974, p. iv.

25. Taylor, *Winchester Churchman* January 1975, p. v.

26. Taylor, 'Rosewindow' 1 in *The Winchester Churchman* January 1975, pp. iii–iv.

27. Ind, interview, 1995: 'The Diocese of Winchester is full of retired generals and admirals, and one in my parish grunted "Bishop's a bloody fool, wear your hat on your head and nobody notices, have it carried on a cushion and every damn idiot sees it." On the other hand, people generally expected oddities from bishops and eccentricity in clergy, and may have been glad it was only to do with his hat!'

28. The Dean of Winchester (Michael Stancliffe), *The Winchester Churchman* January 1975, p. v.

29. Ibid.

30. The honest answer to the question 'Why does a new bishop knock three times on his cathedral doors?' is that no one knows! The practice seems to stem from a confusion between the welcoming of a bishop and the consecration of a church.

See Canon F. Bussby, 'The coming of the bishop', in *The Winchester Churchman* April 1975, p. v.

31. Michael Stancliffe, 'The enthronement of the bishop', *Winchester Churchman* January 1975.
32. J. V. Taylor, Foreword to Michael Stancliffe, *Jacob's Ladder* (SPCK, 1987), p. xii.
33. Ibid., p. x: 'So when the day came for my installation service there, in the planning of which he had shared with such care, there could be no question of any ritual knocking on the door and waiting for admission since that door also was as open as heaven's gate, and I went forward to kneel before the high altar while Michael read T. S. Eliot as only he could.' See T. S. Eliot, 'Little Gidding' from *Four Quartets* in *Collected Poems* (Faber & Faber, 1974), p. 215.
34. J. V. Taylor, *Christ at Both Ends of the Line* (SPCK, 1975).
35. Ibid., p. 4.
36. Ibid.
37. Ibid., p. 6.
38. Dillistone, *Into All the World*, p. 111.
39. Taylor, interview, 1997.
40. Dean Michael Perham, interview, 1995.
41. *The Hampshire Chronicle*, 4 July 1975, p. 8.
42. Bishop David Connor, interview, 1995.
43. Taylor, interview, 1995.
44. Paul Bates, interview, 1995; Canon Ron Diss, interview, 1998.
45. Perham, interview, 1995.
46. Perham, interview, 1997.
47. Ibid.
48. 'Synod condemns sex film proposal', *The Hampshire Chronicle*, 26 November 1976, p. 7.
49. Ibid.
50. 'The fight to save my son's marriage', *Daily Mail*, 23 August 1982.
51. Canon Ron Diss, interview, 1998.
52. Connor, interview, 1995.
53. Paul Bates, Chaplain to Winchester College, later Canon of Westminster, relates this story and the shock which ensued. John Taylor was serious in his ministry with adolescents, and expected parents and school staff to treat them, their ideals and aspirations with the dignity they deserved. Bates, interview, 1995.
54. Diss, interview, 1998.
55. Canon Robert Teare, letter, 6 April 1995.
56. Perham, interview, 1995. The reference is to Anthony Trollope's *Barchester Towers*, first published in 1857, and the other novels in the Barchester series.
57. Teare, interview, 1995.
58. Perham, interview, 1995.
59. M. A. C. Warren, letter, 595/1, 17 April 1977.
60. Taylor, 'Rosewindow' 2, 14 February 1976.
61. 'Rosewindow' 10, October 1975.
62. Perham, interview, 1995.
63. 'Rosewindow' 1, January 1975.
64. 'Rosewindow' 2, January 1975, pp. 1–7.
65. Ibid., p. 7.
66. Ibid.
67. Teare, interview, 1995.
68. Perham, interview, 1995.
69. Teare, interview, 1995.
70. T. S. Eliot, 'Burnt Norton' in *Four Quartets* (*Collected Poems*, 1974, p. 190).
71. Teare, letter, 6 April 1995.
72. Ibid. Bishop Simon Barrington-Ward, JVT's successor as General Secretary of

CMS, excuses this, saying, 'He couldn't help that, because I think that's part of him' (interview, 1995).

73. 'Read my poem *Circus* if you want to know how much I hate my love of applause. My housemaster at school wrote in one honest report that I should learn not to play to the gallery. I still need that' (Bishop John V. Taylor, letter, 9 May 1998).
74. Taylor, *The Christlike God*, pp. 263–4.
75. Taylor, 'Circus' in *A Christmas Sequence and Other Poems*, p. 28.
76. Mark 6.5
77. Ind, interview, 1995.
78. Barrington-Ward, interview, 1995.
79. Ibid.
80. Taylor, interview, 1995.
81. Teare, interview, 1995.
82. Ibid.
83. Ind, interview, 1995.
84. The Revd Ray Bowers, letter, 1995.
85. Bishop Simon Barrington-Ward says that John Taylor's effect is always uneven, and the evidence suggests that John Taylor himself would view this as part of the Christian economy where individuals matter supremely, as opposed to fairness or even-handedness. Barrington-Ward, interview, 1995, and J. V. Taylor, 'Max Warren' in *New Fire*.
86. Teare, interview, 1995.
87. Taylor, 'Max Warren' in *New Fire*.
88. Taylor, interview, BBC Bristol, 1982.
89. Daphne Bowers, interview, 1995.
90. Connor, interview, 1995.
91. Rosemary Hardy, who played the part of Mary Magdalene, said the bishop was 'charismatic' and 'inspiring', while Brian Burrows, who played the part of Pilate, said the bishop had a unique gift as producer, comparable only in his experience to Jonathan Miller (interview, BBC Bristol, 1982).
92. To the choir under the direction of Martin Neary he said, 'You've been working on the sound, but what we are in for is not just an oratorio, it's not just sound, it's a total action, and we are going to make it visual' (interview, BBC Bristol, 1982).
93. 'Observe that African peasant strumming his lyre as he sings at the fireside, or this English girl in the concert-hall, absorbed in a Brahms symphony: you cannot eliminate from their experiences soul or body, spirit or animal, for Man in his totality is involved. God made him so; and what God has joined together let no one attempt to sunder. The blasphemous attempt, alas, is all too often made. What deep horror of sex, what flagellation of the flesh, what strange asceticisms and morbid fancies, what monstrous cruelties and heartless neglect, has Man visited upon himself and his brethren in the execution of this unnatural design! But the Bible knows nothing of this divorce' (Taylor, *Man in the Midst*, pp. 18, 19–20).
94. Taylor, *Man in the Midst*, p. 9.
95. Charles Williams, *The Descent of the Dove: A Short History of the Holy Spirit in the Church* (Longmans Green, 1939), p. vii.
96. Taylor, interview, BBC Bristol, 1982.
97. J. V. Taylor, *The Passion in Africa* (Mowbray, 1957), p. 7.
98. Taylor, interview, BBC Bristol, 1982.
99. Ibid.
100. Ibid.
101. Ibid.
102. Teare, interview, 1995.
103. Michael Stancliffe, *Symbols and Dances* (SPCK, 1986), p. vii.
104. J. V. Taylor's sermon at the Requiem Mass in Winchester Cathedral, published as the Foreword to Michael Stancliffe's posthumous collection of sermons, *Jacob's*

Ladder (SPCK, 1987).

105. Taylor, interview, 1995.
106. Ibid.
107. Ibid.
108. 'Rosewindow' 6, June 1975, p. iii.
109. Ibid.
110. 'Rosewindow' 8, August 1975, pp. i–ii.
111. Ibid., p. iii.
112. Ibid., p. ii.
113. Ibid., p. iii.
114. 'Rosewindow' 10, October 1975, p. ii.
115. Ibid., p. iii.
116. Ibid., p. iv.
117. Ibid., p. v.
118. 'Rosewindow' 3, March 1975, p. ii.
119. 'Rosewindow' 10, October 1975, p. v.
120. *The Hampshire Chronicle*, 10 August 1979, p. 13.
121. Ind, interview, 1995.
122. J. V. Taylor, 'Religion: peace-maker or peace-breaker', in *Islamic Quarterly*, April 1989, p. 53.
123. K. Woolcombe and J. V. Taylor, *No Fundamental Objections to the Ordination of Women to the Priesthood* (addresses to General Synod, 3 July 1975; published by Anglican Group for the Ordination of Women to the Historic Ministry of the Church), p. 4.
124. Ibid., p. 6.
125. Ibid., p. 7.
126. Ibid., pp. 6–7.
127. Walter Freytag 'Changes in the patterns of western missions', in R. K. Orchard (ed.), *The Ghana Assembly of the International Missionary Council* (Edinburgh House Press, 1958).
128. Woolcombe and Taylor, *No Fundamental Objections*, p. 8.
129. J. V. Taylor, Foreword to *A Fearful Symmetry? The Complementarity of Men and Women in the Church* (SPCK, 1992).
130. The Revd Canon Dr Maurice Wiles.
131. *We Believe in God*, Report of the Doctrine Commission of the Church of England (Church House Publishing, 1987), p. ix.
132. Ind, interview, 1995.
133. Ibid.
134. Taylor, interview, 1995.
135. Ind, interview, 1995.
136. John Robinson's *Honest to God* presented in popular form many of the ideas of Dietrich Bonhoeffer, Paul Tillich, and the death of God theologians.
137. Bishop John Austin Baker, letter, 1 August 1998, p. 6. I am grateful for an insider's detailed picture of the workings of the Doctrine Commission. Bishop Baker was a member of the original Archbishops' Commission on Christian Doctrine established by Archbishops Ramsey and Coggan in 1967, and Chairman of the Doctrine Commission of the Church of England after it was reconstituted under the authority of the General Synod and the House of Bishops. As the Doctrine Commission's longest serving member, Bishop Baker is probably in a better position to judge the reports produced than any of my other informants.
138. Perham, interview, 1995.
139. Ibid.
140. Perham, letter, 22 February 1995.
141. Teare, interview, 1995.
142. Perham, interview, 1995.

143. John Taylor lists Klaus Klostermaier's *Hindu and Christian in Vrindaban* (SCM, 1969) as one of the books to influence him most (Taylor, letter, 10 July 1992).

144. Taylor, Foreword to *A Fearful Symmetry?*, p. vii.

145. J. V. Taylor, Introduction to Klaus Klostermaier, *Hindu and Christian in Vrindaban*, p. viii.

146. Perham, interview, 1997.

147. Ind, interview, 1995.

148. J. V. Taylor, 'Farewell Sermon' preached in Winchester Cathedral, 3 March 1985.

149. Taylor, 'Farewell Sermon'.

150. Bishop Bill Ind, Address at the Funeral of John Taylor in Magdalen College Chapel, Oxford, on Friday, 9 February 2001 (unpublished), p. 3.

151. J. V. Taylor, *On Seeing the World Whole* (CMS, 1974).

152. John Taylor hoped that the Church of England would endorse an adventurous theology of God's weakness and suffering, and promoted research into these themes. In the end, however, when the Doctrine Commission refused his vision of the suffering God in favour of the traditional doctrine of God's impassibility, he contributed 'The God in whom we trust'. See *We Believe in God*, pp. 147–62. The Doctrine Commission material would feed his exploration in the Romess Summer School lectures, published as *The Christlike God* (SCM, 1992).

153. Taylor, Acknowledgements in *The Christlike God*.

154. D. L. Edwards, Obituary in *The Church Times*.

155. Taylor, *Weep Not for Me: Meditations on the Cross and the Resurrection* (WCC Risk Books, 1986), p. 13.

156. Apart from the extended treatment of this theme in his greatest book, *The Go-Between God: The Holy Spirit and the Christian Mission*, this special insight runs like a thread of gold through all his works, and he was still thinking and writing about it in his last months. See his Postscript to *The Primal Vision: Christian Presence Amid African Religion* (SCM Classics, 2001), p. 144.

157. Ind, 'Address at the Funeral of John Taylor', p. 1.

158. Ibid., pp. 1–2.

159. Veronica Armstrong, letter, 13 February 2001.

160. Taylor, interview, 1998

161. Taylor, *Weep Not for Me*.

162. J. V. Taylor, *Kingdom Come* (SCM and Trinity Press International, 1989).

163. Taylor, *A Christmas Sequence and Other Poems*.

164. Taylor, Acknowledgements in *The Christlike God*.

165. Veronica Armstrong, letter, 13 February 2001.

166. J. V. Taylor, 'Angels', unpublished poem used in *A Service of Thanksgiving and Farewell: John Vernon Taylor*, Magdalen College Chapel, Oxford, on Friday, 9 February 2001.

167. Genesis 18.1-19

168. J. V. Taylor, 'Divine revelation through human experience', in Ian MacKenzie (ed.), *Bishops on the Bible* (SPCK, 1994), pp. 1–11.

169. Taylor, Author's Note in *A Christmas Sequence and Other Poems*.

170. J. V. Taylor, 'Love's self-opening', unpublished poem used in *A Service of Thanksgiving for the Life of John Vernon Taylor* in Winchester Cathedral on Saturday, 7 April 2001.

Chapter 9: Christlike God

1. Taylor, *Man in the Midst*, pp. 43, 44.

2. Dietrich Bonhoeffer's *Letters and Papers from Prison* was published in English in 1955 and John Taylor seems to have read the book immediately.

3. From first to last John Taylor has been fascinated by the Christian proclamation

of 'a particular kind of God', and has been seeking language and imagery which will not distort the revelation of this distinctively Christian good news. He seeks to allow the whole biblical revelation, 'its record of the acts of God and its inspired interpretation of them, all culminating in the supreme Act, when the Word was made flesh, suffered and died, rose again and ascended – so to dominate and shape our thinking, judging, and feeling that we become more and more intensely aware of the character of God and of His impact upon us' (J. V. Taylor, *Christianity and Politics in Africa*, Penguin, 1957, p. 76).

4. J. V. Taylor, *I Believe in Jesus Christ*, BBC Radio 4 talk on Tuesday, 19 March 1974 (CMS, 1974), p. 1.
5. Taylor, *I Believe in Jesus Christ*, p. 1.
6. Taylor, *Christianity and Politics in Africa*, p. 76.
7. Ibid.
8. Taylor, *Man in the Midst*, p. 49.
9. Taylor, *I Believe in Jesus Christ*, p. 3.
10. L. J. Richard, *A Kenotic Christology* (University of America Press, 1982), p. 168.
11. Taylor, *The Christlike God*, p. 97.
12. Ibid., p. 91.
13. Ibid.
14. Ibid., p. 92.
15. Ibid.
16. Ibid.
17. Ibid.
18. Ibid., p. 91.
19. Taylor, *Man in the Midst*, pp. 52, 81. This is a classic JVT formulation, a coining of the memorable image. It is on a par with, 'Jesus was baptized in the Jordan because it is the lowest river on earth'. Such insights are never forgotten. They become central to the listener's christology, playing a vital role in redefining our doctrine of God. Bishop Bill Ind, interview, 1995.
20. Taylor, *I Believe in Jesus Christ*, p. 6.
21. Taylor, *The Christlike God*, p. 97.
22. Ibid., pp. 99, 98.
23. Ibid., p. 103.
24. Ibid.
25. Ibid., p. 141.
26. Marcus Borg, *Meeting Jesus Again for the First Time* (HarperCollins, 1994).
27. Taylor, *The Christlike God*, p. 117.
28. Justin, *Apology* I, 13.3.
29. Taylor, *The Christlike God*, p. 120.
30. Ibid., p. 121.
31. Ibid., p. 124.
32. Ibid., p. 132.
33. Ibid., p. 124.
34. Ibid., p. 132.
35. Ibid., pp. 134, 135.
36. Frances Young, 'A cloud of witnesses', in John Hick (ed.), *The Myth of God Incarnate* (SCM, 1977), p. 41.
37. This phrase has been popularized by T. S. Eliot. If Eliot's reference to God as 'the still point of the turning world' were left unattended it would certainly be sub-Christian, but he qualifies it by speaking of this point where there is 'neither arrest nor decline', where there is 'neither movement from nor towards', and it cannot be called 'fixity' for 'there the dance is' and 'there is only the dance' (T. S. Eliot, 'Burnt Norton' from *Four Quartets*, in *Collected Poems*, p. 191).
38. Francis House, 'The barrier of impassibility', *Theology* 83 (1880), pp. 410–11.
39. E. Hatch, *The Influence of Greek Ideas and Usages Upon the Christian Church* (William

& Norgate,1892), p. 182. Hatch believed that the writings of Philo largely contributed to the sublimation of the Christian doctrine of God into the hellenistic world-view. See also J. C. McLelland, *God the Anonymous: A Study in Alexandrian Philosophical Theology* (Philadelphia Patristic Foundation, 1976), pp. 23–44; J. M. Hallman, *The Descent of God: Divine Suffering in History and Theology* (Fortress Press, 1991), pp. 23–9.

40. C. C. Richardson (ed.), *Early Christian Fathers*, in *Library of Christian Classics*, 1 (Westminster, 1853), pp. 105, 118–19.

41. Taylor, *The Christlike God*, p. 141.

42. T. E. Pollard, 'The impassibility of God', *Scottish Journal of Theology* 8 (December 1955), pp. 353–64. The Fathers felt that it would not be fitting for the deity to experience emotions! For Irenaeus, it is his sense of the impropriety of divine feelings that seems to be operative.

43. 'It is hardly an exaggeration to say that the theological doctrine of the Divine attributes, handed on from the Early Church, has been shaped by the Platonic and neo-Platonic idea of God, and not by the Biblical Idea.' See Emil Brunner, *The Christian Doctrine of God* (Lutterworth Press, 1949), p. 153.

44. Patripassianism is the technical word for a modalist doctrine of the Trinity which emphasizes the unity of the Trinity at the expense of the plurality. In this understanding, the one God is substantial, while the three differentiations (or modes, or manifestations) are adjectival. See H. E. W. Turner, 'Modalism' in Alan Richardson (ed.), *A Dictionary of Christian Theology* (SCM, 1969), p. 220.

45. R. S. Frank 'Passibility and impassibility', in *Encyclopedia of Religion and Ethics* (Charles Scribner's Sons, 1928), quoting Tertullian's *Adversus Marcionem* ii.27.

46. Hallman, *The Descent of God*, p. 83.

47. *Theological Oration* IV.5 as cited in Pollard, 'The impassibilty of God', p. 359.

48. Hallman, *The Descent of God*, p. 101, quoting Hilary's *De Synodis* 49, in Migne, *Patrologia Latina* 10, 516B–517A.

49. Hallman, *The Descent of God*, p. 102.

50. See Anselm, *Proslogion* 8 in Saint Anselm, *Basic Writings*, p. 13, as cited by Elizabeth Johnson, *She Who Is: The Mystery of God in Feminist Theological Discourse* (Crossroad, 1992), p. 248.

51. See Michael Dodds, 'Aquinas, human suffering and the unchanging God of love', *Theological Studies* 52 (1991), pp. 330–44.

52. J. K. Mozley, *The Impassibility of God: A Survey of Christian Thought* (CUP, 1926), p. 121.

53. The biblical revelation portrays God as one who has suffered in the cross of the Son of God, concerning whom there is no talk of suffering only in human nature, for there is in the New Testament no formulation of a two natures doctrine. It belongs to the person of the Son as mediator, as the eternal high priest, that he is the God-man. See McWilliams, *The Passion of God*, p. 14. Cf. G. Wondra, 'The pathos of God', *The Reformed Review* 18 (December 1964), pp. 28–35.

54. The Chalcedonian Definition, which cannot be called a solution of the christological problem in terms of *how* the two natures are united, remains the measure of christological orthodoxy for the Church. 'Following therefore the holy Fathers, we confess one and the same our Lord Jesus Christ, and we all teach harmoniously that he is the same perfect in Godhead, the same perfect in manhood, truly God and truly man, the same of a reasonable soul and body; consubstantial with the Father in Godhead, and the same consubstantial with us in manhood, like us in all things except sin; begotten before ages of the Father in Godhead, the same in the last days for us and for our salvation born of Mary the virgin *theotokos* in manhood, one and the same Christ, Son, Lord, unique; acknowledged in two natures without confusion, without change, without division, without separation – the difference of the two natures being by no means taken away because of the

union, but rather the distinctive character of each nature being preserved, and each combining in one Person and *hypostasis* – not divided or separated into two Persons, but one and the same Son and only-begotten God, Word, Lord Jesus Christ; as the prophets of old and the Lord Jesus Christ himself taught us about him, and the symbol of the Fathers has handed down to us.' See E. R. Hardy (ed.), *Christology of the Later Fathers* (SCM, 1954), p. 373.

55. See *Luther's Works* 26 (Fortress Press and Concordia Publishing House, 1955), p. 295.
56. See *Luther's Works* 35, p. 236.
57. J. Pelikan, *Luther the Expositor: Introduction to the Reformer's Exegetical Writings* (Concordia Publishing House, 1958), pp. 112–13.
58. Pelikan, *Luther the Expositor*, p. 54.
59. *Luther's Works* 26, p. 29.
60. Walter von Loewenich, *Luther's Theology of the Cross* (Augsburg Publishing House, 1982), p. 13.
61. Alister McGrath, *Luther's Theology of the Cross* (Oxford: Basil Blackwell 1985), p. 174.
62. *Luther's Works* 34, p. 208. See also N. E. Nagel, 'Martinus: Heresy, Doctor Luther, heresy! The person and work of Christ', in *Seven-Headed Luther: Essays in Commemoration of a Quincentenary 1483–1983* (Clarendon Press, 1983), pp. 26ff.
63. *Luthers Werke: Kritische Gesamtausgabe* 10 (Herman Bolaus Nachfolger Weimar, 1883), p. 208, as cited in Marc Lienhard, *Luther: Witness to Jesus Christ* (Augsburg Publishing House, 1982), p. 155. Significantly, John Taylor uses this precise image in working out his own christology. See *The Christlike God*, p. 92.
64. *Luthers Werke* 12, pp. 585–91. See Paul Althaus, *The Theology of Martin Luther* (Fortress Press, 1966), pp. 181–8.
65. *Luther's Works* 22, pp. 492–3.
66. Walter Kasper, *Jesus the Christ* (Routledge & Kegan Paul, 1979), p. 180.
67. 'Est incomprehensibile quod Deus passus est, id quod etiam angeli non satis comprehendunt et admirantur.' Cited in Althaus, *Theology of Martin Luther*, p. 197.
68. *Luther's Works* 24, p. 97; 15, p. 341.
69. Nagel, 'Heresy, Doctor Luther, heresy!', pp. 38–9.
70. Taylor, *The Christlike God*, p. 138.
71. Ibid., p. 273.
72. John Macquarrie, *The Humility of God* (SCM, 1978), p. 65.
73. Taylor, *The Christlike God*, p. 140.
74. Taylor, *Weep Not for Me*, pp. 9–11. The same material is reworked in *The Christlike God*, pp. 139–41, but the treatment lacks the freshness and power of the spoken voice in these Holy Week addresses from the Chapel of the World Council of Churches in Geneva.
75. Taylor, *Weep Not for Me*, p. 9.
76. Taylor, *The Christlike God*, p. 141.
77. Ibid., p. 142.
78. Ibid., p. 143.
79. Charles Hefling (ed.), *Charles Williams: Essential Writings in Spirituality and Theology* (Cowley Publications, 1993), p. 30.
80. Ibid., p. 30.
81. For all the similarities between Max Warren and John Taylor in terms of missionary theology, they are contrasts at this point. 'Warren had little appreciation for the arts and wrote only in prose, whereas Taylor has great insights into music and art, writes poetry and even his prose is poetic.' See Graham Kings, 'Mission and the meeting of faiths: the theologies of Max Warren and John V. Taylor', in K. Ward and B. Stanley (eds), *The Church Mission Society and World Christianity 1799–1999* (W. B. Eerdmans, 2000).
82. Taylor, 'Unicorn', *A Christmas Sequence and Other Poems*, pp. 13–14.

83. Taylor, *Man in the Midst*, p. 22.
84. Taylor, *The Christlike God*, p. 265.
85. Simon Tugwell, Review of *The Go-Between God* in *New Blackfriars*, 54, No. 638, July 1973, p. 334.
86. Taylor, 'Christmas Venite' in *A Christmas Sequence and Other Poems*, p. 15.
87. J. E. Fison, *The Christian Hope* (Longmans, 1954), p. 50. 'The true God of the Bible is a God who is concerned with the events of history and active in them. The religion of the Bible is as much concerned with the things of this world as with the things of the world to come. It shows us quite clearly that men, and not only "souls", are the object of God's love. The righteousness which God requires is a righteousness of the market place, of the law courts, of the palace, a righteousness affecting the policy of land tenure, the maintenance of public health, and the strategy of war' (Taylor, *Christianity and Politics in Africa*, pp. 21, 22–3).
88. Taylor, *Christianity and Politics in Africa*, p. 27.
89. Taylor, *Man in the Midst*, p. 20, and *The Christlike God*, p. 198.
90. Taylor, *Christianity and Politics in Africa*, p. 77.
91. John Wren-Lewis, *They Became Anglicans* (SCM, 1961). p. 165.
92. J. A. T. Robinson, *Honest to God* (SCM, 1963, p. 67).
93. Robinson, *Honest to God*, p. 78.
94. The undercurrent of unease that has always accompanied the traditional assertion of God's impassibility has now in the twentieth century gathered to a concerted rejection of it. 'For the real flaw lies in the projection on to God of a defective analysis of the human person' (Taylor, *The Christlike God*, p. 137).
95. For damaging criticism of modern kenoticism see D. M. Baillie, *God Was in Christ* (Faber and Faber, 1961), pp. 94–8; A. M. Ramsey, *From Gore to Temple* (DLT, 1960), pp. 30–43; John Macquarrie, 'Kenoticism reconsidered', *Theology* 77 (1974), pp. 115–24; C. Welch, *God and Incarnation in Mid-Ninteenth Century German Thought* (SCM, 1965), p. 9, n. 11.
96. John Macquarrie 'Kenoticism reconsidered', p. 122.
97. Ibid., p. 123.
98. Robinson, *Honest to God*, p. 75.
99. Macquarrie, 'Kenoticism reconsidered', p. 123.
100. This idea of the revealed secret is central to John Taylor's formulation of the distinctive contribution Christ makes in dialogue between religions and the human quest for meaning. 'That birth, and the life, death and resurrection which followed, provide the clue by which we can detect this other law at work in the processes of the universe, one which lies at a deeper level than the stimulus to rivalry and self-preservation.' See Taylor, *The Go-Between God*, p. 34, and 'Christian motivation in dialogue', in *Face to Face: Essays on Inter-Faith Dialogue*, pp. 14–15.
101. Taylor, *The Go-Between God*, p. 35.
102. Taylor, 'Christian motivation in dialogue', p. 14. With the exception of the first line, two lines of the same poem are quoted in context at the end of the passage in *The Go-Between God*, p. 35. On neither occasion is any author is acknowledged, but the poem was in fact written by Joseph Mary Plunkett (1887–1916), a signatory of the Proclamation of the Irish Republic who was executed by the British for his part in the 1916 Easter Rising.
103. J. V. Taylor, sermon, Maundy Thursday 1986.
104. Taylor, *The Go-Between God*, p. 35; *Man in the Midst*, p. 54; 'History slows down in the Gospels, until at last all history moves from action to passion, and jerks to a halt before the three hours' silence of Jesus on his Cross' (Gordon Rupp, *Principalities and Powers*, Epworth Press, 1951, p. 32).
105. Taylor, *On Seeing the World Whole* (The John Roberts Press, 1974), p. 12.
106. Taylor, *The Primal Vision*, p. 85.
107. From the time of the Renaissance, with its gathering devotion to the humanity of Jesus, the Christian tradition has been to kneel or bow at the *Incarnatus* in the

Creed of Constantinople-Nicea – 'for us and for our salvation he was incarnate of the Holy Spirit, born of the Virgin Mary, and was made man' (or 'became truly human'). While the creed imagines this making or becoming as the instantaneous result of the virginal conception, John Taylor envisages it as a process, the same process by which any child becomes a human being. Taylor, *The Primal Vision*, pp. 95ff, 122.

108. As Austin Farrer says, 'Jesus was Jesus because of Mary and Joseph and the village Rabbi ... above all of the disciples to whom he gave himself and the poor people to whose need he ministered ... But for these people he would have been another Jesus ... he is what he humanly is by his relation to us'. See A. M. Farrer, *A Celebration of Faith* (Hodder & Stoughton, 1970), pp. 89f., quoted by Taylor, *The Christlike God*, p. 237. There are so many instances of this vision in John Taylor's teaching that it is impossible to catalogue them. See, for example, his 'Farewell Sermon' in Winchester Cathedral, where Jesus' vision of God's will for humanity expands as he looks at the ocean and the horizon.

109. Taylor, *The Primal Vision*, pp. 117–18.

110. Taylor, *Man in the Midst*, p. 60.

111. Taylor, *The Primal Vision*, p. 120, drawing on 1 Corinthians 11.3; Ephesians1.10, 22; 5.23; Colossians 1.20; 2.19.

112. Taylor, *The Go-Between God*, p. 126, and *The Primal Vision*, p. 123.

113. Taylor, *Christianity and Politics in Africa*, pp. 21–34.

114. Taylor, *Man in the Midst*, p. 13.

115. We respond in creative participation because God has chosen the way of incarnation and intends to save the world by being involved in it moment by moment, improvising as each situation arises, rather than following a script (Taylor, *Christianity and Politics in Africa*, p. 27).

116. J. V. Taylor, *The Uncancelled Mandate* (Church House Publishing, 1998), p. 16.

117. Taylor, *Man in the Midst*, pp. 17ff.

118. Ibid., p. 18.

119. Taylor, *The Christlike God*, p. 127. 'If Baptism is the sacrament of our incorporation into Christ, the New Man, it is also that of our immersion into the community of the new Mankind. If in the Lord's Supper we eat the Flesh and drink the Blood of the Son of Man in order to abide in Him and He in us; we are also partaking of the one Loaf that we being many may be one loaf, one body – His Body. And if the selfhood of each of us is something that extends beyond our individuality into the network of inter-relations in which we are enmeshed, then we have no spiritual life of our own apart from that branching organism of inter-penetrating Christian lives which is itself the extension of the Self-hood of Christ' (Taylor, *Man in the Midst*, p. 63).

120. Taylor, *Man in the Midst*, p. 22.

121. Ibid., p. 25.

122. 'In this disharmony even body and soul have been involved, so that three-quarters of the world's religions are built upon fear of the body and the attempt to isolate the soul by asceticism and world-negation' (ibid., pp. 25, 38).

123. Ibid., p. 71.

124. J. V. Taylor, 'This is my Body: a meditation on the Feast of Corpus Christi', 'Rosewindow' 56, *The Winchester Churchman* 197, August 1979, pp. iv–v.

125. Taylor, *The Christlike God*, p. 223.

126. Taylor, *Weep Not for Me*, pp. 11–12.

127. Ibid., p. 12.

128. Harold Kushner, *Why Do Bad Things Happen To Good People?* (Harper & Row, 1980).

129. Taylor, *Weep Not for Me*, p. 13.

130. Charles Williams, *The Descent of the Dove* (Longmans Green, 1939), p. 217. 'God's love for the world is an overflow of the eternal exchange within the Trinity. The response that God waits for from his creation must be in the form of a similar co-

inherence. God has shown us the nature of the divine love through the in-othering of the Incarnation' (Taylor, *The Christlike God*, p. 251).
131. Taylor, *The Christlike God*, p. 239.
132. Williams, *The Descent of the Dove*, p. 69. The Christian's duty is to perceive the declared pattern of the universe and join in the eternal dance of the Trinity. See Humphrey Carpenter, *The Inklings: C. S. Lewis, J. R. R. Tolkien, Charles Williams and Their Friends* (George Allen & Unwin, 1978), p. 103.
133. Taylor, *The Christlike God*, p. 250.
134. Williams, *The Descent of the Dove*, p. 217.
135. Taylor, *The Christlike God*, p. 180.
136. Taylor, *The Primal Vision*, p. 84.
137. Since God is all in all, all there is, how can there be any place that is not God? God makes room for a world of beings other than God by *tsimtsum*, contraction, by inward self-withdrawal, abandoning a space within the divine being and leaving a primordial emptiness and darkness, the non-God, the Void, within which God can 'let be' some Other which is not God, bestowing the gift of being on that which is not Being. See Taylor, *The Christlike God*, p. 192.
138. Taylor, *The Christlike God*, p. 197.
139. Ibid., p. 212.
140. Divine insistence on sharing responsibility with human partners is a very Jewish insight, which is naturally fundamental for God's Jewish Son. It is the notion undergirding the concept of covenant, and it is not confined to human agents. 'Quite apart from God's relation with humanity ... this principle of the creaturely partner appears in the light of this century's physics and molecular chemistry to have characterized God's relation with the universe from the very start.' It is all there in the first chapter of the Book of Genesis, which we routinely misread as though God is the sole actor. 'No sooner have the sun and moon appeared than God gives them sovereignty, dominion, long before the dominion was given to humanity, to rule the whole movement of terrestrial time and to take over from God the separation of light and darkness. God turns to the earth and says, "Bring forth." God didn't just create fishes; somehow the water had to do it' (Taylor, *The Uncancelled Mandate*, pp. 19.
141. Taylor, *The Christlike God*, p. 234.
142. Ibid., p. 233.
143. Ibid., p. 255.
144. W. H. Vanstone, *Love's Endeavour, Love's Expense: The Response of Being to the Love of God* (DLT, 1977).
145. Taylor, *The Christlike God*, p. 205.
146. Taylor, *Enough is Enough* (SCM, 1975), p. 46.
147. Ibid., p. 77.
148. The 'families of defiance' that John Taylor envisages take many forms. 'For the past thirty years and more there have been many experiments in new forms of Christian community, experiments that dispense with life vows, include men and women and family units as well as single people. The Bruderhof movement, the Catholic Action Institutes, the Iona Community, St Julian's Community, Lee Abbey and Scargill, the Taizé Community and that at Grandchamps, the Ecumenical Sisterhood of Mary in Germany and the Evangelical Academies, the Grail, the groups calling themselves L'Arche, the Servants of Christ the King, Focolare – one could go on and on' (Taylor, *Enough is Enough*, pp. 80, 108).
149. Ibid., p. 53.
150. Ibid., p. 51.
151. Ibid., p. 82.
152. Ibid., p. 56.
153. Ibid., pp. 49, 61.
154. Ibid., p. 69.

155. Ibid., p. 60.
156. Ibid., p. 80.
157. Ibid., p. 81.
158. Taylor, *Man in the Midst*, p. 77.
159. Taylor, *The Primal Vision*, p. 188.
160. J. V. Taylor, *On Seeing the World Whole* (Talk at the CMS General Secretary's Breakfast, 30 May 1974; John Roberts Press, 1974), p. 10.
161. Taylor, *The Primal Vision*, p. 189.
162. Ibid., p. 192.
163. Ibid., p. 189.
164. Ibid., p. 195.
165. Taylor, *On Seeing the World Whole*, p. 3.
166. Simple Christian presence was integral to the worker-priest movement in France after the Second World War, where living with and sharing the lives of ordinary people alienated from the Church became an authentic form of ministry and mission. In Protestant circles the concept was launched through the writings of Dietrich Bonhoeffer. Presence was a developing concept, and under the influence of Raimondo Panikkar it clearly came to refer to Christ's own presence. See Raimondo Panikkar, *The Unknown Christ of Hinduism: Towards an Ecumenical Christophany* (Orbis, 1981).
167. Taylor, *The Primal Vision*, p. 190. 'The Cross, after all, was not a symbol of imperial domination but of the *imperium* of sacrifice' (M. A. C. Warren, Introduction to the Christian Presence series in Taylor, *The Primal Vision*, p. 10).
168. Taylor, *On Seeing the World Whole*, p. 3.
169. Taylor, *For All the World*, p. 34.
170. Taylor, *On Seeing the World Whole*, p. 9.
171. Taylor, *The Primal Vision*, p. 195.
172. M. A. C. Warren, Introduction to *The Primal Vision*, p. 10.
173. *The Gospel of Thomas* 77, quoted in M. A. C. Warren, Introduction to *The Primal Vision*, p. 8. See Richard Valantasis (ed.), *The Gospel of Thomas* (Routledge, 1997).
174. Warren, Introduction to *The Primal Vision*, pp. 7–9.
175. Ibid., pp. 9–12.
176. Paul Knitter classifies Max Warren, Kenneth Cragg and John Taylor as typical of the Anglican tradition at this point, and it is pleasing to think that their evangelical credentials are recognized for their essential catholicity. P. F. Knitter, *No Other Name? A Critical Survey of Christian Attitudes Towards the World Religions* (Orbis, 1985), p. 135.
177. J. V. Taylor 'The theological basis of interfaith dialogue', *Crucible*, January–March 1978, p. 4.
178. Ibid., p. 6.
179. Ibid., pp. 6–7.
180. Ibid., p. 11.
181. Ibid., p. 12.
182. Ibid., p. 15.
183. Ibid., pp. 13–14.
184. J. V. Taylor, 'The Christian vision and the way ahead' (Address on being made an Honorary Fellow of the Selly Oak Colleges within the University of Birmingham in June 1987), in *Discernment*, 2:1, Summer 1987, p. 15.
185. Taylor, 'Christian motivation in dialogue', p. 14.
186. Taylor, *For All the World*, p. 42, quoting D. T. Niles, *Upon the Earth* (SCM, 1962), p. 126.
187. Taylor, *For All the World*, p. 44.
188. Williams, *The Descent of the Dove*, p. 3.
189. If the cross of Christ shows us anything about the constitution of the universe we inhabit, then we know that this is what John Taylor calls a *pre-forgiven* universe.

'God had chosen in eternity to take upon himself the risk and the cost of creating this kind of world. As a precondition of creation he took upon himself the judgement and death of the sinner. Being in Christ is a more essential human state than being in ignorance of Christ. So any and every movement of man's mind and will that can properly be called a response of faith is truly faith in Christ to some degree even though Christ is still only the invisible magnetic pole that draws us on' (Taylor, 'The theological basis of inter-faith dialogue', p. 10).

190. Taylor, 'Christian motivation in dialogue', pp. 14–15.
191. Taylor, 'The Christian vision and the way ahead', p. 15.
192. Taylor, *The Uncancelled Mandate*, p. 9.
193. Ibid., p. 10.
194. Taylor, 'The theological basis of interfaith dialogue', p. 6.
195. Ibid., p. 14.
196. In the high priestly prayer in John's Gospel, Jesus prays that his followers 'may be one-in-us, that the world may believe that You have sent me'. Ecumenical enthusiasts make it sound as though the unity of Christians, or even the union of churches, is going to surprise and convince an unbelieving world that Jesus comes from God. The true meaning of the prayer, according to JVT, is that the world may believe that it was You, and not any other kind of God, from whom I came. The prayer is not about the impression the Church might make, or even Jesus's own reputation, but about the glory of God. To do something for the glory of God reveals the true nature of God. 'We cannot bring ourselves to accept one another unconditionally, though we know that this is the only way we could ever have been accepted in Christ. We do not have his faith, nor his Father's faith, to welcome without demanding credentials or to trust without guarantees' (J. V. Taylor, 'Mutual acceptance', sermon for the Week of Prayer for Christian Unity preached in Winchester Cathedral, no date).
197. Taylor, 'The Christian vision and the way ahead', p. 16.
198. Taylor, *The Uncancelled Mandate*, p. 40.
199. Ibid., p. 33.
200. Ibid., p. 34.
201. Ibid., p. 41.
202. Taylor, *For All the World*, p. 82.
203. Roland Allen, *Missionary Principles* (Eerdmans, 1964), p. 67.
204. Taylor, *For All the World*, pp. 90–91.
205. Ibid., p. 91.

Bibliography

Primary sources

THE WRITINGS OF JOHN V. TAYLOR

The Spiritual Equipment of the Local Church and Its Servants, London: Conference of Missionary Societies of GB and Ireland, 1949.

The Spiritual Equipment of the Local Church and Its Servants, London: CMS, 1949.

'The development of African drama for education and evangelism', *International Review of Mission*, 89, No. 155, July 1950.

Were You There? An African Presentation of the Passion Story, London: The Highway Press, 1951.

'Education and the creative Spirit', *Uganda Teachers Journal*, 8, 1953, pp. 22–30.

'Problems of training men for the ministry in Equatorial Africa', *East and West Review*, 20, 1954, pp. 103–9.

Man in the Midst, London: The Highway Press, 1955.

Passion in Africa, London: A. R. Mowbray, 1957.

Christianity and Politics in Africa, London: Penguin, 1957.

'The Uganda Church today', *International Review of Mission*, xlvi, No. 182, April 1957.

'Missionary motives', *Crusade*, September 1957.

Missionary Motives, London: Crusade Booklets, 1957.

The Growth of the Church in Buganda: An Attempt at Understanding, London: SCM, 1958.

'The place and function of the missionary', in R. K. Orchard (ed.), *The Ghana Assembly of the International Missionary Council*, London: Edinburgh House Press, 1958.

Black and White, London: SCM, 1958.

Processes of Growth in an African Church, London: SCM, 1958.

Mukono: An African College Community Experimenting in Wholeness of Life, London: CMS (no date).

The Training of Clergy for the New Africa, London: CMS, 1959.

Christians of the Copperbelt: The Growth of the Church in Northern Rhodesia, London: SCM, 1961 (with Dorothea Lehmann).

'Christianity in Africa', in C. Legum, *Africa: A Handbook to the Continent*, 1961.

The Primal Vision: Christian Presence amid African Religion, London: SCM, 1963.

For All The World: The Christian Mission in the Modern Age, London: Hodder & Stoughton, 1966.

Courts of the Lord's House: A Guide to the Holy Communion, Ibadan: Daystar, 1966.

'Mediators and mediums', in C. Martin (ed.), *Prismatics*, London: SCM, 1966, pp. 65–70.

CMS Newsletter (monthly), No. 263. September 1966 – No. 387, December 1974.

'Missionary responsibility in the Anglican Communion', *International Review of Mission*, lv, No. 218, April 1966.

See for Yourself, London: The Highway Press, 1968.

Change of Address, London: Hodder & Stoughton, 1968.

'Is Christ relevant?', in Hugh Montefiore (ed.), *Sermons from Great St Mary's*, London: Fontana, 1968.

Foreword by Bishop John V. Taylor, in Klaus Klostermaier, *Hindu and Christian in Vrindaban*, London: SCM, 1969.

'Christian motivation in dialogue', *Face to Face: Essays on Inter-Faith Dialogue*, Papers from the CMS Annual School of Mission, January 1970; London: The Highway Press, 1971.

'Small is beautiful', *International Review of Mission*, 60, 1971, pp. 328–38.

The Go-Between God: The Holy Spirit and the Christian Mission, London: SCM, 1972.

Side Shoots and Seeds, London: CMS, 1973.

On Seeing the World Whole, London: John Roberts Press, 1974.

I Believe in Jesus Christ, talk for BBC Radio 4, 19 March 1974, published London: CMS, 1974.

'Rosewindow' (monthly) in *The Winchester Churchman*, No. 162, September 1974 – No. 265, April 1985.

A Church Reshaped, London: CMS, 1975.

Enough is Enough, London: SCM, 1975.

Both Ends of the Line, Enthronement Sermon as Bishop of Winchester given in Winchester Cathedral, 8 February 1975; London: SPCK, 1975.

No Fundamental Objections to the Ordination of Women to the Priesthood, addresses to the General Synod of the Church of England by the Bishops of Oxford and Winchester on 3 July 1975; published by The Anglican Group for the Ordination of Women.

The Secret People, London: CMS, 1977.

'Christ the Kingdom', three lectures at Wycliffe College, Toronto (unpublished, no date).

'The theological basis of inter-faith dialogue', *Crucible*, January–March 1978.

'Bangkok 1972–1973', *International Bulletin of Missionary Research*, 67, No. 267, July 1978.

'Max Warren', *New Fire*, 34, September 1978.

'The Church witnesses to the Kingdom', *Your Kingdom Come: Mission Perspectives*, Geneva: WCC Publications, 1980.

'The Holy Spirit and ecumenism', *Theological Renewal*, No. 18, 1981, pp. 2–14.

'Doing theology', lecture to Aston Training Scheme, 1981 (unpublished).

Believing in the Church: The Corporate Nature of Faith, Report of the Doctrine Commission of the Church of England (JVT, Chairman); London: SPCK, 1981.

'Signs of growth in the Church of England: new shoots from an old tree', in A. Wedderspoon (ed.), *Grow or Die*, Winchester, 1981.

'The temptations of the ministry', *Christian*, 6.5, Epiphany 1982.

'Delhi diary', in *Third Assembly of the World Council of Churches*, Geneva: WCC Publications, 1968.

A Matter of Life and Death, London: SCM, 1986.

Weep Not For Me: Meditations on the Cross and the Resurrection, Geneva: WCC Risk Books, 1986.

'Blake's God', lecture given at St James's, Piccadilly, 28 May 1986 (unpublished).

'The Christian vision and the way ahead', *Discernment*, 2:1, 1987, pp. 13–16.

'The God in whom we trust', in *We Believe in God*, Report of the Doctrine Commission of the Church of England (JVT, Chairman, followed by Bishop John Austin Baker); London: Church House Publishing, 1987 (JVT, anonymous author of Chapter 9, pp. 147–62).

'Homo sapiens within creation under God', in *The Annual Review of St George's House*, Windsor: 1988.

Foreword by Bishop John V. Taylor (Sermon at Michael Stancliffe's Requiem), in Michael Stancliffe, *Jacob's Ladder*, London: SPCK, 1988.

'Religion: peace maker or peace breaker', *Islamic Quarterly*, April 1989.

Kingdom Come, London: SCM, 1989.

A Christmas Sequence and Other Poems, Oxford: The Amate Press, 1989.

The Christlike God, London: SCM, 1992.

Foreword by Bishop John V. Taylor, in *A Fearful Symmetry? The Complementarity of Men and Women in Ministry*, London: SPCK, 1992.

'My pilgrimage in mission', *International Bulletin of Missionary Research*, 17, No. 2, April 1993.

'The future of Christianity', in John MacManners (ed.), *The Oxford History of Christianity*, Oxford: OUP, 1993.

'Making space for transcendence in the school experience', lecture to the Governing Bodies Association, 4 March 1994 (unpublished).

'Divine revelation through human experience', in Iain MacKenzie (ed.). *Bishops on the Bible*, London: SPCK, 1994.

'Christian mission and the next millennium', address given to Partnership for World Mission, General Synod of the Church of England, 19 November 1998 (unpublished).

The Uncancelled Mandate, London: Church House Publishing, 1998.

The Primal Vision: Christian Presence Amid African Religion, Introduction by Jesse N. K. Mugambi, Postscript by J. V. Taylor; London: SCM Classics, 2001.

UNPUBLISHED SERMONS

'The new people', Advent Sunday 1977.

'The crown', 5 June 1977.

'Christmas', 1979.

'Easter', 1982.

'Advent IV', 23 December 1984.

'Law service', 14 October 1984.

'Farewell sermon', Winchester Cathedral, 3 March 1985.

'Maundy Thursday', 1986.

'Utopias', 21 May 1995.

'Selfhood: presence or persona?' (no date).

'Mutual acceptance', Week of Prayer for Christian Unity (no date).

'The law' (no date).

'Five and twenty' (no date).
'There is a man in heaven', Ascension Day (no date).
'The media' (no date).
'World hunger' (no date).
'The family' (no date).
'Music' (no date).
'Who is my mother?', Christmas Day (no date).

TRAVEL DIARIES OF THE GENERAL SECRETARY OF THE CHURCH MISSIONARY SOCIETY

West Africa 1960, pp. 1–177.
USA and Mexico 1963, pp. 1–108.
Iran, Egypt, Jordan, Israel 1964, pp. 1–204.
Malaya, Hong Kong, Japan, New York 1965, pp. 1–115.
Australasia 1966, pp. 1–58.
Elba and Assisi 1966, pp. 1–48.
Pakistan, Nepal, Afghanistan 1970, pp. 1–179.
USA 1970, pp. 1–79.

LETTERS

Bishop John V. Taylor to DGW 10 July 1992
Bishop John V. Taylor to DGW 12 December 1992
Bishop John V. Taylor to DGW 11 March 1995
Bishop John V. Taylor to DGW 9 May 1998
Bishop John V. Taylor to DGW 24 June 1998
Bishop John V. Taylor to DGW 24 July 1998
Bishop John V. Taylor to DGW 20 October 1999
Bishop John V. Taylor to DGW 16 November 2000
Bishop John V. Taylor to Sarah Cawdell 30 March 1995
Bishop Bill Ind to DGW 16 March 1995
Bishop Bill Ind to DGW 4 April 1995
Bishop David Connor to DGW 14 March 1995
The Revd Canon Robert Teare to DGW 6 April 1995
The Revd Jack Hodgins to DGW 13 April 1995
The Revd Canon Ron Diss to DGW 26 January 1995
The Revd Canon Ron Diss to DGW 15 May 1998
The Very Revd Michael Perham to DGW 22 February 1995
The Revd Ray Bowers to DGW 21 April 1995
The Revd Canon Graham Kings to DGW 22 February 1995
The Revd Canon Graham Kings to DGW 23 March 1995
The Revd Canon Graham Kings to DGW 5 August 1995
The Revd Sarah Cawdell to DGW 26 July 1995
The Revd Canon Nigel Harley to DGW 5 April 1995
The Revd Canon Nigel Harley to DGW 13 July 1995
The Rt Revd Lord Coggan of Canterbury & Sissinghurst to DGW 20 July 1996
Bishop Michael Manktelow to DGW 12 May 1998
Bishop Michael Manktelow to DGW 22 June 1998

Graham Phillips to DGW 13 May 1998
Graham Phillips to DGW 17 June 1998
Mary Tomsen (Buckley) to DGW 16 June 1998
Bishop Colin James to DGW 15 May 1998
Bishop John Austin Baker to DGW 1 April 1988

INTERVIEWS

Bishop John V. Taylor 8 September 1992
Bishop John V. Taylor 9 May 1995
Bishop John V. Taylor 19 June 1997
Bishop John V. Taylor 21 July 1998
Bishop Bill Ind 5 May 1995
Bishop David Connor 12 May 1995
Paul Bates 12 May 1995
Paul Bates 29 May 1997
Canon Robert Teare 11 May 1995
Bishop Simon Barrington-Ward 16 May 1995
Bishop Simon Barrington-Ward 18 June 1997
The Revd Ray Bowers 15 May 1995
The Revd Ray Bowers 28 May 1997
Canon Graham Kings 10 May 1995
The Revd Sarah Cawdell 10 May 1995
Canon Michael Perham 12 May 1995
Canon Michael Perham 30 May 1997
Glynne Evans 20 June 1997
Graham Phillips 23 July 1998
Bishop Colin James 28 July 1998
Archdeacon Trevor Nash 27 July 1998
Mary Tomsen (Buckley) 27 July 1998
Bishop Michael Manktelow 30 July 1998
Canon Ronald Diss 31 July 1998

2. Secondary sources

G. H. Anderson and T. F. Stransky (eds), *Christ's Lordship and Religious Pluralism*,
    New York: Orbis, 1983.
W. B. Anderson, *The Church in East Africa 1840–1974*, Dodoma: Central
    Tanganyka Press, 1977.
C. G. Baëta, *Christianity in Tropical Africa: The Renewal of a Non-Western Religion*,
    New York: Edinburgh House Press/Orbis, 1995.
J. A. Baker, *The Foolishness of God*, London: DLT, 1970 (Fontana Books, 1975).
Michael Barnes, *Christian Identity and Religious Pluralism: Religions in
    Conversation*, Nashville: Abingdon, 1989.
Karl Barth, *The Epistle to the Romans*, London: OUP, 1933.
Karl Barth, *Church Dogmatics* (ET by G. T. Thomson, T. F. Torrence and
    G. W. Bromily), Edinburgh: T&T Clark, 13 volumes, 1936–69.

Karl Barth, *Anselm: Fides Quaerens Intellectum*, London: SCM, 1960.

Karl Barth, *The Humanity of God*, Richmond, VA: John Knox Press, 1960.

Stephen Bayne, *Mutual Responsibility and Interdependence in the Body of Christ*, New York: Seabury, 1963; London, SPCK, 1963 (ed. J. Wilkinson).

Kwame Bediako, *Christianity in Africa: The Renewal of a Non-Western Religion*, New York: Edinburgh University Press/Orbis, 1995.

T. A. Beetham, *Christianity and the New Africa*, London: Pall Mall Press, 1967.

Peter Berger, 'Camus, Bonhoeffer and the world come of age', *The Christian Century*, 76: 8 and 15 April 1959.

Daniel Berrigan, 'The passion of Dietrich Bonhoeffer', *Saturday Review*, 30 May 1970.

Eberhard Bethge, 'The challenge of Dietrich Bonhoeffer's life and theology', *Chicago Theological Seminary Register*, 51, No. 2, February 1961.

Eberhard Bethge, 'Bonhoeffer's Christology and his religionless Christianity' in *Union Seminary Quarterly Review*, 23, No.1, Fall 1967

Eberhard Bethge, *Dietrich Bonhoeffer: A Biography*, London: Collins, 1970.

S. B. Bevans, *Models of Contextual Theology*, Maryknoll, NY: Orbis, 1992.

Lionel Blue, *To Heaven with Scribes and Pharisees*, London: DLT, 1975.

D. Bonhoeffer, 'Concerning the Christian idea of God', *The Journal of Religion*, xii, April 1932.

D. Bonhoeffer, *Letters and Papers from Prison*, London: SCM, 1971.

D. Bonhoeffer, *Life Together*, New York: Harper & Row, 1954.

D. Bonhoeffer, *Ethics*, London: SCM, 1955.

D. Bonhoeffer, *Creation and Fall*, London: SCM, 1959.

D. Bonhoeffer, *Act and Being*, New York: Harper & Row, 1962.

D. Bonhoeffer, *Sanctorum Communio*, London: Collins, 1963.

D. Bonhoeffer, *Christ the Centre*, New York: Harper & Row, 1966.

D. Bonhoeffer, *The Cost of Discipleship*, New York: Macmillan, 1966.

John Booty, *An American Apostle: The Life of Stephen Fielding Bayne*, Pennsylvania: Trinity Press, 1997.

Marcus Borg, *Meeting Jesus Again for the First Time*, San Francisco: Harper, 1994.

Marcus Borg, *The God We Never Knew: Beyond Dogmatic Religion to a More Authentic Contemporary Faith*, San Francisco: HarperCollins, 1997.

Marcus Borg and N. T. Wright, *The Meaning of Jesus: Two Visions*, San Francisco: Harper, 1999.

G. Bornkamm, *Jesus of Nazareth*, London: Hodder & Stoughton, 1960.

David Bosch, *Transforming Mission*, New York: Orbis, 1991.

G. Bouma and B. Dixon, *The Religious Factor in Australian Life*, Australia: MARC, 1986.

C. E. Braaten, *Shadow of the Cross*, Toronto: Regis College, 1984.

C. E. Braaten, *Our Naming of God*, Minneapolis: Fortress Press, 1989.

B. R. Brasnett, *The Suffering of the Impassible God*, London: SPCK, 1928.

Ian Breward, *Australia: The Most Godless Place Under Heaven?*, Melbourne: Beacon Hill, 1988.

Michael Brierley, 'Love almighty and love unlimited: the place of W. H. Vanstone in 20th century British theology', unpublished extended essay, Honours School of Theology, Oxford, 1997.

David Brown, *All Their Splendour*, London: Collins Fount, 1982.

Emil Brunner, *Truth as Encounter*, Philadelphia: Westminster Press, 1964.

Martin Buber, *I and Thou*, New York: Charles Scribner & Sons, 1958.

N. M. de S. Cameron (ed.), *The Power and Weakness of God: Impassibility and Orthodoxy*, Edinburgh: Rutherford House, 1990.

D. L. Carmody and J. T. Carmody, *Prayer in the World Religions*, New York: Orbis, 1990.

E. Carpenter, *Archbishop Fisher: His Life and Times*, Norwich: The Canterbury Press, 1991.

H. Carpenter, *The Inklings: C. S. Lewis, J. R. R. Tolkien, Charles Williams and Their Friends*, London: George Allen & Unwin, 1978.

Sarah Cawdell, 'A study of the distinctive theology of mission of John V. Taylor', unpublished essay, Ridley Hall, Cambridge, 1995.

Owen Chadwick, *Michael Ramsey: A Life*, Oxford: OUP, 1990.

J. E. Church, *Quest for the Highest: An Autobiographical Account of the East African Revival*, Exeter: Paternoster Press, 1981.

M. A. Cohen and H. Croner (eds), *Christian Mission – Jewish Mission*, New York: Paulist Press, 1982.

D. Cohn-Sherbok, *Many Mansions: Interfaith and Religious Intolerance*, London: Bellew, 1992.

D. Cohn-Sherbok, *Judaism and Other Faiths*, New York: St Martin's Press, 1994.

C. B. Cousar, *A Theology of the Cross: The Death of Jesus in the Pauline Letters*, Minneapolis: Fortress Press, 1990.

Harold Coward, *Pluralism: Challenge to World Religions*, New York: Orbis, 1985.

Scott Cowdell, *Is Jesus Unique? A Study of Recent Christology*, New York: Paulist Press, 1996.

Harvey Cox, 'Using and misusing Bonhoeffer', *Christianity and Crisis* 24, October 1964.

Harvey Cox, *The Secular City*, New York: Macmillan, 1965.

Harvey Cox, *Many Mansions: A Christian's Encounter with Other Faiths*, Boston: Beacon Press, 1988.

Harvey Cox, *The Secular City*, 25th Anniversary Edition; New York: Macmillan, 1990.

Kenneth Cragg, *The Call of the Minaret*, London: Collins, 1956.

Kenneth Cragg, *Sandals at the Mosque: Christian Presence amid Islam*, London: SCM, 1959.

Kenneth Cragg, *The Dome of the Rock*, London: SPCK, 1964.

Kenneth Cragg, *The Christian and Other Religion*, London: Mowbrays, 1977.

Kenneth Cragg, *This Year in Jerusalem*, London: DLT, 1982.

Kenneth Cragg, *The Christ and the Faiths: Theology in Cross-Reference*, London: SPCK, 1986.

Kenneth Cragg, *What Decided Christianity*, Worthing: Churchman Publishing, 1989.

Kenneth Cragg, *To Meet and to Greet: Faith with Faith*, London: Epworth Press, 1992.

Kenneth Cragg, *Troubled by Truth: Life-Studies in Inter-Faith Concern*, Edinburgh: Pentland Press, 1992.

Kenneth Cragg, *Faith and Life Negotiate: A Christian Story-Study*, Norwich: The Canterbury Press, 1994.

Kenneth Cragg, *The Lively Credentials of God*, London: DLT, 1995.

John Crook (ed.), *Winchester Cathedral: Nine Hundred Years*, Guildford: Phillimore, 1993.

G. Crosse (ed.), *A Dictionary of English Church History*, London: Mowbray, 1912.

O. Cullmann,*The Christology of the New Testament*, London: SCM, 1959.

D. G. Dawe, *The Form of a Servant: A Historical Analysis of the Kenotic Motif*, Philadelphia: Westminster Press, 1963.

D. G. Dawe and J. B. Carman (eds), *Christian Faith in a Religiously Plural World*, New York: Orbis, 1980.

G. D'Costa (ed.), *Christian Uniqueness Reconsidered*, New York: Orbis, 1990.

J. de Gruchy (ed.), *Bonhoeffer for a New Day: Theology in a Time of Transition*, Grand Rapids, MI: W. B. Eerdmans, 1997.

F. W. Dillistone, *Into All the World: A Biography of Max Warren*, London: Hodder & Stoughton, 1980.

F. W. Dillistone, 'The legacy of Max Warren', *International Bulletin of Missionary Research*, July 1981.

F. W. Dillistone, *A Fire for God: The Life of Joe Fison*, Oxford: The Amate Press, 1983.

Doctrine Commission of the Church of England, *The Mystery of Salvation: The Story of God's Gift*, London: Church House Publishing, 1995.

R. H. Drummond, *Toward A New Age in Christian Theology*, New York: Orbis, 1985.

J. D. G. Dunn, *Christology in the Making*, London: SCM, 1980.

D. L. Edwards, *Christian England*, Vols 1 & 2, London: Oxford University Press, 1984.

D. L. Edwards and J. Stott, *Essentials: A Liberal-Evangelical Dialogue*, London: Hodder & Stoughton, 1988.

J.-M. Ela, *My Faith as an African*, New York: Orbis, 1988.

T. S. Eliot, *For Lancelot Andrewes*, London: Faber & Faber, 1928.

E. R. Fairweather (ed.), *Anglican Congress 1963: Report of Proceedings*, Toronto: Anglican Book Centre, 1963.

Richard Fardon, *Mary Douglas: An Intellectual Biography*, London and New York: Routledge, 1999.

Ernst Feil, *Die Theologie Dietrich Bonhoeffers: Hermeneutik, Christologie, Weltverständnis*, Munich: Christian Kaiser Verlag, 1971.

Paul Fiddes, *The Creative Suffering of God*, Oxford: OUP, 1988.

J. E. Fison, *The Blessing of the Holy Spirit*, London: DLT, 1950.

J. E. Fison, *The Christian Hope: The Presence and the Parousia*, London: Longmans Green, 1954.

J. E. Fison, *Fire Upon the Earth*, Edinburgh: Edinburgh House Press, 1958.

Douglas Fletcher, 'An appraisal of Lesslie Newbigin's gospel as public truth proposal', unpublished B.D. Honours thesis, Murdoch University, Perth, 1996.

W. W. Floyd and C. Marsh (eds), *Theology and Practice of Responsibility: Essays on Dietrich Bonhoeffer*, Pennsylvania: Trinity Press International, 1994.

T. E. Fretheim, *The Suffering of God: An Old Testament Perspective*, Philadelphia: Fortress Press, 1984.

Walter Freytag, *Spiritual Revolution in the East*, London: Lutterworth, 1940.

Walter Freytag, *The Gospel and the Religions*, London: SCM, 1957.

M. Fritz, 'A midrash: the self limitation of God', *Journal of Ecumenical Studies* 22/4 (1985), pp. 703–14.

Graeme Garrett, *God Matters: Conversations in Theology*, Collegeville, MN: Liturgical Press, 1999.

Ian Gillman, *Many Faiths One Nation: A Guide to the Major Faiths and Denominations in Australia*, Sydney: Collins, 1988.

J. D. Godsey, *The Theology of Dietrich Bonhoeffer*, Philadelphia: Westminster Press, 1960.

J. D. Godsey, 'Barth and Bonhoeffer: the basic difference', *Quarterly Review* 7, Spring 1987.

Bede Griffiths, *Return to the Center*, Illinois: Templegate, 1976.

Paul Griffiths (ed.), *Christianity Through Non-Christian Eyes*, New York: Orbis, 1990.

Kenneth Grubb, *Crypts of Power*, London: Hodder & Stoughton, 1970.

O. Haaramaki, *The Missionary Ecclesiology of Max A. C. Warren*, Helsinki: The Finnish Society for Missiology and Ecumenism, 1982.

D. J. Hall, *Lighten Our Darkness: Toward An Indigenous Theology of the Cross*, Philadelphia: Westminster Press, 1976.

J. M. Hallman, *The Descent of God: Divine Suffering in History and Theology*, Minneapolis: Fortress Press, 1991.

Ian Hammett (ed.), *Religious Pluralism and Unbelief: Studies Critical and Comparative*, London and New York: Routledge, 1990.

A. T. Hanson, *Grace and Truth*, London: SPCK, 1975.

E. R. Hardy, *The First Apology of Justin Martyr*, in C. C. Richardson, *The Early Christian Fathers*, LCC 1, London: SCM, 1953, pp. 225–89.

A. E. Harvey (ed.), *God Incarnate: Story and Belief*, London: SPCK, 1981.

Adrian Hastings, *Mission and Ministry*, London: SCM, 1971.

Adrian Hastings, *A History of African Christianity 1950–1975*, Cambridge: CUP, 1979.

Adrian Hastings, *African Catholicism*, London: SCM, 1989.

Adrian Hastings, *Robert Runcie*, London: A. R. Mowbray, 1991.

Adrian Hastings, *A History of English Christianity 1920–1990*, London: SCM, 1991.

Adrian Hastings, *The Church in Africa 1450–1950*, Oxford: Clarendon Press, 1994.

B. Hebblethwaite, *Ethics and Religion in a Pluralistic Age*, Edinburgh: T&T Clark, 1997.

P. Hebblethwaite, *Paul VI: The First Modern Pope*, London: HarperCollins, 1993.

C. Hefling (ed.), *Charles Williams: Essential Writings in Spirituality and Theology*, Boston: Cowley Publications, 1993.

J. A. Henley, *Imagination and the Future: Essays on Christian Thought and Practice*, Melbourne: The Hawthorn Press, 1980.

Gordon Hewitt, *The Problem of Success: A History of the CMS 1910–1942*, Vols 1 and 2, London: SCM, 1971 and 1977.

John Hick, *God and the Universe of Faiths*, London: Macmillan, 1973.

John Hick (ed.), *The Myth of God Incarnate*, London: SCM, 1977.

J. Hick and B. Hebblethwaite (eds), *Christianity and Other Religions*, London: Collins, 1980.

J. Hick and P. Knitter (eds), *The Myth of Christian Uniqueness*, London: SCM, 1987.

L. Hickin, 'The Revival of Evangelical Scholarship', *Churchman* 92 (1978), No. 2, pp. 125–33.

D. H. Hopper, *A Dissent on Bonhoeffer*, Philadelphia: Westminster Press, 1975.

Brian Horne (ed.), *Charles Williams: A Celebration*, Leominster: Gracewing, 1995.

Richard Hutch, *The Meaning of Lives: Biography, Autobiography and the Spiritual Quest*, London and Washington: Cassell, 1997.

G. R. James, 'Enduring appeal of kenotic christology', *Theology* 86 (1983), pp. 7–14.

Jakob Jocz, *The Jewish People and Jesus Christ after Auschwitz*, Grand Rapids, MI: Baker House, 1981.

E. Jungel, *The Doctrine of the Trinity*, Edinburgh: Scottish Academic Press, 1975.

Jacob Kavunkal (ed.), *Mission in an Emerging World, Church*, Melbourne: Dove, 1986.

Bruce Kaye, *A Church Without Walls: Being Anglican in Australia*, Melbourne: Dove HarperCollins, 1995.

Bruce Kaye, 'Theology for life in a plural society', *interMission*, 1, No. 1, July 1995, pp. 3–14.

Elliott Kendall, *The End of an Era: Africa and the Missions*, London: SPCK, 1978.

Graham Kings, 'Max Warren: candid comments on mission from his personal letters', *International Bulletin of Missionary Research*, 7, No. 2, April 1993.

Graham Kings, 'Preliminary reflections on a corresponding theology of religion: letters between Max Warren and Pat and Roger Hooker 1965–1977', unpublished paper given at Professor Werner Ustorf's Mission Seminar, University of Birmingham, 15 December 1994.

Graham Kings, 'Immigration, race and grace: Max Warren's letters to Pat and Roger Hooker 1965–1977', in Aasluv Lande and Werner Ustorf (eds), *Mission in a Pluralist World*, Frankfurt am Main: Peter Lang, 1996, pp. 127–51.

Graham Kings, 'Mission and the meeting of faiths: the theologies of Max Warren and John V. Taylor', in K. Ward and B. Stanley (eds), *The Church Mission Society and World Christianity 1799–1999*, Grand Rapids, MI: Eerdmans, 2000.

Kazoh Kitamori, *Theology of the Pain of God*, Richmond, VA: John Knox Press, 1965.

J. Klassen (ed.), *A Bonhoeffer Legacy: Essays in Understanding*, Grand Rapids, MI: W. B. Eerdmans, 1981.

K. Klostermaier, *Hindu and Christian in Vrindaban*, London: SCM, 1969.

Paul Knitter, *No Other Name? A Critical Survey of Christian Attitudes Toward the World Religions*, Maryknoll, NY: Orbis, 1985.

H. Kraemer, *The Communication of the Christian Faith*, Philadelphia: Westminster Press, 1955.

H. Kraemer, *Religion and the Christian Faith*, London: Lutterworth, 1956.

H. Kraemer, *Why Christianity of all Religions?*, Philadelphia: Westminster Press, 1962.

H. Kraemer, *The Christian Message in a Non-Christian World*, Grand Rapids, MI: Kregal, 1963.

Hans Küng, *On Being a Christian*, London: Collins, 1978.

Hans Küng, *Christianity and the World Religions*, London: Collins Fount, 1985.

Hans Küng and J. Moltmann (eds), *Christianity Among World Religions*, Edinburgh: T&T Clark, 1989.

Lester Kurtz, *Gods in the Global Village*, California: Pine Forge Press, 1995.

C. Lamb, *Belief in a Mixed Society*, London: Lion Publishing, 1985.

C. Lamb, *Call to Retrieval: Kenneth Cragg's Christian Vocation to Islam*, London: Grey Seal Books, 1996.

G. W. H. Lampe, *God as Spirit*, Oxford: Clarendon Press, 1977.

Aasluv Lande, 'Witness as Presence', in J. A. Kirk (ed.), *Contemporary Issues in Mission*, Birmingham: Department of Mission, Selly Oak Colleges, 1994.

Aasluv Lande, 'Contemporary Missiology in the Church of England', in A. Lande and W. Ustorf (eds), *Mission in a Pluralist World*, Frankfurt am Main: Peter Lang, 1996, pp. 25–61.

J. Y. Lee, *God Suffers for Us: A Systematic Inquiry into Divine Passibility*, The Hague: Martinus Nihhoff, 1974.

Roger Lloyd, *The Church of England*, London: SCM, 1966.

Nicholas Lossky, *Lancelot Andrewes the Preacher*, Oxford: Clarendon Press, 1991.

David Lyon, 'Jesus in Disneyland: Religion in Postmodern Times', draft of a book contracted with Polity Press, Cambridge, unpublished, no date.

J. P. Mackey, *The Christian Experience of God as Trinity*, London: SCM, 1983.

J. Macquarrie, *Principles of Christian Theology*, New York: Schribners, 1966.

J. Macquarrie, 'Kenoticism reconsidered', *Theology* 77 (1974), pp. 115–24.

J. Macquarrie, *The Humility of God*, Philadelphia: The Westminster Press, 1978.

J. Macquarrie, *Jesus Christ in Modern Thought*, London: SCM, 1990.

J. Macquarrie, *Christology Revisited*, Pennsylvania: Trinity Press International, 1998.

R. Manwaring, *Evangelicals in the Church of England 1914–1980*, Cambridge: CUP, 1980.

Charles Marsh, *Reclaiming Dietrich Bonhoeffer: The Promise of His Theology*, New York: OUP, 1994.

René Marté, *Bonhoeffer: The Man and His Work*, New York: Newman Press, 1967.

Martin Marty (ed.), *The Place of Bonhoeffer*, London: SCM Greenbacks, 1963.

A. McGrath, *Luther's Theology of the Cross*, Oxford: Basil Blackwell, 1985.

John McGuckin, *St Gregory of Nazianzus: An Intellectual Biography*, New York: St Vladimir's Seminary Press, 2001.

D. W. McKain, *Christianity: Some Non-Christian Appraisals*, New York: McGraw-Hill, 1964.

W. McWilliams, *The Passion of God: Divine Suffering in Contemporary Theology*, Atlanta: Mercer University Press, 1985.

J. Moltmann, *The Crucified God*, New York: Harper & Row, 1977.

J. Moltmann, *The Trinity and the Kingdom: The Doctrine of God*, London: SCM, 1981.

J. Moltmann, *God in Creation*, London: SCM 1985.

J. Moltmann, *The Church in the Power of the Spirit*, Minneapolis: Fortress Press, 1993.

Hugh Montefiore, *Oh God, What Next? An Autobiography*, London: Hodder & Stoughton, 1995.

J. R. H. Moorman, *A History of the Church of England*, London: Adam & Charles Black, 1953.

J. K. Mozley, *The Impassibility of God: A Survey of Christian Thought*, Cambridge: CUP, 1926.

Jocelyn Murray, *Proclaim the Good News*, London: Hodder & Stoughton 1985

Stephen Neill, *God's Apprentice*, London: Hodder & Stoughton, 1992.

Lawrence Nemer, *Anglican and Roman Catholic Attitudes on Missions*, St Augustin: Steyler Verlag, 1981.

Jacob Neusner, *Jews and Christians: The Myth of a Common Tradition*, London: SCM, 1991.

Lesslie Newbigin, *Unfinished Agenda: An Autobiography*, SPCK, London 1985.

Lesslie Newbigin, *Foolishness to the Greeks*, Geneva: WCC Mission Studies, 1986.

Lesslie Newbigin, *Mission in Christ's Way: Bible Studies*, Geneva: WCC Mission Series, 1987.

Lesslie Newbigin, *The Gospel in a Pluralist Society*, Geneva: W. B. Eerdmans/WCC, 1989.

Lesslie Newbigin, *Truth to Tell: The Gospel as Public Truth*, Grand Rapids, MI: W. B. Eerdmans, 1991.

Lesslie Newbigin, *A Word in Season*, Edinburgh: W. B. Eerdmans/St Andrew Press, 1994.

Dennis Ngien, *The Suffering of God According to Martin Luther's 'Theologia Crucis'*, New York: Peter Lang, 1995.

R. A. Norris, *The Christological Controversy*, Philadelphia: Fortress Press, 1980.

J. P. O'Donnell, *The Christian Doctrine of God in the Light of Process Theology and the Theology of Hope*, Oxford: OUP, 1983.

Schubert Ogden, *The Point of Christology*, London: SCM, 1982.

R. K. Orchard (ed.), *The Ghana Assembly of the International Missionary Council*, London: Edinburgh House Press, 1958.

R. K. Orchard, *Mission in a Time of Testing*, Philadelphia: Westminster Press, 1964.

Heinrich Ott, *Reality and Faith: The Theological Legacy of Dietrich Bonhoeffer*, Philadelphia: Fortress Press, 1971.

Willard Oxtoby, *The Meaning of Other Faiths*, Philadelphia: Westminster Press, 1983.

C. A. Padwick, *Henry Martyn: Confessor of the Faith*, London: SCM, 1923.

C. A. Padwick, *Temple Gairdner of Cairo*, London: SPCK, 1929.

Bernard Palmer, *High and Mitred: Prime Ministers as Bishop-Makers 1837–1977*, London: SPCK, 1992.

R. Panikkar, *The Unknown Christ of Hinduism*, London: DLT, 1964.

G. Parrinder, *West African Religion*, Oxford: OUP, 1949.

G. Parrinder, *African Traditional Religion*, London: Hutchinson, 1954.

Margaret Pawley, *Donald Coggan: Servant of Christ*, London: SPCK, 1978.

J. T. Pawlikowski, *Christ in the Light of the Christian-Jewish Dialogue*, New York: Paulist Press, 1982.

J. S. Peart-Binns, *Bishop Hugh Montefiore*, London: Anthony Blond, 1990.

J. Pereiro, *Cardinal Manning: An Intellectual Biography*, Oxford: Oxford University Press, 1998.

T. R. Peters, *Die Präsenz des Politischen in der Theologie Dietrich Bonhoeffers*, Munich: Christian Kaiser Verlag, 1976.

J. A. Phillips, *Christ for Us in the Theology of Dietrich Bonhoeffer*, New York: Harper
  & Row, 1967.
G. L. Prestige, *God in Patristic Thought*, London: SPCK, 1952.
Karl Rahner, *Mission and Grace*, 3 vols, London: Sheed & Ward, 1964.
V. Ramachandra, *The Recovery of Mission Beyond the Pluralist Paradigm*, Carlisle:
  Eerdmans; Grand Rapids: Paternoster Press, 1996.
L. L. Rasmussen, *Dietrich Bonhoeffer: Reality and Resistance*, Nashville: Abingdon
  Press, 1972.
Report of the International Missionary Council, Ghana, 1958.
Reports of the WCC Commission on World Mission & Evangelism, Mexico City 1963,
  Bangkok 1973, Melbourne 1980.
L. J. Richard, *What Are They Saying about Christ and World Religions?*, New York:
  Paulist Press, 1981.
L. J. Richard, *A Kenotic Christology*, Washington: University of America Press,
  1982.
L. J. Richard, *Christ: The Self-Emptying God*, New York: Paulist Press, 1997.
Alan Richardson (ed.), *A Dictionary of Christian Theology*, London: SCM, 1969.
E. Robertson, *Bonhoeffer's Legacy: The Christian Way in a World Without Religion*,
  New York: Macmillan Collier Books, 1989.
H. W. Robinson, *Suffering Human and Divine*, London: SCM, 1952.
J. A. T. Robinson, *Honest to God*, London: SCM, 1963.
J. A. T. Robinson, *The Human Face of God*, London: SCM, 1973.
J. A. T. Robinson, *Truth is Two-Eyed*, London: SCM, 1979.
Maggie Ross, *The Fountain and the Furnace: The Way of Tears and Fire*, New York:
  Paulist Press, 1987.
S. Samartha, *One Christ – Many Religions: Towards a Revised Christology*,
  Maryknoll, NY: Orbis, 1991.
S. J. Samartha (ed.), *Faith in the Midst of Faiths*, Geneva: WCC Publications,
  1977.
Dorothy Sayers, 'The shattering dogmas of the Christian tradition', in Dorothy
  Sayers, *Christian Letters to a Post-Christian World*, Grand Rapids, MI: W. B.
  Eerdmans, 1980.
E. Schillebeeckx, *Jesus: An Experiment in Christology*, New York: Seabury Press,
  1979.
E. Schillebeeckx, *Christ: The Experience of Jesus as Lord*, New York: Seabury Press,
  1980.
P. Schonenberg, 'The kenosis or self-emptying of Christ', *Concilium* 1/2 (1966),
  pp. 27–36.
W. R. Shenk, *Henry Venn: Missionary Statesman*, New York: Orbis, 1983.
Edwin Smith, *African Beliefs and Christian Faith*, London: USCL, 1936.
Edwin Smith, *African Ideas of God*, Edinburgh: Edinburgh House Press, 1959.
R. G. Smith, *Secular Christianity*, New York: Harper & Row, 1966.
R. G. Smith (ed.), *World Come of Age: A Symposium on Dietrich Bonhoeffer*,
  Philadelphia: Fortress, 1967.
M. Stancliffe, *Symbols and Dances*, London: SPCK, 1986.
M. Stancliffe, *Jacob's Ladder*, London: SPCK, 1988.
Brian Stanley, *The Bible and the Flag: Protestant Missions and British Imperialism*,
  Leicester: Apollos IVP, 1990.

John Stott, *Christian Mission in the Modern World*, London: Falcon Press, 1975.

John Stott (ed.), *Making Christ Known: Historic Documents from the Lausanne Movement 1974–1989*, Grand Rapids: Eerdmans; Carlisle: Paternoster Press, 1996.

Bengt Sundkler, *The Christian Ministry in Africa*, London: SCM, 1960.

Samuel Terrien, *The Elusive Presence*, New York: Harper & Row, 1978.

M. M. Thomas, *The Acknowledged Christ of the Indian Renaissance*, London: SCM, 1969.

O. C. Thomas (ed.), *Attitudes Towards Other Religions: Some Christian Interpretations*, London: SCM, 1969.

T. F. Torrance, *Karl Barth: An Introduction to His Early Theology*, London: SCM, 1962.

T. Tuma and P. Mutibwa, *A Century of Christianity in Uganda 1877–1977* (no place or publisher), 1978.

B. C. Turner, *A History of Winchester*, Guildford: Phillimore, 1992.

P. M. van Buren, *The Secular Meaning of the Gospel*, New York: Macmillan, 1963.

P. M. van Buren (ed.), *Bonhoeffer in a World Come of Age*, Philadelphia: Fortress, 1968.

A. van Leeuwen, *Christianity in World History*, London: Edinburgh House Press, 1964.

C. A. van Peursen, 'Man and reality: the history of human thought', *Student World*, No. 1, 1963.

Geza Vermes, *Jesus the Jew*, London: Fontana Collins, 1973.

Geza Vermes, *Jesus and the World of Judaism*, Philadelphia: Fortress, 1983.

W. A. Visser 't Hooft, Foreword to J. M. Bailey and D. Gilbert, *The Steps of Bonhoeffer: A Pictorial Album*, New York: Macmillan, 1969.

W. A. Visser 't Hooft, 'Triumphalism in the Gospels', *Scottish Journal of Theology* 28 (1985), pp. 491–501.

Hans Urs von Balthasar, *The Theology of Karl Barth*, New York: Holt, Rinehart & Winston, 1971.

Walter von Loewenich, *Luther's Theology of the Cross*, Philadelphia: Augsburg, 1982.

P. Vorkink (ed.), *Bonhoeffer in a World Come of Age*, Philadelphia: Fortress, 1968.

Keith Ward, *The Concept of God*, Oxford: Blackwell, 1974.

M. A. C. Warren, *Unfolding Purpose*, London: CMS, 1950.

M. A. C. Warren, *Revival: An Enquiry*, London: SCM, 1954.

M. A. C. Warren, *Problems and Promises in Africa Today*, London: Hodder & Stoughton, 1964.

M. A. C. Warren, *The Missionary Movement from Britain in Modern History*, London: SCM, 1965.

M. A. C. Warren, *To Apply the Gospel*, Grand Rapids, MI: W. B. Eerdmans, 1971.

M. A. C. Warren, *Crowded Canvas: Some Experiences of a Lifetime*, London: Hodder & Stoughton, 1974.

M. A. C. Warren, *I Believe in the Great Commission*, London: Hodder & Stoughton, 1971.

D. Webster, *Missionary Societies – One or Many?*, London: The Highway Press, 1960.

C. Welch, *The Trinity in Contemporary Theology*, London: SCM, 1953.

Paul Welsby, *Lancelot Andrewes*, London: SPCK, 1964.

Paul Welsby, *A History of the Church of England 1945–1980*, Oxford: OUP, 1984.

Maurice Wiles, *Christian Theology and Inter-Religious Dialogue*, London: SCM, 1992.

J. Wilkinson (ed.), *Mutual Responsibility and Interdependence in the Body of Christ*, London, SPCK, 1963; New York: Seabury, 1963.

Charles Williams, *Descent into Hell*, London: Faber & Faber, 1937.

Charles Williams, *The Descent of the Dove: A Short History of the Holy Spirit in the Church*, London: Longmans Green, 1939.

Charles Williams, *The Figure of Beatrice*, London: Faber & Faber, 1943.

Charles Williams, 'The way of exchange', in Anne Ridler (ed.), *The Image of the City*, London: OUP, 1958.

Charles Williams, *The Forgiveness of Sins*, Grand Rapids, MI: W. B. Eerdmans, 1984.

D. D. Williams, 'The vulnerable and the invulnerable God', *Christianity and Crisis* 22:3 (5 March 1962), pp. 27–30.

H. R. Williams CR, *Someday I'll Find You*, London: Collins, 1990.

Bryan Wilson, *Religious Toleration and Religious Diversity*, Santa Barbara, CA: California Institute for the Study of American Religion, 1995.

Gibson Winter, *The New Creation As Metropolis*, New York: Macmillan, 1963.

J. W. Woeffel, *Bonhoeffer's Theology: Classical and Revolutionary*, Nashville: Abingdon, 1970.

K. J. Woolcombe, 'The pain of God', *Scottish Journal of Theology* 20 (June 1967), pp. 129–48.

John Wolffe (ed.), *Evangelical Faith and Public Zeal: Evangelicals in Society in Britain 1780–1980*, London: SPCK, 1995.

Robin Woods, *An Autobiography*, London: SCM, 1986.

N. T. Wright, *Who Was Jesus?*, Grand Rapids, MI: W. B. Eerdmans, 1992.

N. T. Wright, 'αρπαγμος and meaning of Philippians 2:5-11', *Journal of Theological Studies* 37 (1986), pp. 321–52.

R. K. Wüstenberg, *A Theology of Life: Dietrich Bonhoeffer's Religionless Christianity*, Grand Rapids, MI: W. B. Eerdmans, 1998.

Timothy Yates, 'Evangelicalism without hyphens: Max Warren, the tradition and theology of mission', *Anvil*, 2, No. 3, 1985.

Timothy Yates, 'Anglican evangelical missiology 1922–1984', in *Missiology: An International Review*, xiv, April 1986.

Timothy Yates, *Christian Mission in the Twentieth Century*, Cambridge: CUP, 1995.

Timothy Yates, 'Newsletter theology: CMS Newsletters since Max Warren 1963–1985', *International Bulletin of Missionary Research*, January 1988, pp. 11–15.

Frances Young, 'God suffered and died', in M. Goulder (ed.), *Incarnation and Myth: The Debate Continued*, London: SCM, 1979.

Ruth Zerner, 'Dietrich Bonhoeffer's vision on the state and history', in J. Klassen (ed.), *A Bonhoeffer Legacy: Essays in Understanding*, Grand Rapids, MI: W. B. Eerdmans, 1981.

W. Zuidema, *God's Partner: An Encounter with Judaism*, London: SCM, 1977.

Index

Note: The following abbreviations are used in the index: CMS = Church Missionary Society; JVT = John V. Taylor

Africanization: and African art forms 39–42, 72
  and Balokole Revival 29–30, 40
  and failure of indigenization 45
Agilberct, Bishop of West Saxons 132
All Souls, Langham Place 19, 20–21
Allen, Roland 222, 253 n.203
Allison, Sherard Falkner, Bishop of Winchester 132, 151, 157
Althaus, Paul 248 nn.64,67
Altizer, T. J. J. 232 n.70
Andrewes, Lancelot, Bishop of Winchester 135
Anglican Communion 5, 81, 112–15
Anglican Congress, Toronto (1963) 7, 112–14, 229 n.38
Anglo-Catholicism 19, 150
Anselm of Canterbury, St 192, 225 n.55, 235 n.6
anthropology 199–212
  and body and soul 34, 55, 102, 159–60, 204–6
  and Christian action 209–11
  and humanity come of age 56–8, 60–65
apathy (*apatheia*) of God 191, 193
Aquinas, St Thomas 71, 192
architecture, ecclesiastical 98–102
Aristotle, and divine impassibility 191, 192
Arius 192
Armstrong, Veronica (daughter of JVT) 45, 180, 245 n.159
arts, value of 92, 97, 101, 121, 139
Athanasius, St 192
atonement 83, 178–9, 208, 234–5 n.6
attention, theology of 72, 91, 92, 118–20, 140, 212
Auden, W. H. 198
Augustine of Hippo, St 71, 192

Baillie, D. M. 249 n.95
Baker, John Austin, Bishop of Salisbury 172, 173, 174–5, 197, 234 n.29
Balokole Revival 26–8
  and Africanization 29–30, 40
  and reconciliation 30, 31–3
  as 'vertical' religion 27, 34
baptism 90,101
Barrington-Ward, Simon (later Bishop of Coventry)
  and Balokole Revival 228 n.9, 229 n.14
  and CMS 91
  and *The Go-Between God* 227 nn.79,81
  on JVT 11, 225 n.46, 243 nn.78, 85
Barth, Karl: and christology 52–4, 55, 62, 123
  and God 184
  influence on JVT 23, 51

  and revelation 66–7, 71, 123
Bates, Paul 242 nn.44,53
Bayne, Bishop Stephen 238 n.40
Believing in the Church (Doctrine Commission) 172, 175
Berrigan, Daniel 64, 232 n.80
Bethge, Eberhard 16, 57, 227 n.86, 231 n.34, 231–2 nn.56,71,75, 233 n.94
Bible: biblical criticism 19–20, 109, 186
  and the Church 123
  verbal inspiration 83
Bible Churchman's Missionary Society 83
biography, and theology 10, 12–16, 59, 66, 159, 186
Birinus, St, Bishop of Winchester 131–2, 169
Birmingham University, Cadbury Lectures 115–21
Bishop, Morris 226 n.66
Bishop Tucker College, Uganda: and Balokole Revival 26–30, 31–3
  and Community 36–9, 42
  and Creativity 39–42, 158
  finances 34
  JVT as Assistant Warden 24, 25–6
  JVT as Warden 26, 30, 31–46, 47, 71–2, 97, 157
  JVT's return to England 47–8
  and nursery school 26
  and political consciousness 42–6
  staff 34
  as teacher-training college 24, 25–6, 33, 34–5
  as theological college 24, 25–6, 34, 36–9, 97
  and Women's Training Centre 26, 37
  and worship 27–8, 30, 31, 39–42
bishops: appointment 134, 240–41 nn.8,9
  JVT on 137
Bissainthe, Gerard 73, 234 n.17
Blake, William, *The Trinity* 121
Bloom, Metropolitan Anthony 120
Bonhoeffer, Dietrich: *Act and Being* 66, 233 n.89
  Christ the Centre 54, 55–7, 62, 67, 231 n.33
  and christology 52–67, 183, 191, 196, 201, 203
  The Cost of Discipleship 59, 60, 62
  and ecclesiology 58, 101
  Ethic 54–5, 57–8, 59, 231 n.35
  and faith 58, 60, 64, 110
  and *Honest to God* 104, 244 n.136
  influence on JVT 12, 15–16, 23, 50–51, 60, 71, 104, 161, 227 n.82
  Letters and Papers from Prison 50, 53, 56, 57–60, 62, 64–5, 71, 245 n.2
  and religionless Christianity 51, 56, 60–67, 231 n.39
  Sanctorum Communio 53

and *theologia crucis* 51–66, 191
and theology of presence 252 n.166
and world come of age 52, 60–65, 106
Borg, Marcus 233 n.83, 246 n.26
Bosch, David 226 n.63
Boulding, Maria 227 n.84
Bowers, Daphne 32, 158, 229 nn.16,22, 243 n.89
Bowers, Ray 30, 32, 157, 228 n.9, 229 nn.13,18,22, 243 n.84
Brunner, Emil 5, 224 n.21, 247 n.43
Buber, Martin 87, 120
Burrows, Brian 160, 243 n.90
Bussby, F. 241–2 n.30

Cadbury Lectures 115–21
Calvin, John 71, 193
Cambridge Inter-Collegiate Christian Union (CICCU) 19, 27–8
Cantess Summer School 180
Carpenter, Edward 240 n.5
Carpenter, Humphrey 251 n.132
Carpenter, S. C. 227 n.10
Cash, Wilson 82–4, 90
Cashmore, Gwen 11, 74, 225 n.47, 234 n.24
catechists 44–5
catholicism 21, 36, 78, 97, 175
Cawdell, Sarah 225 n.40, 227 n.83, 229 n.39, 234 n.20
Chadwick, Owen 133, 237 n.2
Chalcedonian Definition 194, 247–8 n.54
change, reactions to 97–8, 137–8, 168, 221–2
Channel Islands 132, 177
Chavasse Lectures 179, 180
Chesterton, G. K. 226 n.66
Christendom, end of 3, 68, 98, 99, 106, 139
Christian Believing (Doctrine Commission) 173–5
'Christian motivation in dialogue' (JVT) 233 n.97, 238 nn.34, 68, 249 n.100
   and fullness of life 111
   and Jesus Christ 125–6, 129, 202, 219
Christianity: as absolute 7
   African 5, 29–30, 72, 77
   of 'Jerusalem' and 'Galilee' 143–4, 154, 177
   as missionary religion 3–4, 52
   and other faiths 122–9
   'religionless' 51, 56, 60–67, 231 n.39
   of 'Rome' and 'Iona' 88, 143
   unconscious 66–8
The Christlike God (JVT) 78, 155, 243 n.70, 254 n.130
   circumstances of writing 179, 245 n.152
   and co-inherence 208–9
   and creation 200, 207
   and divinity of Jesus 187–8
   and humanity of Jesus 186–7, 198
   and philosophy and theology 188–91
   and suffering of God 196, 198, 207, 210, 249 n.94
christology: and anthropology 200–1
   kenotic 55–6, 101, 186, 201–2, 231 n.40, 232 n.70
   as soteriology 190–91, 207
   and *theologia crucis* 52–68, 101, 111, 128, 191, 193–4
   theology as 52–4, 186–99
Christus Pantocrator 58
Church: as Body of Christ 38, 88, 112, 206, 220
   and Christian unity 221, 253 n.196
   as Christlike 81–2, 220–21
   and diversity 90

and house churches 165–8
and mission to the world 22–3, 51, 64, 94, 110–11, 112–15, 168
and mutual responsibility 38, 112–15, 205–12
for others 57–8, 66–7, 107, 129, 209–10
and reaction to change 97–8, 137–8, 168, 221–2
and religionless Christianity 61–2
and secularization 94, 104–8, 111–12
and whole people of God 107
'and world come of age' 52, 60–65, 99, 104–7
Church of England: and central board of mission 113
   and theology 174
   see also Anglican Communion; Doctrine Commission; General Synod
Church, Joe 27–8
Church Missionary Society: and Africanization 29–30, 79
   Annual School of Mission (1970) 128–9
   and authority of General Secretary 135–6, 140, 145
   change of address 80, 94–8, 234 n.1
   and Chapel of the Living Water 98–102
   and the Church and the world 105
   distinctive ethos 114–15
   and evangelicalism 82–3, 88, 97, 101
   Executive Committee 84
   history 82–4
   JVT as Africa Secretary 8, 80, 93
   JVT as General Secretary 8, 38, 80, 93–102, 103–30, 135–6, 210
   JVT's return from Uganda 48–50
   Newsletters 90–93, 94, 95–101, 104–5
   and voluntary association principle 87–90, 113–15
   and Warren as General Secretary 5, 21–4, 29, 82, 84–90, 93, 94, 145
Church of Uganda 24, 43–4, 48, 78–9
Clement of Alexandria, St 192, 194
clergy: and bishop 137–8, 144, 154–8, 163
   and house groups 167–8
co-inherence 208–9, 221, 226–7 n.78
Coenwalch, King of Wessex 132
Coggan, Donald, Archbishop of Canterbury 141, 240–41 n.8
Commission on World Mission and Evangelism 93, 108
confirmations 149, 150–51
Conner, Bishop David 242 nn.42, 52, 243 n.90
contentment, divine 191
conversion 20, 36
Cowdell, Scott 223 n.3
Cox, Harvey 51–2, 104, 230 n.19
Cragg, Bishop Kenneth: and evangelicalism 20
   Faith and Life Negotiate 12, 13, 21, 225 n.57, 228 nn.16,22
   and inter-faith dialogue 122, 224 n.23, 252 n.176
   Jesus and the Muslim 10, 225 n.38
   and Taylor 12, 76
   and theology of cross-reference 223 n.7
   Troubled by Truth 10, 12, 225 n.39
cross *see theologia crucis*
Crosse, Gordon 240 n.2
culture, and mission 17, 21, 23, 29–30, 72–4, 97, 188
Cynegils, King of Wessex 131–2
Cyril of Alexandria, St 193

Davidson, Randall Thomas, Archbishop of
    Canterbury 135
'death of God' school 60, 174, 232 n.70, 244 n.136
dependence, in mission 37–8
diaconate, revival 168
dialogue, inter-faith 6–7, 12–13, 81–2, 116, 122–30,
    176, 214–21
Dillistone, F. W.: *Into All the World* 29–30, 85–9, 93,
    145, 224 n.33, 228 n.12, 235 nn.7, 20, 23, 237 n.3,
    240 n.5, 241 n.16
  'The Legacy of Max Warren' 85, 235 n.16
  as teacher 18
direction, spiritual 79
Diss, Ron 242 nn.44, 51
diversity, and mission 9, 71, 82, 88, 114
Doctrine Commission 145, 169–70, 172–6, 178–9
Dodd, C. H. 18
Dodds, Michael 247 n.51
'Doing Theology' (JVT) 234 n.32
  and Bonhoeffer 237 n.5
  and experience and theology 8, 77, 92–3, 98, 224
    n.34
  and the Holy Spirit 120, 238 n.52
drama: African 28, 39, 40–42, 72, 158
  and architecture 101–2
  in Winchester 158–61
Duke, David 13, 226 n.66

Earnshaw-Smith, Harold 19, 20
East African Balokole Revival *see* Balokole Revival
ecclesiology: of Bonhoeffer 58, 101
  and voluntary organizations 90, 113–15
  in young Churches 69–70
ecumenism: and missionary societies 89–90
  and mutuality 112–15
  and ordination of women to priesthood 170
Edington, William 132
Edwards, D. L. 179, 245 n.154
Eliot, T. S. 142–3, 154, 246 n.37
Ellis, Bob 225 n.48
Emerson, Ralph Waldo 15
Eucharist: and Body of Christ 205–6
  and presence of Christ 127
evangelicalism: and All Souls, Langham Place 19,
    20
  and Articles of Religion 83, 172–3
  and biblical criticism 19–20
  and Bonhoeffer 61
  and CMS 82–3, 88, 97, 101
  conservative 19, 27, 83, 236–7 n.72
  and Doctrine Commission 175
  and inter-faith dialogue 126, 252 n.177
  and JVT 17–21, 23–4, 36, 61, 78, 97, 101, 141
  and mission 23–4, 36
  and pastoral care 78
  and reserved sacrament 101
  and Wycliffe Hall 18, 19
evangelism: and dialogue 127
  and propagation of Christianity 122
  see also listening; mission; presence
exchange, doctrine of 208
excommunication, in Church of Uganda 44–5, 46
experience: and revelation 35, 70, 181, 185
  and theology 8, 9–10, 21, 23, 35–6, 48, 59, 69–70,
    92, 130, 176
  and the Trinity 189–90
  and witness 10

facts: and christology 161, 186, 193
  of experience 8, 21, 70, 92, 98, 216
Fairweather, E. R. 224 n.32, 225 n.56, 233 n.6
faith: in Bonhoeffer 58, 60, 64, 110
  and certainty 130
  and salvation 110, 126, 128, 194
'families of defiance' 251 n.148
Fardon, Richard 225 n.52, 226 n.72
Farnham Castle 133
Farrer, Austin 250 n.108
Fison, Joe (Joseph Edward; later Bishop of
    Salisbury) 18, 92, 97, 104, 117, 236 n.39, 249
    n.87
forgiveness 121, 125, 128, 167
Fowler, James *et al.* 226 n.66
Francis of Assisi, St 212, 220
Frank, R. S. 247 n.45
Freytag, Walter 51, 172, 244 n.127

Ganda Church 27–8
Garbett, Cyril, as Bishop of Winchester 133, 135,
    142
Gardiner, Stephen, Bishop of Winchester 133, 135,
    139, 240 n.7
Garrett, Graeme 70–71
General Synod 170–72, 174
geography, and mission 17, 22
Gibbs, Mark and Morton, Ralph 237 n.6
globalization 5–6, 68, 138–9, 213, 224 n.25
The Go-Between God (JVT): and Christ 124–5, 127,
    129–30, 202–3
  circumstances of writing 118–20, 238 n.52
  as fragmentary 227 n.79
  and Holy Spirit 11–12, 120–25
  and human brokenness 52, 121
  importance of 238 n.66
  and inter-faith dialogue 249 n.100
  and mission 16, 224 n.21
  and religion 122–4, 230 n.17
  and truth 13
God: in African religion 77–8
  as changeless 188, 190, 191–2, 218
  as Christlike 1, 2, 9–10, 38, 53, 63, 65, 67, 81, 168,
    184–99, 220–21
  economy of 235–6 n.22
  as God of history 85–6, 91–2, 95, 97, 106, 109,
    136, 185
  as impassible 191–2, 193–6, 218, 245 n.152, 249 n.94
  as love 4, 128, 190, 192, 196, 202–3, 206, 208–10, 222
  as missionary 4–5, 9, 102, 222, 226 n.63
  as omnipotent 53, 58, 197, 201, 208
  as transcendent and immanent 58, 102, 128, 187,
    189–90
  weakness of 38, 53, 56, 64–5, 101, 179, 192, 198,
    200, 245 n.152
  and the world 105
  see also Holy Spirit; Jesus Christ; suffering
Godsey, John 52, 230 n.21, 232–3 nn.82, 85
Goldberg, Michael 226 n.66
Gospel of Thomas 213, 252 n.173
'great commission' 3–5
Green, Michael 173
Gregory of Nazianzus, St 192

Hallman, J. M. 246–7 n.39
Hammond, Peter 98–9
Hardy, E. R. 247–8 n.54

Hardy, Rosemary 159, 243 n.91
Harper, Ralph 240 n.111
Harrison, Douglas 18
Harvey, Jonathan 158–61, 181
Hastings, Adrian 26, 27, 45, 69, 228 n.6, 229 n.57
Hatch, E. 246 n.39
Haughton, Rosemary 110–11, 237 n.32
Hebblethwaite, P. 225 n.49
Hedda, Bishop of Winchester 132, 169
Hefling, Charles 198, 248 n.79
Hewitt, G. H. G. 235 n.7
Hilary of Poitiers, St 192
history: and JVT 95, 97, 105–6, 109, 135, 144,
      146–7, 152–3
   and Warren 51, 86–7, 91–2, 109, 136
Holy Spirit: and Calvary 116, 117, 120–21
   and co-inherence 208, 226–7 n.78
   as go-between 10, 12, 104, 118–21, 122–5, 127,
      139
   in inter-faith dialogue 2, 116, 125–7, 130, 216
   and JVT's Cadbury lectures 116
Holy Trinity, Cambridge 19, 84
Hooker, Pat (daughter of Max Warren) 241
      nn.10,15
Hooker, Roger (son-in-law of Max Warren) 241
      nn.10,15
House of Bishops 145
house churches 165–8
House, Francis 246 n.38
Huddleston, Archbishop Trevor CR 69
humanity, and fullness of life 64–5, 68, 104, 111,
      119, 125, 219–20

Ignatius of Antioch, St 85, 191
'in-othering' 208–9, 221
Incarnation: and anthropology 199–209
   in Bonhoeffer 54–6, 65
   and impassibility of God 191–2, 193–7, 218
   and inculturation 73
   and mission 9–10, 34–5, 220
   and modalism 232 n.70
   and theology 35, 37, 51, 101, 124–5
   and union of sacred and secular 51, 94, 102, 200
inculturation 72–4, 234 n.16
Ind, Bill (later Bishop of Truro) 227 n.8, 246 n.19
   and Church Missionary Society 241 n.13
   and Doctrine Commission 173–4, 176
   and JVT as Bishop of Winchester 137, 141, 169,
      241 nn.17, 27, 243 nn.77, 83
   and JVT's education 18
   and JVT's funeral 178, 179
International Missionary Council: and JVT 8, 43,
      47–8, 69, 89, 227 n.4
   and World Council of Churches 89
intimacy, in the Church 166–7
Irenaeus, St 191, 247 n.42

James, Colin, Bishop of Winchester 157, 165
Jesuits, and mission 82
Jesus Christ: and Christlikeness of God 1, 2, 9–10,
      38, 53, 63, 65, 67, 81, 168, 184–99
   as Christus Pantocrator 58, 116
   divinity of 117, 190, 192, 194–5, 201
   humanity of 62, 116, 156, 186–7, 190, 192, 194–5,
      198, 201–3, 220, 231 n.32
   and Kingdom of God 3, 218
   as logos 124, 189

as man-for-others 56–60, 65–7, 128, 185, 201–3
   as measure of mankind 183–4
   and other faiths 129–30
   and reality 54–6, 58–9, 61, 65–7, 187, 200, 219
   as secular 102, 106
   uniqueness 1–2, 8
   see also christology; Incarnation
Johnson, Elizabeth 71, 247 n.50
Jones, John C., Bishop of Bangor 26, 28, 30, 35, 228
      n.5
Judaism 106, 188
Justin Martyr, St, Apology 189, 246 n.28

Kant, Immanuel 62–3
Kasper, Walter 195, 248 n.66
Keller, Hans 14
Kelley, Geoffrey 227 n.82
Keswick Convention 27, 228 n.7
Kierkegaard, Søren 71, 190
Kigosi, Blasio 27
Kingdom of God: minority images 3, 68
   and politics 43, 95
   in proclamation of Jesus 3, 218
Kings, Graham 241 n.10, 248 n.81
Klassen, A. J. 227 n.82
Klostermaier, Klaus 234 n.3, 245 n.143
Knitter, Paul 252 n.176
knowledge, and truth 6–7, 10–11, 92–3, 139
Kraemer, Hendrik 1, 2, 5, 7, 8, 51, 123, 224 n.28
Küng, Hans 6, 224 n.27
Kurtz, Lester 1, 223 n.2
Kushner, Harold 250 n.128

laity: and knowledge of theology 107–8
   and ministry of whole people of God 88–9, 107,
      138, 171
Lehman, Paul 227 n.82
listening, role of 69, 72, 74, 77, 129, 214–16
liturgy 20, 99, 150–51
   and drama 28, 159
   see also worship
Loewenich, Walter von 194, 248 n.60
logos 124, 189
London House 152–3
Lothere, Bishop of Winchester 132
Luganda (language) 35
Luther, Martin 61, 64, 71, 183, 191, 192–6

McCaughey, Davis 225 n.54, 227 n.85
McClendon, James 13–14, 226 n.66
McGrath, Alister 194, 248 n.61
McKay, Alexander 92
McLelland, J. C. 246–7 n.39
Macquarrie, John 95, 202, 248 n.72, 249 n.99
McWilliams, Warren 247 n.53
Magdalen College, Oxford 132
Man in the Midst (JVT) 226–7 n.78, 246 n.19
   and Body of Christ 250 n.119
   circumstances of writing 50, 225 n.59
   and human wholeness 243 n.93
   and Jesus as measure of Man and God 183, 185,
      204–5
Manning, F. X. 231 n.38
marriage, and Church of Uganda 44, 45–6, 78
Marshall, J. T. 239 n.104
metanoia 60, 204
ministry: as response 32, 137

of whole people of God 107, 138, 171
see also clergy
mission 212–22
and baptism 90
context 91, 92, 94
as corporate 111
and geography 17, 22
as God's mission 4–5, 9, 102, 222, 226 n.63
as Incarnational 9–10, 34–5, 220
and mutual responsibility 112, 221
in New Testament 3–4
romantic view of 18, 47–8, 49
as sending 22
and theology 93
and the Trinity 4, 13, 122, 226 n.63
and worship 94, 100
see also culture; diversity; evangelism
missionary societies 87–8, 113–14
mitre, episcopal 140–41
modalism 232 n.70
Montefiore, C. G. and Loewe, H. 240
Morley, George, Bishop of Winchester 133
Mott, John 93
Mozley, J. K. 247 n.52
Mukono *see* Bishop Tucker College
Murray, Les 11, 225 nn.48,51
*Mutual Responsibility and Interdependence in the
Body of Christ* 113
mutuality, in the Church 167

Nagel, N. E. 248 nn.62,69
Nagenda, William 28
Neary, Martin 243 n.92
Neill, Bishop Stephen 18
Newbigin, Lesslie: *Mission in Christ's Way* 224
nn.18,20, 240 n.114
and mutual responsibility 112
'On being the Church in the world' 224 n.16
Truth to Tell 6, 8, 11, 224 n.26, 224 n.36, 225 n.45
Niles, D. T. 219
Noetus 192
Nouwen, Henri 226 n.66
Nsibambi, Simeoni 27–8
Nsubuga, Dunstan 31

Ogletree, T. W. 232 n.70
Origen 71, 192
Oxford Group (Moral Rearmament) 27

Palmer, Bernard 240–41 n.8
Panikkar, Raimondo 252 n.166
Parrinder, Geoffrey 69
Partnership House: chapel 98–102
JVT's move from 145–6
move to 80, 94–8, 234 n.1
and USPG 236 n.72
Pascal, Blaise 184
Passion and Resurrection (drama) 158–61
patripassianism 192, 232 n.70, 247 n.44
Paul, St 71, 72
Pelikan, J. 248 n.57
Penman, David, Archbishop of Melbourne 223
n.10
Perham, Michael, Dean of Derby 152, 154, 175,
242 nn.40, 56, 244 n.138
personality, and salvation 10
Phillips, Graham 164–5

Phillips, J. A. 233 nn.87,91
Phillips, James M. 12, 225 n.50
Philo Judaeus 191
philosophy, and theology 53, 116, 188–9, 191–7,
218, 234 n.16
Pittenger, Norman 118
Plunkett, Joseph Mary 249 n.102
pluralism, religious 8, 12, 68, 81
and Christianity 1–2, 214–19
as God-given 9, 71
and relativism 3, 6–7
poetry, and theology 11–12, 50, 74, 92, 129, 139,
148, 198–9
politics: and Bonhoeffer 60, 66
and JVT 95, 201, 210, 218
in Uganda 42–6
Pollard, T. E. 247 nn.42,47
polygamy 27, 45
Praxeas 192, 232 n.70
prayer 218
presence: of Christ 127, 150, 220
evangelism as 71, 127–9, 212–15, 220–22
of God 91, 128–9, 213
priesthood, and women 170–72
priesthood of all believers 87, 88, 107, 140, 171
The Primal Vision (JVT) 226–7 n.78, 245 n.156
and African religion 73, 77–8
and anthropology 203–4
and the cross 128
and failure of the Church 75–6
importance of 76–7, 238 n.66
and Incarnation 72–3, 225 n.60, 249–50 n.107
and inculturation 72–3, 234 n.16
and presence of God 213
and value of listening 70, 72, 74, 77, 129

Rajasheker, J. P. 2, 223 n.4
Ramsey, Michael, Archbishop of Canterbury 223
n.8, 249 n.95
and diocese of Winchester 133–4, 240–41 n.8
and *Honest to God* 103, 104
and *Mutual Responsibility and Interdependence*
112, 115, 238 nn.38,41
Rasmussen, L. L. 66, 230 n.22, 231 n.55, 233
nn.86,91
reality: and Christ 54–6, 58–9, 61, 65–7, 187, 200,
219
and nature of God 199–200, 202, 206
relativism 2–3, 7
religion: as dynamic 126
as response 122–3, 216
responsibility: in Bonhoeffer 62, 63–5
in Christian anthropology 204–6, 208–12, 251
n.140
in mission 112, 221
and secularization 56, 106–7, 111, 112–15
revelation: in art 97
in Bonhoeffer 62–3, 67
and experience 35, 70, 181, 185
and the Holy Spirit 120, 124
responses to 122, 124–5, 183, 216
and suffering of God 190, 193, 196, 197
and the world 105
and world religions 2, 216
Richard, L. J. 246 n.10
Richardson, Alan 232 n.70, 235 n.6
Richardson, C. C. 54, 231 n.31, 247 n.40

Ridley Hall, Cambridge 18
Robinson, Bishop John A. T. 103–4, 174, 201, 223
    n.11, 231 n.32, 249 n.92
Rolt, C. E. 197
Romess Summer School lectures 179, 245 n.152
Rotherham, Thomas, Bishop of Lincoln 132
Rupp, Gordon 249 n.104
Rwanda Mission 27

sacrament, reserved 101
sacramentalism 78–9, 97, 129, 158, 168, 205–6
St Catherine's College, Oxford 18
St Helen's, as JVT's second curacy 21
St Lawrence's School, Ramsgate 17
salvation: and cross-bearing 219
    and faith 110, 125, 128, 194
    as indiscriminate 125–6
    and personality 10
    and secularization 104–5, 107, 111–12
    and society 34, 42–3
secularism: in Bonhoeffer 56, 59–61
    and responsibility 56, 106–7, 111, 112–15
    and theology 104–12, 161
sexuality 149, 159, 163, 205
Shevill, Ian 236 n.72
Simeon, Charles 19, 82
Smyth, Charles 133, 240 n.3
society, and salvation 34, 42–3, 104–5, 107
Society of Jesus, and mission 82
Society for Ordained Scientists 179
Sölle, D. 232 n.70
soteriology, christology as 190–91, 207
'South Bank religion' 103–4, 161, 174
Stackhouse, Reginald 47, 230 n.3
Stancliffe, Michael, Dean of Winchester 141–2,
    161–3, 240 n.116
Stendahl, Krister 68, 122, 238 n.65
Stephens, David 133, 240 n.4
Stock, Eugene 95, 236 n.51
Stroup, George 3–14, 226 n.71
Student Christian Movement (SCM) 19, 27
suffering: of the Church and the Christian 59–60,
    64, 214
    of God 4, 9–10, 53, 56, 64–5, 179, 188, 191–6, 203,
        207, 218, 232 n.70
    of Jesus 53, 63, 186, 191–3, 196–7
    of others 64, 209
Sundkler, Bengt 69
Swithun, St, Bishop of Winchester 135
syncretism 78, 126, 214

Takenawa, Masao 104
Taylor, Joanna (daughter of JVT) 24, 47, 180
Taylor, John Ralph Strickland, Bishop of Sodor
    and Man (JVT's father) 17, 18
Taylor, John V.:
    biography:
    death 178, 180, funeral service 180–81;
        memorial service 181
    family background, and interest in mission 17–18
    education, diploma in education 24; universities
        18; theological college 18–20
    health, depression 47–50, 52, 118; eyesight
        problems 179, 181
    retirement 178–80
    character: capacity for work 157; creativity 15,
        48–50, 158–63; graciousness 93; honesty 22–3,

33, 79, 130, 149–50; hospitality 32; humility 33,
    38–9, 130, 141, 159; leadership style 136–40,
    144, 156–8, 175–6, 235–6 n.22; as musician 32;
    needs and weaknesses 93, 121, 149–50, 154–6,
    243 n.72; patience 30, 31, 38–9; personal
    magnetism 11; as reconciler 30, 31–5, 175;
    romanticism 135; sense of humour 19, 32, 80;
    sensitivity 31, 32, 43, 71, 141, 156, 177;
    spontaneity 32, 38, 136; as visionary 38, 79, 96,
    114, 164–8, 177, 210, 178
    creative life:
    poems and verses: 'Angels' 181, 245 n.166;
        'Christmas Venite' 200, 249 n.86; 'Circus' 155,
        243 n.73; 'Easter' 10, 130, 225 n.42; 'Kestrels
        Returning to Winchester Cathedral' 131, 240
        n.1; 'Love's self-opening' 182, 245 n.170;
        'Vespers' 103
    prayers 144
    sermons and addresses: 'Christian mission and the
        next Millennium' 224 n.25; 'The Christian
        vision and the way ahead' 218–21, 252 n.184;
        'Farewell Sermon' 177–8, 245 n.149, 250 n.108;
        'Is Christ relevant to the non-European?' 230
        n.18; Maundy Thursday 1986 202–3; 'Mutual
        acceptance' 253 n.196; 'This is my Body' 206;
        see also 'Doing theology'
    writings: Christ at Both Ends of the Line 143, 242
        n.34; Christ is the Kingdom 47; Christianity and
        Politics in Africa 50, 69, 185, 200–1, 245–6 n.3,
        249 n.87, 250 n.115; Christians of the Copperbelt
        70; CMS Newsletters 10, 94, 95–101, 104–11,
        122, 225 n.41, 236 n.43; 'The development of
        African drama for education and evangelism'
        229 n.41; 'Divine revelation through human
        experience' 237 n.26, 239 n.75, 246 n.168;
        Enough is Enough 89, 151, 210–12, 252
        nn.146,148; A Fearful Symmetry? 176, 244 n.129;
        For All the World 220, 222, 224 n.19, 225 n.40,
        226 n.63, 229 n.29, 238 n.35, 252 nn.186–7; The
        Growth of the Church in Buganda 69–70, 229
        n.58; I Believe in Jesus Christ 185, 186, 187, 246
        n.4; Kingdom Come 180; A Matter of Life and
        Death 117–18, 180, 238 nn.48,52; 'Max Warren'
        22, 85, 86, 157, 228 n.23, 235 n.19, 243 n.85;
        'Missionary responsibility in the Anglican
        Communion' 112–13, 115, 238 nn.37,46;
        Mukono: An African College Community 25–6,
        37, 40, 46, 228 n.1, 229 n.36; 'My pilgrimage in
        mission' 9, 17–18, 35, 39, 43, 47, 225 n.37, 227
        n.1, 229 nn.34,50; No Fundamental Objections to
        the Ordination of Women to the Priesthood (with
        Woolcombe) 171, 172, 244 n.123; On Seeing the
        World Whole 245 n.151, 249 n.105, 252 n.160;
        The Passion in Africa 243 n.97; 'The place and
        function of the missionary' 4, 22–3, 224 n.17,
        228 n.24; Processes of Growth in an African
        Church 70; 'Religion; peace-maker or peace-
        breaker' 169, 244 n.122; 'The theological basis
        of inter-faith dialogue' 126, 215, 217–18, 220,
        239 n.93, 252–3 n.189; 'The Uganda Church
        today' 72, 74, 78–9, 81, 233 n.5, 234 n.33; The
        Uncancelled Mandate 205, 220, 221–2, 224 n.22,
        251 n.140; Weep Not for Me 121, 180, 197, 207,
        225 n.47, 238 n.62, 245 n.155; Were You There?
        40–42, 229 n.46; see also 'Christian motivation
        in dialogue'; The Christlike God; The Go-Between
        God; Man in the Midst; The Primal Vision

private life: marriage 21, 149–50; children 24, 47, 70, 179–80; friendships 32, 72, 137, 146, 150, 156, 161–3, 169, 180, 240 n.116

religious life: ordination 19; first curacy 19, 20–21; second curacy 21; anger with God 49; call to mission 21–2; and catholicism 21, 36, 78, 97; crisis in faith 47–51, 52; and evangelicalism 17–21, 23–4, 36, 61, 78, 97, 101, 141; and sacramentalism 78–9, 97, 129, 158, 168, 205–6

working life:

Bishop Tucker College 8, 9, 24, 25–46, 47–8, 71–2, 97

International Missionary Council 8, 43, 47–8, 70–72; and African religion 77–8; and inculturation 72–4; and theology of diversity 71; and value of listening 69–70, 71–2, 74, 77, 227 n.4; and World Council of Churches 89

CMS 5; as Africa Secretary 8, 80, 93; centralization and voluntary principle 113–15; and change of address 94–8; and Chapel of the Living Water 98–102; as General Secretary 8, 38, 80, 93–102, 103–30, 145, 210; and inter-faith dialogue 122–30; and *Newsletters* 91, 92, 122; resignation 135–6, 165; and World Council of Churches 93, 108–10

as Bishop of Winchester 8, 38, 134–82; and administration 139, 151–4; appointment 134–5, 136–9; and cathedral and dean 161–3; and chaplains 146, 149, 151–2, 169–70; and clergy 137–8, 154–8, 163; consecration and enthronement 141–4; and Diocesan Pilgrimage 169, 179; and Doctrine Commission 145, 169–70, 172–6, 178–9; and end of Christendom 98, 99, 106, 139; and episcopal vestments 140–41, 150; favouritism 154–8, 235–6 n.22; and General Synod 70–72; and House of Bishops 145; and liturgy 150–51; and ordinations 151; and *Passion and Resurrection* 158–61; as pastor 137, 149–50, 151, 154–8, 163; as performer 154–6; and senior staff 162–3; sermons 148–9, 177–8, 202–3; and *Towards Full Responsibility* 164–8; and *Winchester Churchman* 136, 137–42, 152–3; and young people 147–8, 150–51, 160, 242 n.53

as theologian 14–16, 183–4; and Cadbury Lectures 115–21; christocentrism 109–11, 117, 124–5, 184; on the Church 22–3; and church architecture 98–102; contribution to missiology 9, 10; as diversifier 70–71; and growth in local churches 69–70; and inter-faith dialogue 122–30, 215–21; on mission of God 4, 102; as poet 74, 148, 151, 155, 158–63, 178, 180, 181, 198–9; on religion 122–3; and religious pluralism 2, 13, 214–18; and 'South Bank religion' 103–4, 161, 174; and *theologia crucis* 51–2, 60, 65, 68, 101, 111, 128; transcendence and immanence of God 102, 128, 187, 189–90; and the world 95–7, 104–7; as writer 50, 74–6

Taylor, Peggy (wife of JVT) 151
    and children 24, 47, 70
    marriage 21, 118, 149–50
    and Max Warren 86
    and retirement 180, 181
    and return from Uganda 49–50

Taylor, Peter (son of JVT) 24, 47, 180

Taylor, Veronica (daughter of JVT) *see* Armstrong, Veronica

Teare, Robert 154, 156, 162, 175, 242 nn.55, 57, 67, 244 n.141

technology, and secularization 105–6, 111, 211

Templeton, Elizabeth 225 n.62

Tertullian 71, 192

Theodore of Tarsus, St, Archbishop of Canterbury 132

theologia crucis: of Bonhoeffer 51–66, 191
    of Luther 193–6
    and mission 222
    of JVT 51–2, 60, 65, 68, 101, 111, 128, 190–91

theology: biblical 237 n.26
    as christology 52–4, 186–99
    in Church of England 174
    as come of age 103–30
    of 'cross-reference' 2, 223 n.7
    and experience 8, 9–10, 21, 23, 35–6, 48, 59, 69–70, 92, 130, 176, 189–90
    as Incarnational 35, 37, 51, 101, 124–5
    Jewish 106, 188
    and the laity 89, 107–8
    and mission 93
    and poetry 11–12, 50, 74, 92, 129, 139, 148, 198–9
    'South Bank' 103–4, 161, 174
    systematic and unsystematic 11–12, 14–15, 67–8, 69–71
    see also attention; biography; 'death of God' school; philosophy

Thornhill, Alan 18

Thorold, Anthony Wilson, Bishop of Winchester 133

Tillich, Paul 71, 104, 230–31 n.28, 244 n.136

Tomsen, Mary (JVT's secretary) 151

Trinity: and co-inherence 208–9, 221
    icon by St Andrei Rublev 181–2
    and mission 4, 13, 122, 226 n.63
    modalist doctrine 247 n.44
    and monotheism 189–90

Trinity College, Bristol 20

Trinity College, Cambridge 18

truth: and inter-faith dialogue 6, 126, 129, 216
    and knowledge 6–7, 10–11, 92–3, 139
    as relational 12–13, 29, 185
    and religious response 122, 216

Tucker, Alfred 25

Tugwell, Simon 200, 249 n.85

Turner, H. E. W. 247 n.44

Tutu, Desmond, Archbishop of Cape Town 141

Uganda: JVT in 8, 9, 70–72
    see also Bishop Tucker College

United Society for the Propagation of the Gospel 236 n.72

unity of Christianity 101, 221, 253 n.196

Updike, John 14, 226 n.73

Vahanian, G. 232 n.70

Van Buren, Paul 54, 231 n.29

Van Leeuwen, Arend 107, 237 n.14

Vanstone, W. H. 251 n.144

Venn, Henry 82, 85

Venn, John 82

violence 153, 161

Warren, Max 1, 90, 235 n.31
    and the arts 248 n.81
    and Balokole Revival 29–30, 31–2

and bishoprics 133–4, 135–6, 145, 240 n.5
as Canon of Westminster 93
and Christian Presence series 214, 224 n.23, 252
  n.167
and Christianity 7, 88, 143
and church structures 87–8, 135
and CMS 5, 21–2, 29, 69, 82, 84–7, 93, 94, 145
  and Cash 83–4
  Newsletters 90–93
  and voluntary principle 87–90, 113
and diversity 88, 90
and God of history 51, 86–7, 91–2, 109, 136
and Holy Spirit 116, 117
and inculturation 74
influence on JVT 19, 21–2, 23–4, 29, 49–50, 84
and inter-faith dialogue 122, 214
and JVT as bishop 152
leadership style 84–8, 90, 157, 235 n.22
as missionary 50, 224 n.33
and praise for *The Primal Vision* 76–7
and 'South Bank religion' 103, 237 n.3
Towards 1999 89, 235 n.27
and uniqueness of Christ 7–8
and World Council of Churches 89
We Believe in God (Doctrine Commission) 172, 245
  n.152
Webster, Douglas 50, 238 n.42
Welch, C. 249 n.95
Welsh, James 120
Wiles, Maurice 172, 173, 227 n.79, 239 nn.73,74,92
Wilcken, John 60, 232 n.68
William of Wykeham, Bishop of Winchester 135,
  147
Williams, Charles 160, 198, 208, 220, 226–7 n.78,
  243 n.95
Williams, Harry CR 226 n.69
Wilson, Harold 240–41 n.8
The Winchester Churchman 136, 137–42, 152–4,
  166–7, 206, 241 n.19
Winchester College 147–8, 150–51
Winchester diocese: and administration 139, 151–4
  bishops 133–4
  boundaries 132
  as conservative 133, 177
  history 131–3, 141, 146–7
  JVT's appointment 134–5, 136–9
  JVT's consecration and enthronement 141–4
Wini, Bishop of Winchester 132
Winnington-Ingram, Arthur Foley, Bishop of
  London 19
Winter, Gibson 104, 106, 237 nn.13,17
witness, as way of living 10
Woelfel, J. W. 227 n.82, 230 n.27, 230–31 n.28, 231
  n.39
Wolsey, Card. Thomas 135
Wolvesey House 133, 145–6, 162
women, ordination to priesthood 170–72
Wondra, G. 247 n.53
Woodd, Joanna (daughter of JVT) *see* Taylor, Joanna

Woods, Frank, Archbishop of Melbourne 227–8 n.13
Woods, Robin, Bishop of Worcester 19, 227–8 n.13
Woods, Samuel Edward 227–8 n.13
Woolcombe, Kenneth, Bishop of Oxford 170
work, and faith 143–4
World Council of Churches: Commission on
  World Mission and Evangelism 93, 108
  and International Missionary Council 89
  and JVT 43, 104, 108–10, 180
  Uppsala assembly (1968) 93, 108–10
worship: as active and corporate 99
  in Bishop Tucker College 27–8, 30, 31, 39–42
  in house groups 167–8
  and mission 94, 100
  and secularization 107
  and work 143–4
Wren, Sir Christopher 133
Wren-Lewis, John 201, 249 n.91
Wycliffe College, Toronto 47–8
Wycliffe Hall, Oxford 18–20, 97, 117, 179, 236 n.39

Yates, Timothy 236 n.45
Young, Frances 246 n.36

Zerner, Ruth 227 n.82, 233 n.92

Index of Biblical References

Old Testament
Gen. 18.1-19 245 n.167
Amos 9.7 124
New Testament
Matt.
  12.30 59
  16.13-23 231 n.50
  28.18-20 4, 224 n.14
Mark
  6.5 156
  9.40 59
John 20.19-23 4, 224 n.15
Acts
  1.1ff. 239 n.80
  1.6-8 224 n.14
Rom. 1.4 239 n.83
1 Cor.
  8.6 239 n.83
  9.20-22 72, 233–4 n.13
  11.3 250 n.111
2 Cor. 13.13-14 238 n.53
Eph.
  1.10, 22 250 n.111
  5.23 250 n.111
Phil. 2.5-11 231 n.40, 239 n.83
Col.
  1.16 239 n.83
  1.20 250 n.111
  1.7 55
  2.19 250 n.111